# STUDY GUIDE

## Chapters 10-15

# College Accounting

## 20th EDITION

## James A. Heintz, DBA, CPA

Professor of Accounting
School of Business
University of Kansas

## Robert W. Parry, Jr., Ph.D.

Professor of Accounting
Kelley School of Business
Indiana University

SOUTH-WESTERN
CENGAGE Learning™

Australia • Brazil • Japan • Korea • Mexico • Singapore • Spain • United Kingdom • United States

SOUTH-WESTERN
CENGAGE Learning

**Study Guide and Working Papers for College Accounting, 20th edition**
**Chapters 10-15**
**James A. Heintz and Robert W. Parry, Jr.**

Vice President of Editorial, Business: Jack W. Calhoun

Editor-in-Chief: Rob Dewey

Executive Editor: Sharon Oblinger

Developmental Editor: Sara Wilson, CPA, CATS Publishing

Associate Marketing Manager: Laura Stopa

Marketing Coordinator: Heather Mooney

Senior Content Project Manager: Tim Bailey

Director of Media Development: Rick Lindgren

Media Editor: Bryan England

Senior Frontlist Buyer, Manufacturing: Doug Wilke

Production Service: LEAP Publishing Services, Inc.

Senior Art Director: Stacy Jenkins Shirley

Cover and Internal Designer: Grannan Graphic Design

Cover Image: Digital Vision/Juice Images

Rights Acquisition Account Manager- Image: John Hill

Photo Researcher: Megan Lessard, Pre-PressPMG

For product information and technology assistance, contact us at **Cengage Learning Customer & Sales Support, 1-800-354-9706**

For permission to use material from this text or product, submit all requests online at **www.cengage.com/permissions**
Further permissions questions can be emailed to **permissionrequest@cengage.com**

ISBN-13: 978-0-538-73706-7
ISBN-10: 0-538-73706-9

Chapters 1-9 + 10-15 Package
ISBN-13: 978-0-538-73704-3
ISBN-10: 0-538-73704-2

**South-Western Cengage Learning**
5191 Natorp Boulevard
Mason, OH 45040
USA

Cengage Learning products are represented in Canada by Nelson Education, Ltd.

For your course and learning solutions, visit www.cengage.com
Purchase any of our products at your local college store or at our preferred online store **www.ichapters.com**

Printed in the United States of America
1 2 3 4 5 6 7 14 13 12 11 10

# Table of Contents

# CHAPTER 10
# ACCOUNTING FOR SALES AND CASH RECEIPTS

## LEARNING OBJECTIVES

Chapter 10 introduces the merchandising business: sales transactions and the related new accounts, a new ledger, and a new schedule. Merchandise sales transactions are shown in general journal format.

**Objective 1.     Describe merchandise sales transactions.**

Retail businesses make sales on account, as well as cash sales and credit card sales. Sales tickets and cash register receipts are produced for customers and for accounting purposes.

Wholesale businesses also make sales on account, but the process is more complicated and includes purchase orders and sales invoices. Credit approval is required for sales on account.

Both types of businesses have sales returns (merchandise returned for a refund) and allowances (reductions in price because of defects, damage, or other problems with the merchandise).

**Objective 2.     Describe and use merchandise sales accounts.**

Accounting for sales transactions requires four general ledger accounts: Sales, Sales Tax Payable, Sales Returns and Allowances, and Sales Discounts. Sales is a revenue account; Sales Tax Payable is a liability account; and Sales Returns and Allowances and Sales Discounts are contra-revenue accounts.

When a sale is made and sales tax is added to the sale, the liability account (Sales Tax Payable) is credited for the amount of tax that will be remitted to the government. Therefore, when merchandise is returned for a credit (Sales Returns and Allowances), the customer is also refunded the amount of the sales tax (Sales Tax Payable is debited).

Cash discounts are given to business customers who pay within a discount period such as 10 days. This encourages prompt payment of bills. When a discount is taken, the sales discounts account is debited for the amount of the discount.

Net sales is determined by deducting the contra-revenue accounts (Sales Returns and Allowances and Sales Discounts) from gross sales.

**Objective 3.     Describe and use the accounts receivable ledger.**

The accounts receivable account in the general ledger provides a record of the total amount owed to a business by its customers. To help run the business, a record also is needed of the amount owed by individual customers. The accounts receivable subsidiary ledger provides this information.

When an accounts receivable subsidiary ledger is used, the accounts receivable account in the general ledger is a "controlling account." The accounts receivable ledger is "subsidiary" to this account. Transactions are posted daily from the general journal to both the general ledger and the accounts receivable ledger.

**Objective 4.     Prepare a schedule of accounts receivable.**

Once all daily postings are completed to individual accounts, the balance in the accounts receivable general ledger account must agree with the sum of the customer balances in the accounts receivable ledger. The schedule of accounts receivable is prepared at the end of the month to verify that the total of customer balances equals the balance in the controlling account, Accounts Receivable.

# REVIEW QUESTIONS

**Instructions:** Analyze each of the following items carefully before writing your answer in the column at the right.

| | **Question** | **Answer** |
|---|---|---|

**LO 1**   1. A(n) _____ business purchases merchandise such as clothing, furniture, or computers to sell to its customers. ...........................   _____

**LO 1**   2. A(n) _____ is a transfer of merchandise from one individual or business to another in exchange for cash or a promise to pay cash.   _____

**LO 1**   3. A(n) _____ is a document created as evidence of a sale for a retail business. ..................................................   _____

**LO 1**   4. A written order to buy merchandise, called a(n) _____, is received from a customer. ............................................   _____

**LO 1**   5. A(n) _____ is prepared when merchandise ordered is shipped to a customer. ..................................................   _____

**LO 1**   6. Merchandise returned by a customer for a refund is called a(n) _____. ..................................................   _____

**LO 1**   7. Reductions in price of merchandise granted because of defect or damage are called _____. ......................................   _____

**LO 1**   8. When credit is given for merchandise returned or for an allowance, a(n) _____ is issued. .....................................   _____

**LO 2**   9. The sales account is a _____ account. ....................................   _____

**LO 2** 10. When a sale on account is made, _____ is debited. ...............   _____

**LO 2** 11. When a sale is made with sales tax, a liability account, called _____, is credited for the amount of the sales tax. ..................   _____

**LO 2** 12. Sales Returns and Allowances is a contra- _____ account. ....   _____

**LO 2** 13. A(n) _____ is granted for prompt payment by customers who buy merchandise on account. ......................................   _____

**LO 2** 14. Sales Discounts is a contra- _____ account. .........................   _____

**LO 3** 15. A record of each customer's account balance is contained in the _____ ledger. ..................................................   _____

**LO 3** 16. To indicate that the accounts receivable ledger has been posted, a slash and a _____ are entered in the Posting Reference column of the general journal. ......................................   _____

**LO 3** 17. Sales returns and allowances are posted to both the general ledger and the _____ ledger. ..........................................   _____

**LO 3** 18. When a collection is received on account, _____ is credited.   _____

**LO 4** 19. The _____ is a listing of the balances of all customers who owe money at the end of the month. ...........................................   _____

**LO 4** 20. The schedule of accounts receivable is used to verify that the sum of the accounts receivable ledger balances equals the _____ balance. ..................................................   _____

## EXERCISES

### Exercise 1  (LO 1)  SALES DOCUMENTS

The following is a copy of a purchase order received from Custom Builders, Inc., by Rogers Building Supplies, Inc. Assuming you are employed by Rogers Building Supplies, Inc., prepare a sales invoice (No. 491) dated July 18 billing Custom Builders, Inc., for the items specified in their Order No. A208. The unit prices are as follows: #6 insulated steel doors, $290.00 each and #28 pine, six-panel doors, $125 each. Indicate terms of 30 days.

| | *Purchase Order* | *Order No.*  **A208** |
|---|---|---|
| *Date*   July 15, 20--  *Terms*   30 days | **CUSTOM BUILDERS, INC.**<br>**2001 HILLSIDE DR.**<br>**BLOOMINGTON, IN 47401-2287** | |

*To*
Rogers Building Supplies, Inc.
So. Adams
Bloomington, IN 47401-3663

| Quantity | Description | Price |
|---|---|---|
| 10 | #6 Insulated steel doors | 290.00 |
| 15 | #28 Pine, six-panel doors | 125.00 |

*Deliver no goods without a written order on this form.*      *By*  ___E. Taylor___

**Exercise 1 (Concluded)**

| Invoice | **ROGERS BUILDING SUPPLIES, INC.** | | | |
|---|---|---|---|---|
| Invoice No. | **So. Adams,** | | | |
| Date | **Bloomington, IN 47401-3663** | | | |
| Your Order No. | | | | |
| | Sold to | | | |
| Terms | | | | |

| Quantity | Description | Unit Price | Amount |
|---|---|---|---|
| | | | |
| | | | |
| | | | |
| | | | |
| | | | |

## Exercise 2  (LO 1)  SALES DOCUMENTS

On July 28, Custom Builders, Inc., returned one #6 insulated steel door to Rogers Building Supplies, Inc., for credit. Using the blank form on page 147, prepare a credit memorandum (No. 17) covering the cost of the door sold on July 18.

**Exercise 2 (Concluded)**

| Credit Memorandum | **ROGERS BUILDING SUPPLIES, INC.** |
|---|---|
| | **So. Adams,** |
| No. | **Bloomington, IN 47401-3663** |

Date                    To

We credit your account as follows:

| Quantity | Description | Unit Price | Amount |
|---|---|---|---|
| | | | |
| | | | |
| | | | |
| | | | |
| | | | |
| | | | |

**Exercise 3  (LO 2/3)  SALES AND SALES RETURNS AND ALLOWANCES TRANSACTIONS**

Record the following transactions in a general journal, assuming a 5% sales tax.

(a)  Sold $230.00 of merchandise, plus sales tax, on account. R. B. Jones, Sale No. 28.
(b)  R. B. Jones returned $30 worth of merchandise for a credit.
(c)  R. B. Jones paid the balance of the account in cash.
(d)  Sold $300.00 of merchandise, plus sales tax, for cash.
(e)  Merchandise returned for cash refund, $15.

**Exercise 3 (Concluded)**

## GENERAL JOURNAL

PAGE _____

| | DATE | DESCRIPTION | POST. REF. | DEBIT | CREDIT | |
|---|---|---|---|---|---|---|
| 1 | | | | | | 1 |
| 2 | | | | | | 2 |
| 3 | | | | | | 3 |
| 4 | | | | | | 4 |
| 5 | | | | | | 5 |
| 6 | | | | | | 6 |
| 7 | | | | | | 7 |
| 8 | | | | | | 8 |
| 9 | | | | | | 9 |
| 10 | | | | | | 10 |
| 11 | | | | | | 11 |
| 12 | | | | | | 12 |
| 13 | | | | | | 13 |
| 14 | | | | | | 14 |
| 15 | | | | | | 15 |
| 16 | | | | | | 16 |
| 17 | | | | | | 17 |
| 18 | | | | | | 18 |
| 19 | | | | | | 19 |
| 20 | | | | | | 20 |
| 21 | | | | | | 21 |
| 22 | | | | | | 22 |
| 23 | | | | | | 23 |
| 24 | | | | | | 24 |

## Exercise 4  (LO2)  COMPUTING NET SALES

Based on the following information, compute net sales.

| | |
|---|---|
| Gross sales | $5,010 |
| Sales returns and allowances | 565 |
| Sales discounts | 97 |

_____

_____

_____

_____

## Exercise 5 (LO3) SALES TRANSACTIONS

Diana Brewer operates the Floor and Window Treatment Center and completed the following transactions related to sales of merchandise on account during the month of February. Sales tax of 5% was included in the amount of each sale.

Feb.  2  Sold wallpaper supplies to Dresson Homes, $98.95; terms, n/30. Sale No. 255.
      12  Sold paint to Ray Acuff, $105.00; terms, n/30. Sale No. 256.
      23  Sold miniblinds to Clydette Rupert, $114.83; terms, n/30. Sale No. 257.
      24  Sold decorator items to Marty Staple, $35.55; terms, n/30. Sale No. 258.
      25  Sold paint to Angel Burtin, $25.57; terms, n/30. Sale No. 259.

*Required:*

Enter the above transactions in a general journal.

### GENERAL JOURNAL                                    PAGE ____

| | DATE | | DESCRIPTION | POST. REF. | DEBIT | CREDIT | |
|---|---|---|---|---|---|---|---|
| 1 | | | | | | | 1 |
| 2 | | | | | | | 2 |
| 3 | | | | | | | 3 |
| 4 | | | | | | | 4 |
| 5 | | | | | | | 5 |
| 6 | | | | | | | 6 |
| 7 | | | | | | | 7 |
| 8 | | | | | | | 8 |
| 9 | | | | | | | 9 |
| 10 | | | | | | | 10 |
| 11 | | | | | | | 11 |
| 12 | | | | | | | 12 |
| 13 | | | | | | | 13 |
| 14 | | | | | | | 14 |
| 15 | | | | | | | 15 |
| 16 | | | | | | | 16 |
| 17 | | | | | | | 17 |
| 18 | | | | | | | 18 |
| 19 | | | | | | | 19 |
| 20 | | | | | | | 20 |
| 21 | | | | | | | 21 |
| 22 | | | | | | | 22 |
| 23 | | | | | | | 23 |
| 24 | | | | | | | 24 |
| 25 | | | | | | | 25 |

### Exercise 6  (LO 3)  CASH RECEIPTS TRANSACTIONS

Diana Brewer of the Floor and Window Treatment Center received cash during the month of March as described below.

Mar.  2  Received cash from Dresson Homes on account, $98.95.
    12  Received cash from Ray Acuff on account, $105.00.
    15  Made cash sale to Jean Granite, $404.76, plus 5% sales tax.
    18  Made cash sale to Bill Green, $2,380.95, plus 5% sales tax.
    23  Received cash from Clydette Rupert on account, $114.83.
    24  Received cash from Marty Staple on account, $35.55.
    25  Received cash from Angel Burtin on account, $25.57.
    31  Cash sales for the month were $22,000.00, including 5% sales tax (from cash register tape).
    31  Credit card sales for the month were $28,000.00, including 5% sales tax. Bank credit card expense is $560.

*Required:*

Enter the above transactions in the general journal below and on the next page.

## GENERAL JOURNAL

PAGE

| | DATE | DESCRIPTION | POST. REF. | DEBIT | CREDIT | |
|---|---|---|---|---|---|---|
| 1 | | | | | | 1 |
| 2 | | | | | | 2 |
| 3 | | | | | | 3 |
| 4 | | | | | | 4 |
| 5 | | | | | | 5 |
| 6 | | | | | | 6 |
| 7 | | | | | | 7 |
| 8 | | | | | | 8 |
| 9 | | | | | | 9 |
| 10 | | | | | | 10 |
| 11 | | | | | | 11 |
| 12 | | | | | | 12 |
| 13 | | | | | | 13 |
| 14 | | | | | | 14 |
| 15 | | | | | | 15 |
| 16 | | | | | | 16 |
| 17 | | | | | | 17 |
| 18 | | | | | | 18 |
| 19 | | | | | | 19 |
| 20 | | | | | | 20 |

## Exercise 6 (Concluded)

**GENERAL JOURNAL**                                                    PAGE

| | DATE | | DESCRIPTION | POST. REF. | DEBIT | CREDIT | |
|---|---|---|---|---|---|---|---|
| 1 | | | | | | | 1 |
| 2 | | | | | | | 2 |
| 3 | | | | | | | 3 |
| 4 | | | | | | | 4 |
| 5 | | | | | | | 5 |
| 6 | | | | | | | 6 |
| 7 | | | | | | | 7 |
| 8 | | | | | | | 8 |
| 9 | | | | | | | 9 |
| 10 | | | | | | | 10 |
| 11 | | | | | | | 11 |
| 12 | | | | | | | 12 |
| 13 | | | | | | | 13 |
| 14 | | | | | | | 14 |
| 15 | | | | | | | 15 |
| 16 | | | | | | | 16 |
| 17 | | | | | | | 17 |
| 18 | | | | | | | 18 |
| 19 | | | | | | | 19 |
| 20 | | | | | | | 20 |
| 21 | | | | | | | 21 |
| 22 | | | | | | | 22 |
| 23 | | | | | | | 23 |
| 24 | | | | | | | 24 |
| 25 | | | | | | | 25 |
| 26 | | | | | | | 26 |
| 27 | | | | | | | 27 |
| 28 | | | | | | | 28 |
| 29 | | | | | | | 29 |
| 30 | | | | | | | 30 |
| 31 | | | | | | | 31 |
| 32 | | | | | | | 32 |
| 33 | | | | | | | 33 |
| 34 | | | | | | | 34 |

# PROBLEMS

## Problem 7  (LO 2/3)  SALES, SALES RETURNS AND ALLOWANCES, AND CASH RECEIPTS TRANSACTIONS

The following information represents transactions for Kwan Chu's Fish Market for the month of July 20--. Sales tax is 6%.

July   1  Sold merchandise on account to B. A. Smith, $137.50, plus sales tax. Sale No. 33.

3  B. A. Smith returned merchandise worth $15.00, plus sales tax, for a credit. Credit Memo No.11.

5  Sold merchandise on account to L. L. Unis, $218.00, plus sales tax. Sale No. 34.

7  Cash sales for the week were $325.44, plus sales tax.

10  Sold merchandise on account to W. P. Clark, $208.00, plus sales tax. Sale No. 35.

11  Received $129.85 from B. A. Smith, on account.

13  W. P. Clark returned merchandise worth $22.00, plus sales tax, for a credit. Credit Memo No. 12.

14  Cash sales for the week were $411.20, plus sales tax.

16  Sold merchandise on account to B. A. Smith, $282.50, plus sales tax. Sale No. 36.

17  Received $231.08 from L. L. Unis, on account.

21  Cash sales for the week were $292.50, plus sales tax.

24  Sold merchandise on account to L. L. Unis, $224.50, plus sales tax. Sale No. 37.

28  Cash sales for the week were $300.50, plus sales tax.

31  Received $197.16 from W. P. Clark, on account.

*Required:*

Using the information provided, record the transactions in the general journal below and on pages 153–154.

## GENERAL JOURNAL

PAGE

| | DATE | DESCRIPTION | POST. REF. | DEBIT | CREDIT | |
|---|---|---|---|---|---|---|
| 1 | | | | | | 1 |
| 2 | | | | | | 2 |
| 3 | | | | | | 3 |
| 4 | | | | | | 4 |
| 5 | | | | | | 5 |
| 6 | | | | | | 6 |
| 7 | | | | | | 7 |
| 8 | | | | | | 8 |
| 9 | | | | | | 9 |
| 10 | | | | | | 10 |
| 11 | | | | | | 11 |
| 12 | | | | | | 12 |
| 13 | | | | | | 13 |
| 14 | | | | | | 14 |
| 15 | | | | | | 15 |

## Problem 7 (Continued)

### GENERAL JOURNAL                                    PAGE _____

| | DATE | | DESCRIPTION | POST. REF. | DEBIT | CREDIT | |
|---|---|---|---|---|---|---|---|
| 1 | | | | | | | 1 |
| 2 | | | | | | | 2 |
| 3 | | | | | | | 3 |
| 4 | | | | | | | 4 |
| 5 | | | | | | | 5 |
| 6 | | | | | | | 6 |
| 7 | | | | | | | 7 |
| 8 | | | | | | | 8 |
| 9 | | | | | | | 9 |
| 10 | | | | | | | 10 |
| 11 | | | | | | | 11 |
| 12 | | | | | | | 12 |
| 13 | | | | | | | 13 |
| 14 | | | | | | | 14 |
| 15 | | | | | | | 15 |
| 16 | | | | | | | 16 |
| 17 | | | | | | | 17 |
| 18 | | | | | | | 18 |
| 19 | | | | | | | 19 |
| 20 | | | | | | | 20 |
| 21 | | | | | | | 21 |
| 22 | | | | | | | 22 |
| 23 | | | | | | | 23 |
| 24 | | | | | | | 24 |
| 25 | | | | | | | 25 |
| 26 | | | | | | | 26 |
| 27 | | | | | | | 27 |
| 28 | | | | | | | 28 |
| 29 | | | | | | | 29 |
| 30 | | | | | | | 30 |

## Problem 7 (Concluded)

**GENERAL JOURNAL**                                                    PAGE

| | DATE | | DESCRIPTION | POST. REF. | DEBIT | CREDIT | |
|---|---|---|---|---|---|---|---|
| 1 | | | | | | | 1 |
| 2 | | | | | | | 2 |
| 3 | | | | | | | 3 |
| 4 | | | | | | | 4 |
| 5 | | | | | | | 5 |
| 6 | | | | | | | 6 |
| 7 | | | | | | | 7 |
| 8 | | | | | | | 8 |
| 9 | | | | | | | 9 |
| 10 | | | | | | | 10 |
| 11 | | | | | | | 11 |
| 12 | | | | | | | 12 |
| 13 | | | | | | | 13 |
| 14 | | | | | | | 14 |
| 15 | | | | | | | 15 |
| 16 | | | | | | | 16 |
| 17 | | | | | | | 17 |
| 18 | | | | | | | 18 |
| 19 | | | | | | | 19 |
| 20 | | | | | | | 20 |
| 21 | | | | | | | 21 |
| 22 | | | | | | | 22 |
| 23 | | | | | | | 23 |
| 24 | | | | | | | 24 |
| 25 | | | | | | | 25 |
| 26 | | | | | | | 26 |
| 27 | | | | | | | 27 |
| 28 | | | | | | | 28 |
| 29 | | | | | | | 29 |
| 30 | | | | | | | 30 |
| 31 | | | | | | | 31 |

## Problem 8 (LO 3/4) SALES, LEDGERS, AND SCHEDULE OF ACCOUNTS RECEIVABLE

H. K. Smythe operates Leather All, a leather shop that sells luggage, handbags, business cases, and other leather goods. During the month of May, the following sales on account were made:

| May | 3 | Sold merchandise on account to T. A. Pigdon, $247.50, plus sales tax of $14.85. Sale No. 51. |
| | 4 | Sold merchandise on account to J. R. Feyton, $55.00, plus sales tax of $3.30. Sale No. 52. |
| | 6 | Sold merchandise on account to P. C. McMurdy, $99.00, plus sales tax of $5.94. Sale No. 53. |
| | 10 | Sold merchandise on account to J. T. Messer, $175.00, plus sales tax of $10.50. Sale No. 54. |
| | 12 | Sold merchandise on account to A. F. Schlitz, $355.00, plus sales tax of $21.30. Sale No. 55. |
| | 13 | Sold merchandise on account to J. R. Feyton, $215.00, plus sales tax of $12.90. Sale No. 56. |
| | 20 | Sold merchandise on account to P. C. McMurdy, $400.00, plus sales tax of $24.00. Sale No. 57. |
| | 28 | Sold merchandise on account to J. T. Messer, $255.00, plus sales tax of $15.30. Sale No. 58. |

*Required:*

1. Enter the above transactions in the general journal provided below and on page 156 (start with page 7).
2. Post the entries to the general ledger and accounts receivable ledger on pages 156–158.
3. Prepare a schedule of accounts receivable as of May 31.

**1.**                                     **GENERAL JOURNAL**                                     PAGE

| | DATE | | DESCRIPTION | POST. REF. | DEBIT | CREDIT | |
|---|---|---|---|---|---|---|---|
| 1 | | | | | | | 1 |
| 2 | | | | | | | 2 |
| 3 | | | | | | | 3 |
| 4 | | | | | | | 4 |
| 5 | | | | | | | 5 |
| 6 | | | | | | | 6 |
| 7 | | | | | | | 7 |
| 8 | | | | | | | 8 |
| 9 | | | | | | | 9 |
| 10 | | | | | | | 10 |
| 11 | | | | | | | 11 |
| 12 | | | | | | | 12 |
| 13 | | | | | | | 13 |
| 14 | | | | | | | 14 |
| 15 | | | | | | | 15 |
| 16 | | | | | | | 16 |
| 17 | | | | | | | 17 |
| 18 | | | | | | | 18 |
| 19 | | | | | | | 19 |
| 20 | | | | | | | 20 |

**Problem 8 (Continued)**

## GENERAL JOURNAL

PAGE

| | DATE | DESCRIPTION | POST. REF. | DEBIT | CREDIT | |
|---|---|---|---|---|---|---|
| 1 | | | | | | 1 |
| 2 | | | | | | 2 |
| 3 | | | | | | 3 |
| 4 | | | | | | 4 |
| 5 | | | | | | 5 |
| 6 | | | | | | 6 |
| 7 | | | | | | 7 |
| 8 | | | | | | 8 |
| 9 | | | | | | 9 |
| 10 | | | | | | 10 |
| 11 | | | | | | 11 |
| 12 | | | | | | 12 |
| 13 | | | | | | 13 |
| 14 | | | | | | 14 |
| 15 | | | | | | 15 |
| 16 | | | | | | 16 |
| 17 | | | | | | 17 |
| 18 | | | | | | 18 |
| 19 | | | | | | 19 |

**2.**

## GENERAL LEDGER

ACCOUNT   Accounts Receivable                                      ACCOUNT NO.   122

| DATE | | ITEM | POST. REF. | DEBIT | CREDIT | BALANCE DEBIT | BALANCE CREDIT |
|---|---|---|---|---|---|---|---|
| 20-- May | 1 | Balance | ✓ | | | 8 3 4 00 | |
| | | | | | | | |
| | | | | | | | |
| | | | | | | | |
| | | | | | | | |
| | | | | | | | |
| | | | | | | | |

**Problem 8 (Continued)**

ACCOUNT  Sales Tax Payable                                          ACCOUNT NO.  231

| DATE | ITEM | POST. REF. | DEBIT | CREDIT | BALANCE | |
|------|------|-----------|-------|--------|---------|--|
| | | | | | DEBIT | CREDIT |
| | | | | | | |
| | | | | | | |
| | | | | | | |
| | | | | | | |
| | | | | | | |
| | | | | | | |
| | | | | | | |
| | | | | | | |

ACCOUNT  Sales                                                     ACCOUNT NO.  401

| DATE | ITEM | POST. REF. | DEBIT | CREDIT | BALANCE | |
|------|------|-----------|-------|--------|---------|--|
| | | | | | DEBIT | CREDIT |
| | | | | | | |
| | | | | | | |
| | | | | | | |
| | | | | | | |
| | | | | | | |
| | | | | | | |
| | | | | | | |
| | | | | | | |

## ACCOUNTS RECEIVABLE LEDGER

**NAME**  J. R. Feyton

**ADDRESS**  6022 Columbia, St. Louis, MO  63139-1906

| DATE | ITEM | POST. REF. | DEBIT | CREDIT | BALANCE |
|------|------|-----------|-------|--------|---------|
| | | | | | |
| | | | | | |
| | | | | | |

**Problem 8 (Continued)**

**NAME** P. C. McMurdy

**ADDRESS** 1214 N. 2nd St., E. St. Louis, IL  62201-2679

| DATE | | ITEM | POST. REF. | DEBIT | CREDIT | BALANCE |
|---|---|---|---|---|---|---|
| 20-- May | 1 | Balance | ✓ | | | 1 2 5 00 |
| | | | | | | |
| | | | | | | |

**NAME** J. T. Messer

**ADDRESS** P.O. Box 249, Chesterfield, MO  63017-3901

| DATE | | ITEM | POST. REF. | DEBIT | CREDIT | BALANCE |
|---|---|---|---|---|---|---|
| 20-- May | 1 | Balance | ✓ | | | 1 7 7 00 |
| | | | | | | |
| | | | | | | |

**NAME** T. A. Pigdon

**ADDRESS** 1070 Purcell, University City, MO  63130-1546

| DATE | | ITEM | POST. REF. | DEBIT | CREDIT | BALANCE |
|---|---|---|---|---|---|---|
| 20-- May | 1 | Balance | ✓ | | | 2 8 0 00 |
| | | | | | | |
| | | | | | | |

**NAME** A. F. Schlitz

**ADDRESS** 800 Lindbergh Blvd., St. Louis, MO  63166-1546

| DATE | | ITEM | POST. REF. | DEBIT | CREDIT | BALANCE |
|---|---|---|---|---|---|---|
| 20-- May | 1 | Balance | ✓ | | | 2 5 2 00 |
| | | | | | | |
| | | | | | | |

**Problem 8 (Concluded)**

**3.** _____

_____

| | | | | | | |
|---|---|---|---|---|---|---|
| | | | | | | |
| | | | | | | |
| | | | | | | |
| | | | | | | |
| | | | | | | |
| | | | | | | |
| | | | | | | |
| | | | | | | |
| | | | | | | |
| | | | | | | |
| | | | | | | |
| | | | | | | |

## Problem 9  (LO 2/3)  SALES, SALES RETURNS AND ALLOWANCES, CASH RECEIPTS, AND LEDGERS

Paula Angelillis operates the Hard-to-Find Auto Parts Store. Much of her business is by mail. The following transactions related to sales and cash receipts occurred during June:

| | | |
|---|---|---|
| June | 1 | Received $300 from A. K. Wells, including $14.29 of sales tax, for field cash sale. (Field cash sales are not included in cash register tapes.) |
| | 5 | Received $125.60 from L. Strous on account. |
| | 10 | Received $263.25 from D. Manning on account. |
| | 12 | Q. Striker returned merchandise for credit. The sales price was $215.00, plus sales tax of $10.75. |
| | 18 | Received $58.25 from D. Warding on account. |
| | 20 | Received $1,000 from B. L. Stryker, including $47.62 tax (field cash sale). |
| | 21 | Received $29.99 from L. Clese on account. |
| | 24 | R. Popielarz returned merchandise for credit. Sales price was $116.25, plus sales tax of $5.81. |
| | 27 | Received $426.00 from L. LeCount on account. |
| | 30 | Cash and bank credit card sales for the month were $8,200, plus sales tax of $410.00. Bank credit card expense is $80. |

*Required:*

1. Enter each transaction in the general journal provided on pages 160–161 (start with page 8).
2. Post the entries to the general and accounts receivable ledgers (pages 161–164).

**Problem 9 (Continued)**

**1.**
GENERAL JOURNAL

PAGE

| | DATE | DESCRIPTION | POST. REF. | DEBIT | CREDIT | |
|---|---|---|---|---|---|---|
| 1 | | | | | | 1 |
| 2 | | | | | | 2 |
| 3 | | | | | | 3 |
| 4 | | | | | | 4 |
| 5 | | | | | | 5 |
| 6 | | | | | | 6 |
| 7 | | | | | | 7 |
| 8 | | | | | | 8 |
| 9 | | | | | | 9 |
| 10 | | | | | | 10 |
| 11 | | | | | | 11 |
| 12 | | | | | | 12 |
| 13 | | | | | | 13 |
| 14 | | | | | | 14 |
| 15 | | | | | | 15 |
| 16 | | | | | | 16 |
| 17 | | | | | | 17 |
| 18 | | | | | | 18 |
| 19 | | | | | | 19 |
| 20 | | | | | | 20 |
| 21 | | | | | | 21 |
| 22 | | | | | | 22 |
| 23 | | | | | | 23 |
| 24 | | | | | | 24 |
| 25 | | | | | | 25 |
| 26 | | | | | | 26 |
| 27 | | | | | | 27 |
| 28 | | | | | | 28 |
| 29 | | | | | | 29 |
| 30 | | | | | | 30 |
| 31 | | | | | | 31 |
| 32 | | | | | | 32 |
| 33 | | | | | | 33 |
| 34 | | | | | | 34 |
| 35 | | | | | | 35 |
| 36 | | | | | | 36 |

**Problem 9 (Continued)**

## GENERAL JOURNAL                                           PAGE ____

| | DATE | | DESCRIPTION | POST. REF. | DEBIT | CREDIT | |
|---|---|---|---|---|---|---|---|
| 1 | | | | | | | 1 |
| 2 | | | | | | | 2 |
| 3 | | | | | | | 3 |
| 4 | | | | | | | 4 |
| 5 | | | | | | | 5 |
| 6 | | | | | | | 6 |
| 7 | | | | | | | 7 |
| 8 | | | | | | | 8 |
| 9 | | | | | | | 9 |
| 10 | | | | | | | 10 |
| 11 | | | | | | | 11 |
| 12 | | | | | | | 12 |
| 13 | | | | | | | 13 |
| 14 | | | | | | | 14 |
| 15 | | | | | | | 15 |
| 16 | | | | | | | 16 |
| 17 | | | | | | | 17 |

**2.**                       ## GENERAL LEDGER

ACCOUNT  Cash                                    ACCOUNT NO.  101

| DATE | | ITEM | POST. REF. | DEBIT | CREDIT | BALANCE | |
|---|---|---|---|---|---|---|---|
| | | | | | | DEBIT | CREDIT |
| 20-- June | 1 | Balance | ✓ | | | 13 2 0 0 25 | |
| | | | | | | | |
| | | | | | | | |
| | | | | | | | |
| | | | | | | | |
| | | | | | | | |
| | | | | | | | |
| | | | | | | | |

**Problem 9 (Continued)**

ACCOUNT  Accounts Receivable                                           ACCOUNT NO.  122

| DATE | | ITEM | POST. REF. | DEBIT | CREDIT | BALANCE | |
|---|---|---|---|---|---|---|---|
| | | | | | | DEBIT | CREDIT |
| 20-- June | 1 | Balance | ✓ | | | 1 2 5 0 90 | |
| | | | | | | | |
| | | | | | | | |
| | | | | | | | |
| | | | | | | | |
| | | | | | | | |
| | | | | | | | |

ACCOUNT  Sales Tax Payable                                             ACCOUNT NO.  231

| DATE | | ITEM | POST. REF. | DEBIT | CREDIT | BALANCE | |
|---|---|---|---|---|---|---|---|
| | | | | | | DEBIT | CREDIT |
| 20-- June | 1 | Balance | ✓ | | | | 1 2 5 00 |
| | | | | | | | |
| | | | | | | | |
| | | | | | | | |
| | | | | | | | |
| | | | | | | | |
| | | | | | | | |

ACCOUNT  Sales                                                        ACCOUNT NO.  401

| DATE | | ITEM | POST. REF. | DEBIT | CREDIT | BALANCE | |
|---|---|---|---|---|---|---|---|
| | | | | | | DEBIT | CREDIT |
| | | | | | | | |
| | | | | | | | |
| | | | | | | | |

ACCOUNT  Sales Returns and Allowances                                 ACCOUNT NO.  401.1

| DATE | | ITEM | POST. REF. | DEBIT | CREDIT | BALANCE | |
|---|---|---|---|---|---|---|---|
| | | | | | | DEBIT | CREDIT |
| | | | | | | | |
| | | | | | | | |
| | | | | | | | |

## Problem 9 (Continued)

ACCOUNT   Bank Credit Card Expense                                ACCOUNT NO. 513

| DATE | ITEM | POST. REF. | DEBIT | CREDIT | BALANCE | |
|---|---|---|---|---|---|---|
| | | | | | DEBIT | CREDIT |
| | | | | | | |
| | | | | | | |
| | | | | | | |

## ACCOUNTS RECEIVABLE LEDGER

**NAME** L. Clese

**ADDRESS** 875 Glenway Drive, Glendale, MO 63122-4112

| DATE | | ITEM | POST. REF. | DEBIT | CREDIT | BALANCE |
|---|---|---|---|---|---|---|
| 20--<br>June | 1 | Balance | ✓ | | | 2 9 99 |
| | | | | | | |
| | | | | | | |
| | | | | | | |

**NAME** L. LeCount

**ADDRESS** 1439 East Broad Street, Columbus, OH 43205-9892

| DATE | | ITEM | POST. REF. | DEBIT | CREDIT | BALANCE |
|---|---|---|---|---|---|---|
| 20--<br>June | 1 | Balance | ✓ | | | 4 2 6 00 |
| | | | | | | |
| | | | | | | |
| | | | | | | |

**NAME** D. Manning

**ADDRESS** 2101 Cumberland Road, Noblesville, IN 47870-2435

| DATE | | ITEM | POST. REF. | DEBIT | CREDIT | BALANCE |
|---|---|---|---|---|---|---|
| 20--<br>June | 1 | Balance | ✓ | | | 2 6 3 25 |
| | | | | | | |
| | | | | | | |
| | | | | | | |

## Problem 9 (Concluded)

**NAME** R. Popielarz

**ADDRESS** 3001 Hillcrest Drive, Dallas, PA  18612-6854

| DATE | | ITEM | POST. REF. | DEBIT | CREDIT | BALANCE |
|---|---|---|---|---|---|---|
| 20--<br>June | 1 | Balance | ✓ | | | 1 2 2 06 |
| | | | | | | |
| | | | | | | |

**NAME** Q. Striker

**ADDRESS** 4113 Main Street, Beech Grove, IN  46107-9643

| DATE | | ITEM | POST. REF. | DEBIT | CREDIT | BALANCE |
|---|---|---|---|---|---|---|
| 20--<br>June | 1 | Balance | ✓ | | | 2 2 5 75 |
| | | | | | | |
| | | | | | | |
| | | | | | | |

**NAME** L. Strous

**ADDRESS** 2215 N. State Road 135, Greenwood, IN  46142-6432

| DATE | | ITEM | POST. REF. | DEBIT | CREDIT | BALANCE |
|---|---|---|---|---|---|---|
| 20--<br>June | 1 | Balance | ✓ | | | 1 2 5 60 |
| | | | | | | |
| | | | | | | |
| | | | | | | |

**NAME** D. Warding

**ADDRESS** 1100 W. Main Street, Carmel, IN  46032-2364

| DATE | | ITEM | POST. REF. | DEBIT | CREDIT | BALANCE |
|---|---|---|---|---|---|---|
| 20--<br>June | 1 | Balance | ✓ | | | 5 8 25 |
| | | | | | | |
| | | | | | | |
| | | | | | | |

# CHAPTER 11
# ACCOUNTING FOR PURCHASES AND CASH PAYMENTS

## LEARNING OBJECTIVES

Chapter 11 continues the study of merchandise transactions. In this chapter, purchases and cash payments are emphasized, and another new ledger and new schedule are introduced. As was done in Chapter 10, merchandise purchases transactions are shown in general journal format.

**Objective 1.    Define merchandise purchases transactions.**

For a merchandising business, **purchases** refers to merchandise acquired for resale. Several important documents are used in the purchasing process of a merchandising business. A **purchase requisition** is a form used to request the purchasing department to purchase merchandise or other property. A **purchase order** is a written order to buy goods from a specific vendor (supplier). A **receiving report** is prepared upon receipt of merchandise and indicates what merchandise has been received. An **invoice** is a document prepared by the seller as a bill for the merchandise shipped. To the seller, this is a sales invoice. To the buyer, it is called a **purchase invoice.**

The accounting department compares the purchase invoice with the purchase requisition, purchase order, and receiving report. If the invoice is for the goods ordered at the correct price, the invoice is paid by the due date.

When credit terms such as 2/10, n/30 are offered by the seller, a **cash discount** is available to the buyer if the bill is paid within the discount period. Another type of discount, called a **trade discount,** is often offered by manufacturers and wholesalers. This discount is a reduction from the list or catalog price. By simply adjusting the trade discount percentages, companies can avoid the cost of reprinting catalogs every time there is a change in price.

**Objective 2.    Describe and use merchandise purchases accounts and compute gross profit.**

To account for merchandise purchases transactions, four new accounts are used. These are **Purchases, Purchases Returns and Allowances, Purchases Discounts,** and **Freight-In.**

**Purchases** is an account to which the cost of merchandise (i.e., inventory acquired for resale) is debited.

**Purchases Returns and Allowances** is a contra-purchases account to which returns of merchandise and price reductions are credited. This account is subtracted from Purchases on the income statement.

**Purchases Discounts** is a contra-purchases account to which any cash discounts allowed on purchases are credited. This account is subtracted from Purchases on the income statement.

**Freight-In** is an adjunct-purchases account to which transportation charges on merchandise purchases are debited. This account is added to Purchases on the income statement.

**FOB shipping point** means that transportation charges are paid by the buyer. **FOB destination** means that transportation charges are paid by the seller.

Gross profit is computed using the following format:

| | | | | | |
|---|---|---|---|---|---|
| Sales | | | | $xxxx | |
| | Less: | Sales returns and allowances | $xxxx | | |
| | | Sales discounts | xxxx | xxxx | |
| | Net sales | | | | $xxxx |
| Cost of goods sold: | | | | | |
| | Merchandise inventory, beginning of period | | | $xxxx | |
| | Purchases | | $xxxx | | |
| | Less: | Purchases returns and allowances | $xxxx | | |
| | | Purchases discounts | xxxx | xxxx | |
| | Net purchases | | $xxxx | | |
| | Add freight-in | | xxxx | | |
| | Cost of goods purchased | | | xxxx | |
| | Goods available for sale | | | $xxxx | |
| | Less merchandise inventory, end of period | | | xxxx | |
| | Cost of goods sold | | | | xxxx |
| Gross profit | | | | | $xxxx |

**Objective 3.  Describe and use the accounts payable ledger.**

The accounts payable account in the general ledger provides a record of the total amount owed by a business to its suppliers. To help run the business, a record also is needed of the amount owed to each supplier. The accounts payable subsidiary ledger provides this information.

When an accounts payable subsidiary ledger is used, the accounts payable account in the general ledger is a "controlling account." The accounts payable ledger is "subsidiary" to this account. Transactions are posted daily from the general journal to both the general ledger and the accounts payable ledger.

**Objective 4.  Prepare a schedule of accounts payable.**

The Accounts Payable balance in the general ledger should equal the sum of the supplier balances in the accounts payable ledger. A listing of supplier accounts and balances is called a **schedule of accounts payable.** This schedule is usually prepared at the end of the month to verify that the sum of the accounts payable ledger balances equals the Accounts Payable balance.

## REVIEW QUESTIONS

**Instructions:** Analyze each of the following items carefully before writing your answer in the column at the right.

| | Question | Answer |
|---|---|---|
| | **Question** | **Answer** |
| **LO 1** | **1.** For a merchandising business, _____ refers to merchandise acquired for resale. ................................................................ | _____ |
| **LO 1** | **2.** A(n) _____ is a form used to request the purchasing department to purchase merchandise or other property. .............. | _____ |
| **LO 1** | **3.** A(n) _____ is a written order to buy goods from a specific vendor (supplier). ........................................................... | _____ |

**LO 1**   **4.** When the merchandise is received, a(n) _____ indicating what has been received is prepared. .............................................   _____

**LO 1**   **5.** To the buyer, a document prepared by the seller as a bill for the merchandise shipped is called a(n) _____. .............................   _____

**LO 1**   **6.** In the credit terms 2/10, n/30, the 2 represents a(n) _____. ....   _____

**LO 1**   **7.** A(n) _____ is a type of discount offered by manufacturers and wholesalers as a reduction from the list or catalog price offered to different classes of customers. ......................................   _____

**LO 2**   **8.** List the four accounts used with merchandise purchases transactions. ......................................................................   _____

_____

_____

_____

**LO 2**   **9.** FOB shipping point means that transportation charges are paid by the _____. ......................................................................   _____

**LO 2**   **10.** FOB destination means that transportation charges are paid by the _____. ......................................................................   _____

**LO 2**   **11.** Cost of merchandise available for sale less the end-of-period merchandise inventory is called _____. ...............................   _____

**LO 2**   **12.** Net sales minus cost of merchandise sold is called _____. .....   _____

**LO 3**   **13.** A separate ledger containing an individual account payable for each supplier is called a(n) _____. .........................................   _____

**LO 3**   **14.** To indicate that the accounts payable ledger has been posted, a slash and a _____ are entered in the Posting Reference column of the general journal. ..................................................................   _____

**LO 3**   **15.** If a buyer returns merchandise or is given an allowance for damaged merchandise, the account _____ is credited for the dollar amount. ......................................................................   _____

**LO 3**   **16.** Purchases returns and allowances are posted to both the general ledger and the _____ ledger. ....................................................   _____

**LO 3**   **17.** When a payment is made on account, _____ is debited. ..........   _____

**LO 4**   **18.** To verify that the sum of the accounts payable ledger balances equals the Accounts Payable balance, a(n) _____ is prepared.   _____

# EXERCISES

## Exercise 1 (LO 1) PURCHASE REQUISITION

You are employed by Eberle Hardware, a retail hardware business, as manager of the lawn and garden department. On October 1, 20--, after completing an inventory, you decide that the following merchandise should be ordered:

| | | | |
|---|---|---|---|
| 15 | All steel rubber-tire wheelbarrows | 24 | Spade shovels |
| 25 | Garden hose, 1/2", 50 ft. | 6 | Long-handle spade shovels |
| 3 | Power mower, 21" cut | 12 | Spade forks |
| 5 | Heavy duty rototillers | | |

You would like delivery within 10 days and should be notified upon receipt of the merchandise. Using the form provided below, prepare the purchase requisition.

---

**Eberle Hardware**

110 E. Kirkwood Ave.
Indianapolis, IN 46011-3274

**Purchase Requisition**

Requisition No. _502_

Required for Department _____     Date Issued _____

Advise _____  On Delivery     Date Required _____

| Quantity | Description |
|---|---|
| | |
| | |
| | |
| | |
| | |

Approved By _____     Requisition Placed By _____

**DEPARTMENT MANAGER'S MEMORANDUM**

Issued To _____

Purchase Order No. _____     _____

Date _____     _____

---

*NOTE: The department manager's memorandum at the bottom of the form should not be completed until after the purchase order is placed in Exercise 2.*

## Exercise 2  (LO 1)  PURCHASE ORDER

Assume you are acting as purchasing agent for Eberle Hardware. On October 2, 20--, order the merchandise specified on Requisition No. 502 in Exercise 1 from Wesner's Supply, 1476 S. Spurr Drive, Miami, FL 33161-1516. Use the purchase order form provided below specifying shipment by AAA freight FOB destination; unit prices as follows:

| | |
|---|---|
| All steel rubber-tire wheelbarrows | $ 20.35 |
| Garden hose, 1/2", 50 ft. | 4.65 |
| Power mower, 21" cut | 180.75 |
| Heavy duty rototillers | 291.50 |
| Spade shovels | 7.45 |
| Long-handle spade shovels | 9.30 |
| Spade forks | 7.70 |

After preparing the purchase order, fill in the department manager's memorandum at the bottom of Purchase Requisition No. 502 prepared in Exercise 1. Assume the requisition was approved by Scott Roturt.

**Eberle Hardware**

110 E. Kirkwood Ave.
Indianapolis, IN 46011-3274

**Purchase Order**

Order No.  361

Date _____

To _____

_____

_____

Deliver By _____

Ship via _____

FOB _____

| Quantity | Description | Unit Price | Total |
|---|---|---|---|
| | | | |
| | | | |
| | | | |
| | | | |
| | | | |

By _____

## Exercise 3  (LO 1)  PURCHASE INVOICES

The purchase invoice below received from Wesner's Supply has been referred to you for verification. Compare it with Purchase Order No. 361 in Exercise 2 and verify (a) the quantities ordered, (b) the quantities shipped, (c) the unit prices, (d) the extensions, and (e) the total amount of the invoice. For each item that has been verified, report any discrepancies detected.

| INVOICE NO | SOLD TO | SHIP TO |
|---|---|---|
| | Eberle Hardware<br>110 E. Kirkwood Ave.<br>Indianapolis, IN 46011-3274 | same |

**W S  Wesner's Supply**

1476 S. Spurr Drive, Miami, FL  33161-1516

| INVOICE DATE | YOUR ORDER NO & DATE | DATE SHIPPED |
|---|---|---|
| Oct. 7, 20-- | 361 Oct. 2, 20-- | Oct. 7, 20-- |
| | REQUISITION NO | OUR ORDER NO |
| | | |

| TERMS | FOB | CAR INITIALS & NO | HOW SHIPPED & ROUTE | SHIPPED FROM |
|---|---|---|---|---|
| 2/10, n/30 | Destination | | Freight AAA | Miami |

| QUANTITY SHIPPED | DESCRIPTION | UNIT PRICE | EXTENSION |
|---|---|---|---|
| 15 | All steel rubber-tire wheelbarrows | $ 20.35 | $   305.25 |
| 25 | Garden hose, 1/2", 50 ft. | 4.65 | 116.25 |
| 4 | Power mower, 21" cut | 291.50 | 1,166.00 |
| 5 | Heavy duty rototillers | 180.75 | 903.75 |
| 24 | Spade shovels | 7.95 | 178.80 |
| 6 | Long-handle spade shovels | 9.30 | 57.00 |
| 12 | Spade forks | 7.70 | 92.40 |
| | | | $2,819.45 |

_____

_____

_____

_____

_____

_____

_____

_____

_____

## Exercise 4  (LO 1)  TRADE DISCOUNT

Skirvin Enterprises purchased merchandise with a list price of $800, less a trade discount of 10%. Compute the amount to be paid.

_____

_____

_____

## Exercise 5  (LO1)  CASH DISCOUNT

Geisel's Boating Supplies purchased life preservers and other boating equipment for resale costing $1,200, terms 3/10, n/60.

1.  If Geisel makes payment within the discount period, how much will be paid?

_____

_____

2.  If the invoice terms were 2/10, n/30, compute the cash discount available to Geisel's if payment is made within the discount period.

_____

_____

## Exercise 6  (LO2)  GROSS PROFIT

The following information was taken from the records of Hi-Fi Specialists for the month of August 20--:

| | |
|---|---:|
| Sales | $257,800 |
| Sales returns and allowances | 1,900 |
| Sales discounts | 400 |
| Merchandise inventory, August 1 | 38,000 |
| Merchandise inventory, August 31 | 32,000 |
| Purchases | 200,000 |
| Purchases returns and allowances | 10,200 |
| Purchases discounts | 4,000 |
| Freight-In | 2,000 |

*Required:*

Using the form on page 172, show the computation of gross profit on the income statement for the month of August.

## Exercise 6 (Concluded)

### Exercise 7  (LO 3)  JOURNALIZING PURCHASES AND CASH PAYMENTS

The following transactions occurred during the month of November at O'Henesy Office Equipment and Supply:

Nov.  5   Purchased the following merchandise on account; unit prices are given:

| | | |
|---|---|---|
| 20 | Mini-shredders | $    63.95 |
| 10 | Hi-speed printer-scanners | 900.00 |
| 5 | Laptop computers | 1,995.00 |

The purchase has a trade discount of 15% and credit terms of 2/10, n/30.

15   Issued a check for the amount due on the November 5 purchase.

*Required:*

1. Journalize the above transactions in the general journal below.
2. Give the appropriate general journal entry if the payment is not made until December 5.

### 1. and 2.

**GENERAL JOURNAL**                                  PAGE _____

| | DATE | DESCRIPTION | POST. REF. | DEBIT | CREDIT | |
|---|---|---|---|---|---|---|
| 1 | | | | | | 1 |
| 2 | | | | | | 2 |
| 3 | | | | | | 3 |
| 4 | | | | | | 4 |
| 5 | | | | | | 5 |
| 6 | | | | | | 6 |
| 7 | | | | | | 7 |
| 8 | | | | | | 8 |
| 9 | | | | | | 9 |
| 10 | | | | | | 10 |
| 11 | | | | | | 11 |

*Supporting calculations:*

_____

_____

_____

_____

_____

_____

_____

# PROBLEMS

## Problem 8  (LO3)  JOURNALIZING AND POSTING PURCHASES TRANSACTIONS

J. R. Lang, owner of Lang's Galleria, made the following purchases of merchandise on account during the month of November 20--:

Nov.  2   Purchase Invoice No. 611, $4,145, from Ford Distributors.

5   Purchase Invoice No. 216, $2,165, from Mueller Wholesaler.

15   Purchase Invoice No. 399, $2,895, from Grant White & Co.

19   Purchase Invoice No. 106, $1,845, from Bailey & Hinds, Inc.

22   Purchase Invoice No. 914, $3,225, from Ford Distributors.

28   Purchase Invoice No. 661, $2,175, from Jackson Company.

30   Purchase Invoice No. 716, $3,500, from Mueller Wholesaler.

*Required:*

1. Record the transactions in the general journal (page 9) on page 175.
2. Post from the journal to the general ledger accounts and the accounts payable ledger accounts (pages 176–177).

**Problem 8 (Continued)**

**1.**

## GENERAL JOURNAL                                            PAGE ____

| | DATE | | DESCRIPTION | POST. REF. | DEBIT | CREDIT | |
|---|---|---|---|---|---|---|---|
| 1 | | | | | | | 1 |
| 2 | | | | | | | 2 |
| 3 | | | | | | | 3 |
| 4 | | | | | | | 4 |
| 5 | | | | | | | 5 |
| 6 | | | | | | | 6 |
| 7 | | | | | | | 7 |
| 8 | | | | | | | 8 |
| 9 | | | | | | | 9 |
| 10 | | | | | | | 10 |
| 11 | | | | | | | 11 |
| 12 | | | | | | | 12 |
| 13 | | | | | | | 13 |
| 14 | | | | | | | 14 |
| 15 | | | | | | | 15 |
| 16 | | | | | | | 16 |
| 17 | | | | | | | 17 |
| 18 | | | | | | | 18 |
| 19 | | | | | | | 19 |
| 20 | | | | | | | 20 |
| 21 | | | | | | | 21 |
| 22 | | | | | | | 22 |
| 23 | | | | | | | 23 |
| 24 | | | | | | | 24 |
| 25 | | | | | | | 25 |
| 26 | | | | | | | 26 |
| 27 | | | | | | | 27 |
| 28 | | | | | | | 28 |
| 29 | | | | | | | 29 |
| 30 | | | | | | | 30 |

**Problem 8 (Continued)**

2.

## GENERAL LEDGER

ACCOUNT  Accounts Payable                                                      ACCOUNT NO.  202

| DATE | ITEM | POST. REF. | DEBIT | CREDIT | BALANCE DEBIT | BALANCE CREDIT |
|------|------|-----------|-------|--------|---------------|----------------|
|      |      |           |       |        |               |                |
|      |      |           |       |        |               |                |
|      |      |           |       |        |               |                |
|      |      |           |       |        |               |                |
|      |      |           |       |        |               |                |
|      |      |           |       |        |               |                |
|      |      |           |       |        |               |                |
|      |      |           |       |        |               |                |

ACCOUNT  Purchases                                                             ACCOUNT NO.  501

| DATE | ITEM | POST. REF. | DEBIT | CREDIT | BALANCE DEBIT | BALANCE CREDIT |
|------|------|-----------|-------|--------|---------------|----------------|
|      |      |           |       |        |               |                |
|      |      |           |       |        |               |                |
|      |      |           |       |        |               |                |
|      |      |           |       |        |               |                |
|      |      |           |       |        |               |                |
|      |      |           |       |        |               |                |
|      |      |           |       |        |               |                |
|      |      |           |       |        |               |                |

## ACCOUNTS PAYABLE LEDGER

**NAME**  Bailey & Hinds, Inc.

**ADDRESS**

| DATE | ITEM | POST. REF. | DEBIT | CREDIT | BALANCE |
|------|------|-----------|-------|--------|---------|
|      |      |           |       |        |         |
|      |      |           |       |        |         |
|      |      |           |       |        |         |
|      |      |           |       |        |         |

## Problem 8 (Concluded)

**NAME** Ford Distributors

**ADDRESS**

| DATE | | ITEM | POST. REF. | DEBIT | CREDIT | BALANCE |
|---|---|---|---|---|---|---|
| | | | | | | |
| | | | | | | |
| | | | | | | |

**NAME** Grant White & Co.

**ADDRESS**

| DATE | | ITEM | POST. REF. | DEBIT | CREDIT | BALANCE |
|---|---|---|---|---|---|---|
| | | | | | | |
| | | | | | | |
| | | | | | | |

**NAME** Jackson Company

**ADDRESS**

| DATE | | ITEM | POST. REF. | DEBIT | CREDIT | BALANCE |
|---|---|---|---|---|---|---|
| | | | | | | |
| | | | | | | |
| | | | | | | |

**NAME** Mueller Wholesaler

**ADDRESS**

| DATE | | ITEM | POST. REF. | DEBIT | CREDIT | BALANCE |
|---|---|---|---|---|---|---|
| | | | | | | |
| | | | | | | |
| | | | | | | |

### Problem 9  (LO 3/4)  PURCHASES TRANSACTIONS AND SCHEDULE OF ACCOUNTS PAYABLE

Tom Bowers operates a business under the name of Tom's Sporting Goods. The books include a general journal and an accounts payable ledger. The following transactions are related to purchases for the month of February:

| Feb. | 3 | Purchased merchandise from Ringer's on account, $498.64. Invoice No. 611; terms 2/10, n/30. |
|------|----|---------|
| | 4 | Purchased merchandise on account from Klein Brothers, $780.11. Invoice No. 112; terms 30 days. |
| | 11 | Purchased merchandise from Corleon's on account, $2,300.00. Invoice No. 432; terms 30 days. |
| | 15 | Received a credit memorandum from Ringer's for $30.00 for merchandise returned that had been purchased on account. |

*Required:*
1. Enter the above transactions in the general journal provided below (page 5).
2. Post from the journal to the general ledger and accounts payable ledger on pages 179–180.
3. Prepare a schedule of accounts payable as of February 28.

**1.**

## GENERAL JOURNAL

PAGE

| | DATE | DESCRIPTION | POST. REF. | DEBIT | CREDIT | |
|----|------|-------------|-----------|-------|--------|----|
| 1 | | | | | | 1 |
| 2 | | | | | | 2 |
| 3 | | | | | | 3 |
| 4 | | | | | | 4 |
| 5 | | | | | | 5 |
| 6 | | | | | | 6 |
| 7 | | | | | | 7 |
| 8 | | | | | | 8 |
| 9 | | | | | | 9 |
| 10 | | | | | | 10 |
| 11 | | | | | | 11 |
| 12 | | | | | | 12 |
| 13 | | | | | | 13 |
| 14 | | | | | | 14 |
| 15 | | | | | | 15 |

**Problem 9 (Continued)**

**2.**

## GENERAL LEDGER

ACCOUNT   Accounts Payable                                                    ACCOUNT NO.   202

| DATE | | ITEM | POST. REF. | DEBIT | CREDIT | BALANCE | |
|---|---|---|---|---|---|---|---|
| | | | | | | DEBIT | CREDIT |
| 20-- Feb. | 1 | Balance | ✓ | | | | 3 1 2 5 50 |
| | | | | | | | |
| | | | | | | | |
| | | | | | | | |
| | | | | | | | |
| | | | | | | | |

ACCOUNT   Purchases                                                          ACCOUNT NO.   501

| DATE | | ITEM | POST. REF. | DEBIT | CREDIT | BALANCE | |
|---|---|---|---|---|---|---|---|
| | | | | | | DEBIT | CREDIT |
| 20-- Feb. | 1 | Balance | ✓ | | | 2 5 0 0 00 | |
| | | | | | | | |
| | | | | | | | |
| | | | | | | | |
| | | | | | | | |

ACCOUNT   Purchases Returns and Allowances                                   ACCOUNT NO.   501.1

| DATE | | ITEM | POST. REF. | DEBIT | CREDIT | BALANCE | |
|---|---|---|---|---|---|---|---|
| | | | | | | DEBIT | CREDIT |
| 20-- Feb. | 1 | Balance | ✓ | | | | 2 0 0 00 |
| | | | | | | | |
| | | | | | | | |
| | | | | | | | |

**Problem 9 (Concluded)**

**ACCOUNTS PAYABLE LEDGER**

**NAME** Corleon's

**ADDRESS** 1894 Winthrop Ave., White Plains, NY  10606-6915

| DATE | | ITEM | POST. REF. | DEBIT | CREDIT | BALANCE |
|---|---|---|---|---|---|---|
| 20--<br>Feb. | 1 | Balance | ✓ | | | 1 6 2 5 50 |
| | | | | | | |
| | | | | | | |

**NAME** Klein Brothers

**ADDRESS** 1728 Camino Real, San Antonio, TX  78238-4420

| DATE | | ITEM | POST. REF. | DEBIT | CREDIT | BALANCE |
|---|---|---|---|---|---|---|
| 20--<br>Feb. | 1 | Balance | ✓ | | | 6 2 5 00 |
| | | | | | | |
| | | | | | | |
| | | | | | | |

**NAME** Ringer's

**ADDRESS** 1500 North Street, Bakersfield, CA  93301-4747

| DATE | | ITEM | POST. REF. | DEBIT | CREDIT | BALANCE |
|---|---|---|---|---|---|---|
| 20--<br>Feb. | 1 | Balance | ✓ | | | 8 7 5 00 |
| | | | | | | |
| | | | | | | |
| | | | | | | |

**3.**

| | | |
|---|---|---|
| | | |
| | | |
| | | |
| | | |
| | | |

## Problem 10 (LO 3/4) CASH PAYMENTS TRANSACTIONS AND SCHEDULE OF ACCOUNTS PAYABLE

Chris Bultman operates a retail shoe store called Bultman Shoes. The books include a general journal and an accounts payable ledger. The following transactions are related to cash payments for the month of August:

Aug. 1 Issued Check No. 47 for $900.00 in payment of rent (Rent Expense) for August.

3 Issued Check No. 48 to Blue Suede Shoes Company in payment on account, $640.00, less 2% discount.

9 Issued Check No. 49 to Style-Rite in payment on account, $800.00, less 3% discount.

14 Issued Check No. 50 for $125.28 in payment of utility bill (Utilities Expense).

20 Issued Check No. 51 to Baldo Company in payment for cash purchase, $525.00.

22 Issued Check No. 52 to West Coast Shoes in payment on account, $625.00. A discount of 2% was lost because Bultman neglected to pay the invoice within the discount period.

27 Issued Check No. 53 for $2,000.00 to Bultman for a cash withdrawal for personal use.

*Required:*

1. Enter the above transactions in the general journal (page 4) on page 182.
2. Post from the journal to the general ledger and accounts payable ledger accounts provided on pages 183–185.
3. Prepare a schedule of accounts payable for Bultman Shoes on August 31, 20--, using the form on page 185.

**Problem 10 (Continued)**

**1.**

## GENERAL JOURNAL

| | DATE | DESCRIPTION | POST. REF. | DEBIT | CREDIT | |
|---|---|---|---|---|---|---|
| 1 | | | | | | 1 |
| 2 | | | | | | 2 |
| 3 | | | | | | 3 |
| 4 | | | | | | 4 |
| 5 | | | | | | 5 |
| 6 | | | | | | 6 |
| 7 | | | | | | 7 |
| 8 | | | | | | 8 |
| 9 | | | | | | 9 |
| 10 | | | | | | 10 |
| 11 | | | | | | 11 |
| 12 | | | | | | 12 |
| 13 | | | | | | 13 |
| 14 | | | | | | 14 |
| 15 | | | | | | 15 |
| 16 | | | | | | 16 |
| 17 | | | | | | 17 |
| 18 | | | | | | 18 |
| 19 | | | | | | 19 |
| 20 | | | | | | 20 |
| 21 | | | | | | 21 |
| 22 | | | | | | 22 |
| 23 | | | | | | 23 |
| 24 | | | | | | 24 |
| 25 | | | | | | 25 |
| 26 | | | | | | 26 |
| 27 | | | | | | 27 |
| 28 | | | | | | 28 |
| 29 | | | | | | 29 |
| 30 | | | | | | 30 |

**Problem 10 (Continued)**
**2.**

## GENERAL LEDGER

ACCOUNT   Cash                                                      ACCOUNT NO.   101

| DATE | | ITEM | POST. REF. | DEBIT | CREDIT | BALANCE | |
|---|---|---|---|---|---|---|---|
| | | | | | | DEBIT | CREDIT |
| 20-- Aug. | 1 | Balance | ✓ | | | 25 0 0 0 00 | |
| | | | | | | | |
| | | | | | | | |
| | | | | | | | |
| | | | | | | | |
| | | | | | | | |
| | | | | | | | |
| | | | | | | | |

ACCOUNT   Accounts Payable                                         ACCOUNT NO.   202

| DATE | | ITEM | POST. REF. | DEBIT | CREDIT | BALANCE | |
|---|---|---|---|---|---|---|---|
| | | | | | | DEBIT | CREDIT |
| 20-- Aug. | 1 | Balance | ✓ | | | | 3 3 6 6 00 |
| | | | | | | | |
| | | | | | | | |
| | | | | | | | |
| | | | | | | | |

ACCOUNT   C. Bultman, Drawing                                      ACCOUNT NO.   312

| DATE | | ITEM | POST. REF. | DEBIT | CREDIT | BALANCE | |
|---|---|---|---|---|---|---|---|
| | | | | | | DEBIT | CREDIT |
| 20-- Aug. | 1 | Balance | ✓ | | | 14 0 0 0 00 | |

ACCOUNT   Purchases                                                ACCOUNT NO.   501

| DATE | | ITEM | POST. REF. | DEBIT | CREDIT | BALANCE | |
|---|---|---|---|---|---|---|---|
| | | | | | | DEBIT | CREDIT |
| 20-- Aug. | 1 | Balance | ✓ | | | 54 2 6 5 43 | |
| | | | | | | | |
| | | | | | | | |

**Problem 10 (Continued)**

ACCOUNT   Purchases Discounts                                                           ACCOUNT NO.   501.2

| DATE | | ITEM | POST. REF. | DEBIT | CREDIT | BALANCE | | | |
|---|---|---|---|---|---|---|---|---|---|
| | | | | | | DEBIT | | CREDIT | |
| 20--<br>Aug. | 1 | Balance | ✓ | | | | | 3 2 5 20 | |
| | | | | | | | | | |
| | | | | | | | | | |

ACCOUNT   Rent Expense                                                           ACCOUNT NO.   521

| DATE | | ITEM | POST. REF. | DEBIT | CREDIT | BALANCE | | | |
|---|---|---|---|---|---|---|---|---|---|
| | | | | | | DEBIT | | CREDIT | |
| 20--<br>Aug. | 1 | Balance | ✓ | | | 7 2 0 0 00 | | | |
| | | | | | | | | | |
| | | | | | | | | | |

ACCOUNT   Utilities Expense                                                           ACCOUNT NO.   533

| DATE | | ITEM | POST. REF. | DEBIT | CREDIT | BALANCE | | | |
|---|---|---|---|---|---|---|---|---|---|
| | | | | | | DEBIT | | CREDIT | |
| 20--<br>Aug. | 1 | Balance | ✓ | | | 8 2 2 87 | | | |
| | | | | | | | | | |
| | | | | | | | | | |

## ACCOUNTS PAYABLE LEDGER

**NAME**  Blue Suede Shoes Company

**ADDRESS**  2805 South Meridian, Indianapolis, IN  46225-3460

| DATE | | ITEM | POST. REF. | DEBIT | CREDIT | BALANCE |
|---|---|---|---|---|---|---|
| 20--<br>Aug. | 1 | Balance | ✓ | | | 6 4 0 00 |
| | | | | | | |
| | | | | | | |

**Problem 10 (Concluded)**

**NAME** Style-Rite

**ADDRESS** 6500 9th Street, New Orleans, LA  70115-1122

| DATE | | ITEM | POST. REF. | DEBIT | CREDIT | BALANCE |
|---|---|---|---|---|---|---|
| 20-- Aug. | 1 | Balance | ✓ | | | 1 2 0 0 00 |
| | | | | | | |
| | | | | | | |
| | | | | | | |

**NAME** West Coast Shoes

**ADDRESS** 705 Rialto Avenue, Fresno, CA  93705-7845

| DATE | | ITEM | POST. REF. | DEBIT | CREDIT | BALANCE |
|---|---|---|---|---|---|---|
| 20-- Aug. | 1 | Balance | ✓ | | | 1 5 2 6 00 |
| | | | | | | |
| | | | | | | |
| | | | | | | |

**3.**

## Problem 11  (LO 3)  CASH PAYMENTS TRANSACTIONS

The following cash payments were made by Demis Music Company during the month of July:

July   5   Paid $600 for rent. Issued Check No. 222.

12   Purchased $3,250 in merchandise from Hamilton Music Company. Issued Check No. 223.

18   Made a payment on account to Martinez Guitar Company for $4,500, less a 2% discount for paying within the discount period. Issued Check No. 224.

25   Paid $2,000 to First National Bank to pay off a note. Issued Check No. 225.

31   Anna Demis withdrew $5,500 from the business for personal use. Issued Check No. 226.

*Required:*

Enter the above transactions in a general journal.

### GENERAL JOURNAL                                    PAGE

| | DATE | | DESCRIPTION | POST. REF. | DEBIT | CREDIT | |
|---|---|---|---|---|---|---|---|
| 1 | | | | | | | 1 |
| 2 | | | | | | | 2 |
| 3 | | | | | | | 3 |
| 4 | | | | | | | 4 |
| 5 | | | | | | | 5 |
| 6 | | | | | | | 6 |
| 7 | | | | | | | 7 |
| 8 | | | | | | | 8 |
| 9 | | | | | | | 9 |
| 10 | | | | | | | 10 |
| 11 | | | | | | | 11 |
| 12 | | | | | | | 12 |
| 13 | | | | | | | 13 |
| 14 | | | | | | | 14 |
| 15 | | | | | | | 15 |
| 16 | | | | | | | 16 |
| 17 | | | | | | | 17 |
| 18 | | | | | | | 18 |
| 19 | | | | | | | 19 |
| 20 | | | | | | | 20 |

# CHAPTER 11 APPENDIX
# THE NET-PRICE METHOD OF RECORDING PURCHASES

## LEARNING OBJECTIVES

**Objective 1.    Describe the net-price method of recording purchases.**

Under the net-price method, purchases are recorded at the net amount, assuming that all cash discounts will be taken.

**Objective 2.    Record purchases and cash payments using the net-price method.**

At the time of purchase, Purchases is debited and Accounts Payable is credited for the gross price less the cash discount. If payment is made within the discount period, Accounts Payable is debited and Cash is credited for the net price. If payment is not made until after the discount period, Accounts Payable is debited for the net price, Purchases Discounts Lost is debited for the discount lost, and Cash is credited for the gross price.

### Apx. Exercise  (LO 1/2 )  PURCHASES AND CASH PAYMENTS TRANSACTIONS

Jiang's Accessory Shop had the following transactions during April:

| Apr. | 2 | Purchased merchandise on account from Sag's Apparel for $2,000, terms 2/10, n/30. |
| | 5 | Purchased merchandise on account from Lee's Wholesale for $1,800, terms 1/10, n/30. |
| | 11 | Paid the amount due to Sag's Apparel for the purchase on April 2. |
| | 25 | Paid the amount due to Lee's Wholesale for the purchase on April 5. |

*Required:*

1. Prepare general journal entries for these transactions using the gross-price method.
2. Prepare general journal entries for these transactions using the net-price method.

**1.**

### GENERAL JOURNAL                                    PAGE

| | DATE | | DESCRIPTION | POST. REF. | DEBIT | CREDIT | |
|---|---|---|---|---|---|---|---|
| 1 | | | | | | | 1 |
| 2 | | | | | | | 2 |
| 3 | | | | | | | 3 |
| 4 | | | | | | | 4 |
| 5 | | | | | | | 5 |
| 6 | | | | | | | 6 |
| 7 | | | | | | | 7 |
| 8 | | | | | | | 8 |
| 9 | | | | | | | 9 |
| 10 | | | | | | | 10 |
| 11 | | | | | | | 11 |
| 12 | | | | | | | 12 |
| 13 | | | | | | | 13 |

**2.**

## GENERAL JOURNAL

| | DATE | DESCRIPTION | POST. REF. | DEBIT | CREDIT | |
|---|---|---|---|---|---|---|
| 1 | | | | | | 1 |
| 2 | | | | | | 2 |
| 3 | | | | | | 3 |
| 4 | | | | | | 4 |
| 5 | | | | | | 5 |
| 6 | | | | | | 6 |
| 7 | | | | | | 7 |
| 8 | | | | | | 8 |
| 9 | | | | | | 9 |
| 10 | | | | | | 10 |
| 11 | | | | | | 11 |
| 12 | | | | | | 12 |
| 13 | | | | | | 13 |
| 14 | | | | | | 14 |
| 15 | | | | | | 15 |
| 16 | | | | | | 16 |
| 17 | | | | | | 17 |
| 18 | | | | | | 18 |
| 19 | | | | | | 19 |
| 20 | | | | | | 20 |
| 21 | | | | | | 21 |
| 22 | | | | | | 22 |
| 23 | | | | | | 23 |
| 24 | | | | | | 24 |
| 25 | | | | | | 25 |
| 26 | | | | | | 26 |
| 27 | | | | | | 27 |
| 28 | | | | | | 28 |
| 29 | | | | | | 29 |
| 30 | | | | | | 30 |

# CHAPTER 12
# SPECIAL JOURNALS

## LEARNING OBJECTIVES

Chapter 12 continues the study of sales, cash receipts, purchases, and cash payments transactions in a merchandising business. The focus is on how to account for these transactions more efficiently. Four special journals that speed up and simplify the recording process are introduced.

**Objective 1.     Describe, explain the purpose of, and identify transactions recorded in special journals.**

A **special journal** is a journal designed for recording only certain kinds of transactions. The types of special journals used by a business should depend on the types of transactions that occur frequently for the business. Four special journals commonly used by businesses are the sales journal, cash receipts journal, purchases journal, and cash payments journal.

**Objective 2.     Describe and use the sales journal.**

The **sales journal** saves time and energy by simplifying the recording and posting of transactions. It is a "special journal" used to record only credit sales of merchandise.

Credit sales affect Accounts Receivable (debit), Sales (credit), and, if there is a sales tax, Sales Tax Payable (credit). The sales journal provides separate columns for Accounts Receivable Debit, Sales Credit, and Sales Tax Payable Credit. The column totals are posted monthly to the general ledger accounts. Individual customer accounts in the accounts receivable ledger are posted daily.

**Objective 3.     Describe and use the cash receipts journal.**

Like the sales journal, a **cash receipts journal** saves time and energy in recording and posting transactions. Any time cash is received, the cash receipts journal is the book of original entry, and Cash is always debited. Column headings are established for Cash and other accounts that are frequently used, such as Sales (credit), Accounts Receivable (credit), Bank Credit Card Expense (debit), and Sales Tax Payable (credit). There usually also is a General Credit column for accounts that do not have a special column.

As with other special journals, column totals are posted at the end of the month. Daily postings are made for items in the General Credit column, as well as to the accounts receivable ledger.

**Objective 4.     Describe and use the purchases journal.**

A **purchases journal** is a special journal used to record only purchases of merchandise on account. This journal may have only a single column for Purchases Debit/Accounts Payable Credit Alternatively, there may be three columns for Purchases Debit, Freight-In Debit, and Accounts Payable Credit.

Each general ledger account used in the purchases journal requires only one posting each period. Individual supplier accounts in the accounts payable ledger are posted daily.

**Objective 5.     Describe and use the cash payments journal.**

A **cash payments journal** is a special journal used to record only cash payments transactions. The column headings of the cash payments journal will be those accounts that are most frequently affected by the company's cash payments transactions. Column totals are posted to the general ledger accounts at the end of the month. Items in the General Debit column are posted daily.  Individual supplier accounts in the accounts payable ledger also are posted daily.

# REVIEW QUESTIONS

**Instructions:** Analyze each of the following items carefully before writing your answer in the column at the right.

| | | **Question** | **Answer** |
|---|---|---|---|
| **LO 1** | **1.** | A journal designed for recording only certain kinds of transactions is called a _____. ............................... | _____ |
| **LO 1** | **2.** | Transactions that occur infrequently, and adjusting and closing entries usually are recorded in the _____. ........................... | _____ |
| **LO 2** | **3.** | A sale is recorded in a sales journal by entering what four pieces of information? ................................... | _____ |
| | | | _____ |
| | | | _____ |
| | | | _____ |
| **LO 2** | **4.** | A(n) _____ journal is a special journal used to record only sales of merchandise on account. ........................ | _____ |
| **LO 2** | **5.** | Sales returns and allowances are generally recorded in the _____ journal. ........................................ | _____ |
| **LO 2** | **6.** | Each sales journal entry is posted to the accounts receivable ledger _____. ....................................... | _____ |
| **LO 3** | **7.** | Any time the cash receipts journal is used, a debit is made to _____. ........................................... | _____ |
| **LO 3** | **8.** | The cash receipts journal is a special journal used to record only _____ transactions. ........................... | _____ |
| **LO 3** | **9.** | Each amount in the General Credit column of the cash receipts journal is posted _____. ........................... | _____ |
| **LO 4** | **10.** | A(n) _____ is a special journal used to record only purchases of merchandise on account. ........................ | _____ |
| **LO 4** | **11.** | Purchases returns and allowances are recorded in the _____. | _____ |
| **LO 4** | **12.** | The purchases journal for a company like Northern Micro, whose suppliers generally pay the freight charges, would have only a single column labeled Purchases Debit/_____. ..................... | _____ |
| **LO 4** | **13.** | A separate ledger containing an individual account payable for each supplier is called a(n) _____. ........................ | _____ |
| **LO 4** | **14.** | Each purchases journal entry is posted to the accounts payable ledger _____. ...................................... | _____ |
| **LO 5** | **15.** | A(n) _____ is a special journal used to record only cash payments transactions. ................................ | _____ |

**LO 5 16.** Any time the cash payments journal is used, a credit is made to the account called _____. ...................................................... _____

**LO 5 17.** A cash payment is recorded in the cash payments journal by entering what four pieces of information? .................................... _____

 _____

 _____

 _____

**LO 5 18.** Each amount in the General Debit column of the cash payments journal is posted _____. ...................................................... _____

## EXERCISES

### Exercise 1  (LO 1)  RECORDING TRANSACTIONS IN THE PROPER JOURNAL

Indicate the proper journal in which to record each transaction below by placing an "X" in the appropriate box.

| | Journal | | | | |
|---|---|---|---|---|---|
| **Transaction** | **Sales** | **Cash Receipts** | **Purchases** | **Cash Payments** | **General** |
| a.  Made payment to supplier on account. | | | | | |
| b.  Sold old delivery equipment for cash. | | | | | |
| c.  Sold merchandise on account. | | | | | |
| d.  Purchased merchandise for cash. | | | | | |
| e.  Returned merchandise to supplier for credit. | | | | | |
| f.  Invested additional funds in the business. | | | | | |
| g.  Purchased merchandise on account. | | | | | |

### Exercise 2  (LO 2)  SALES JOURNAL

Diana Brewer operates the Floor and Window Treatment Center and completed the following transactions related to sales of merchandise on account during the month of February. Sales tax of 5% was included in the amount of each sale.

Feb.  2 Sold wallpaper supplies to Dresson Homes, $98.95, terms n/30. Sale No. 255.
   12 Sold paint to Ray Acuff, $105.00, terms n/30. Sale No. 256.
   23 Sold miniblinds to Clydette Rupert, $114.83, terms n/30. Sale No. 257.
   24 Sold decorator items to Marty Staple, $35.55, terms n/30. Sale No. 258.
   25 Sold paint to Angel Burtin, $25.57, terms n/30. Sale No. 259.

## Exercise 2 (Concluded)

*Required:*

1. Enter the transactions from the previous page in the sales journal.
2. Total and rule the journal.

**1. and 2.**

### SALES JOURNAL                                                    PAGE

| | DATE | SALE NO. | TO WHOM SOLD | POST. REF. | ACCOUNTS RECEIVABLE DEBIT | SALES CREDIT | SALES TAX PAYABLE CREDIT | |
|---|---|---|---|---|---|---|---|---|
| 1 | | | | | | | | 1 |
| 2 | | | | | | | | 2 |
| 3 | | | | | | | | 3 |
| 4 | | | | | | | | 4 |
| 5 | | | | | | | | 5 |
| 6 | | | | | | | | 6 |
| 7 | | | | | | | | 7 |

## Exercise 3  (LO 3)  CASH RECEIPTS JOURNAL

Diana Brewer of the Floor and Window Treatment Center received cash during the month of March as described below.

| Mar. | 2 | Received cash from Dresson Homes on account, $98.95. |
|---|---|---|
| | 12 | Received cash from Ray Acuff on account, $105.00. |
| | 15 | Made cash sale to Jean Granite, $404.76, plus 5% sales tax. |
| | 18 | Made cash sale to Bill Green, $2,380.95, plus 5% sales tax. |
| | 23 | Received cash from Clydette Rupert on account, $114.83. |
| | 24 | Received cash from Marty Staple on account, $35.55. |
| | 25 | Received cash from Angel Burtin on account, $25.57. |
| | 31 | Made cash sales for the month of $22,000.00, including 5% sales tax (from cash register tape). |
| | 31 | Made credit card sales for the month of $28,000.00, including 5% sales tax. |

*Required:*

1. Enter the above transactions in the cash receipts journal on page 193.
2. Total and rule the journal.

**Exercise 3 (Concluded)**
**1. and 2.**               **CASH RECEIPTS JOURNAL**                   PAGE

| | DATE | ACCOUNT CREDITED | POST. REF. | GENERAL CREDIT | ACCOUNTS RECEIVABLE CREDIT | SALES CREDIT | SALES TAX PAYABLE CREDIT | CASH DEBIT | |
|---|---|---|---|---|---|---|---|---|---|
| 1 | | | | | | | | | 1 |
| 2 | | | | | | | | | 2 |
| 3 | | | | | | | | | 3 |
| 4 | | | | | | | | | 4 |
| 5 | | | | | | | | | 5 |
| 6 | | | | | | | | | 6 |
| 7 | | | | | | | | | 7 |
| 8 | | | | | | | | | 8 |
| 9 | | | | | | | | | 9 |
| 10 | | | | | | | | | 10 |
| 11 | | | | | | | | | 11 |

## Exercise 4 (LO 4) PURCHASES JOURNAL

Tom Bowers operates a business under the name of Tom's Sporting Goods. The books of original entry include a purchases journal and a general journal, in which entries such as Purchase Returns and Allowances are recorded. An accounts payable ledger is used to maintain a record of the amount owed to suppliers. The following transactions are related to purchases for the month of February:

Feb. 3   Purchased merchandise from Ringer's on account, $498.64, Invoice No. 611, terms 2/10, n/30.

4   Purchased merchandise on account from Klein Brothers, $780.11, Invoice No. 112, terms 30 days.

11   Purchased merchandise from Corleon's on account, $2,300.00, Invoice No. 432, terms 30 days.

15   Received a credit memo from Ringer's for $30.00 for merchandise returned that had been purchased on account.

*Required:*

Enter the above transactions in the following purchases journal and general journal:

### PURCHASES JOURNAL                   PAGE

| | DATE | INVOICE NO. | FROM WHOM PURCHASED | POST. REF. | PURCHASES DEBIT ACCTS. PAY. CREDIT | |
|---|---|---|---|---|---|---|
| 1 | | | | | | 1 |
| 2 | | | | | | 2 |
| 3 | | | | | | 3 |
| 4 | | | | | | 4 |
| 5 | | | | | | 5 |

**Exercise 4 (Concluded)**

GENERAL JOURNAL PAGE

| | DATE | | DESCRIPTION | POST. REF. | DEBIT | CREDIT | |
|---|---|---|---|---|---|---|---|
| 1 | | | | | | | 1 |
| 2 | | | | | | | 2 |
| 3 | | | | | | | 3 |

**Exercise 5 (LO 5) CASH PAYMENTS JOURNAL**

The following cash payments were made by Demis Music Company during the month of July:

July   5   Paid $600 for rent. Issued Check No. 222.

      12   Purchased $3,250 in merchandise from Hamilton Music Company. Issued Check No. 223.

      18   Made a payment on account to Martinez Guitar Company for $4,500, less a 2% discount for paying within the discount period. Issued Check No. 224.

      25   Paid $2,000 to First National Bank to pay off a note. Issued Check No. 225.

      31   Anna Demis withdrew $5,500 from the business for personal use. Issued Check No. 226.

*Required:*

1. Enter the above transactions in the cash payments journal.
2. Total, rule, and prove the journal.

**1. and 2.**

CASH PAYMENTS JOURNAL PAGE

| | DATE | CK. NO. | ACCOUNT DEBITED | POST. REF. | GENERAL DEBIT | ACCOUNTS PAYABLE DEBIT | PURCHASES DEBIT | PURCHASES DISCOUNTS CREDIT | CASH CREDIT | |
|---|---|---|---|---|---|---|---|---|---|---|
| 1 | | | | | | | | | | 1 |
| 2 | | | | | | | | | | 2 |
| 3 | | | | | | | | | | 3 |
| 4 | | | | | | | | | | 4 |
| 5 | | | | | | | | | | 5 |
| 6 | | | | | | | | | | 6 |
| 7 | | | | | | | | | | 7 |

## PROBLEMS

### Problem 6 (LO 2/3) SALES JOURNAL AND CASH RECEIPTS JOURNAL

The following information represents transactions for Kwan Chu's Fish Market for the month of July 20--. Sales tax is 6%.

| July | | |
|---|---|---|
| | 1 | Sold merchandise on account to B. A. Smith, $137.50, plus sales tax. Sale No. 33. |
| | 3 | B. A. Smith returned merchandise, $15.00, plus sales tax, for a credit. Credit Memo No. 11. |
| | 5 | Sold merchandise on account to L. L. Unis, $218.00, plus sales tax. Sale No. 34. |
| | 7 | Made cash sales for the week, $325.44, plus sales tax. |
| | 10 | Sold merchandise on account to W. P. Clark, $208.00, plus sales tax. Sale No. 35. |
| | 11 | Received $129.85 from B. A. Smith, on account. |
| | 13 | W. P. Clark returned merchandise, $22.00, plus sales tax, for a credit. Credit Memo No. 12. |
| | 14 | Made cash sales for the week, $411.20, plus sales tax. |
| | 16 | Sold merchandise on account to B. A. Smith, $282.50, plus sales tax. Sale No. 36. |
| | 17 | Received $231.08 from L. L. Unis, on account. |
| | 21 | Made cash sales for the week, $292.50, plus sales tax. |
| | 24 | Sold merchandise on account to L. L. Unis, $224.50, plus sales tax. Sale No. 37. |
| | 28 | Made cash sales for the week, $300.50, plus sales tax. |
| | 31 | Received $197.16 from W. P. Clark, on account. |

*Required:*

1. Using the information provided, record the transactions in the sales journal, cash receipts journal, or general journal as required.

2. Total and rule the column totals.

### 1. and 2.

**GENERAL JOURNAL**                                    PAGE _____

| | DATE | DESCRIPTION | POST. REF. | DEBIT | CREDIT | |
|---|---|---|---|---|---|---|
| 1 | | | | | | 1 |
| 2 | | | | | | 2 |
| 3 | | | | | | 3 |
| 4 | | | | | | 4 |
| 5 | | | | | | 5 |
| 6 | | | | | | 6 |
| 7 | | | | | | 7 |
| 8 | | | | | | 8 |
| 9 | | | | | | 9 |
| 10 | | | | | | 10 |

## Problem 6 (Concluded)

### SALES JOURNAL

PAGE

| | DATE | | SALE NO. | TO WHOM SOLD | POST. REF. | ACCOUNTS RECEIVABLE DEBIT | SALES CREDIT | SALES TAX PAYABLE CREDIT | |
|---|---|---|---|---|---|---|---|---|---|
| 1 | | | | | | | | | 1 |
| 2 | | | | | | | | | 2 |
| 3 | | | | | | | | | 3 |
| 4 | | | | | | | | | 4 |
| 5 | | | | | | | | | 5 |
| 6 | | | | | | | | | 6 |
| 7 | | | | | | | | | 7 |
| 8 | | | | | | | | | 8 |

### CASH RECEIPTS JOURNAL

PAGE

| | DATE | | ACCOUNT CREDITED | POST. REF. | GENERAL CREDIT | ACCOUNTS RECEIVABLE CREDIT | SALES CREDIT | SALES TAX PAYABLE CREDIT | CASH DEBIT | |
|---|---|---|---|---|---|---|---|---|---|---|
| 1 | | | | | | | | | | 1 |
| 2 | | | | | | | | | | 2 |
| 3 | | | | | | | | | | 3 |
| 4 | | | | | | | | | | 4 |
| 5 | | | | | | | | | | 5 |
| 6 | | | | | | | | | | 6 |
| 7 | | | | | | | | | | 7 |
| 8 | | | | | | | | | | 8 |
| 9 | | | | | | | | | | 9 |
| 10 | | | | | | | | | | 10 |

### Problem 7  (LO 2)  SALES JOURNAL, GENERAL LEDGER, AND ACCOUNTS RECEIVABLE LEDGER

H. K. Smythe operates Leather All, a leather shop that sells luggage, handbags, business cases, and other leather goods. During the month of May, the following sales on account were made:

May  3    Sold merchandise on account to T. A. Pigdon, $247.50, plus sales tax of $14.85. Sale No. 51.

4    Sold merchandise on account to J. R. Feyton, $55.00, plus sales tax of $3.30. Sale No. 52.

6    Sold merchandise on account to P. C. McMurdy, $99.00, plus sales tax of $5.94. Sale No. 53.

10    Sold merchandise on account to J. T. Messer, $175.00, plus sales tax of $10.50. Sale No. 54.

12    Sold merchandise on account to A. F. Schlitz, $355.00, plus sales tax of $21.30. Sale No. 55.

13    Sold merchandise on account to J. R. Feyton, $215.00, plus sales tax of $12.90. Sale No. 56.

20    Sold merchandise on account to P. C. McMurdy, $400.00, plus sales tax of $24.00. Sale No. 57.

28    Sold merchandise on account to J. T. Messer, $255.00, plus sales tax of $15.30. Sale No. 58.

*Required:*

1.  Enter the above transactions in the sales journal (page 1) provided below.
2.  Post the entries in the sales journal to the accounts receivable ledger on pages 198–199.
3.  Total and verify the column totals and rule the sales journal. Complete the summary postings to the general ledger on page 198.

### 1. and 3.

**SALES JOURNAL**                                                                     PAGE 1

| | DATE | SALE NO. | TO WHOM SOLD | POST. REF. | ACCOUNTS RECEIVABLE DEBIT | SALES CREDIT | SALES TAX PAYABLE CREDIT | |
|---|---|---|---|---|---|---|---|---|
| 1 | | | | | | | | 1 |
| 2 | | | | | | | | 2 |
| 3 | | | | | | | | 3 |
| 4 | | | | | | | | 4 |
| 5 | | | | | | | | 5 |
| 6 | | | | | | | | 6 |
| 7 | | | | | | | | 7 |
| 8 | | | | | | | | 8 |
| 9 | | | | | | | | 9 |
| 10 | | | | | | | | 10 |

**Problem 7 (Continued)**

**3.**                              **GENERAL LEDGER**

ACCOUNT  Accounts Receivable                              ACCOUNT NO.  122

| DATE | | ITEM | POST. REF. | DEBIT | CREDIT | BALANCE | |
|---|---|---|---|---|---|---|---|
| | | | | | | DEBIT | CREDIT |
| 20--<br>May | 1 | Balance | ✓ | | | 8 3 4 00 | |
| | | | | | | | |
| | | | | | | | |

ACCOUNT  Sales Tax Payable                              ACCOUNT NO.  231

| DATE | ITEM | POST. REF. | DEBIT | CREDIT | BALANCE | |
|---|---|---|---|---|---|---|
| | | | | | DEBIT | CREDIT |
| | | | | | | |
| | | | | | | |
| | | | | | | |
| | | | | | | |

ACCOUNT  Sales                              ACCOUNT NO.  401

| DATE | ITEM | POST. REF. | DEBIT | CREDIT | BALANCE | |
|---|---|---|---|---|---|---|
| | | | | | DEBIT | CREDIT |
| | | | | | | |
| | | | | | | |
| | | | | | | |
| | | | | | | |

**2.**                    **ACCOUNTS RECEIVABLE LEDGER**

**NAME**  J. R. Feyton

**ADDRESS**  6022 Columbia, St. Louis, MO  63139-1906

| DATE | ITEM | POST. REF. | DEBIT | CREDIT | BALANCE |
|---|---|---|---|---|---|
| | | | | | |
| | | | | | |
| | | | | | |
| | | | | | |

**Problem 7 (Concluded)**

**NAME** P. C. McMurdy

**ADDRESS** 1214 N. 2nd St., E. St. Louis, IL  62201-2679

| DATE | | ITEM | POST. REF. | DEBIT | CREDIT | BALANCE |
|---|---|---|---|---|---|---|
| 20-- May | 1 | Balance | ✓ | | | 1 2 5 00 |
| | | | | | | |
| | | | | | | |

**NAME** J. T. Messer

**ADDRESS** P.O. Box 249, Chesterfield, MO  63017-3901

| DATE | | ITEM | POST. REF. | DEBIT | CREDIT | BALANCE |
|---|---|---|---|---|---|---|
| 20-- May | 1 | Balance | ✓ | | | 1 7 7 00 |
| | | | | | | |
| | | | | | | |

**NAME** T. A. Pigdon

**ADDRESS** 1070 Purcell, University City, MO  63130-1546

| DATE | | ITEM | POST. REF. | DEBIT | CREDIT | BALANCE |
|---|---|---|---|---|---|---|
| 20-- May | 1 | Balance | ✓ | | | 2 8 0 00 |
| | | | | | | |
| | | | | | | |

**NAME** A. F. Schlitz

**ADDRESS** 800 Lindbergh Blvd., St. Louis, MO  63166-1546

| DATE | | ITEM | POST. REF. | DEBIT | CREDIT | BALANCE |
|---|---|---|---|---|---|---|
| 20-- May | 1 | Balance | ✓ | | | 2 5 2 00 |
| | | | | | | |
| | | | | | | |

### Problem 8 (LO 3) CASH RECEIPTS JOURNAL, GENERAL JOURNAL, GENERAL LEDGER, AND ACCOUNTS RECEIVABLE LEDGER

Paula Angelillis operates Hard-to-Find Auto Parts Store. Much of her business is by mail. The books of original entry include a cash receipts journal and a general journal. The following transactions related to sales and cash receipts occurred during June:

June 1 Received $300 from A. K. Wells, including $14.29 of sales tax, for field cash sale. (Field cash sales are not included in cash register tapes.)

5 Received $125.60 from L. Strous on account.

10 Received $263.25 from D. Manning on account.

12 Q. Striker returned merchandise for credit. The sales price was $215.00, plus sales tax of $10.75.

18 Received $58.25 from D. Warding on account.

20 Received $1,000 from B. L. Stryker, including $47.62 tax (field cash sale).

21 Received $29.99 from L. Clese on account.

24 R. Popielarz returned merchandise for credit. The sales price was $116.25, plus sales tax of $5.81.

27 Received $426.00 from L. LeCount on account.

30 Made cash and bank credit card sales for the month of $8,200, plus sales tax of $410.00. Bank credit card expense is $80.

*Required:*

1. Enter each transaction in either the cash receipts journal (page 18) or the general journal (page 5) provided. Total, verify the totals, and rule the cash receipts journal.

2. Make the individual postings required from the cash receipts journal and the general journal to the general and accounts receivable ledgers.

3. Make the summary postings from the cash receipts journal to the general ledger.

**1.**

## GENERAL JOURNAL

PAGE 5

| | DATE | | DESCRIPTION | POST. REF. | DEBIT | CREDIT | |
|---|---|---|---|---|---|---|---|
| 1 | | | | | | | 1 |
| 2 | | | | | | | 2 |
| 3 | | | | | | | 3 |
| 4 | | | | | | | 4 |
| 5 | | | | | | | 5 |
| 6 | | | | | | | 6 |
| 7 | | | | | | | 7 |
| 8 | | | | | | | 8 |
| 9 | | | | | | | 9 |
| 10 | | | | | | | 10 |

## Problem 8 (Continued)

### CASH RECEIPTS JOURNAL

| | DATE | ACCOUNT CREDITED | POST. REF. | GENERAL CREDIT | ACCOUNTS REC. CREDIT | SALES CREDIT | SALES TAX PAYABLE CREDIT | BANK CR. CARD EXP. DEBIT | CASH DEBIT | |
|---|---|---|---|---|---|---|---|---|---|---|
| 1 | | | | | | | | | | 1 |
| 2 | | | | | | | | | | 2 |
| 3 | | | | | | | | | | 3 |
| 4 | | | | | | | | | | 4 |
| 5 | | | | | | | | | | 5 |
| 6 | | | | | | | | | | 6 |
| 7 | | | | | | | | | | 7 |
| 8 | | | | | | | | | | 8 |
| 9 | | | | | | | | | | 9 |
| 10 | | | | | | | | | | 10 |
| 11 | | | | | | | | | | 11 |
| 12 | | | | | | | | | | 12 |

## 2. and 3.

### GENERAL LEDGER

ACCOUNT   Cash                                                      ACCOUNT NO.   101

| DATE | | ITEM | POST. REF. | DEBIT | CREDIT | BALANCE DEBIT | BALANCE CREDIT |
|---|---|---|---|---|---|---|---|
| 20-- June | 1 | Balance | ✓ | | | 13 2 0 0 25 | |
| | | | | | | | |

ACCOUNT   Accounts Receivable                                      ACCOUNT NO.   122

| DATE | | ITEM | POST. REF. | DEBIT | CREDIT | BALANCE DEBIT | BALANCE CREDIT |
|---|---|---|---|---|---|---|---|
| 20-- June | 1 | Balance | ✓ | | | 1 2 5 0 90 | |
| | | | | | | | |
| | | | | | | | |
| | | | | | | | |

**Problem 8 (Continued)**

ACCOUNT Sales Tax Payable                                           ACCOUNT NO. 231

| DATE | | ITEM | POST. REF. | DEBIT | CREDIT | BALANCE | |
|---|---|---|---|---|---|---|---|
| | | | | | | DEBIT | CREDIT |
| 20--<br>June | 1 | Balance | ✓ | | | | 1 2 5 00 |
| | | | | | | | |
| | | | | | | | |
| | | | | | | | |

ACCOUNT Sales                                                      ACCOUNT NO. 401

| DATE | ITEM | POST. REF. | DEBIT | CREDIT | BALANCE | |
|---|---|---|---|---|---|---|
| | | | | | DEBIT | CREDIT |
| | | | | | | |
| | | | | | | |
| | | | | | | |
| | | | | | | |

ACCOUNT Sales Returns and Allowances                               ACCOUNT NO. 401.1

| DATE | ITEM | POST. REF. | DEBIT | CREDIT | BALANCE | |
|---|---|---|---|---|---|---|
| | | | | | DEBIT | CREDIT |
| | | | | | | |
| | | | | | | |
| | | | | | | |
| | | | | | | |

ACCOUNT Bank Credit Card Expense                                   ACCOUNT NO. 513

| DATE | ITEM | POST. REF. | DEBIT | CREDIT | BALANCE | |
|---|---|---|---|---|---|---|
| | | | | | DEBIT | CREDIT |
| | | | | | | |
| | | | | | | |
| | | | | | | |

**Problem 8 (Continued)**

## ACCOUNTS RECEIVABLE LEDGER

**NAME**  L. Clese

**ADDRESS** 875 Glenway Drive, Glendale, MO  63122-4112

| DATE | | ITEM | POST. REF. | DEBIT | CREDIT | BALANCE |
|---|---|---|---|---|---|---|
| 20-- June | 1 | Balance | ✓ | | | 2 9 99 |
| | | | | | | |
| | | | | | | |
| | | | | | | |

**NAME**  L. LeCount

**ADDRESS** 1439 East Broad Street, Columbus, OH  43205-9892

| DATE | | ITEM | POST. REF. | DEBIT | CREDIT | BALANCE |
|---|---|---|---|---|---|---|
| 20-- June | 1 | Balance | ✓ | | | 4 2 6 00 |
| | | | | | | |
| | | | | | | |
| | | | | | | |

**NAME**  D. Manning

**ADDRESS** 2101 Cumberland Road, Noblesville, IN  47870-2435

| DATE | | ITEM | POST. REF. | DEBIT | CREDIT | BALANCE |
|---|---|---|---|---|---|---|
| 20-- June | 1 | Balance | ✓ | | | 2 6 3 25 |
| | | | | | | |
| | | | | | | |
| | | | | | | |

**Problem 8 (Concluded)**

**NAME** R. Popielarz

**ADDRESS** 3001 Hillcrest Drive, Dallas, PA  18612-6854

| DATE | | ITEM | POST. REF. | DEBIT | CREDIT | BALANCE |
|---|---|---|---|---|---|---|
| 20-- June | 1 | Balance | ✓ | | | 1 2 2 06 |
| | | | | | | |
| | | | | | | |

**NAME** Q. Striker

**ADDRESS** 4113 Main Street, Beech Grove, IN  46107-9643

| DATE | | ITEM | POST. REF. | DEBIT | CREDIT | BALANCE |
|---|---|---|---|---|---|---|
| 20-- June | 1 | Balance | ✓ | | | 2 2 5 75 |
| | | | | | | |
| | | | | | | |

**NAME** L. Strous

**ADDRESS** 2215 N. State Road 135, Greenwood, IN  46142-6432

| DATE | | ITEM | POST. REF. | DEBIT | CREDIT | BALANCE |
|---|---|---|---|---|---|---|
| 20-- June | 1 | Balance | ✓ | | | 1 2 5 60 |
| | | | | | | |
| | | | | | | |

**NAME** D. Warding

**ADDRESS** 1100 W. Main Street, Carmel, IN  46032-2364

| DATE | | ITEM | POST. REF. | DEBIT | CREDIT | BALANCE |
|---|---|---|---|---|---|---|
| 20-- June | 1 | Balance | ✓ | | | 5 8 25 |
| | | | | | | |
| | | | | | | |

### Problem 9  (LO 4)  PURCHASES JOURNAL, GENERAL LEDGER, AND ACCOUNTS PAYABLE LEDGER

J. R. Lang, owner of Lang's Galleria, made the following purchases of merchandise on account during the month of November 20--.

Nov. 2   Purchase Invoice No. 611, $4,145, from Ford Distributors.

     5   Purchase Invoice No. 216, $2,165, from Mueller Wholesaler.

  15   Purchase Invoice No. 399, $2,895, from Grant White & Co.

  19   Purchase Invoice No. 106, $1,845, from Bailey & Hinds, Inc.

  22   Purchase Invoice No. 914, $3,225, from Ford Distributors.

  28   Purchase Invoice No. 661, $2,175, from Jackson Company.

  30   Purchase Invoice No. 716, $3,500, from Mueller Wholesaler.

*Required:*

1. Record the transactions in the purchases journal (page 9). Total and rule the journal.
2. Post from the purchases journal to the general ledger accounts and to the accounts payable ledger accounts.

**1.**

**PURCHASES JOURNAL**                                    PAGE    9

| | DATE | INVOICE NO. | FROM WHOM PURCHASED | POST. REF. | PURCHASES DEBIT ACCTS. PAY. CREDIT | |
|---|---|---|---|---|---|---|
| 1 | | | | | | 1 |
| 2 | | | | | | 2 |
| 3 | | | | | | 3 |
| 4 | | | | | | 4 |
| 5 | | | | | | 5 |
| 6 | | | | | | 6 |
| 7 | | | | | | 7 |
| 8 | | | | | | 8 |
| 9 | | | | | | 9 |
| 10 | | | | | | 10 |

**2.**

**GENERAL LEDGER**

ACCOUNT   Accounts Payable                                    ACCOUNT NO.   202

| | DATE | ITEM | POST. REF. | DEBIT | CREDIT | BALANCE DEBIT | BALANCE CREDIT |
|---|---|---|---|---|---|---|---|
| | | | | | | | |
| | | | | | | | |
| | | | | | | | |

**Problem 9 (Continued)**

ACCOUNT  Purchases                                                    ACCOUNT NO.  501

| DATE | ITEM | POST. REF. | DEBIT | CREDIT | BALANCE | |
|---|---|---|---|---|---|---|
| | | | | | DEBIT | CREDIT |
| | | | | | | |
| | | | | | | |
| | | | | | | |

## ACCOUNTS PAYABLE LEDGER

**NAME**  Bailey & Hinds, Inc.

**ADDRESS**

| DATE | ITEM | POST. REF. | DEBIT | CREDIT | BALANCE |
|---|---|---|---|---|---|
| | | | | | |
| | | | | | |
| | | | | | |

**NAME**  Ford Distributors

**ADDRESS**

| DATE | ITEM | POST. REF. | DEBIT | CREDIT | BALANCE |
|---|---|---|---|---|---|
| | | | | | |
| | | | | | |
| | | | | | |

**NAME**  Grant White & Co.

**ADDRESS**

| DATE | ITEM | POST. REF. | DEBIT | CREDIT | BALANCE |
|---|---|---|---|---|---|
| | | | | | |
| | | | | | |
| | | | | | |

## Problem 9 (Concluded)

**NAME**   Jackson Company
**ADDRESS**

| DATE | ITEM | POST. REF. | DEBIT | CREDIT | BALANCE |
|------|------|-----------|-------|--------|---------|
|      |      |           |       |        |         |
|      |      |           |       |        |         |
|      |      |           |       |        |         |
|      |      |           |       |        |         |

**NAME**   Mueller Wholesaler
**ADDRESS**

| DATE | ITEM | POST. REF. | DEBIT | CREDIT | BALANCE |
|------|------|-----------|-------|--------|---------|
|      |      |           |       |        |         |
|      |      |           |       |        |         |
|      |      |           |       |        |         |
|      |      |           |       |        |         |

## Problem 10  (LO 5)  CASH PAYMENTS JOURNAL, GENERAL LEDGER, AND ACCOUNTS PAYABLE LEDGER

Chris Bultman operates a retail shoe store. The following transactions are related to cash payments for the month of August:

Aug.  1   Issued Check No. 47 for $900.00 in payment of rent (Rent Expense) for August.
     3   Issued Check No. 48 to Blue Suede Shoes Company in payment on account, $640.00, less 2% discount.
     9   Issued Check No. 49 to Style-Rite in payment on account, $800.00, less 3% discount.
    14   Issued Check No. 50 for $125.28 in payment of utility bill (Utilities Expense).
    20   Issued Check No. 51 to Baldo Company in payment for cash purchase, $525.00.
    22   Issued Check No. 52 to West Coast Shoes in payment on account, $625.00. A discount of 2% was lost because Bultman neglected to pay the invoice within the discount period.
    27   Issued Check No. 53 for $2,000.00 to Bultman for a cash withdrawal for personal use.

*Required:*

1. Enter the above transactions in the cash payments journal (page 9).
2. Enter the totals, rule, and prove the journal.
3. Complete individual postings to the general ledger and accounts payable ledger and summary postings to the general ledger. The relevant accounts are provided on pages 208–210.

**Problem 10 (Continued)**

**1. and 2.**

## CASH PAYMENTS JOURNAL

| | DATE | CK. NO. | ACCOUNT DEBITED | POST. REF. | GENERAL DEBIT | ACCOUNTS PAYABLE DEBIT | PURCHASES DEBIT | PURCHASES DISCOUNTS CREDIT | CASH CREDIT | |
|---|---|---|---|---|---|---|---|---|---|---|
| 1 | | | | | | | | | | 1 |
| 2 | | | | | | | | | | 2 |
| 3 | | | | | | | | | | 3 |
| 4 | | | | | | | | | | 4 |
| 5 | | | | | | | | | | 5 |
| 6 | | | | | | | | | | 6 |
| 7 | | | | | | | | | | 7 |
| 8 | | | | | | | | | | 8 |
| 9 | | | | | | | | | | 9 |
| 10 | | | | | | | | | | 10 |

**3.**

## GENERAL LEDGER

ACCOUNT   Cash                                              ACCOUNT NO.   101

| DATE | ITEM | POST. REF. | DEBIT | CREDIT | BALANCE DEBIT | BALANCE CREDIT |
|---|---|---|---|---|---|---|
| 20--<br>Aug. 1 | Balance | ✓ | | | 25 0 0 0 00 | |
| | | | | | | |
| | | | | | | |

ACCOUNT   Accounts Payable                                  ACCOUNT NO.   202

| DATE | ITEM | POST. REF. | DEBIT | CREDIT | BALANCE DEBIT | BALANCE CREDIT |
|---|---|---|---|---|---|---|
| 20--<br>Aug. 1 | Balance | ✓ | | | | 3 3 6 6 00 |
| | | | | | | |
| | | | | | | |

## Problem 10 (Continued)

ACCOUNT   C. Bultman, Drawing                    ACCOUNT NO.  312

| DATE | | ITEM | POST. REF. | DEBIT | CREDIT | BALANCE | |
|---|---|---|---|---|---|---|---|
| | | | | | | DEBIT | CREDIT |
| 20--<br>Aug. | 1 | Balance | ✓ | | | 14 0 0 0 00 | |
| | | | | | | | |
| | | | | | | | |

ACCOUNT   Purchases                    ACCOUNT NO.  501

| DATE | | ITEM | POST. REF. | DEBIT | CREDIT | BALANCE | |
|---|---|---|---|---|---|---|---|
| | | | | | | DEBIT | CREDIT |
| 20--<br>Aug. | 1 | Balance | ✓ | | | 54 2 6 5 43 | |
| | | | | | | | |
| | | | | | | | |

ACCOUNT   Purchases Discounts                    ACCOUNT NO.  501.2

| DATE | | ITEM | POST. REF. | DEBIT | CREDIT | BALANCE | |
|---|---|---|---|---|---|---|---|
| | | | | | | DEBIT | CREDIT |
| 20--<br>Aug. | 1 | Balance | ✓ | | | | 3 2 5 20 |
| | | | | | | | |
| | | | | | | | |

ACCOUNT   Rent Expense                    ACCOUNT NO.  521

| DATE | | ITEM | POST. REF. | DEBIT | CREDIT | BALANCE | |
|---|---|---|---|---|---|---|---|
| | | | | | | DEBIT | CREDIT |
| 20--<br>Aug. | 1 | Balance | ✓ | | | 7 2 0 0 00 | |
| | | | | | | | |
| | | | | | | | |

ACCOUNT   Utilities Expense                    ACCOUNT NO.  533

| DATE | | ITEM | POST. REF. | DEBIT | CREDIT | BALANCE | |
|---|---|---|---|---|---|---|---|
| | | | | | | DEBIT | CREDIT |
| 20--<br>Aug. | 1 | Balance | ✓ | | | 8 2 2 87 | |
| | | | | | | | |
| | | | | | | | |

**Problem 10 (Concluded)**

## ACCOUNTS PAYABLE LEDGER

**NAME**  Blue Suede Shoes Company

**ADDRESS**

| DATE | | ITEM | POST. REF. | DEBIT | CREDIT | BALANCE |
|---|---|---|---|---|---|---|
| 20-- Aug. | 1 | Balance | ✓ | | | 6 4 0 00 |
| | | | | | | |
| | | | | | | |

**NAME**  Style-Rite

**ADDRESS**

| DATE | | ITEM | POST. REF. | DEBIT | CREDIT | BALANCE |
|---|---|---|---|---|---|---|
| 20-- Aug. | 1 | Balance | ✓ | | | 1 2 0 0 00 |
| | | | | | | |
| | | | | | | |

**NAME**  West Coast Shoes

**ADDRESS**

| DATE | | ITEM | POST. REF. | DEBIT | CREDIT | BALANCE |
|---|---|---|---|---|---|---|
| 20-- Aug. | 1 | Balance | ✓ | | | 1 5 2 6 00 |
| | | | | | | |
| | | | | | | |

# CHAPTER 13
# ACCOUNTING FOR MERCHANDISE INVENTORY

## LEARNING OBJECTIVES

Merchandise inventory plays an important role in determining the amount of net income on the income statement. For a merchandising business, the cost of goods sold is the largest individual expense on the income statement. In this chapter, you will learn how to determine the dollar amounts assigned to the cost of goods sold and ending merchandise inventory.

**Objective 1.     Explain the impact of merchandise inventory on the financial statements.**

It is important to report accurately the dollar amount of merchandise inventory on the income statement. An error in counting the physical ending merchandise inventory will not only affect the current year's net income but will also affect the following year's net income. This is because the ending merchandise inventory for the current year becomes the beginning merchandise inventory for the following year. In the year that the error in counting the merchandise inventory is made, the statement of owner's equity and balance sheet will also be in error. However, at the end of the second year, the income statement will be in error, but the statement of owner's equity and balance sheet will be correctly stated. This is because an ending inventory error in the first year "washes out" over the two-year period.

**Objective 2.     Describe the two principal systems of accounting for merchandise inventory—the periodic system and the perpetual system.**

There are two principal systems of accounting for inventory: (1) the periodic system and (2) the perpetual system.

Under the **periodic system**, the current merchandise inventory and the cost of goods sold are not determined until the end of the accounting period when a **physical inventory** is taken. The purchases account is debited for the cost of all goods purchased. The balance in the merchandise inventory account is merely a record of the most recent physical inventory.

Under the **perpetual system**, the merchandise inventory account is debited for the cost of all goods bought, including freight charges, and credited for the cost of all goods sold. In addition, this account is debited when customers return merchandise and credited when returns, allowances, and discounts are granted by suppliers. The balance of the merchandise inventory account represents the cost of goods on hand at all times.

**Objective 3.     Compute the costs allocated to the ending inventory and cost of goods sold using different inventory methods.**

A **physical inventory** is a count of all the goods that have not been sold. This is normally done when the inventory is at its lowest level, which corresponds with the end of the company's **natural business year**. Only goods that are the property of the firm should be included in a physical inventory. Goods held on **consignment** and goods shipped **FOB shipping point** as of the balance sheet date should be excluded. Goods shipped **FOB destination** and in transit as of the balance sheet date should be included in the inventory count. Because prices are constantly changing, there are four acceptable methods to assigning costs to the ending inventory.

When each unit of inventory can be specifically identified, the **specific identification method** can be used. To use this method, inventory items must be physically different from each other or must have serial numbers.

The **first-in, first-out (FIFO)** method assumes that the first goods bought are the first goods sold. Therefore, the latest goods bought remain in inventory.

Another method of allocating merchandise cost is called the **weighted-average cost method**. This costing method is based on the average cost of identical units. The weighted average is calculated by dividing the total cost of merchandise available for sale by the total number of units available for sale. To compute the cost of goods sold, simply multiply the number of units sold by the weighted-average cost per unit.

A fourth method of allocating merchandise cost is called the **last-in, first-out (LIFO) method**. It assumes that the sales in the period were made from the most recently purchased goods. Therefore, the earliest goods bought remain in inventory. It is important to emphasize that this method is used to allocate costs to inventory. In most cases, it does not correspond to the physical flow of merchandise. When prices are rising, net income calculated by using the LIFO method will be less than net income calculated by using either the FIFO or the weighted-average method.

When a firm uses a **perpetual inventory system**, a continuous record is maintained for the quantities and costs of goods on hand at all times. Perpetual inventories do not eliminate the need for taking periodic physical inventories. If a difference is found between the physical count and the amount in the perpetual inventory records, the adjustment to merchandise inventory is required. This adjustment is illustrated in Chapter 14.

The **lower-of-cost-or-market method** is used whenever the replacement cost of the ending inventory is less than its actual cost. When this happens, the following entry is made:

| | | |
|---|---|---|
| Loss on Write-Down of Inventory | xxx | |
|     Merchandise Inventory | | xxx |

This practice is consistent with the practice of conservatism.

**Objective 4.**    **Estimate the ending inventory and cost of goods sold by using the gross profit and retail inventory methods.**

Businesses using the periodic inventory method must estimate their ending inventory and cost of goods sold in order to provide interim financial statements. Two generally accepted methods are the gross profit method and the retail inventory method.

Under the **gross profit method**, the firm's normal gross profit percentage [(net sales – cost of goods sold)/net sales] can be used to estimate the cost of goods sold and ending inventory. Cost of goods sold can be estimated by multiplying the gross profit percentage by the net sales and subtracting this amount from net sales.

The **retail inventory method** requires keeping records of both the cost and selling (retail) prices of all goods purchased. The percentage of total goods available for sale at cost divided by the total goods available for sale at retail is used to estimate cost of goods sold and ending inventory.

## REVIEW QUESTIONS

**Instructions:** Analyze each of the following items carefully before writing your answer in the column at the right.

| | Question | Answer |
|---|---|---|
| LO 1 | **1.** Understating the ending inventory for the year 20-1 will cause net income for the year 20-1 to be _____. .................................... | _____ |
| LO 1 | **2.** Overstating the ending inventory for the year 20-1 will cause net income for the year 20-2 to be _____. ......................................... | _____ |
| LO 2 | **3.** The two principal systems of accounting for inventory are the _____ and _____. ........................................................ | _____ |
| | | _____ |

**LO 2**   **4.** Under the _____ system, the merchandise inventory
account is debited for the cost of all goods purchased. ........................   _____

**LO 3**   **5.** The process of counting all the goods on hand at the end of the
period is called taking a(n) _____. ..................................   _____

**LO 3**   **6.** A fiscal year that starts and ends at the time the stock of goods is
normally at its lowest level is known as a(n) _____. ....................   _____

**LO 3**   **7.** A special form used to record information when taking a
physical inventory is called a(n) _____. ....................................   _____

**LO 3**   **8.** In the term "FOB shipping point," FOB stands for _____. ...........   _____

**LO 3**   **9.** If goods are shipped "FOB _____ ," the seller pays for shipping
and the goods are the property of the selling company until
received by the buying company. ........................................................   _____

**LO 3**   **10.** Name the four methods of assigning cost to the ending inventory
and cost of goods sold. ........................................................................   _____

_____

_____

_____

**LO 3**   **11.** A costing method that assumes the first goods bought were the first
goods sold and, therefore, the latest goods bought remain in
inventory is called _____. ...............................................................   _____

**LO 3**   **12.** A costing method that assumes the sales in the period were made
from the most recently purchased goods and, therefore, the earliest
goods bought remain in inventory is called _____. .........................   _____

**LO 3**   **13.** When prices are rising, the cost method that will result in the highest
net income is _____. .......................................................................   _____

**LO 3**   **14.** When prices are rising, the cost method that will result in the lowest
ending inventory is _____. ...............................................................   _____

**LO 3**   **15.** In the application of "lower-of-cost-or-market," the term "market"
refers to _____. ...............................................................................   _____

**LO 3**   **16.** The practice of conservatism states we should never anticipate
_____ but always anticipate _____. .........................................   _____

_____

**LO 3**   **17.** The difference between the cost and market value is considered a
loss due to holding _____. ..............................................................   _____

**LO 3**   **18.** The dollar amount of the loss due to holding inventory is normally
charged to an account entitled _____. ..........................................   _____

**LO 4**   **19.** Under the _____ method, the firm's normal gross profit can be
used to estimate the cost of goods sold and ending inventory. ............   _____

**LO 4**   **20.** The _____ method of estimating inventory requires keeping records
of both the cost and selling (retail) prices of all goods purchased ........   _____

## EXERCISES

### Exercise 1  (LO 2)  JOURNAL ENTRIES FOR PERIODIC AND PERPETUAL INVENTORY METHODS

The following inventory transactions occurred for Riegler Company during the month of April:

Apr.  2    Purchased merchandise on account, $2,500.
      5    Purchased merchandise for cash, $3,000.
     10    Sold merchandise on account for $500. The cost of the merchandise sold was $300.
     15    Sold merchandise that cost $250 for $400 cash.

*Required:*

1.   Prepare general journal entries for the above transactions. Assume the periodic inventory system is used.
2.   Prepare general journal entries for the above transactions. Assume the perpetual inventory system is used.

**Exercise 1 (Continued)**
**1. Periodic Inventory System**

## GENERAL JOURNAL

PAGE

| | DATE | | DESCRIPTION | POST. REF. | DEBIT | CREDIT | |
|---|---|---|---|---|---|---|---|
| 1 | | | | | | | 1 |
| 2 | | | | | | | 2 |
| 3 | | | | | | | 3 |
| 4 | | | | | | | 4 |
| 5 | | | | | | | 5 |
| 6 | | | | | | | 6 |
| 7 | | | | | | | 7 |
| 8 | | | | | | | 8 |
| 9 | | | | | | | 9 |
| 10 | | | | | | | 10 |
| 11 | | | | | | | 11 |
| 12 | | | | | | | 12 |
| 13 | | | | | | | 13 |
| 14 | | | | | | | 14 |
| 15 | | | | | | | 15 |
| 16 | | | | | | | 16 |
| 17 | | | | | | | 17 |
| 18 | | | | | | | 18 |
| 19 | | | | | | | 19 |
| 20 | | | | | | | 20 |
| 21 | | | | | | | 21 |
| 22 | | | | | | | 22 |
| 23 | | | | | | | 23 |
| 24 | | | | | | | 24 |
| 25 | | | | | | | 25 |
| 26 | | | | | | | 26 |
| 27 | | | | | | | 27 |
| 28 | | | | | | | 28 |
| 29 | | | | | | | 29 |
| 30 | | | | | | | 30 |
| 31 | | | | | | | 31 |
| 32 | | | | | | | 32 |
| 33 | | | | | | | 33 |

**Exercise 1 (Concluded)**
**2. Perpetual Inventory System**

### GENERAL JOURNAL

PAGE

| | DATE | DESCRIPTION | POST. REF. | DEBIT | CREDIT | |
|---|---|---|---|---|---|---|
| 1 | | | | | | 1 |
| 2 | | | | | | 2 |
| 3 | | | | | | 3 |
| 4 | | | | | | 4 |
| 5 | | | | | | 5 |
| 6 | | | | | | 6 |
| 7 | | | | | | 7 |
| 8 | | | | | | 8 |
| 9 | | | | | | 9 |
| 10 | | | | | | 10 |
| 11 | | | | | | 11 |
| 12 | | | | | | 12 |
| 13 | | | | | | 13 |
| 14 | | | | | | 14 |
| 15 | | | | | | 15 |
| 16 | | | | | | 16 |
| 17 | | | | | | 17 |
| 18 | | | | | | 18 |
| 19 | | | | | | 19 |
| 20 | | | | | | 20 |
| 21 | | | | | | 21 |
| 22 | | | | | | 22 |
| 23 | | | | | | 23 |
| 24 | | | | | | 24 |
| 25 | | | | | | 25 |
| 26 | | | | | | 26 |
| 27 | | | | | | 27 |
| 28 | | | | | | 28 |
| 29 | | | | | | 29 |
| 30 | | | | | | 30 |
| 31 | | | | | | 31 |
| 32 | | | | | | 32 |
| 33 | | | | | | 33 |

**Exercise 2  (LO 3)  COMPUTING COST OF GOODS SOLD, ENDING INVENTORY, AND GROSS PROFIT**

Sally Holvey operates Sally's Used Cars. Sally uses the specific identification costing method for determining ending inventory and cost of goods sold. Provided below is a list of the cars that were available for sale during the past month with the cost and selling price if sold. Based on this information, compute the cost of goods sold, cost of the ending inventory, and gross profit.

| Year | Model | Cost | Selling Price |
|------|-------|------|---------------|
| 2009 | Mercury Grand Marquis | $12,000 | $13,450 |
| 2008 | Ford Explorer | 21,500 | |
| 2008 | Ford Focus | 12,400 | 13,992 |
| 2006 | Ford Mustang | 13,200 | 14,450 |
| 2005 | Honda Accord | 10,200 | 12,900 |
| 2005 | Jeep Wrangler | 11,400 | |
| 2005 | Porsche 911 | 42,500 | 49,900 |
| 2007 | Porsche Boxster | 32,500 | 34,200 |
| 2004 | Honda CR-V | 10,500 | |
| 2006 | BMW M5 | 39,500 | |
| 1990 | BMW 325i | 4,200 | |

_____

_____

_____

_____

_____

_____

_____

_____

_____

_____

_____

_____

_____

_____

_____

_____

_____

_____

_____

_____

## Exercise 3  (LO 3)  LOWER-OF-COST-OR-MARKET

Keast Enterprises has four items of inventory with costs and market values at year-end as follows:

| Item | Cost | Market Value |
|------|------|--------------|
| 1 | $20,000 | $18,000 |
| 2 | 45,000 | 48,000 |
| 3 | 18,000 | 16,000 |
| 4 | 88,000 | 90,000 |

Compute the amount of Keast's inventory at year-end using the lower-of-cost-or-market method applied to:

a.   The total inventory.

b.   Each item in the inventory.

## Exercise 4  (LO 4)  RETAIL INVENTORY METHOD

Tyrone Sales Company started in the retail business on July 1. Net purchases to December 31 amounted to $140,000, and the goods were marked to sell at retail for $200,000. Net sales amounted to $160,000. Using the retail method, compute the approximate cost of the inventory on December 31.

_____

_____

_____

_____

_____

_____

_____

_____

_____

_____

_____

_____

_____

_____

_____

_____

_____

_____

_____

_____

_____

_____

_____

_____

_____

_____

_____

_____

_____

## PROBLEMS

### Problem 5  (LO 3)  FIFO, LIFO, AND WEIGHTED-AVERAGE

Hickman Equipment Co. sells stereo equipment and is interested in the effect that the inventory method has on the information provided in the financial statements. You have been asked to demonstrate the impact of various inventory methods for one item of merchandise handled by Hickman. Use the information provided below for your analysis.

|  | Units | Unit Price | Total Cost |
|---|---|---|---|
| Beginning inventory | 50 | $120 | $ 6,000 |
| Purchases during period: | | | |
| 1st purchase | 80 | 130 | 10,400 |
| 2nd purchase | 100 | 150 | 15,000 |
| 3rd purchase | 70 | 160 | 11,200 |
| Total | 300 | | $42,600 |

Number of units sold: 280
Net sales revenue for the period: $54,000

*Required:*

Compute cost of goods sold, ending inventory, and gross profit using the FIFO, LIFO, and weighted-average cost methods.

### FIFO Inventory Method

| Date 20-1/ 20-2 | | Cost of Goods Sold | | | Cost of Ending Inventory | | |
|---|---|---|---|---|---|---|---|
| | | Units | Unit Price | Total | Units | Unit Price | Total |
| | | | | | | | |
| | | | | | | | |
| | | | | | | | |
| | | | | | | | |
| | | | | | | | |
| | | | | | | | |
| | | | | | | | |
| | | | | | | | |
| | | | | | | | |
| | | | | | | | |

## Problem 5 (Concluded)

### LIFO Inventory Method

| Date 20-1/ 20-2 | | Cost of Goods Sold | | | Cost of Ending Inventory | | |
|---|---|---|---|---|---|---|---|
| | | Units | Unit Price | Total | Units | Unit Price | Total |
| | | | | | | | |
| | | | | | | | |
| | | | | | | | |
| | | | | | | | |
| | | | | | | | |
| | | | | | | | |
| | | | | | | | |
| | | | | | | | |

_____
_____
_____
_____

### Weighted-Average Method

_____
_____
_____
_____
_____
_____
_____
_____
_____
_____
_____

## Problem 6 (LO 4) GROSS PROFIT METHOD OF ESTIMATING INVENTORY

The normal gross profit of Zello Company is 30%. The store was destroyed by fire the night of May 27, but the records were saved. The accounts show that the inventory at the start of the year cost $120,000, net purchases to May 27 were $140,000, and net sales to date were $230,000.

*Required:*

Calculate the estimated cost of the goods destroyed by the fire.

## Problem 7  (LO 4)  RETAIL INVENTORY METHOD

Assume the following information for Vargo Company:

|                         | Cost      | Retail    |
|-------------------------|-----------|-----------|
| Inventory, June 1       | $200,000  | $300,000  |
| Net purchases for June  | 400,000   | 700,000   |
| Net sales for June      |           | 780,000   |

*Required:*

Estimate the June 30 inventory using the retail inventory method.

_____

_____

_____

_____

_____

_____

_____

_____

_____

_____

_____

_____

_____

_____

_____

_____

_____

_____

_____

_____

_____

_____

_____

_____

_____

_____

# CHAPTER 13 APPENDIX
# PERPETUAL INVENTORY METHOD:
# LIFO AND MOVING-AVERAGE METHODS

## APPENDIX LEARNING OBJECTIVES

In Chapter 13, you learned how to apply the LIFO and weighted-average inventory methods under the **periodic inventory system**. In the appendix to Chapter 13, the **perpetual inventory system** is illustrated. Recall that all calculations under the periodic system are done at the end of the accounting period. Under the perpetual system, costs are computed every time merchandise is purchased and sold. These costs are used to maintain a running record of the cost of goods sold to date and the balance of inventory on hand.

**Objective 1.**    **Compute the costs allocated to the ending inventory and cost of goods sold using the perpetual LIFO inventory method.**

LIFO has layers. Under perpetual LIFO, each time inventory is purchased, a new layer of inventory is formed. Each time inventory is sold, it is assumed that the units came from the most recently purchased layer, followed by the next most recently purchased layer.

**Objective 2.**    **Compute the costs allocated to the ending inventory and cost of goods sold using the perpetual moving-average inventory method.**

When using the perpetual moving-average inventory method, each time inventory is purchased, a new average cost per unit is calculated. When inventory is sold, the most recent average cost is used to measure cost of goods sold and the remaining inventory on hand.

## APPENDIX EXERCISES
### Apx. Exercise 1 (LO 1) PERPETUAL LIFO INVENTORY METHOD

The beginning inventory, purchases, and sales for Smaltz Sailing Company for the month of September are provided below.

| Date | Beginning Inventory and Purchases | | Sales |
|---|---|---|---|
| | Units | Cost/Unit | Units |
| Sept. 1 (BI) | 100 | $6.00 | |
| | 100 | 6.20 | |
| | 200 | 6.30 | |
| Sept. 10 | | | 250 |
| Sept. 15 | 600 | 6.50 | |
| Sept. 30 | | | 300 |
| BI: Beginning Inventory | | | |

*Required:*

Calculate the total amount assigned to cost of goods sold during September and the ending inventory on September 30 using the perpetual LIFO inventory method.

**Apx. Exercise 1 (Concluded)**

| Date | Purchases | | | Cost of Goods Sold | | | | Inventory on Hand | | | | |
|---|---|---|---|---|---|---|---|---|---|---|---|---|
| | Units | Cost/ Unit | Total | Units | Cost/ Unit | CGS | Cum. CGS | Layer | Units | Cost/ Unit | Layer Cost | Total |
| 9/1 (BI) | | | | | | | | | | | | |
| | | | | | | | | | | | | |
| 9/10 | | | | | | | | | | | | |
| 9/15 | | | | | | | | | | | | |
| | | | | | | | | | | | | |
| 9/30 | | | | | | | | | | | | |
| | | | | | | | | | | | | |
| Cost of Goods Sold during September | | | | | | | | | | | | |

BI: Beginning Inventory

## Apx. Exercise 2 (LO 2) PERPETUAL MOVING-AVERAGE INVENTORY METHOD

*Required:*

Using the inventory data provided in Apx. Exercise 1, calculate the total amount assigned to cost of goods sold during September and the ending inventory on September 30 using the perpetual moving-average inventory method.

**Apx. Exercise 2 (Concluded)**

| Date | Purchases | | | Cost of Goods Sold | | | | Inventory on Hand and Average Cost per Unit | | | |
|---|---|---|---|---|---|---|---|---|---|---|---|
| | Units | Cost/ Unit | Total | Units | Cost/ Unit | CGS | Cum. CGS | Cost of Purchase or (Sale) | Cost of Inventory on Hand | Units on Hand | Average Cost/ Unit |
| 9/1 (BI) | | | | | | | | | | | |
| 9/10 | | | | | | | | | | | |
| 9/15 | | | | | | | | | | | |
| 9/30 | | | | | | | | | | | |
| Cost of Goods Sold during September | | | | | | | | | | | |

BI: Beginning Inventory

## Apx. Exercise 3 (LO 1) PERPETUAL LIFO INVENTORY METHOD

The beginning inventory, purchases, and sales for McGuire Flag Company for the month of October are provided below.

| Date | Beginning Inventory and Purchases | | Sales |
|------|-------|-----------|-------|
|      | Units | Cost/Unit | Units |
| Oct. 1 (BI) | 100 | $3.00 | |
|  | 150 | 3.20 | |
|  | 250 | 3.50 | |
| Oct. 8 | | | 450 |
| Oct. 20 | 300 | 3.80 | |
| Oct. 31 | | | 200 |
| BI: Beginning Inventory | | | |

*Required:*

Calculate the total amount to be assigned to cost of goods sold during October and the ending inventory on October 31 using the perpetual LIFO inventory method.

**Apx. Exercise 3 (Concluded)**

| Date | Purchases | | | Cost of Goods Sold | | | | Inventory on Hand | | | | |
|---|---|---|---|---|---|---|---|---|---|---|---|---|
| | Units | Cost/ Unit | Total | Units | Cost/ Unit | CGS | Cum. CGS | Layer | Units | Cost/ Unit | Layer Cost | Total |
| 10/1 (BI) | | | | | | | | | | | | |
| | | | | | | | | | | | | |
| 10/8 | | | | | | | | | | | | |
| | | | | | | | | | | | | |
| 10/20 | | | | | | | | | | | | |
| 10/31 | | | | | | | | | | | | |
| Cost of Goods Sold during October | | | | | | | | | | | | |

BI:  Beginning Inventory

## Apx. Exercise 4 (LO 2) PERPETUAL MOVING-AVERAGE INVENTORY METHOD

*Required:*

Using the inventory data provided in Apx. Exercise 3, calculate the total amount assigned to cost of goods sold during October and the ending inventory on October 31 using the perpetual moving-average inventory method.

**Apx. Exercise 4 (Concluded)**

| Date | Purchases | | | Cost of Goods Sold | | | | Inventory on Hand and Average Cost per Unit | | | |
|---|---|---|---|---|---|---|---|---|---|---|---|
| | Units | Cost/ Unit | Total | Units | Cost/ Unit | CGS | Cum. CGS | Cost of Purchase or (Sale) | Cost of Inventory on Hand | Units on Hand | Average Cost/ Unit |
| 10/1 (BI) | | | | | | | | | | | |
| 10/8 | | | | | | | | | | | |
| 10/20 | | | | | | | | | | | |
| 10/31 | | | | | | | | | | | |
| Cost of Goods Sold during October | | | | | | | | | | | |

BI: Beginning Inventory

# APPENDIX PROBLEMS

## Apx. Problem 5 (LO 1) PERPETUAL LIFO INVENTORY METHOD

The beginning inventory, purchases, and sales for Snyder Ball Company for the month of February are provided below.

| Date | Beginning Inventory and Purchases | | Sales |
|------|------|------|------|
| | Units | Cost/ Unit | Units |
| Feb. 1 | 30 | $6.70 | |
| (BI) | 70 | 6.90 | |
| Feb. 3 | 400 | 7.10 | |
| Feb. 5 | | | 250 |
| Feb. 11 | 700 | 7.20 | |
| Feb. 13 | | | 500 |
| Feb. 16 | 300 | 7.50 | |
| Feb. 18 | 500 | 7.70 | |
| Feb. 24 | | | 600 |
| Feb. 25 | | | 50 |
| Feb. 28 | 300 | 8.00 | |
| BI: Beginning Inventory | | | |

*Required:*

Calculate the total amount to be assigned to cost of goods sold during February and the ending inventory on February 28 using the perpetual LIFO inventory method.

**Apx. Problem 5 (Continued)**

| Date | Purchases Units | Purchases Cost/ Unit | Purchases Total | Cost of Goods Sold Units | Cost of Goods Sold Cost/ Unit | Cost of Goods Sold CGS | Cost of Goods Sold Cum. CGS | Inventory on Hand Layer | Inventory on Hand Units | Inventory on Hand Cost/ Unit | Inventory on Hand Layer Cost | Inventory on Hand Total |
|------|-----|-----|-----|-----|-----|-----|-----|-----|-----|-----|-----|-----|
| 2/1 (BI) | | | | | | | | | | | | |
| 2/3 | | | | | | | | | | | | |
| 2/5 | | | | | | | | | | | | |
| 2/11 | | | | | | | | | | | | |
| 2/13 | | | | | | | | | | | | |
| 2/16 | | | | | | | | | | | | |

**Apx. Problem 5 (Concluded)**

| Date | Purchases | | | Cost of Goods Sold | | | | Inventory on Hand | | | | |
|------|-----------|-----------|-------|-------|-------------|-----|----------|-------|-------|-------------|------------|-------|
| | Units | Cost/ Unit | Total | Units | Cost/ Unit | CGS | Cum. CGS | Layer | Units | Cost/ Unit | Layer Cost | Total |
| 2/18 | | | | | | | | | | | | |
| | | | | | | | | | | | | |
| | | | | | | | | | | | | |
| 2/24 | | | | | | | | | | | | |
| | | | | | | | | | | | | |
| 2/25 | | | | | | | | | | | | |
| | | | | | | | | | | | | |
| 2/28 | | | | | | | | | | | | |
| Cost of Goods Sold during February | | | | | | | | | | | | |

BI:  Beginning Inventory

## Apx. Problem 6 (LO 2) PERPETUAL MOVING-AVERAGE INVENTORY METHOD

*Required:*

Using the inventory data provided in Apx. Problem 5, calculate the total amount assigned to cost of goods sold during February and the ending inventory on February 28 using the perpetual moving-average inventory method.

**Apx. Problem 6 (Concluded)**

| Date | Purchases | | | Cost of Goods Sold | | | | Inventory on Hand and Average Cost per Unit | | | |
| | Units | Cost/ Unit | Total | Units | Cost/ Unit | CGS | Cum. CGS | Cost of Purchase or (Sale) | Cost of Inventory on Hand | Units on Hand | Average Cost/ Unit |
| --- | --- | --- | --- | --- | --- | --- | --- | --- | --- | --- | --- |
| 2/1 (BI) | | | | | | | | | | | |
| 2/3 | | | | | | | | | | | |
| 2/5 | | | | | | | | | | | |
| 2/11 | | | | | | | | | | | |
| 2/13 | | | | | | | | | | | |
| 2/16 | | | | | | | | | | | |
| 2/18 | | | | | | | | | | | |
| 2/24 | | | | | | | | | | | |
| 2/25 | | | | | | | | | | | |
| 2/28 | | | | | | | | | | | |

Cost of Goods Sold during February

BI: Beginning Inventory

## Apx. Problem 7 (LO 1)   PERPETUAL LIFO INVENTORY METHOD

The beginning inventory, purchases, and sales for Rafalko Candy Company for the month of July are provided below.

| Date | Beginning Inventory and Purchases | | Sales |
| --- | --- | --- | --- |
| | Units | Cost/ Unit | Units |
| July 1 | 50 | $5.90 | |
| (BI) | 50 | 6.10 | |
| July 5 | 400 | 6.20 | |
| July 7 | | | 300 |
| July 12 | 300 | 6.40 | |
| July 15 | | | 200 |
| July 18 | 100 | 6.50 | |
| July 20 | 600 | 6.80 | |
| July 24 | | | 800 |
| July 27 | | | 100 |
| July 31 | 100 | 6.90 | |
| BI: Beginning Inventory | | | |

*Required:*

Calculate the total amount to be assigned to cost of goods sold during July and the ending inventory on July 31 using the perpetual LIFO inventory method.

**Apx. Problem 7 (Continued)**

| Date | Purchases | | | Cost of Goods Sold | | | | Inventory on Hand | | | |
|---|---|---|---|---|---|---|---|---|---|---|---|
| | Units | Cost/ Unit | Total | Units | Cost/ Unit | CGS | Cum. CGS | Layer | Units | Cost/ Unit | Layer Cost | Total |
| 7/1 (BI) | | | | | | | | | | | | |
| 7/5 | | | | | | | | | | | | |
| 7/7 | | | | | | | | | | | | |
| 7/12 | | | | | | | | | | | | |
| 7/15 | | | | | | | | | | | | |
| 7/18 | | | | | | | | | | | | |

## Apx. Problem 7 (Concluded)

| Date | Purchases | | | Cost of Goods Sold | | | | | Inventory on Hand | | | | |
|---|---|---|---|---|---|---|---|---|---|---|---|---|---|
| | Units | Cost/ Unit | Total | Units | Cost/ Unit | CGS | Cum. CGS | | Layer | Units | Cost/ Unit | Layer Cost | Total |
| 7/20 | | | | | | | | | | | | | |
| | | | | | | | | | | | | | |
| | | | | | | | | | | | | | |
| | | | | | | | | | | | | | |
| | | | | | | | | | | | | | |
| 7/24 | | | | | | | | | | | | | |
| | | | | | | | | | | | | | |
| 7/27 | | | | | | | | | | | | | |
| 7/31 | | | | | | | | | | | | | |
| | | | | | | | | | | | | | |
| Cost of Goods Sold during July | | | | | | | | | | | | | |

BI:  Beginning Inventory

## Apx. Problem 8  (LO 2)  PERPETUAL MOVING-AVERAGE INVENTORY METHOD

*Required:*

Using the inventory data provided in Apx. Problem 7, calculate the total amount assigned to cost of goods sold during July and the ending inventory on July 31 using the perpetual moving-average inventory method.

**Apx. Problem 8 (Concluded)**

| Date | Purchases | | | Cost of Goods Sold | | | | Inventory on Hand and Average Cost per Unit | | | |
|---|---|---|---|---|---|---|---|---|---|---|---|
| | Units | Cost/ Unit | Total | Units | Cost/ Unit | CGS | Cum. CGS | Cost of Purchase or (Sale) | Cost of Inventory on Hand | Units on Hand | Average Cost/ Unit |
| 7/1 (BI) | | | | | | | | | | | |
| 7/5 | | | | | | | | | | | |
| 7/7 | | | | | | | | | | | |
| 7/12 | | | | | | | | | | | |
| 7/15 | | | | | | | | | | | |
| 7/18 | | | | | | | | | | | |
| 7/20 | | | | | | | | | | | |
| 7/24 | | | | | | | | | | | |
| 7/27 | | | | | | | | | | | |
| 7/31 | | | | | | | | | | | |
| | | | | | | | | | | | |

Cost of Goods Sold during July

BI: Beginning Inventory

# CHAPTER 14
# ADJUSTMENTS AND THE WORK SHEET
# FOR A MERCHANDISING BUSINESS

## LEARNING OBJECTIVES

Chapter 14 covers the end-of-period adjustments and the preparation of a work sheet for a merchandising business. Adjustments for merchandise inventory and unearned revenue are emphasized.

**Objective 1.    Prepare an adjustment for merchandise inventory using the periodic inventory system.**

During the year, the purchase and sale of merchandise is not entered in the merchandise inventory account. Thus, at the end of the year, it is necessary to adjust the merchandise inventory account to properly reflect the amount of inventory on hand. This is accomplished by removing the beginning inventory from the books (the current balance), and entering the ending inventory, based on a physical count. This adjustment is made on the work sheet in a two-step process as shown below. This technique is used so that all of the information required to compute cost of goods sold is available in the Income Statement columns of the work sheet.

| Account Title | Trial Balance | | Adjustments | | | | Adjusted Trial Balance | | Income Statement | | Balance Sheet | |
|---|---|---|---|---|---|---|---|---|---|---|---|---|
| | Debit | Credit | | Debit | Credit | | Debit | Credit | Debit | Credit | Debit | Credit |
| Merchandise Inventory | 20 | | **(Step 2)** | **30** | 20 | (Step 1) | 30 | | BI | EI | 30 | |
| Income Summary | | | (Step 1) | 20 | 30 | **(Step 2)** | 20 | 30 | -- 20 | 30 | | |
| Purchases | 80 | | | | | | | | 80 | Purchases | | |

Step 1:  Remove beginning inventory        Income Summary                                20
                                                         Merchandise Inventory                              20

**Step 2:  Insert ending inventory**         **Merchandise Inventory**               30
                                                         **Income Summary**                                 30

BI:  Beginning Inventory ($20);  EI:  Ending Inventory ($30)

Cost of goods sold:

| | |
|---|---|
| Merchandise inventory, January 1 | $ 20 |
| Purchases | 80 |
| Goods available for sale | $100 |
| **Less merchandise inventory, December 31** | 30 |
| Cost of goods sold | $ 70 |

**Objective 2.    Prepare an adjustment for unearned revenue.**

A liability account is created when cash is received before the product or service is provided. This liability is called **unearned revenue**. If all, or part, of the revenue has been earned by the end of the period, an adjustment is made in order to reduce the liability, Unearned Revenue, and increase the related revenue account.

The entry to record receipt of cash for revenue to be earned later is as follows:

Cash                                  xxx
     Unearned Revenue                          xxx

The entry when all, or part, of revenue has been earned is as follows:

| | | |
|---|---|---|
| Unearned Revenue | xxx | |
| Sales | | xxx |

### Objective 3.   Prepare a work sheet for a merchandising business.

At the end of the accounting period, a work sheet is prepared to make the remaining steps of the accounting cycle easier. The work sheet is similar to the one you learned about in Chapter 5 for a service business, except for the new accounts introduced for a merchandising business and the unearned revenue account that was introduced in this chapter.

Adjusting entries are entered on the work sheet, including adjustments for supplies used, insurance expired, depreciation, and wages earned but not paid. From the Adjusted Trial Balance columns, all amounts are extended to either the Income Statement columns or the Balance Sheet columns of the work sheet.

Of particular importance is the method of extending the amounts for Merchandise Inventory and Income Summary on the work sheet. Merchandise Inventory is extended in the usual manner. The adjusted balance is extended to the Adjusted Trial Balance columns and then to the Balance Sheet columns. However, both the debit *and* credit adjustments to Income Summary are extended to the Adjusted Trial Balance columns and then to the Income Statement columns (see table below). The debit to Income Summary represents the beginning balance of Merchandise Inventory. The credit to Income Summary represents the ending balance of Merchandise Inventory. Both amounts are used on the income statement. Thus, both amounts are extended to the Income Statement columns.

The other accounts identified with merchandise accounting will be extended into the Income Statement columns of the work sheet. Also, any unearned revenue that has been earned as of the balance sheet date will be adjusted into revenue (see table below).

## WORK SHEET

| | Trial Balance | | Adjustments | | Adj. Trial Balance | | Income Statement | | Balance Sheet | |
|---|---|---|---|---|---|---|---|---|---|---|
| | Dr. | Cr. | Dr. | Cr. | Dr. | Cr. | Dr. | Cr. | Dr. | Cr. |
| Merchandise Inv. | BI | | EI | BI | EI | | | | EI | |
| Unearned Rev. | | xx | xx | | | xx | | | | xx |
| Income Summary | | | BI | EI | BI | EI | BI | EI | | |
| Revenue | | xx | | xx | | xx | | xx | | |
| Sales | | xx | | | | xx | | xx | | |
| Sales Ret. & Allow. | xx | | | | xx | | xx | | | |
| Sales Discounts | xx | | | | xx | | xx | | | |
| Purchases | xx | | | | xx | | xx | | | |
| Purch. Ret. & Allow. | | xx | | | | xx | | xx | | |
| Purch. Discounts | | xx | | | | xx | | xx | | |
| Freight-In | xx | | | | xx | | xx | | | |

All of the accounts needed to arrive at net income for a merchandising business are in the Income Statement columns of the work sheet. The difference between the debits and credits in the Income Statement columns and between the debits and credits in the Balance Sheet columns will equal either net income or net loss.

**Objective 4.    Journalize adjusting entries for a merchandising business.**

Just because adjusting entries were analyzed and placed on the work sheet does not mean that they have been entered into the accounts in the general ledger. Adjusting entries need to be entered in the general journal and posted to the general ledger. This information can be taken from the Adjustments columns of the work sheet.

**Objective 5.    Prepare adjusting journal entries under the perpetual inventory system.**

Under the perpetual inventory system, the merchandise inventory and cost of goods sold accounts are continually updated throughout the year to reflect purchases and sales of inventory. Comparative entries under the periodic and perpetual inventory systems are shown below.

| Transaction | Periodic System | | Perpetual System | |
|---|---|---|---|---|
| 1.  Purchased merchandise on account, $100. | Purchases                    100 <br>    Accounts Payable | 100 | Merchandise Inventory          100 <br>    Accounts Payable | 100 |
| 2.  Sold merchandise on account, $60. The cost of the merchandise sold was $50. | Accounts Receivable          60 <br>    Sales | 60 | Accounts Receivable           60 <br>    Sales <br><br> Cost of Goods Sold             50 <br>    Merchandise Inventory | 60 <br><br><br> 50 |
| 3.  Periodic system: Beginning inventory, $40. Ending inventory, $90. | Income Summary               40 <br>    Merchandise Inventory <br><br> Merchandise Inventory        90 <br>    Income Summary | 40 <br><br><br> 90 | | |
| 4.  Perpetual system: Ending balance of merchandise inventory, $100. Ending inventory based on physical count, $90. | | | Inventory Short and Over       10 <br>    Merchandise Inventory | 10 |

## REVIEW QUESTIONS

**Instructions:** Analyze each of the following items carefully before writing your answer in the column at the right.

| | **Question** | **Answer** |
|---|---|---|
| LO 1 | **1.** At the end of an accounting period, a(n) _____ is used to analyze and prepare adjustments and to determine the amount of net income or net loss for the time period. .................................... | _____ |
| LO 1 | **2.** The amount of inventory on hand at the end of the accounting period is determined by taking a(n) _____ of the goods on hand. | _____ |
| LO 1 | **3.** Under the periodic system of adjusting for the ending inventory, the beginning inventory is removed from the merchandise inventory account with a(n) _____ , and a debit is entered into ...............................................the _____ account. | _____ <br><br> _____ |
| LO 1 | **4.** Under the periodic system of accounting for the ending inventory, the ending inventory is entered by debiting Merchandise Inventory and crediting the _____ account. ............................... | _____ |

**LO 1**   5.  Purchases less purchases returns and allowances and purchases discounts equals _____. ....................................................   _____

**LO 1**   6.  Beginning inventory plus net purchases and freight-in equals _____. .......................................................................   _____

**LO 1**   7.  Merchandise available for sale less ending inventory is equal to _____. .......................................................................   _____

**LO 1**   8.  On the work sheet, both the debit and credit amounts of the income summary account are extended to the _____ and the _____ columns of the work sheet. ...........................................................   _____

_____

**LO 1**   9.  Purchases Returns and Allowances and Purchases Discounts are deducted from the _____ account on the income statement. .....   _____

**LO 2**  10.  The cash received in advance of delivering a product or performing a service is called _____. ..................................................   _____

**LO 2**  11.  Unearned revenue is reported as a(n) _____ on the balance sheet.   _____

**LO 2**  12.  At the end of an accounting period, unearned revenue is adjusted into a(n) _____ account for the amount of revenue that has been earned. ..................................................................................   _____

**LO 2**  13.  Purchases Returns and Allowances and Purchases Discounts are classified as _____ accounts. .....................................................   _____

**LO 3**  14.  The first step in preparing a work sheet is to prepare the _____.   _____

**LO 3**  15.  On the work sheet, amounts are extended from the Adjusted Trial Balance columns to the _____ and _____ columns. ...........   _____

_____

**LO 3**  16.  If credits exceed debits on the Income Statement columns of the work sheet, this represents a net _____. ....................................   _____

**LO 3**  17.  The most helpful aid in entering adjustments into the general journal is the _____. .......................................................................   _____

**LO 5**  18.  Under the perpetual inventory system, _____ is debited when inventory is purchased. .........................................................   _____

**LO 5**  19.  Under the perpetual inventory system, _____ is (are) debited when inventory is sold. .................................................................   _____

# EXERCISES

## Exercise 1 (LO 1) ADJUSTING ENTRIES FOR MERCHANDISE INVENTORY

Kendall's TV and Appliances had merchandise inventory of $60,300 at the beginning of the year and $54,800 at the end of the year. Prepare the necessary adjusting entries in a general journal.

### GENERAL JOURNAL

PAGE

| | DATE | | DESCRIPTION | POST. REF. | DEBIT | CREDIT | |
|---|---|---|---|---|---|---|---|
| 1 | | | | | | | 1 |
| 2 | | | | | | | 2 |
| 3 | | | | | | | 3 |
| 4 | | | | | | | 4 |
| 5 | | | | | | | 5 |
| 6 | | | | | | | 6 |
| 7 | | | | | | | 7 |

## Exercise 2 (LO 1) CALCULATION OF COST OF GOODS SOLD

The following amounts are known for Casey's Card and Gift Shop:

| | |
|---|---|
| Beginning merchandise inventory | $33,000 |
| Ending merchandise inventory | 41,000 |
| Purchases | 86,000 |
| Purchases returns and allowances | 4,500 |
| Purchases discounts | 2,500 |
| Freight-in | 1,000 |

Prepare the cost of goods sold section of the income statement for Casey's Card and Gift Shop.

## Exercise 3 (LO 2) ADJUSTMENT FOR UNEARNED REVENUE

The following transactions took place for Hamilton Theaters. Journalize these transactions in a general journal.

Feb.  22  Sold 2,000 season tickets at $25 each, receiving cash of $50,000. Received cash before the services were provided.

Dec.  31  An end-of-period adjustment is needed to recognize that $45,000 in ticket revenue has been earned.

**GENERAL JOURNAL**                                                      PAGE

| | DATE | DESCRIPTION | POST. REF. | DEBIT | CREDIT | |
|---|---|---|---|---|---|---|
| 1 | | | | | | 1 |
| 2 | | | | | | 2 |
| 3 | | | | | | 3 |
| 4 | | | | | | 4 |
| 5 | | | | | | 5 |
| 6 | | | | | | 6 |
| 7 | | | | | | 7 |

## Exercise 4 (LO 4) JOURNALIZING ADJUSTING ENTRIES

The partial work sheet below is taken from the books of Long Auto Repair for the year ended December 31, 20--.

Long Auto Repair

Work Sheet (Partial)

For Year Ended December 31, 20--

| | ACCOUNT TITLE | TRIAL BALANCE DEBIT | TRIAL BALANCE CREDIT | ADJUSTMENTS DEBIT | ADJUSTMENTS CREDIT | |
|---|---|---|---|---|---|---|
| 1 | Merchandise Inventory | 60 0 0 0 00 | | (b) 57 0 0 0 00 | (a) 60 0 0 0 00 | 1 |
| 2 | Supplies | 6 0 0 0 00 | | | (d) 3 2 0 0 00 | 2 |
| 3 | Building | 150 0 0 0 00 | | | | 3 |
| 4 | Accum. Depr.—Building | | 45 0 0 0 00 | | (e) 8 0 0 0 00 | 4 |
| 5 | Wages Payable | | | | (f) 2 4 0 0 00 | 5 |
| 6 | Unearned Repair Revenue | | 6 0 0 0 00 | (c) 5 0 0 0 00 | | 6 |
| 7 | Income Summary | | | (a) 60 0 0 0 00 | (b) 57 0 0 0 00 | 7 |
| 8 | Repair Revenue | | 30 0 0 0 00 | | (c) 5 0 0 0 00 | 8 |
| 9 | Wages Expense | 39 0 0 0 00 | | (f) 2 4 0 0 00 | | 9 |
| 10 | Supplies Expense | | | (d) 3 2 0 0 00 | | 10 |
| 11 | Depr. Exp.—Building | | | (e) 8 0 0 0 00 | | 11 |
| 12 | | | | | | 12 |
| 13 | | | | | | 13 |
| 14 | | | | | | 14 |
| 15 | | | | | | 15 |

Journalize the above adjustments in a general journal.

## Exercise 4 (Concluded)

**GENERAL JOURNAL**                                    PAGE

| | DATE | | DESCRIPTION | POST. REF. | DEBIT | CREDIT | |
|---|---|---|---|---|---|---|---|
| 1 | | | | | | | 1 |
| 2 | | | | | | | 2 |
| 3 | | | | | | | 3 |
| 4 | | | | | | | 4 |
| 5 | | | | | | | 5 |
| 6 | | | | | | | 6 |
| 7 | | | | | | | 7 |
| 8 | | | | | | | 8 |
| 9 | | | | | | | 9 |
| 10 | | | | | | | 10 |
| 11 | | | | | | | 11 |
| 12 | | | | | | | 12 |
| 13 | | | | | | | 13 |
| 14 | | | | | | | 14 |
| 15 | | | | | | | 15 |
| 16 | | | | | | | 16 |
| 17 | | | | | | | 17 |
| 18 | | | | | | | 18 |
| 19 | | | | | | | 19 |
| 20 | | | | | | | 20 |

## Exercise 5 (LO 5) JOURNAL ENTRIES UNDER THE PERPETUAL INVENTORY SYSTEM

Bahita Business Supplies entered into the following transactions. Prepare journal entries under the perpetual inventory system.

Aug.  1   Purchased merchandise on account from Gul Paper, $10,000.
      5   Purchased merchandise for cash, $5,000.
      10  Sold merchandise on account to Padam Medical Services for $2,000. The merchandise cost $1,500.

### GENERAL JOURNAL                                                    PAGE

| | DATE | | DESCRIPTION | POST. REF. | DEBIT | CREDIT | |
|---|---|---|---|---|---|---|---|
| 1 | | | | | | | 1 |
| 2 | | | | | | | 2 |
| 3 | | | | | | | 3 |
| 4 | | | | | | | 4 |
| 5 | | | | | | | 5 |
| 6 | | | | | | | 6 |
| 7 | | | | | | | 7 |
| 8 | | | | | | | 8 |
| 9 | | | | | | | 9 |
| 10 | | | | | | | 10 |
| 11 | | | | | | | 11 |
| 12 | | | | | | | 12 |
| 13 | | | | | | | 13 |

**Exercise 6  (LO 5)  PREPARE ADJUSTING ENTRY FOR A MERCHANDISING BUSINESS: PERPETUAL INVENTORY SYSTEM**

On December 31, Ranjit Enterprises completed a physical count of its inventory.  Although the merchandise inventory account shows a balance of $8,000, the physical count comes to $7,800.  Prepare the appropriate adjusting entry under the perpetual inventory system.

### GENERAL JOURNAL                                        PAGE

| | DATE | | DESCRIPTION | POST. REF. | DEBIT | CREDIT | |
|---|---|---|---|---|---|---|---|
| 1 | | | | | | | 1 |
| 2 | | | | | | | 2 |
| 3 | | | | | | | 3 |
| 4 | | | | | | | 4 |
| 5 | | | | | | | 5 |
| 6 | | | | | | | 6 |
| 7 | | | | | | | 7 |
| 8 | | | | | | | 8 |

## PROBLEMS

### Problem 7  (LO 1/2/3)  PREPARE A WORK SHEET

The work sheet provided on pages 252–253 is taken from the books of Ocean Beach Sail Shop, a business owned by Nicole Smith. Adjustment information is provided below. Smith uses the periodic inventory system.

(a and b)   Based on a physical count, merchandise inventory on hand as of December 31, 20--, $36,000.
(c)   Supplies remaining at end of the year, $2,350.
(d)   Unexpired insurance on December 31, $1,875.
(e)   Depreciation expense on the building for 20--, $7,000.
(f)   Depreciation expense on the store equipment for 20--, $2,800.
(g)   Unearned tour revenue as of December 31, $2,700.
(h)   Wages earned but not paid as of December 31, $1,100.

*Required:*

1.  Complete the Adjustments columns. Identify each adjustment with its corresponding letter.
2.  Complete the work sheet.

**Problem 7 (Continued)**
**1. and 2.**

Ocean Beach

Work

For Year Ended

| | ACCOUNT TITLE | TRIAL BALANCE | | | | | | | | | | ADJUSTMENTS | | | | | | | | | |
|---|---|---|---|---|---|---|---|---|---|---|---|---|---|---|---|---|---|---|---|---|---|---|
| | | DEBIT | | | | | CREDIT | | | | | DEBIT | | | | | CREDIT | | | | |
| 1 | Cash | 27 | 0 | 0 | 0 | 00 | | | | | | | | | | | | | | | |
| 2 | Accounts Receivable | 9 | 0 | 0 | 0 | 00 | | | | | | | | | | | | | | | |
| 3 | Merchandise Inventory | 31 | 0 | 0 | 0 | 00 | | | | | | | | | | | | | | | |
| 4 | Supplies | 7 | 5 | 0 | 0 | 00 | | | | | | | | | | | | | | | |
| 5 | Prepaid Insurance | 4 | 9 | 0 | 0 | 00 | | | | | | | | | | | | | | | |
| 6 | Land | 40 | 0 | 0 | 0 | 00 | | | | | | | | | | | | | | | |
| 7 | Building | 60 | 0 | 0 | 0 | 00 | | | | | | | | | | | | | | | |
| 8 | Accum. Depr.—Building | | | | | | 25 | 0 | 0 | 0 | 00 | | | | | | | | | | |
| 9 | Store Equipment | 29 | 0 | 0 | 0 | 00 | | | | | | | | | | | | | | | |
| 10 | Accum. Depr.—Store Equipment | | | | | | 9 | 0 | 0 | 0 | 00 | | | | | | | | | | |
| 11 | Accounts Payable | | | | | | 7 | 6 | 0 | 0 | 00 | | | | | | | | | | |
| 12 | Wages Payable | | | | | | | | | | | | | | | | | | | | |
| 13 | Sales Tax Payable | | | | | | 6 | 1 | 0 | 0 | 00 | | | | | | | | | | |
| 14 | Unearned Tour Revenue | | | | | | 6 | 8 | 0 | 0 | 00 | | | | | | | | | | |
| 15 | Mortgage Payable | | | | | | 43 | 0 | 0 | 0 | 00 | | | | | | | | | | |
| 16 | N. Smith, Capital | | | | | | 124 | 5 | 9 | 0 | 00 | | | | | | | | | | |
| 17 | N. Smith, Drawing | 33 | 0 | 0 | 0 | 00 | | | | | | | | | | | | | | | |
| 18 | Income Summary | | | | | | | | | | | | | | | | | | | | |
| 19 | Sales | | | | | | 122 | 0 | 0 | 0 | 00 | | | | | | | | | | |
| 20 | Sales Returns and Allowances | 4 | 2 | 0 | 0 | 00 | | | | | | | | | | | | | | | |
| 21 | Tour Revenue | | | | | | | | | | | | | | | | | | | | |
| 22 | Purchases | 38 | 0 | 0 | 0 | 00 | | | | | | | | | | | | | | | |
| 23 | Purchases Returns and Allowances | | | | | | 2 | 6 | 0 | 0 | 00 | | | | | | | | | | |
| 24 | Purchases Discounts | | | | | | 1 | 4 | 0 | 0 | 00 | | | | | | | | | | |
| 25 | Freight-In | 2 | 5 | 0 | 0 | 00 | | | | | | | | | | | | | | | |
| 26 | Wages Expense | 47 | 0 | 0 | 0 | 00 | | | | | | | | | | | | | | | |
| 27 | Advertising Expense | 4 | 8 | 0 | 0 | 00 | | | | | | | | | | | | | | | |
| 28 | Supplies Expense | | | | | | | | | | | | | | | | | | | | |
| 29 | Telephone Expense | 1 | 8 | 0 | 0 | 00 | | | | | | | | | | | | | | | |
| 30 | Utilities Expense | 7 | 6 | 0 | 0 | 00 | | | | | | | | | | | | | | | |
| 31 | Insurance Expense | | | | | | | | | | | | | | | | | | | | |
| 32 | Depr. Expense—Building | | | | | | | | | | | | | | | | | | | | |
| 33 | Depr. Expense—Store Equipment | | | | | | | | | | | | | | | | | | | | |
| 34 | Miscellaneous Expense | | 7 | 9 | 0 | 00 | | | | | | | | | | | | | | | |
| 35 | | 348 | 0 | 9 | 0 | 00 | 348 | 0 | 9 | 0 | 00 | | | | | | | | | | |
| 36 | | | | | | | | | | | | | | | | | | | | | |
| 37 | | | | | | | | | | | | | | | | | | | | | |
| 38 | | | | | | | | | | | | | | | | | | | | | |

## Problem 7 (Concluded)

**Sail Shop**

**Sheet**

**December 31, 20--**

| ADJUSTED TRIAL BALANCE | | INCOME STATEMENT | | BALANCE SHEET | | |
|---|---|---|---|---|---|---|
| DEBIT | CREDIT | DEBIT | CREDIT | DEBIT | CREDIT | |
| | | | | | | 1 |
| | | | | | | 2 |
| | | | | | | 3 |
| | | | | | | 4 |
| | | | | | | 5 |
| | | | | | | 6 |
| | | | | | | 7 |
| | | | | | | 8 |
| | | | | | | 9 |
| | | | | | | 10 |
| | | | | | | 11 |
| | | | | | | 12 |
| | | | | | | 13 |
| | | | | | | 14 |
| | | | | | | 15 |
| | | | | | | 16 |
| | | | | | | 17 |
| | | | | | | 18 |
| | | | | | | 19 |
| | | | | | | 20 |
| | | | | | | 21 |
| | | | | | | 22 |
| | | | | | | 23 |
| | | | | | | 24 |
| | | | | | | 25 |
| | | | | | | 26 |
| | | | | | | 27 |
| | | | | | | 28 |
| | | | | | | 29 |
| | | | | | | 30 |
| | | | | | | 31 |
| | | | | | | 32 |
| | | | | | | 33 |
| | | | | | | 34 |
| | | | | | | 35 |
| | | | | | | 36 |
| | | | | | | 37 |
| | | | | | | 38 |

## Problem 8  (LO 4)  JOURNALIZING ADJUSTING ENTRIES

From the work sheet prepared for Ocean Beach Sail Shop (Problem 7), record the adjusting entries in a general journal.

**GENERAL JOURNAL**                                        PAGE

| | DATE | DESCRIPTION | POST. REF. | DEBIT | CREDIT | |
|---|---|---|---|---|---|---|
| 1 | | | | | | 1 |
| 2 | | | | | | 2 |
| 3 | | | | | | 3 |
| 4 | | | | | | 4 |
| 5 | | | | | | 5 |
| 6 | | | | | | 6 |
| 7 | | | | | | 7 |
| 8 | | | | | | 8 |
| 9 | | | | | | 9 |
| 10 | | | | | | 10 |
| 11 | | | | | | 11 |
| 12 | | | | | | 12 |
| 13 | | | | | | 13 |
| 14 | | | | | | 14 |
| 15 | | | | | | 15 |
| 16 | | | | | | 16 |
| 17 | | | | | | 17 |
| 18 | | | | | | 18 |
| 19 | | | | | | 19 |
| 20 | | | | | | 20 |
| 21 | | | | | | 21 |
| 22 | | | | | | 22 |
| 23 | | | | | | 23 |
| 24 | | | | | | 24 |
| 25 | | | | | | 25 |
| 26 | | | | | | 26 |
| 27 | | | | | | 27 |
| 28 | | | | | | 28 |
| 29 | | | | | | 29 |
| 30 | | | | | | 30 |

# CHAPTER 14 APPENDIX
# EXPENSE METHOD OF ACCOUNTING FOR PREPAID EXPENSES

## LEARNING OBJECTIVES

The appendix to Chapter 14 covers the expense method of accounting for prepaid expenses.

**Objective 1. Use the expense method of accounting for prepaid expenses.**

Under the **expense method** of accounting for prepaid expenses, supplies and other prepaid items are entered as **expenses** when purchased. Under this method, we must adjust the accounts at the end of each accounting period to record the **unused** portions as assets.

**Objective 2. Make the appropriate adjusting entries when the expense method is used for prepaid expenses.**

To illustrate the appropriate entries, let's assume that the following entry was made on November 1, 20--, when six months' office rent was paid in advance:

| 20-- | | | |
|---|---|---|---|
| Nov. 1 | Office Rent Expense | 6,000 | |
| |  Cash | | 6,000 |
| |   Paid six months' office | | |
| |   rent in advance | | |

At the end of December, adjusting entries must be made to prepare year-end financial statements. The office has been used for two months. Thus, the office expense for the year should be $2,000 ($1,000 per month $\times$ 2). This leaves $4,000 that should be recorded as an asset, Prepaid Office Rent. The following adjusting entry is made for office rent:

| 20-- | Adjusting Entry | | |
|---|---|---|---|
| Dec. 31 | Prepaid Office Rent | 4,000 | |
| |  Office Rent Expense | | 4,000 |

As shown in the T accounts below, after this entry is posted, the office rent expense account has a debit balance of $2,000 ($6,000 – $4,000). This amount is reported on the income statement as an operating expense. The prepaid office rent account has a debit balance of $4,000. It is reported on the balance sheet as a current asset.

| Prepaid Office Rent | | Office Rent Expense | |
|---|---|---|---|
| | | Nov. 1 6,000 | |
| Adj. Dec. 31 4,000 | | | Adj. Dec. 31 4,000 |
| | | Bal. Dec. 31 2,000 | |

## Apx. Exercise 1 (LO 2) EXPENSE METHOD OF ACCOUNTING FOR PREPAID EXPENSES

Dalton's Fishery paid $2,400 for a one-year insurance premium on its delivery van on October 1. The following entry was made:

20--

Oct. 1   Insurance Expense                 2,400

        Cash                                          2,400

            Paid insurance premium

Insurance coverage started on October 1. Prepare the adjusting entry on December 31.

### GENERAL JOURNAL                                                  PAGE

| | DATE | DESCRIPTION | POST. REF. | DEBIT | CREDIT | |
|---|---|---|---|---|---|---|
| 1 | | | | | | 1 |
| 2 | | | | | | 2 |
| 3 | | | | | | 3 |
| 4 | | | | | | 4 |
| 5 | | | | | | 5 |

## Apx. Exercise 2 (LO 1/2) EXPENSE METHOD OF ACCOUNTING FOR PREPAID EXPENSES

On August 21, Georgio's Dry Goods purchased supplies costing $6,000 for cash. This amount was debited to the supplies expense account. At the end of the year, an inventory shows that supplies costing $1,000 still remain. Prepare the entries for the purchase and year-end adjustment.

### GENERAL JOURNAL                                                  PAGE

| | DATE | DESCRIPTION | POST. REF. | DEBIT | CREDIT | |
|---|---|---|---|---|---|---|
| 1 | | | | | | 1 |
| 2 | | | | | | 2 |
| 3 | | | | | | 3 |
| 4 | | | | | | 4 |
| 5 | | | | | | 5 |
| 6 | | | | | | 6 |
| 7 | | | | | | 7 |
| 8 | | | | | | 8 |
| 9 | | | | | | 9 |
| 10 | | | | | | 10 |

# CHAPTER 15
# FINANCIAL STATEMENTS AND YEAR-END
# ACCOUNTING FOR A MERCHANDISING BUSINESS

## LEARNING OBJECTIVES

Chapter 15 covers the year-end accounting process as it applies to a merchandising business—the work sheet, closing and reversing entries, and the financial statements. In addition, financial ratios are introduced for the merchandising business.

**Objective 1.    Prepare a single-step and multiple-step income statement for a merchandising business.**

The **single-step** form of income statement lists all revenue items and their total first, followed by all expense items and their total. The difference, which is either net income or net loss, is then calculated.

The **multiple-step income statement** contains the computation of net sales and cost of goods sold. It also reports gross profit, income from operations, and net income. The multiple-step income statement begins with gross sales less deductions to arrive at *net sales*. Then, cost of goods sold is calculated—beginning inventory plus net purchases and freight-in, less ending inventory. Net sales minus cost of goods sold results in *gross profit*. Then, operating expenses are subtracted, resulting in income from operations. Finally, other revenue and expenses not from operations (such as interest) are included to compute *net income.*

**Objective 2.    Prepare a statement of owner's equity.**

The statement of owner's equity summarizes all changes in the owner's equity, including net income or loss and any additional investments or withdrawals by the owner.

**Objective 3.    Prepare a classified balance sheet.**

The **classified balance sheet** distinguishes between *current* and long-term assets and liabilities. Current assets include cash and assets that will be converted to cash or consumed within the year or operating cycle (whichever is longer). Property, plant, and equipment are assets with long useful lives and much less liquidity. Current liabilities are generally due within a year and require the use of current assets. Long-term liabilities extend longer than one year.

**Objective 4.    Compute standard financial ratios.**

Financial ratios help evaluate the current financial condition and profitability of a company. **Working capital** is current assets minus current liabilities; it tells whether a business has enough current assets to meet current operating debts.

The **current** and **quick ratios** measure a firm's ability to pay its current liabilities. The current ratio is calculated by dividing current assets by current liabilities. The desirable ratio is 2:1 ($2 of current assets for every $1 of current liabilities). **Quick assets** include cash and other very liquid assets—such as accounts receivable. The quick ratio is calculated by dividing quick assets by current liabilities. The desirable ratio is 1:1.

**Return on owner's equity** is calculated by dividing net income by average owner's equity (beginning equity plus ending equity, divided by 2). This rate of return can be compared with other years' rates and with other businesses' rates.

The **accounts receivable turnover** is determined by dividing net credit sales by average accounts receivable. This number is then divided into 365 days to determine the average number of days credit customers are taking to pay for their purchases.

**Inventory turnover** reveals how many times merchandise inventory "turned over" or was sold during the period. It is calculated by dividing cost of goods sold by the average inventory (beginning inventory plus ending inventory, divided by 2). This number is then divided into 365 days to determine the average number of days merchandise is held before it is sold.

### Objective 5.    Prepare closing entries for a merchandising business.

As with a service business, closing entries for a merchandising business are facilitated by the work sheet. All temporary accounts are closed—sales, contra-sales accounts, purchases, contra-purchases accounts, and expenses. The income summary account already contains two entries for merchandise inventory adjustments (debited to remove the old balance; credited to enter the new balance). First, all income statement accounts with credit balances are debited, crediting the income summary account. Then, all income statement accounts with debit balances are credited, debiting the income summary account. The balance in the income summary account is then transferred to the owner's equity account; a credit balance (indicating net income) is debited to close the income summary account. Finally, the drawing account is closed to the owner's capital account.

After the closing entries are posted, the post-closing trial balance is prepared. It reflects balances after the adjusting and closing entries are posted; only permanent accounts still have balances.

### Objective 6.    Prepare reversing entries.

Year-end adjusting entries may be reversed in the next accounting period if it helps to simplify entries to be made in the new year. Except for the first year of operation, **reversing entries** are helpful whenever an adjusting entry has increased an asset or liability account from a zero balance. The reversing entries are made on the first day of the new accounting period.

## REVIEW QUESTIONS

**Instructions:** Analyze each of the following items carefully before writing your answer in the column at the right.

| | Question | Answer |
|---|---|---|
| **LO 1**   1. | The primary purpose of the _____ is to serve as an aid in preparing the financial statements. ................................... | _____ |
| **LO 1**   2. | The _____ form of income statement lists all revenue items first, followed by all expense items and their totals. .................... | _____ |
| **LO 1**   3. | Gross sales less sales returns and allowances is called _____. ..... | _____ |
| **LO 1**   4. | _____ is the result of net sales less cost of goods sold. ................. | _____ |
| **LO 1**   5. | When operating expenses are subtracted from gross profit, the result is called _____. ............................................... | _____ |
| **LO 1**   6. | After other revenues are added and other expenses are subtracted, the final result is called _____. ................................. | _____ |

LO 2   **7.** The statement of owner's equity shows the net _____ or _____ in owner's equity for the period. ......................................................

_____

_____

LO 3   **8.** The report form of a(n) _____ balance sheet distinguishes between current and long-term assets and between current and long-term liabilities. ......................................................

_____

LO 3   **9.** The speed with which assets can be converted to cash is called _____. ......................................................

_____

LO 3   **10.** The difference between the cost of a long-term asset and the amount of accumulated depreciation is called _____ or book value. .......

_____

LO 3   **11.** _____ are obligations that are due within one year or during the normal operating cycle of the business, whichever is longer. ...........

_____

LO 3   **12.** A(n) _____ is an example of a long-term liability based on a written agreement evidencing a debt secured by property. ...............

_____

LO 4   **13.** The difference between current assets and current liabilities is called _____. ......................................................

_____

LO 4   **14.** The _____ ratio is current assets divided by current liabilities. ......................................................

_____

LO 4   **15.** _____ assets include cash and all other current assets that can be quickly converted to cash. ......................................................

_____

LO 4   **16.** The _____ ratio is calculated by dividing net income by average owner's equity. ......................................................

_____

LO 4   **17.** The _____ measures the number of times the accounts receivable were collected during the accounting period. ...............................

_____

LO 4   **18.** The _____ measures the number of times merchandise is sold during the accounting period. ......................................................

_____

LO 5   **19.** All _____ owner's equity accounts are closed at the end of the accounting period. ......................................................

_____

LO 5   **20.** The purpose of the _____ is to prove that the general ledger is in balance at the beginning of the new accounting period and that all temporary accounts have zero balances. ......................................

_____

LO 6   **21.** A reversing entry is the opposite of a(n) _____ entry. .............

_____

LO 6   **22.** Adjusting entries that increase an asset or liability account from a(n) _____ balance may be reversed. ......................................

_____

# EXERCISES

## Exercise 1  (LO 1)  MULTIPLE-STEP INCOME STATEMENT

From the information below, prepare a multiple-step income statement for Morse Motor Company for the year ended December 31, 20-1.

| | |
|---|---:|
| Merchandise Inventory, January 1, 20-1 | $ 28,900 |
| Merchandise Inventory, December 31, 20-1 | 29,600 |
| Sales | 118,300 |
| Sales Returns and Allowances | 1,000 |
| Sales Discounts | 280 |
| Interest Revenue | 1,900 |
| Purchases | 68,000 |
| Purchases Returns and Allowances | 2,140 |
| Purchases Discounts | 1,360 |
| Freight-In | 540 |
| Wages Expense | 23,200 |
| Rent Expense | 8,000 |
| Supplies Expense | 900 |
| Telephone Expense | 2,600 |
| Utilities Expense | 3,800 |
| Insurance Expense | 1,000 |
| Depreciation Expense—Equipment | 2,000 |
| Miscellaneous Expense | 300 |
| Interest Expense | 700 |

**Exercise 1 (Concluded)**

**Exercise 2 (LO 2/3) PREPARE A STATEMENT OF OWNER'S EQUITY AND CLASSIFIED BALANCE SHEET**

From the information below and the income statement prepared for Exercise 1, prepare a statement of owner's equity and a report form of a classified balance sheet for Morse Motor Company as of December 31, 20-1.

| | |
|---|---|
| Cash | $19,200 |
| Accounts Receivable | 28,500 |
| Merchandise Inventory | 29,600 |
| Supplies | 1,800 |
| Prepaid Insurance | 1,100 |
| Equipment | 32,000 |
| Accumulated Depreciation—Equipment | 4,000 |
| Accounts Payable | 18,620 |
| Wages Payable | 280 |
| Sales Tax Payable | 480 |
| Mortgage Payable—current portion | 1,200 |
| Mortgage Payable | 8,000 |
| K. T. Morse, Capital, January 1, 20-1 | 66,740 |
| K. T. Morse, Drawing (during year) | 8,000 |
| Additional investment by K. T. Morse, May 1, 20-1 | 10,000 |

**Exercise 2 (Concluded)**

## Exercise 3  (LO 4)  FINANCIAL RATIOS

From the Morse Motor Company financial statements prepared in Exercises 1 and 2, compute the following ratios: (Net credit sales for the year were $88,000; accounts receivable on January 1 was $24,200.)

1.  Working capital

_____

_____

_____

_____

2.  Current ratio

_____

_____

_____

_____

3.  Quick ratio

_____

_____

_____

_____

4.  Return on owner's equity

_____

_____

_____

_____

5.  Accounts receivable turnover

_____

_____

_____

_____

6.  Inventory turnover

_____

_____

_____

_____

## Exercise 4  (LO 5/6)  CLOSING AND REVERSING ENTRIES

Based on the foregoing information provided for Morse Motor Company in Exercises 1-3, prepare closing and reversing entries in the general journal on page 266. Adjusting entries are shown below.

| | | |
|---|---|---|
| Income Summary | 28,900 | |
|     Merchandise Inventory | | 28,900 |
| | | |
| Merchandise Inventory | 29,600 | |
|     Income Summary | | 29,600 |
| | | |
| Insurance Expense | 1,000 | |
|     Prepaid Insurance | | 1,000 |
| | | |
| Depreciation Expense | 2,000 | |
|     Accumulated Depreciation—Equipment | | 2,000 |
| | | |
| Supplies Expense | 900 | |
|     Supplies | | 900 |
| | | |
| Wages Expense | 280 | |
|     Wages Payable | | 280 |

**Exercise 4 (Concluded)**

**GENERAL JOURNAL**                                           PAGE _____

| | DATE | DESCRIPTION | POST. REF. | DEBIT | CREDIT | |
|---|---|---|---|---|---|---|
| 1 | | | | | | 1 |
| 2 | | | | | | 2 |
| 3 | | | | | | 3 |
| 4 | | | | | | 4 |
| 5 | | | | | | 5 |
| 6 | | | | | | 6 |
| 7 | | | | | | 7 |
| 8 | | | | | | 8 |
| 9 | | | | | | 9 |
| 10 | | | | | | 10 |
| 11 | | | | | | 11 |
| 12 | | | | | | 12 |
| 13 | | | | | | 13 |
| 14 | | | | | | 14 |
| 15 | | | | | | 15 |
| 16 | | | | | | 16 |
| 17 | | | | | | 17 |
| 18 | | | | | | 18 |
| 19 | | | | | | 19 |
| 20 | | | | | | 20 |
| 21 | | | | | | 21 |
| 22 | | | | | | 22 |
| 23 | | | | | | 23 |
| 24 | | | | | | 24 |
| 25 | | | | | | 25 |
| 26 | | | | | | 26 |
| 27 | | | | | | 27 |
| 28 | | | | | | 28 |
| 29 | | | | | | 29 |
| 30 | | | | | | 30 |
| 31 | | | | | | 31 |

## PROBLEMS

### Problem 5  (REVIEW)  COMPLETE A WORK SHEET

Complete the work sheet for Clark's Clothing Store on pages 268–269 by using the adjustment information provided below.

(a and b)    Merchandise Inventory, December 31, 20-1, $12,400.

(c)    Unused supplies on December 31, 20-1, $2,100.

(d)    Expired insurance on December 31, 20-1, $500.

(e)    Depreciation expense on building for the year, $10,000.

(f)    Depreciation expense on fixtures for the year, $2,000.

(g)    Wages accrued (earned but not yet paid), $380.

(h)    Unearned revenues on December 31, 20-1, $3,000.

## Problem 5  (Continued)

Clark's Clothing
Work
For Year Ended

| | ACCOUNT TITLE | TRIAL BALANCE DEBIT | TRIAL BALANCE CREDIT | ADJUSTMENTS DEBIT | ADJUSTMENTS CREDIT |
|---|---|---|---|---|---|
| 1 | Cash | 16 4 0 0 00 | | | |
| 2 | Accounts Receivable | 7 1 0 0 00 | | | |
| 3 | Merchandise Inventory | 28 0 0 0 00 | | | |
| 4 | Supplies | 3 0 0 0 00 | | | |
| 5 | Prepaid Insurance | 2 0 0 0 00 | | | |
| 6 | Land | 10 0 0 0 00 | | | |
| 7 | Building | 100 0 0 0 00 | | | |
| 8 | Accum. Depr.—Building | | 10 0 0 0 00 | | |
| 9 | Fixtures | 33 0 0 0 00 | | | |
| 10 | Accum. Depr.—Fixtures | | 6 0 0 0 00 | | |
| 11 | Accounts Payable | | 9 0 0 0 00 | | |
| 12 | Wages Payable | | | | |
| 13 | Sales Tax Payable | | 1 2 0 0 00 | | |
| 14 | Unearned Revenue | | 10 0 0 0 00 | | |
| 15 | Mortgage Payable | | 58 0 0 0 00 | | |
| 16 | Alex Clark, Capital | | 73 3 0 0 00 | | |
| 17 | Alex Clark, Drawing | 12 5 0 0 00 | | | |
| 18 | Income Summary | | | | |
| 19 | Sales | | 225 5 0 0 00 | | |
| 20 | Sales Returns and Allowances | 2 0 0 0 00 | | | |
| 21 | Sales Discounts | 5 0 0 00 | | | |
| 22 | Purchases | 68 5 0 0 00 | | | |
| 23 | Purchases Returns and Allowances | | 1 2 0 0 00 | | |
| 24 | Purchases Discounts | | 1 3 0 0 00 | | |
| 25 | Freight-In | 4 4 0 00 | | | |
| 26 | Wages Expense | 19 8 0 0 00 | | | |
| 27 | Advertising Expense | 7 0 0 00 | | | |
| 28 | Rent Expense | 82 6 6 0 00 | | | |
| 29 | Supplies Expense | | | | |
| 30 | Telephone Expense | 2 1 0 0 00 | | | |
| 31 | Utilities Expense | 1 8 0 0 00 | | | |
| 32 | Insurance Expense | | | | |
| 33 | Depr. Expense—Building | | | | |
| 34 | Depr. Expense—Fixtures | | | | |
| 35 | Miscellaneous Expense | 6 0 0 00 | | | |
| 36 | Interest Expense | 4 4 0 0 00 | | | |
| 37 | | 395 5 0 0 00 | 395 5 0 0 00 | | |
| 38 | Net Income | | | | |
| 39 | | | | | |

## Problem 5 (Concluded)

**Store** _____

**Sheet** _____

**December 31, 20-1**

| ADJUSTED TRIAL BALANCE | | INCOME STATEMENT | | BALANCE SHEET | | |
|---|---|---|---|---|---|---|
| DEBIT | CREDIT | DEBIT | CREDIT | DEBIT | CREDIT | |
| | | | | | | 1 |
| | | | | | | 2 |
| | | | | | | 3 |
| | | | | | | 4 |
| | | | | | | 5 |
| | | | | | | 6 |
| | | | | | | 7 |
| | | | | | | 8 |
| | | | | | | 9 |
| | | | | | | 10 |
| | | | | | | 11 |
| | | | | | | 12 |
| | | | | | | 13 |
| | | | | | | 14 |
| | | | | | | 15 |
| | | | | | | 16 |
| | | | | | | 17 |
| | | | | | | 18 |
| | | | | | | 19 |
| | | | | | | 20 |
| | | | | | | 21 |
| | | | | | | 22 |
| | | | | | | 23 |
| | | | | | | 24 |
| | | | | | | 25 |
| | | | | | | 26 |
| | | | | | | 27 |
| | | | | | | 28 |
| | | | | | | 29 |
| | | | | | | 30 |
| | | | | | | 31 |
| | | | | | | 32 |
| | | | | | | 33 |
| | | | | | | 34 |
| | | | | | | 35 |
| | | | | | | 36 |
| | | | | | | 37 |
| | | | | | | 38 |
| | | | | | | 39 |

### Problem 6  (LO 1/2/3)  PREPARATION OF AN INCOME STATEMENT, STATEMENT OF OWNER'S EQUITY, AND BALANCE SHEET

Based on the work sheet for Clark's Clothing Store, prepare the following financial statements:

1.  Multiple-step income statement.
2.  Statement of owner's equity. (Alex made no additional investments during the year.)
3.  Classified balance sheet. (Mortgage Payable—current portion is $1,000.)

**1. (See page 271)**

**2.**

**Problem 6 (Continued)**

**1.** _____

_____

**Problem 6 (Concluded)**

**3.**

## Problem 7  (LO 4)  FINANCIAL RATIOS

For Clark's Clothing Store, calculate the following financial statement ratios. (*Note*: Net credit sales for the year were $115,000, and accounts receivable on January 1 was $8,400.)

1.  Working capital

_____

_____

_____

_____

2.  Current ratio

_____

_____

_____

3.  Quick ratio

_____

_____

_____

_____

4.  Return on owner's equity

_____

_____

_____

_____

5.  Accounts receivable turnover

_____

_____

_____

6.  Inventory turnover

_____

_____

_____

_____

## Problem 8  (LO 5/6)  ADJUSTING, CLOSING, AND REVERSING ENTRIES

From the work sheet prepared for Clark's Clothing Store (Problem 5), record the adjusting, closing, and reversing entries on the general journal page below and on the next page.

**GENERAL JOURNAL**                                    PAGE

| | DATE | DESCRIPTION | POST. REF. | DEBIT | CREDIT | |
|---|---|---|---|---|---|---|
| 1 | | | | | | 1 |
| 2 | | | | | | 2 |
| 3 | | | | | | 3 |
| 4 | | | | | | 4 |
| 5 | | | | | | 5 |
| 6 | | | | | | 6 |
| 7 | | | | | | 7 |
| 8 | | | | | | 8 |
| 9 | | | | | | 9 |
| 10 | | | | | | 10 |
| 11 | | | | | | 11 |
| 12 | | | | | | 12 |
| 13 | | | | | | 13 |
| 14 | | | | | | 14 |
| 15 | | | | | | 15 |
| 16 | | | | | | 16 |
| 17 | | | | | | 17 |
| 18 | | | | | | 18 |
| 19 | | | | | | 19 |
| 20 | | | | | | 20 |
| 21 | | | | | | 21 |
| 22 | | | | | | 22 |
| 23 | | | | | | 23 |
| 24 | | | | | | 24 |
| 25 | | | | | | 25 |
| 26 | | | | | | 26 |
| 27 | | | | | | 27 |
| 28 | | | | | | 28 |
| 29 | | | | | | 29 |

**Problem 8 (Concluded)**

**GENERAL JOURNAL**                          PAGE _____

| | DATE | | DESCRIPTION | POST. REF. | DEBIT | CREDIT | |
|---|---|---|---|---|---|---|---|
| 1 | | | | | | | 1 |
| 2 | | | | | | | 2 |
| 3 | | | | | | | 3 |
| 4 | | | | | | | 4 |
| 5 | | | | | | | 5 |
| 6 | | | | | | | 6 |
| 7 | | | | | | | 7 |
| 8 | | | | | | | 8 |
| 9 | | | | | | | 9 |
| 10 | | | | | | | 10 |
| 11 | | | | | | | 11 |
| 12 | | | | | | | 12 |
| 13 | | | | | | | 13 |
| 14 | | | | | | | 14 |
| 15 | | | | | | | 15 |
| 16 | | | | | | | 16 |
| 17 | | | | | | | 17 |
| 18 | | | | | | | 18 |
| 19 | | | | | | | 19 |
| 20 | | | | | | | 20 |
| 21 | | | | | | | 21 |
| 22 | | | | | | | 22 |
| 23 | | | | | | | 23 |
| 24 | | | | | | | 24 |
| 25 | | | | | | | 25 |
| 26 | | | | | | | 26 |
| 27 | | | | | | | 27 |
| 28 | | | | | | | 28 |
| 29 | | | | | | | 29 |
| 30 | | | | | | | 30 |
| 31 | | | | | | | 31 |

# NOTES

# WORKING PAPERS

### Chapters 10-15

# College Accounting

### 20th EDITION

## James A. Heintz, DBA, CPA

Professor of Accounting
School of Business
University of Kansas

## Robert W. Parry, Jr., Ph.D.

Professor of Accounting
Kelley School of Business
Indiana University

SOUTH-WESTERN
CENGAGE Learning

Australia • Brazil • Japan • Korea • Mexico • Singapore • Spain • United Kingdom • United States

**SOUTH-WESTERN**
CENGAGE Learning

**Study Guide and Working Papers for College Accounting, 20th edition Chapters 10-15**
**James A. Heintz and Robert W. Parry, Jr.**

Vice President of Editorial, Business: Jack W. Calhoun

Editor-in-Chief: Rob Dewey

Executive Editor: Sharon Oblinger

Developmental Editor: Sara Wilson, CPA, CATS Publishing

Associate Marketing Manager: Laura Stopa

Marketing Coordinator: Heather Mooney

Senior Content Project Manager: Tim Bailey

Director of Media Development: Rick Lindgren

Media Editor: Bryan England

Senior Frontlist Buyer, Manufacturing: Doug Wilke

Production Service: LEAP Publishing Services, Inc.

Senior Art Director: Stacy Jenkins Shirley

Cover and Internal Designer: Grannan Graphic Design

Cover Image: Digital Vision/Juice Images

Rights Acquisition Account Manager-Image: John Hill

Photo Researcher: Megan Lessard, Pre-PressPMG

For product information and technology assistance, contact us at **Cengage Learning Customer & Sales Support, 1-800-354-9706**

For permission to use material from this text or product, submit all requests online at **www.cengage.com/permissions**
Further permissions questions can be emailed to **permissionrequest@cengage.com**

ISBN-13: 978-0-538-73706-7
ISBN-10: 0-538-73706-9

Chapters 1-9 + 10-15 Package
ISBN-13: 978-0-538-73704-3
ISBN-10: 0-538-73704-2

**South-Western Cengage Learning**
5191 Natorp Boulevard
Mason, OH 45040
USA

Cengage Learning products are represented in Canada by Nelson Education, Ltd.

For your course and learning solutions, visit www.cengage.com
Purchase any of our products at your local college store or at our preferred online store **www.ichapters.com**

Printed in the United States of America
1 2 3 4 5 6 7 14 13 12 11 10

# Table of Contents

## Exercise 10-1A

1. _____    4. _____

2. _____    5. _____

3. _____    6. _____

## Exercise 10-2A
**1.**

| Cash | Accounts Receivable |
|---|---|
| | |

| Sales Tax Payable | Sales |
|---|---|
| | |

| Sales Returns and Allowances | Sales Discounts |
|---|---|
| | |

**2.**

| Cash | Accounts Receivable |
|---|---|
| | |

| Sales Tax Payable | Sales |
|---|---|
| | |

| Sales Returns and Allowances | Sales Discounts |
|---|---|
| | |

**Exercise 10-2A (Concluded)**

3.

| Cash | | Accounts Receivable |
|---|---|---|
| | | |

| Sales Tax Payable | | Sales |
|---|---|---|
| | | |

| Sales Returns and Allowances | | Sales Discounts |
|---|---|---|
| | | |

4.

| Cash | | Accounts Receivable |
|---|---|---|
| | | |

| Sales Tax Payable | | Sales |
|---|---|---|
| | | |

| Sales Returns and Allowances | | Sales Discounts |
|---|---|---|
| | | |

5.

| Cash | | Accounts Receivable |
|---|---|---|
| | | |

| Sales Tax Payable | | Sales |
|---|---|---|
| | | |

| Sales Returns and Allowances | | Sales Discounts |
|---|---|---|
| | | |

**Exercise 10-6A**

## GENERAL JOURNAL

| | DATE | | DESCRIPTION | POST. REF. | DEBIT | CREDIT | |
|---|---|---|---|---|---|---|---|
| 1 | | | | | | | 1 |
| 2 | | | | | | | 2 |
| 3 | | | | | | | 3 |
| 4 | | | | | | | 4 |
| 5 | | | | | | | 5 |
| 6 | | | | | | | 6 |
| 7 | | | | | | | 7 |
| 8 | | | | | | | 8 |
| 9 | | | | | | | 9 |
| 10 | | | | | | | 10 |
| 11 | | | | | | | 11 |
| 12 | | | | | | | 12 |
| 13 | | | | | | | 13 |
| 14 | | | | | | | 14 |
| 15 | | | | | | | 15 |

## GENERAL LEDGER

ACCOUNT  Accounts Receivable                    ACCOUNT NO.  122

| DATE | | ITEM | POST. REF. | DEBIT | CREDIT | BALANCE DEBIT | BALANCE CREDIT |
|---|---|---|---|---|---|---|---|
| 20–– June | 1 | Balance | ✓ | | | 4 2 0 0 00 | |
| | | | | | | | |
| | | | | | | | |
| | | | | | | | |

ACCOUNT  Sales Returns and Allowances              ACCOUNT NO.  401.1

| DATE | ITEM | POST. REF. | DEBIT | CREDIT | BALANCE DEBIT | BALANCE CREDIT |
|---|---|---|---|---|---|---|
| | | | | | | |
| | | | | | | |
| | | | | | | |
| | | | | | | |

## Exercise 10-6A (Concluded)

### ACCOUNTS RECEIVABLE LEDGER

**NAME**  John B. Abramowitz

**ADDRESS**  3201 West Judkins Road, Seattle, WA 98201-1079

| DATE | | ITEM | POST. REF. | DEBIT | CREDIT | BALANCE |
|---|---|---|---|---|---|---|
| 20-- June | 1 | Balance | ✓ | | | 8 5 0 00 |
| | | | | | | |
| | | | | | | |

**NAME**  L. B. Gruder

**ADDRESS**  44 Western Blvd., Spokane, WA 98601-4092

| DATE | | ITEM | POST. REF. | DEBIT | CREDIT | BALANCE |
|---|---|---|---|---|---|---|
| 20-- June | 1 | Balance | ✓ | | | 4 2 8 00 |
| | | | | | | |
| | | | | | | |

**NAME**  Marie L. Perez

**ADDRESS**  158 West Adams Point, Bellevue, WA 98401-0663

| DATE | | ITEM | POST. REF. | DEBIT | CREDIT | BALANCE |
|---|---|---|---|---|---|---|
| 20-- June | 1 | Balance | ✓ | | | 1 0 1 8 00 |
| | | | | | | |
| | | | | | | |

## Exercise 10-7A

**GENERAL JOURNAL**                                                PAGE _____

| | DATE | | DESCRIPTION | POST. REF. | DEBIT | CREDIT | |
|---|---|---|---|---|---|---|---|
| 1 | | | | | | | 1 |
| 2 | | | | | | | 2 |
| 3 | | | | | | | 3 |
| 4 | | | | | | | 4 |
| 5 | | | | | | | 5 |
| 6 | | | | | | | 6 |
| 7 | | | | | | | 7 |
| 8 | | | | | | | 8 |
| 9 | | | | | | | 9 |
| 10 | | | | | | | 10 |
| 11 | | | | | | | 11 |
| 12 | | | | | | | 12 |
| 13 | | | | | | | 13 |
| 14 | | | | | | | 14 |
| 15 | | | | | | | 15 |
| 16 | | | | | | | 16 |
| 17 | | | | | | | 17 |
| 18 | | | | | | | 18 |
| 19 | | | | | | | 19 |
| 20 | | | | | | | 20 |
| 21 | | | | | | | 21 |
| 22 | | | | | | | 22 |

## Exercise 10-8A

## Problem 10-9A

1.

**GENERAL JOURNAL**

| | DATE | | DESCRIPTION | POST. REF. | DEBIT | CREDIT | |
|---|---|---|---|---|---|---|---|
| 1 | | | | | | | 1 |
| 2 | | | | | | | 2 |
| 3 | | | | | | | 3 |
| 4 | | | | | | | 4 |
| 5 | | | | | | | 5 |
| 6 | | | | | | | 6 |
| 7 | | | | | | | 7 |
| 8 | | | | | | | 8 |
| 9 | | | | | | | 9 |
| 10 | | | | | | | 10 |
| 11 | | | | | | | 11 |
| 12 | | | | | | | 12 |
| 13 | | | | | | | 13 |
| 14 | | | | | | | 14 |
| 15 | | | | | | | 15 |
| 16 | | | | | | | 16 |
| 17 | | | | | | | 17 |
| 18 | | | | | | | 18 |
| 19 | | | | | | | 19 |
| 20 | | | | | | | 20 |
| 21 | | | | | | | 21 |
| 22 | | | | | | | 22 |
| 23 | | | | | | | 23 |
| 24 | | | | | | | 24 |
| 25 | | | | | | | 25 |
| 26 | | | | | | | 26 |
| 27 | | | | | | | 27 |
| 28 | | | | | | | 28 |
| 29 | | | | | | | 29 |
| 30 | | | | | | | 30 |
| 31 | | | | | | | 31 |
| 32 | | | | | | | 32 |
| 33 | | | | | | | 33 |
| 34 | | | | | | | 34 |

**Problem 10-9A (Continued)**

2.

## GENERAL LEDGER

ACCOUNT   Accounts Receivable                                      ACCOUNT NO.   122

| DATE | ITEM | POST. REF. | DEBIT | CREDIT | BALANCE DEBIT | BALANCE CREDIT |
|------|------|------------|-------|--------|---------------|----------------|
|      |      |            |       |        |               |                |
|      |      |            |       |        |               |                |
|      |      |            |       |        |               |                |
|      |      |            |       |        |               |                |
|      |      |            |       |        |               |                |
|      |      |            |       |        |               |                |
|      |      |            |       |        |               |                |

ACCOUNT   Sales Tax Payable                                        ACCOUNT NO.   231

| DATE | ITEM | POST. REF. | DEBIT | CREDIT | BALANCE DEBIT | BALANCE CREDIT |
|------|------|------------|-------|--------|---------------|----------------|
|      |      |            |       |        |               |                |
|      |      |            |       |        |               |                |
|      |      |            |       |        |               |                |
|      |      |            |       |        |               |                |
|      |      |            |       |        |               |                |
|      |      |            |       |        |               |                |
|      |      |            |       |        |               |                |
|      |      |            |       |        |               |                |
|      |      |            |       |        |               |                |

ACCOUNT   Sales                                                    ACCOUNT NO.   401

| DATE | ITEM | POST. REF. | DEBIT | CREDIT | BALANCE DEBIT | BALANCE CREDIT |
|------|------|------------|-------|--------|---------------|----------------|
|      |      |            |       |        |               |                |
|      |      |            |       |        |               |                |
|      |      |            |       |        |               |                |
|      |      |            |       |        |               |                |
|      |      |            |       |        |               |                |
|      |      |            |       |        |               |                |

## Problem 10-9A (Concluded)

### ACCOUNTS RECEIVABLE LEDGER

**NAME** Hassad Co.

**ADDRESS** 1225 W. Temperance Street, Elletsville, IN 47429-9976

| DATE | ITEM | POST. REF. | DEBIT | CREDIT | BALANCE |
|------|------|------------|-------|--------|---------|
|      |      |            |       |        |         |
|      |      |            |       |        |         |
|      |      |            |       |        |         |

**NAME** Helsinki, Inc.

**ADDRESS** 125 Fishers Drive, Noblesville, IN 47870-8867

| DATE | ITEM | POST. REF. | DEBIT | CREDIT | BALANCE |
|------|------|------------|-------|--------|---------|
|      |      |            |       |        |         |
|      |      |            |       |        |         |
|      |      |            |       |        |         |

**NAME** Jung Manufacturing Co.

**ADDRESS** 8825 Old State Road, Bloomington, IN 47401-8823

| DATE | ITEM | POST. REF. | DEBIT | CREDIT | BALANCE |
|------|------|------------|-------|--------|---------|
|      |      |            |       |        |         |
|      |      |            |       |        |         |
|      |      |            |       |        |         |

**NAME** Ardis Myler

**ADDRESS** 2100 Greer Lane, Bedford, IN 47421-8876

| DATE | ITEM | POST. REF. | DEBIT | CREDIT | BALANCE |
|------|------|------------|-------|--------|---------|
|      |      |            |       |        |         |
|      |      |            |       |        |         |
|      |      |            |       |        |         |

**Exercise 10-1B**

1. _____     4. _____

2. _____     5. _____

3. _____     6. _____


**Exercise 10-2B**

**1.**

| Cash | Accounts Receivable |
|------|---------------------|
|      |                     |

| Sales Tax Payable | Sales |
|-------------------|-------|
|                   |       |

| Sales Returns and Allowances | Sales Discounts |
|------------------------------|-----------------|
|                              |                 |


**2.**

| Cash | Accounts Receivable |
|------|---------------------|
|      |                     |

| Sales Tax Payable | Sales |
|-------------------|-------|
|                   |       |

| Sales Returns and Allowances | Sales Discounts |
|------------------------------|-----------------|
|                              |                 |

## Exercise 10-2B (Concluded)

**3.**

| Cash | Accounts Receivable |
|---|---|

| Sales Tax Payable | Sales |
|---|---|

| Sales Returns and Allowances | Sales Discounts |
|---|---|

**4.**

| Cash | Accounts Receivable |
|---|---|

| Sales Tax Payable | Sales |
|---|---|

| Sales Returns and Allowances | Sales Discounts |
|---|---|

**5.**

| Cash | Accounts Receivable |
|---|---|

| Sales Tax Payable | Sales |
|---|---|

| Sales Returns and Allowances | Sales Discounts |
|---|---|

**Exercise 10-3B**

_____

_____

_____

_____

_____

_____

**Exercise 10-4B**

### GENERAL JOURNAL    PAGE

| | DATE | DESCRIPTION | POST. REF. | DEBIT | CREDIT | |
|---|---|---|---|---|---|---|
| 1 | | | | | | 1 |
| 2 | | | | | | 2 |
| 3 | | | | | | 3 |
| 4 | | | | | | 4 |
| 5 | | | | | | 5 |
| 6 | | | | | | 6 |
| 7 | | | | | | 7 |
| 8 | | | | | | 8 |
| 9 | | | | | | 9 |
| 10 | | | | | | 10 |
| 11 | | | | | | 11 |
| 12 | | | | | | 12 |
| 13 | | | | | | 13 |
| 14 | | | | | | 14 |
| 15 | | | | | | 15 |
| 16 | | | | | | 16 |
| 17 | | | | | | 17 |
| 18 | | | | | | 18 |
| 19 | | | | | | 19 |
| 20 | | | | | | 20 |

## Exercise 10-4B (Concluded)

**GENERAL JOURNAL**                                        PAGE

| | DATE | | DESCRIPTION | POST. REF. | DEBIT | CREDIT | |
|---|---|---|---|---|---|---|---|
| 21 | | | | | | | 21 |
| 22 | | | | | | | 22 |
| 23 | | | | | | | 23 |
| 24 | | | | | | | 24 |
| 25 | | | | | | | 25 |
| 26 | | | | | | | 26 |
| 27 | | | | | | | 27 |
| 28 | | | | | | | 28 |

## Exercise 10-5B

**GENERAL JOURNAL**                                        PAGE

| | DATE | | DESCRIPTION | POST. REF. | DEBIT | CREDIT | |
|---|---|---|---|---|---|---|---|
| 1 | | | | | | | 1 |
| 2 | | | | | | | 2 |
| 3 | | | | | | | 3 |
| 4 | | | | | | | 4 |
| 5 | | | | | | | 5 |
| 6 | | | | | | | 6 |
| 7 | | | | | | | 7 |
| 8 | | | | | | | 8 |
| 9 | | | | | | | 9 |
| 10 | | | | | | | 10 |
| 11 | | | | | | | 11 |
| 12 | | | | | | | 12 |
| 13 | | | | | | | 13 |
| 14 | | | | | | | 14 |
| 15 | | | | | | | 15 |
| 16 | | | | | | | 16 |
| 17 | | | | | | | 17 |
| 18 | | | | | | | 18 |
| 19 | | | | | | | 19 |
| 20 | | | | | | | 20 |
| 21 | | | | | | | 21 |
| 22 | | | | | | | 22 |

**Exercise 10-6B**

## GENERAL JOURNAL

PAGE 60

| | DATE | DESCRIPTION | POST. REF. | DEBIT | CREDIT | |
|---|---|---|---|---|---|---|
| 1 | | | | | | 1 |
| 2 | | | | | | 2 |
| 3 | | | | | | 3 |
| 4 | | | | | | 4 |
| 5 | | | | | | 5 |
| 6 | | | | | | 6 |
| 7 | | | | | | 7 |
| 8 | | | | | | 8 |
| 9 | | | | | | 9 |
| 10 | | | | | | 10 |
| 11 | | | | | | 11 |
| 12 | | | | | | 12 |
| 13 | | | | | | 13 |
| 14 | | | | | | 14 |

## GENERAL LEDGER

ACCOUNT   Accounts Receivable                                    ACCOUNT NO.   122

| DATE | ITEM | POST. REF. | DEBIT | CREDIT | BALANCE DEBIT | BALANCE CREDIT |
|---|---|---|---|---|---|---|
| 20-- June 1 | Balance | ✓ | | | 3 9 0 0 00 | |
| | | | | | | |
| | | | | | | |
| | | | | | | |

ACCOUNT   Sales Returns and Allowances                          ACCOUNT NO.   401.1

| DATE | ITEM | POST. REF. | DEBIT | CREDIT | BALANCE DEBIT | BALANCE CREDIT |
|---|---|---|---|---|---|---|
| | | | | | | |
| | | | | | | |
| | | | | | | |
| | | | | | | |

## Exercise 10-6B (Concluded)

### ACCOUNTS RECEIVABLE LEDGER

**NAME**  John B. Adams

**ADDRESS**  127 Strawberry Lane, Manchester, CT 06040-0865

| DATE | | ITEM | POST. REF. | DEBIT | CREDIT | BALANCE |
|---|---|---|---|---|---|---|
| 20-- June | 1 | Balance | ✓ | | | 8 5 0 00 |
| | | | | | | |
| | | | | | | |
| | | | | | | |
| | | | | | | |

**NAME**  L. B. Greene

**ADDRESS**  2254 Blackrock, Bronx, NY 10472-1974

| DATE | | ITEM | POST. REF. | DEBIT | CREDIT | BALANCE |
|---|---|---|---|---|---|---|
| 20-- June | 1 | Balance | ✓ | | | 4 2 8 00 |
| | | | | | | |
| | | | | | | |
| | | | | | | |
| | | | | | | |

**NAME**  Marie L. Phillips

**ADDRESS**  334 Fern St., W. Hartford, CT 06119-2314

| DATE | | ITEM | POST. REF. | DEBIT | CREDIT | BALANCE |
|---|---|---|---|---|---|---|
| 20-- June | 1 | Balance | ✓ | | | 1 0 1 8 00 |
| | | | | | | |
| | | | | | | |
| | | | | | | |
| | | | | | | |

**Exercise 10-7B**

## GENERAL JOURNAL

| | DATE | | DESCRIPTION | POST. REF. | DEBIT | CREDIT | |
|---|---|---|---|---|---|---|---|
| 1 | | | | | | | 1 |
| 2 | | | | | | | 2 |
| 3 | | | | | | | 3 |
| 4 | | | | | | | 4 |
| 5 | | | | | | | 5 |
| 6 | | | | | | | 6 |
| 7 | | | | | | | 7 |
| 8 | | | | | | | 8 |
| 9 | | | | | | | 9 |
| 10 | | | | | | | 10 |
| 11 | | | | | | | 11 |
| 12 | | | | | | | 12 |
| 13 | | | | | | | 13 |
| 14 | | | | | | | 14 |
| 15 | | | | | | | 15 |
| 16 | | | | | | | 16 |
| 17 | | | | | | | 17 |
| 18 | | | | | | | 18 |
| 19 | | | | | | | 19 |
| 20 | | | | | | | 20 |
| 21 | | | | | | | 21 |
| 22 | | | | | | | 22 |
| 23 | | | | | | | 23 |

**Exercise 10-8B**

**Problem 10-9B**

1.

**GENERAL JOURNAL**                                    PAGE 15

| | DATE | | DESCRIPTION | POST. REF. | DEBIT | CREDIT | |
|---|---|---|---|---|---|---|---|
| 1 | | | | | | | 1 |
| 2 | | | | | | | 2 |
| 3 | | | | | | | 3 |
| 4 | | | | | | | 4 |
| 5 | | | | | | | 5 |
| 6 | | | | | | | 6 |
| 7 | | | | | | | 7 |
| 8 | | | | | | | 8 |
| 9 | | | | | | | 9 |
| 10 | | | | | | | 10 |
| 11 | | | | | | | 11 |
| 12 | | | | | | | 12 |
| 13 | | | | | | | 13 |
| 14 | | | | | | | 14 |
| 15 | | | | | | | 15 |
| 16 | | | | | | | 16 |
| 17 | | | | | | | 17 |
| 18 | | | | | | | 18 |
| 19 | | | | | | | 19 |
| 20 | | | | | | | 20 |
| 21 | | | | | | | 21 |
| 22 | | | | | | | 22 |
| 23 | | | | | | | 23 |
| 24 | | | | | | | 24 |
| 25 | | | | | | | 25 |
| 26 | | | | | | | 26 |
| 27 | | | | | | | 27 |
| 28 | | | | | | | 28 |
| 29 | | | | | | | 29 |
| 30 | | | | | | | 30 |
| 31 | | | | | | | 31 |
| 32 | | | | | | | 32 |
| 33 | | | | | | | 33 |
| 34 | | | | | | | 34 |

**Problem 10-9B (Continued)**

2.

## GENERAL LEDGER

ACCOUNT   Accounts Receivable                                    ACCOUNT NO.   122

| DATE | ITEM | POST. REF. | DEBIT | CREDIT | BALANCE | |
|------|------|------------|-------|--------|---------|---|
| | | | | | DEBIT | CREDIT |
| | | | | | | |
| | | | | | | |
| | | | | | | |
| | | | | | | |
| | | | | | | |
| | | | | | | |
| | | | | | | |

ACCOUNT   Sales Tax Payable                                      ACCOUNT NO.   231

| DATE | ITEM | POST. REF. | DEBIT | CREDIT | BALANCE | |
|------|------|------------|-------|--------|---------|---|
| | | | | | DEBIT | CREDIT |
| | | | | | | |
| | | | | | | |
| | | | | | | |
| | | | | | | |
| | | | | | | |
| | | | | | | |
| | | | | | | |
| | | | | | | |

ACCOUNT   Sales                                                  ACCOUNT NO.   401

| DATE | ITEM | POST. REF. | DEBIT | CREDIT | BALANCE | |
|------|------|------------|-------|--------|---------|---|
| | | | | | DEBIT | CREDIT |
| | | | | | | |
| | | | | | | |
| | | | | | | |
| | | | | | | |
| | | | | | | |
| | | | | | | |

## Problem 10-9B (Concluded)

### ACCOUNTS RECEIVABLE LEDGER

**NAME** Dvorak Manufacturing

**ADDRESS** 2105 Williams Drive, Muncie, IN 47304-2437

| DATE | ITEM | POST. REF. | DEBIT | CREDIT | BALANCE |
|------|------|------------|-------|--------|---------|
|      |      |            |       |        |         |
|      |      |            |       |        |         |
|      |      |            |       |        |         |
|      |      |            |       |        |         |

**NAME** Saga, Inc.

**ADDRESS** 1453 Parnell Avenue, Indianapolis, IN 46201-6870

| DATE | ITEM | POST. REF. | DEBIT | CREDIT | BALANCE |
|------|------|------------|-------|--------|---------|
|      |      |            |       |        |         |
|      |      |            |       |        |         |
|      |      |            |       |        |         |
|      |      |            |       |        |         |

**NAME** Vinnie Ward

**ADDRESS** 308 So. Muirhead Drive, Okemos, MI 48864-5356

| DATE | ITEM | POST. REF. | DEBIT | CREDIT | BALANCE |
|------|------|------------|-------|--------|---------|
|      |      |            |       |        |         |
|      |      |            |       |        |         |
|      |      |            |       |        |         |
|      |      |            |       |        |         |

**NAME** Zapata Co.

**ADDRESS** 789 N. Stafford Dr., Bloomington, IN 47401-6201

| DATE | ITEM | POST. REF. | DEBIT | CREDIT | BALANCE |
|------|------|------------|-------|--------|---------|
|      |      |            |       |        |         |
|      |      |            |       |        |         |
|      |      |            |       |        |         |
|      |      |            |       |        |         |

**Problem 10-10B**

**1.**

## GENERAL JOURNAL

| | DATE | DESCRIPTION | POST. REF. | DEBIT | CREDIT | |
|---|---|---|---|---|---|---|
| 1 | | | | | | 1 |
| 2 | | | | | | 2 |
| 3 | | | | | | 3 |
| 4 | | | | | | 4 |
| 5 | | | | | | 5 |
| 6 | | | | | | 6 |
| 7 | | | | | | 7 |
| 8 | | | | | | 8 |
| 9 | | | | | | 9 |
| 10 | | | | | | 10 |
| 11 | | | | | | 11 |
| 12 | | | | | | 12 |
| 13 | | | | | | 13 |
| 14 | | | | | | 14 |
| 15 | | | | | | 15 |
| 16 | | | | | | 16 |
| 17 | | | | | | 17 |
| 18 | | | | | | 18 |
| 19 | | | | | | 19 |
| 20 | | | | | | 20 |
| 21 | | | | | | 21 |
| 22 | | | | | | 22 |
| 23 | | | | | | 23 |
| 24 | | | | | | 24 |
| 25 | | | | | | 25 |
| 26 | | | | | | 26 |
| 27 | | | | | | 27 |
| 28 | | | | | | 28 |
| 29 | | | | | | 29 |
| 30 | | | | | | 30 |
| 31 | | | | | | 31 |
| 32 | | | | | | 32 |
| 33 | | | | | | 33 |
| 34 | | | | | | 34 |

## Problem 10-10B (Continued)

**GENERAL JOURNAL**

| | DATE | | DESCRIPTION | POST. REF. | DEBIT | CREDIT | |
|---|---|---|---|---|---|---|---|
| 1 | | | | | | | 1 |
| 2 | | | | | | | 2 |
| 3 | | | | | | | 3 |
| 4 | | | | | | | 4 |
| 5 | | | | | | | 5 |
| 6 | | | | | | | 6 |
| 7 | | | | | | | 7 |
| 8 | | | | | | | 8 |
| 9 | | | | | | | 9 |
| 10 | | | | | | | 10 |
| 11 | | | | | | | 11 |
| 12 | | | | | | | 12 |
| 13 | | | | | | | 13 |
| 14 | | | | | | | 14 |
| 15 | | | | | | | 15 |
| 16 | | | | | | | 16 |
| 17 | | | | | | | 17 |
| 18 | | | | | | | 18 |
| 19 | | | | | | | 19 |
| 20 | | | | | | | 20 |
| 21 | | | | | | | 21 |
| 22 | | | | | | | 22 |
| 23 | | | | | | | 23 |
| 24 | | | | | | | 24 |
| 25 | | | | | | | 25 |
| 26 | | | | | | | 26 |
| 27 | | | | | | | 27 |
| 28 | | | | | | | 28 |
| 29 | | | | | | | 29 |
| 30 | | | | | | | 30 |
| 31 | | | | | | | 31 |
| 32 | | | | | | | 32 |
| 33 | | | | | | | 33 |
| 34 | | | | | | | 34 |

## Problem 10-10B (Continued)

2.

## GENERAL LEDGER

ACCOUNT    Cash                                                    ACCOUNT NO.    101

| DATE | | ITEM | POST. REF. | DEBIT | CREDIT | BALANCE DEBIT | BALANCE CREDIT |
|---|---|---|---|---|---|---|---|
| 20-- Jan. | 1 | Balance | ✓ | | | 2 8 9 0 75 | |
| | | | | | | | |
| | | | | | | | |
| | | | | | | | |
| | | | | | | | |
| | | | | | | | |
| | | | | | | | |
| | | | | | | | |
| | | | | | | | |
| | | | | | | | |
| | | | | | | | |

ACCOUNT    Accounts Receivable                                     ACCOUNT NO.    122

| DATE | | ITEM | POST. REF. | DEBIT | CREDIT | BALANCE DEBIT | BALANCE CREDIT |
|---|---|---|---|---|---|---|---|
| 20-- Jan. | 1 | Balance | ✓ | | | 6 3 0 0 00 | |
| | | | | | | | |
| | | | | | | | |
| | | | | | | | |
| | | | | | | | |
| | | | | | | | |
| | | | | | | | |
| | | | | | | | |
| | | | | | | | |

## Problem 10-10B (Continued)

ACCOUNT Sales Tax Payable                               ACCOUNT NO. 231

| DATE | ITEM | POST. REF. | DEBIT | CREDIT | BALANCE DEBIT | BALANCE CREDIT |
|------|------|-----------|-------|--------|-------|--------|
|  |  |  |  |  |  |  |
|  |  |  |  |  |  |  |
|  |  |  |  |  |  |  |
|  |  |  |  |  |  |  |
|  |  |  |  |  |  |  |
|  |  |  |  |  |  |  |
|  |  |  |  |  |  |  |
|  |  |  |  |  |  |  |

ACCOUNT Sales                                            ACCOUNT NO. 401

| DATE | ITEM | POST. REF. | DEBIT | CREDIT | BALANCE DEBIT | BALANCE CREDIT |
|------|------|-----------|-------|--------|-------|--------|
|  |  |  |  |  |  |  |
|  |  |  |  |  |  |  |
|  |  |  |  |  |  |  |
|  |  |  |  |  |  |  |
|  |  |  |  |  |  |  |
|  |  |  |  |  |  |  |
|  |  |  |  |  |  |  |
|  |  |  |  |  |  |  |

ACCOUNT Sales Returns and Allowances                     ACCOUNT NO. 401.1

| DATE | ITEM | POST. REF. | DEBIT | CREDIT | BALANCE DEBIT | BALANCE CREDIT |
|------|------|-----------|-------|--------|-------|--------|
|  |  |  |  |  |  |  |
|  |  |  |  |  |  |  |
|  |  |  |  |  |  |  |

ACCOUNT Bank Credit Card Expense                         ACCOUNT NO. 513

| DATE | ITEM | POST. REF. | DEBIT | CREDIT | BALANCE DEBIT | BALANCE CREDIT |
|------|------|-----------|-------|--------|-------|--------|
|  |  |  |  |  |  |  |
|  |  |  |  |  |  |  |
|  |  |  |  |  |  |  |
|  |  |  |  |  |  |  |

**Problem 10-10B (Continued)**

## ACCOUNTS RECEIVABLE LEDGER

**NAME** Ray Boyd

**ADDRESS** 229 SE 65th Avenue, Portland, OR 97215-1451

| DATE | | ITEM | POST. REF. | DEBIT | CREDIT | BALANCE |
|---|---|---|---|---|---|---|
| 20–<br>Jan. | 1 | Balance | ✓ | | | 1 4 0 0 00 |
| | | | | | | |
| | | | | | | |
| | | | | | | |

**NAME** Dazai Manufacturing

**ADDRESS** 447 6th Avenue, Flagstaff, AZ 86004-6842

| DATE | | ITEM | POST. REF. | DEBIT | CREDIT | BALANCE |
|---|---|---|---|---|---|---|
| 20–<br>Jan. | 1 | Balance | ✓ | | | 3 1 8 00 |
| | | | | | | |
| | | | | | | |
| | | | | | | |

**NAME** Clint Hassell

**ADDRESS** 1462 N. Steves Blvd., Los Cruces, NM 88012-7791

| DATE | | ITEM | POST. REF. | DEBIT | CREDIT | BALANCE |
|---|---|---|---|---|---|---|
| 20–<br>Jan. | 1 | Balance | ✓ | | | 8 1 5 00 |
| | | | | | | |
| | | | | | | |
| | | | | | | |

## Problem 10-10B (Concluded)

**NAME** Jan Sowada

**ADDRESS** 5997 Blackgold Lane, Grapevine, TX 76051-2366

| DATE | | ITEM | POST. REF. | DEBIT | CREDIT | BALANCE |
|---|---|---|---|---|---|---|
| 20-- Jan. | 1 | Balance | ✓ | | | 1 4 8 1 00 |
| | | | | | | |
| | | | | | | |
| | | | | | | |
| | | | | | | |

**NAME** Robert Zehnle

**ADDRESS** 6881 Seneca Drive, San Diego, CA 92127-8671

| DATE | | ITEM | POST. REF. | DEBIT | CREDIT | BALANCE |
|---|---|---|---|---|---|---|
| 20-- Jan. | 1 | Balance | ✓ | | | 2 2 8 6 00 |
| | | | | | | |
| | | | | | | |
| | | | | | | |
| | | | | | | |

**Problem 10-11B**

1.

## GENERAL JOURNAL

| | DATE | | DESCRIPTION | POST. REF. | DEBIT | CREDIT | |
|---|---|---|---|---|---|---|---|
| 1 | | | | | | | 1 |
| 2 | | | | | | | 2 |
| 3 | | | | | | | 3 |
| 4 | | | | | | | 4 |
| 5 | | | | | | | 5 |
| 6 | | | | | | | 6 |
| 7 | | | | | | | 7 |
| 8 | | | | | | | 8 |
| 9 | | | | | | | 9 |
| 10 | | | | | | | 10 |
| 11 | | | | | | | 11 |
| 12 | | | | | | | 12 |
| 13 | | | | | | | 13 |
| 14 | | | | | | | 14 |
| 15 | | | | | | | 15 |
| 16 | | | | | | | 16 |
| 17 | | | | | | | 17 |
| 18 | | | | | | | 18 |
| 19 | | | | | | | 19 |
| 20 | | | | | | | 20 |
| 21 | | | | | | | 21 |
| 22 | | | | | | | 22 |
| 23 | | | | | | | 23 |
| 24 | | | | | | | 24 |
| 25 | | | | | | | 25 |
| 26 | | | | | | | 26 |
| 27 | | | | | | | 27 |
| 28 | | | | | | | 28 |
| 29 | | | | | | | 29 |
| 30 | | | | | | | 30 |
| 31 | | | | | | | 31 |
| 32 | | | | | | | 32 |
| 33 | | | | | | | 33 |
| 34 | | | | | | | 34 |

**Problem 10-11B (Continued)**

| | | | | | |
|---|---|---|---|---|---|
| **GENERAL JOURNAL** | | | | PAGE | 8 |

| | DATE | | DESCRIPTION | POST. REF. | DEBIT | CREDIT | |
|---|---|---|---|---|---|---|---|
| 1 | | | | | | | 1 |
| 2 | | | | | | | 2 |
| 3 | | | | | | | 3 |
| 4 | | | | | | | 4 |
| 5 | | | | | | | 5 |
| 6 | | | | | | | 6 |
| 7 | | | | | | | 7 |
| 8 | | | | | | | 8 |
| 9 | | | | | | | 9 |
| 10 | | | | | | | 10 |
| 11 | | | | | | | 11 |
| 12 | | | | | | | 12 |
| 13 | | | | | | | 13 |
| 14 | | | | | | | 14 |
| 15 | | | | | | | 15 |
| 16 | | | | | | | 16 |
| 17 | | | | | | | 17 |
| 18 | | | | | | | 18 |
| 19 | | | | | | | 19 |
| 20 | | | | | | | 20 |
| 21 | | | | | | | 21 |
| 22 | | | | | | | 22 |
| 23 | | | | | | | 23 |
| 24 | | | | | | | 24 |
| 25 | | | | | | | 25 |
| 26 | | | | | | | 26 |
| 27 | | | | | | | 27 |
| 28 | | | | | | | 28 |
| 29 | | | | | | | 29 |
| 30 | | | | | | | 30 |
| 31 | | | | | | | 31 |
| 32 | | | | | | | 32 |
| 33 | | | | | | | 33 |
| 34 | | | | | | | 34 |

## Problem 10-11B (Continued)

2.

**GENERAL LEDGER**

ACCOUNT  Cash                                                                    ACCOUNT NO.  101

| DATE | | ITEM | POST. REF. | DEBIT | CREDIT | BALANCE | |
|---|---|---|---|---|---|---|---|
| | | | | | | DEBIT | CREDIT |
| 20-- Apr. | 1 | Balance | ✓ | | | 2 8 6 4 54 | |
| | | | | | | | |
| | | | | | | | |
| | | | | | | | |
| | | | | | | | |
| | | | | | | | |
| | | | | | | | |
| | | | | | | | |

ACCOUNT  Accounts Receivable                                                     ACCOUNT NO.  122

| DATE | | ITEM | POST. REF. | DEBIT | CREDIT | BALANCE | |
|---|---|---|---|---|---|---|---|
| | | | | | | DEBIT | CREDIT |
| 20-- Apr. | 1 | Balance | ✓ | | | 2 7 2 6 25 | |
| | | | | | | | |
| | | | | | | | |
| | | | | | | | |
| | | | | | | | |
| | | | | | | | |
| | | | | | | | |
| | | | | | | | |
| | | | | | | | |
| | | | | | | | |
| | | | | | | | |
| | | | | | | | |

## Problem 10-11B (Continued)

ACCOUNT  Sales Tax Payable                    ACCOUNT NO.  231

| DATE | ITEM | POST. REF. | DEBIT | CREDIT | BALANCE DEBIT | BALANCE CREDIT |
|------|------|-----------|-------|--------|-------|--------|
| | | | | | | |
| | | | | | | |
| | | | | | | |
| | | | | | | |
| | | | | | | |
| | | | | | | |
| | | | | | | |
| | | | | | | |
| | | | | | | |
| | | | | | | |
| | | | | | | |
| | | | | | | |
| | | | | | | |

ACCOUNT  Sales                    ACCOUNT NO.  401

| DATE | ITEM | POST. REF. | DEBIT | CREDIT | BALANCE DEBIT | BALANCE CREDIT |
|------|------|-----------|-------|--------|-------|--------|
| | | | | | | |
| | | | | | | |
| | | | | | | |
| | | | | | | |
| | | | | | | |
| | | | | | | |
| | | | | | | |
| | | | | | | |
| | | | | | | |
| | | | | | | |
| | | | | | | |
| | | | | | | |

ACCOUNT  Sales Returns and Allowances                    ACCOUNT NO.  401.1

| DATE | ITEM | POST. REF. | DEBIT | CREDIT | BALANCE DEBIT | BALANCE CREDIT |
|------|------|-----------|-------|--------|-------|--------|
| | | | | | | |
| | | | | | | |
| | | | | | | |

**Problem 10-11B (Concluded)**

## ACCOUNTS RECEIVABLE LEDGER

**NAME** O. L. Meyers

**ADDRESS** 119 Hartford Turnpike, Vernon, CT 06066-0113

| DATE | ITEM | POST. REF. | DEBIT | CREDIT | BALANCE |
|------|------|-----------|-------|--------|---------|
|  |  |  |  |  |  |
|  |  |  |  |  |  |
|  |  |  |  |  |  |
|  |  |  |  |  |  |
|  |  |  |  |  |  |
|  |  |  |  |  |  |

**NAME** Kelsay Munkres

**ADDRESS** 233 Cambridge Dr., Branford, CT 06405-9276

| DATE | | ITEM | POST. REF. | DEBIT | CREDIT | BALANCE |
|------|--|------|-----------|-------|--------|---------|
| 20-- Apr. | 1 | Balance | ✓ |  |  | 4 8 2 00 |
|  |  |  |  |  |  |  |
|  |  |  |  |  |  |  |

**NAME** Andrew Plaa

**ADDRESS** 51 Bissell Ave., Old Saybrook, CT 06475-0212

| DATE | ITEM | POST. REF. | DEBIT | CREDIT | BALANCE |
|------|------|-----------|-------|--------|---------|
|  |  |  |  |  |  |
|  |  |  |  |  |  |
|  |  |  |  |  |  |
|  |  |  |  |  |  |

**NAME** Melissa Richfield

**ADDRESS** 1107 Silver Lane, East Hartford, CT 06108-1907

| DATE | | ITEM | POST. REF. | DEBIT | CREDIT | BALANCE |
|------|--|------|-----------|-------|--------|---------|
| 20-- Apr. | 1 | Balance | ✓ |  |  | 2 2 4 4 25 |
|  |  |  |  |  |  |  |
|  |  |  |  |  |  |  |
|  |  |  |  |  |  |  |

**Problem 10-12B**

**Challenge Problem**

## GENERAL JOURNAL

PAGE _____

| | DATE | | DESCRIPTION | POST. REF. | DEBIT | CREDIT | |
|---|---|---|---|---|---|---|---|
| 1 | | | | | | | 1 |
| 2 | | | | | | | 2 |
| 3 | | | | | | | 3 |
| 4 | | | | | | | 4 |
| 5 | | | | | | | 5 |
| 6 | | | | | | | 6 |
| 7 | | | | | | | 7 |
| 8 | | | | | | | 8 |
| 9 | | | | | | | 9 |
| 10 | | | | | | | 10 |
| 11 | | | | | | | 11 |
| 12 | | | | | | | 12 |
| 13 | | | | | | | 13 |
| 14 | | | | | | | 14 |
| 15 | | | | | | | 15 |
| 16 | | | | | | | 16 |
| 17 | | | | | | | 17 |
| 18 | | | | | | | 18 |
| 19 | | | | | | | 19 |
| 20 | | | | | | | 20 |
| 21 | | | | | | | 21 |
| 22 | | | | | | | 22 |
| 23 | | | | | | | 23 |
| 24 | | | | | | | 24 |
| 25 | | | | | | | 25 |
| 26 | | | | | | | 26 |
| 27 | | | | | | | 27 |
| 28 | | | | | | | 28 |
| 29 | | | | | | | 29 |
| 30 | | | | | | | 30 |
| 31 | | | | | | | 31 |
| 32 | | | | | | | 32 |
| 33 | | | | | | | 33 |
| 34 | | | | | | | 34 |

**Exercise 11-1A**

1. _____

2. Purchase order _____

3. _____

4. _____

**Exercise 11-2A**

1.

_____

_____

_____

_____

2.

_____

_____

_____

_____

3.

**GENERAL JOURNAL**                                          PAGE _____

| | DATE | | DESCRIPTION | POST. REF. | DEBIT | CREDIT | |
|---|---|---|---|---|---|---|---|
| 1 | | | | | | | 1 |
| 2 | | | | | | | 2 |
| 3 | | | | | | | 3 |
| 4 | | | | | | | 4 |
| 5 | | | | | | | 5 |
| 6 | | | | | | | 6 |
| 7 | | | | | | | 7 |
| 8 | | | | | | | 8 |
| 9 | | | | | | | 9 |
| 10 | | | | | | | 10 |
| 11 | | | | | | | 11 |
| 12 | | | | | | | 12 |
| 13 | | | | | | | 13 |
| 14 | | | | | | | 14 |
| 15 | | | | | | | 15 |

**Exercise 11-3A**

1.

|  Cash  |  | Accounts Payable  |
|---|---|---|

|  Purchases  |  | Purchases Returns and Allowances  |
|---|---|---|

|  Purchases Discounts  |  | Freight-In  |
|---|---|---|

2.

|  Cash  |  | Accounts Payable  |
|---|---|---|

|  Purchases  |  | Purchases Returns and Allowances  |
|---|---|---|

|  Purchases Discounts  |  | Freight-In  |
|---|---|---|

**Exercise 11-3A (Concluded)**

**3.**

| Cash | | Accounts Payable | |
|---|---|---|---|
| | | | |

| Purchases | | Purchases Returns and Allowances | |
|---|---|---|---|
| | | | |

| Purchases Discounts | | Freight-In | |
|---|---|---|---|
| | | | |

**4.**

| Cash | | Accounts Payable | |
|---|---|---|---|
| | | | |

| Purchases | | Purchases Returns and Allowances | |
|---|---|---|---|
| | | | |

| Purchases Discounts | | Freight-In | |
|---|---|---|---|
| | | | |

**Exercise 11-4A**

Name _____

**Exercise 11-5A**

## GENERAL JOURNAL

PAGE

| | DATE | DESCRIPTION | POST. REF. | DEBIT | CREDIT | |
|---|---|---|---|---|---|---|
| 1 | | | | | | 1 |
| 2 | | | | | | 2 |
| 3 | | | | | | 3 |
| 4 | | | | | | 4 |
| 5 | | | | | | 5 |
| 6 | | | | | | 6 |
| 7 | | | | | | 7 |
| 8 | | | | | | 8 |
| 9 | | | | | | 9 |
| 10 | | | | | | 10 |
| 11 | | | | | | 11 |
| 12 | | | | | | 12 |
| 13 | | | | | | 13 |
| 14 | | | | | | 14 |
| 15 | | | | | | 15 |
| 16 | | | | | | 16 |
| 17 | | | | | | 17 |
| 18 | | | | | | 18 |
| 19 | | | | | | 19 |
| 20 | | | | | | 20 |
| 21 | | | | | | 21 |
| 22 | | | | | | 22 |
| 23 | | | | | | 23 |
| 24 | | | | | | 24 |
| 25 | | | | | | 25 |
| 26 | | | | | | 26 |
| 27 | | | | | | 27 |
| 28 | | | | | | 28 |
| 29 | | | | | | 29 |
| 30 | | | | | | 30 |
| 31 | | | | | | 31 |
| 32 | | | | | | 32 |
| 33 | | | | | | 33 |
| 34 | | | | | | 34 |

**Exercise 11-6A**

## GENERAL JOURNAL

| | DATE | DESCRIPTION | POST. REF. | DEBIT | CREDIT | |
|---|---|---|---|---|---|---|
| 1 | | | | | | 1 |
| 2 | | | | | | 2 |
| 3 | | | | | | 3 |
| 4 | | | | | | 4 |
| 5 | | | | | | 5 |
| 6 | | | | | | 6 |
| 7 | | | | | | 7 |
| 8 | | | | | | 8 |
| 9 | | | | | | 9 |
| 10 | | | | | | 10 |
| 11 | | | | | | 11 |
| 12 | | | | | | 12 |

## GENERAL LEDGER

ACCOUNT   Accounts Payable                               ACCOUNT NO.   202

| DATE | | ITEM | POST. REF. | DEBIT | CREDIT | BALANCE DEBIT | BALANCE CREDIT |
|---|---|---|---|---|---|---|---|
| 20--<br>July | 1 | Balance | ✓ | | | | 10 6 5 0 00 |
| | | | | | | | |
| | | | | | | | |
| | | | | | | | |

ACCOUNT   Purchases Returns and Allowances               ACCOUNT NO.   501.1

| DATE | ITEM | POST. REF. | DEBIT | CREDIT | BALANCE DEBIT | BALANCE CREDIT |
|---|---|---|---|---|---|---|
| | | | | | | |
| | | | | | | |
| | | | | | | |
| | | | | | | |

**Exercise 11-6A (Concluded)**

## ACCOUNTS PAYABLE LEDGER

**NAME** Datamagic

**ADDRESS**

| DATE | | ITEM | POST. REF. | DEBIT | CREDIT | BALANCE |
|---|---|---|---|---|---|---|
| 20-- July | 1 | Balance | ✓ | | | 2 6 0 0 00 |
| | | | | | | |
| | | | | | | |
| | | | | | | |
| | | | | | | |

**NAME** Starcraft Industries

**ADDRESS**

| DATE | | ITEM | POST. REF. | DEBIT | CREDIT | BALANCE |
|---|---|---|---|---|---|---|
| 20-- July | 1 | Balance | ✓ | | | 4 3 0 0 00 |
| | | | | | | |
| | | | | | | |
| | | | | | | |
| | | | | | | |

**NAME** XYZ, Inc.

**ADDRESS**

| DATE | | ITEM | POST. REF. | DEBIT | CREDIT | BALANCE |
|---|---|---|---|---|---|---|
| 20-- July | 1 | Balance | ✓ | | | 3 7 5 0 00 |
| | | | | | | |
| | | | | | | |
| | | | | | | |
| | | | | | | |

## Exercise 11-7A

**GENERAL JOURNAL**

| | DATE | | DESCRIPTION | POST. REF. | DEBIT | CREDIT | |
|---|---|---|---|---|---|---|---|
| 1 | | | | | | | 1 |
| 2 | | | | | | | 2 |
| 3 | | | | | | | 3 |
| 4 | | | | | | | 4 |
| 5 | | | | | | | 5 |
| 6 | | | | | | | 6 |
| 7 | | | | | | | 7 |
| 8 | | | | | | | 8 |
| 9 | | | | | | | 9 |
| 10 | | | | | | | 10 |
| 11 | | | | | | | 11 |
| 12 | | | | | | | 12 |
| 13 | | | | | | | 13 |
| 14 | | | | | | | 14 |
| 15 | | | | | | | 15 |
| 16 | | | | | | | 16 |
| 17 | | | | | | | 17 |
| 18 | | | | | | | 18 |
| 19 | | | | | | | 19 |
| 20 | | | | | | | 20 |
| 21 | | | | | | | 21 |

## Exercise 11-8A

**Problem 11-9A**

1.

## GENERAL JOURNAL

| | DATE | | DESCRIPTION | POST. REF. | DEBIT | CREDIT | |
|---|---|---|---|---|---|---|---|
| 1 | | | | | | | 1 |
| 2 | | | | | | | 2 |
| 3 | | | | | | | 3 |
| 4 | | | | | | | 4 |
| 5 | | | | | | | 5 |
| 6 | | | | | | | 6 |
| 7 | | | | | | | 7 |
| 8 | | | | | | | 8 |
| 9 | | | | | | | 9 |
| 10 | | | | | | | 10 |
| 11 | | | | | | | 11 |
| 12 | | | | | | | 12 |
| 13 | | | | | | | 13 |
| 14 | | | | | | | 14 |
| 15 | | | | | | | 15 |
| 16 | | | | | | | 16 |
| 17 | | | | | | | 17 |
| 18 | | | | | | | 18 |
| 19 | | | | | | | 19 |
| 20 | | | | | | | 20 |
| 21 | | | | | | | 21 |
| 22 | | | | | | | 22 |
| 23 | | | | | | | 23 |
| 24 | | | | | | | 24 |
| 25 | | | | | | | 25 |
| 26 | | | | | | | 26 |
| 27 | | | | | | | 27 |
| 28 | | | | | | | 28 |
| 29 | | | | | | | 29 |
| 30 | | | | | | | 30 |
| 31 | | | | | | | 31 |
| 32 | | | | | | | 32 |
| 33 | | | | | | | 33 |
| 34 | | | | | | | 34 |

## Problem 11-9A (Continued)

2.

### GENERAL LEDGER

ACCOUNT  Accounts Payable                                         ACCOUNT NO.  202

| DATE | ITEM | POST. REF. | DEBIT | CREDIT | BALANCE | |
|------|------|------------|-------|--------|---------|---|
| | | | | | DEBIT | CREDIT |
| | | | | | | |
| | | | | | | |
| | | | | | | |
| | | | | | | |
| | | | | | | |
| | | | | | | |
| | | | | | | |
| | | | | | | |

ACCOUNT  Purchases                                                ACCOUNT NO.  501

| DATE | ITEM | POST. REF. | DEBIT | CREDIT | BALANCE | |
|------|------|------------|-------|--------|---------|---|
| | | | | | DEBIT | CREDIT |
| | | | | | | |
| | | | | | | |
| | | | | | | |
| | | | | | | |
| | | | | | | |
| | | | | | | |
| | | | | | | |
| | | | | | | |

### ACCOUNTS PAYABLE LEDGER

**NAME**

**ADDRESS**

| DATE | ITEM | POST. REF. | DEBIT | CREDIT | BALANCE |
|------|------|------------|-------|--------|---------|
| | | | | | |
| | | | | | |
| | | | | | |
| | | | | | |

**Problem 11-9A (Concluded)**

### NAME

### ADDRESS

| DATE | ITEM | POST. REF. | DEBIT | CREDIT | BALANCE |
|------|------|------------|-------|--------|---------|
|      |      |            |       |        |         |
|      |      |            |       |        |         |
|      |      |            |       |        |         |
|      |      |            |       |        |         |

### NAME

### ADDRESS

| DATE | ITEM | POST. REF. | DEBIT | CREDIT | BALANCE |
|------|------|------------|-------|--------|---------|
|      |      |            |       |        |         |
|      |      |            |       |        |         |
|      |      |            |       |        |         |
|      |      |            |       |        |         |

### NAME

### ADDRESS

| DATE | ITEM | POST. REF. | DEBIT | CREDIT | BALANCE |
|------|------|------------|-------|--------|---------|
|      |      |            |       |        |         |
|      |      |            |       |        |         |
|      |      |            |       |        |         |
|      |      |            |       |        |         |

### NAME

### ADDRESS

| DATE | ITEM | POST. REF. | DEBIT | CREDIT | BALANCE |
|------|------|------------|-------|--------|---------|
|      |      |            |       |        |         |
|      |      |            |       |        |         |
|      |      |            |       |        |         |
|      |      |            |       |        |         |

**Problem 11-10A**

1.

## GENERAL JOURNAL

| | DATE | | DESCRIPTION | POST. REF. | DEBIT | CREDIT | |
|---|---|---|---|---|---|---|---|
| 1 | | | | | | | 1 |
| 2 | | | | | | | 2 |
| 3 | | | | | | | 3 |
| 4 | | | | | | | 4 |
| 5 | | | | | | | 5 |
| 6 | | | | | | | 6 |
| 7 | | | | | | | 7 |
| 8 | | | | | | | 8 |
| 9 | | | | | | | 9 |
| 10 | | | | | | | 10 |
| 11 | | | | | | | 11 |
| 12 | | | | | | | 12 |
| 13 | | | | | | | 13 |
| 14 | | | | | | | 14 |
| 15 | | | | | | | 15 |
| 16 | | | | | | | 16 |
| 17 | | | | | | | 17 |
| 18 | | | | | | | 18 |
| 19 | | | | | | | 19 |
| 20 | | | | | | | 20 |
| 21 | | | | | | | 21 |
| 22 | | | | | | | 22 |
| 23 | | | | | | | 23 |
| 24 | | | | | | | 24 |
| 25 | | | | | | | 25 |
| 26 | | | | | | | 26 |
| 27 | | | | | | | 27 |
| 28 | | | | | | | 28 |
| 29 | | | | | | | 29 |
| 30 | | | | | | | 30 |
| 31 | | | | | | | 31 |
| 32 | | | | | | | 32 |
| 33 | | | | | | | 33 |
| 34 | | | | | | | 34 |

**Problem 11-10A (Continued)**

## GENERAL JOURNAL

PAGE 10

| | DATE | | DESCRIPTION | POST. REF. | DEBIT | CREDIT | |
|---|---|---|---|---|---|---|---|
| 1 | | | | | | | 1 |
| 2 | | | | | | | 2 |
| 3 | | | | | | | 3 |
| 4 | | | | | | | 4 |
| 5 | | | | | | | 5 |

**2.**

## GENERAL LEDGER

ACCOUNT    Cash                                    ACCOUNT NO.    101

| DATE | | ITEM | POST. REF. | DEBIT | CREDIT | BALANCE DEBIT | BALANCE CREDIT |
|---|---|---|---|---|---|---|---|
| 20-- May | 1 | Balance | ✓ | | | 40 0 0 0 00 | |
| | | | | | | | |
| | | | | | | | |
| | | | | | | | |
| | | | | | | | |
| | | | | | | | |
| | | | | | | | |
| | | | | | | | |
| | | | | | | | |
| | | | | | | | |
| | | | | | | | |

ACCOUNT    Accounts Payable                        ACCOUNT NO.    202

| DATE | | ITEM | POST. REF. | DEBIT | CREDIT | BALANCE DEBIT | BALANCE CREDIT |
|---|---|---|---|---|---|---|---|
| 20-- May | 1 | Balance | ✓ | | | | 20 0 0 0 00 |
| | | | | | | | |
| | | | | | | | |
| | | | | | | | |
| | | | | | | | |

## Problem 11-10A (Continued)

ACCOUNT   Purchases                                         ACCOUNT NO.   501

| DATE | ITEM | POST. REF. | DEBIT | CREDIT | BALANCE | |
|------|------|------------|-------|--------|---------|---|
| | | | | | DEBIT | CREDIT |
| | | | | | | |
| | | | | | | |
| | | | | | | |
| | | | | | | |

ACCOUNT   Purchases Discounts                               ACCOUNT NO.   501.2

| DATE | ITEM | POST. REF. | DEBIT | CREDIT | BALANCE | |
|------|------|------------|-------|--------|---------|---|
| | | | | | DEBIT | CREDIT |
| | | | | | | |
| | | | | | | |
| | | | | | | |
| | | | | | | |

ACCOUNT   Freight-In                                        ACCOUNT NO.   502

| DATE | ITEM | POST. REF. | DEBIT | CREDIT | BALANCE | |
|------|------|------------|-------|--------|---------|---|
| | | | | | DEBIT | CREDIT |
| | | | | | | |
| | | | | | | |
| | | | | | | |
| | | | | | | |

ACCOUNT   Rent Expense                                      ACCOUNT NO.   521

| DATE | ITEM | POST. REF. | DEBIT | CREDIT | BALANCE | |
|------|------|------------|-------|--------|---------|---|
| | | | | | DEBIT | CREDIT |
| | | | | | | |
| | | | | | | |
| | | | | | | |

ACCOUNT   Utilities Expense                                 ACCOUNT NO.   533

| DATE | ITEM | POST. REF. | DEBIT | CREDIT | BALANCE | |
|------|------|------------|-------|--------|---------|---|
| | | | | | DEBIT | CREDIT |
| | | | | | | |
| | | | | | | |
| | | | | | | |

**Problem 11-10A (Concluded)**

## ACCOUNTS PAYABLE LEDGER

**NAME** Fantastic Toys

**ADDRESS**

| DATE | | ITEM | POST. REF. | DEBIT | CREDIT | BALANCE |
|---|---|---|---|---|---|---|
| 20--<br>May | 1 | Balance | ✓ | | | 5 2 0 0 00 |
| | | | | | | |
| | | | | | | |

**NAME** Goya Outlet

**ADDRESS**

| DATE | | ITEM | POST. REF. | DEBIT | CREDIT | BALANCE |
|---|---|---|---|---|---|---|
| 20--<br>May | 1 | Balance | ✓ | | | 3 8 0 0 00 |
| | | | | | | |
| | | | | | | |
| | | | | | | |

**NAME** Mueller's Distributors

**ADDRESS**

| DATE | | ITEM | POST. REF. | DEBIT | CREDIT | BALANCE |
|---|---|---|---|---|---|---|
| 20--<br>May | 1 | Balance | ✓ | | | 3 6 0 0 00 |
| | | | | | | |
| | | | | | | |
| | | | | | | |

**NAME** Van Kooning

**ADDRESS**

| DATE | | ITEM | POST. REF. | DEBIT | CREDIT | BALANCE |
|---|---|---|---|---|---|---|
| 20--<br>May | 1 | Balance | ✓ | | | 7 4 0 0 00 |
| | | | | | | |
| | | | | | | |
| | | | | | | |

## Problem 11-11A

**1.**

**GENERAL JOURNAL**

| | DATE | | DESCRIPTION | POST. REF. | DEBIT | CREDIT | |
|---|---|---|---|---|---|---|---|
| 1 | | | | | | | 1 |
| 2 | | | | | | | 2 |
| 3 | | | | | | | 3 |
| 4 | | | | | | | 4 |
| 5 | | | | | | | 5 |
| 6 | | | | | | | 6 |
| 7 | | | | | | | 7 |
| 8 | | | | | | | 8 |
| 9 | | | | | | | 9 |
| 10 | | | | | | | 10 |
| 11 | | | | | | | 11 |
| 12 | | | | | | | 12 |
| 13 | | | | | | | 13 |
| 14 | | | | | | | 14 |
| 15 | | | | | | | 15 |
| 16 | | | | | | | 16 |
| 17 | | | | | | | 17 |
| 18 | | | | | | | 18 |
| 19 | | | | | | | 19 |
| 20 | | | | | | | 20 |
| 21 | | | | | | | 21 |
| 22 | | | | | | | 22 |
| 23 | | | | | | | 23 |
| 24 | | | | | | | 24 |
| 25 | | | | | | | 25 |
| 26 | | | | | | | 26 |
| 27 | | | | | | | 27 |
| 28 | | | | | | | 28 |
| 29 | | | | | | | 29 |
| 30 | | | | | | | 30 |
| 31 | | | | | | | 31 |
| 32 | | | | | | | 32 |
| 33 | | | | | | | 33 |
| 34 | | | | | | | 34 |

**Problem 11-11A (Continued)**

**GENERAL JOURNAL**                                      PAGE 17

| | DATE | | DESCRIPTION | POST. REF. | DEBIT | CREDIT | |
|---|---|---|---|---|---|---|---|
| 1 | | | | | | | 1 |
| 2 | | | | | | | 2 |
| 3 | | | | | | | 3 |
| 4 | | | | | | | 4 |
| 5 | | | | | | | 5 |
| 6 | | | | | | | 6 |
| 7 | | | | | | | 7 |
| 8 | | | | | | | 8 |
| 9 | | | | | | | 9 |
| 10 | | | | | | | 10 |
| 11 | | | | | | | 11 |
| 12 | | | | | | | 12 |
| 13 | | | | | | | 13 |
| 14 | | | | | | | 14 |
| 15 | | | | | | | 15 |
| 16 | | | | | | | 16 |
| 17 | | | | | | | 17 |
| 18 | | | | | | | 18 |
| 19 | | | | | | | 19 |
| 20 | | | | | | | 20 |
| 21 | | | | | | | 21 |
| 22 | | | | | | | 22 |
| 23 | | | | | | | 23 |
| 24 | | | | | | | 24 |
| 25 | | | | | | | 25 |
| 26 | | | | | | | 26 |
| 27 | | | | | | | 27 |
| 28 | | | | | | | 28 |
| 29 | | | | | | | 29 |
| 30 | | | | | | | 30 |
| 31 | | | | | | | 31 |
| 32 | | | | | | | 32 |
| 33 | | | | | | | 33 |
| 34 | | | | | | | 34 |

## Problem 11-11A (Continued)

**2.**

## GENERAL LEDGER

ACCOUNT   Cash                                                                                      ACCOUNT NO.   101

| DATE | | ITEM | POST. REF. | DEBIT | CREDIT | BALANCE | |
|---|---|---|---|---|---|---|---|
| | | | | | | DEBIT | CREDIT |
| 20-- July | 1 | Balance | ✓ | | | 20 0 0 0 00 | |
| | | | | | | | |
| | | | | | | | |
| | | | | | | | |
| | | | | | | | |
| | | | | | | | |
| | | | | | | | |
| | | | | | | | |
| | | | | | | | |

ACCOUNT   Accounts Payable                                                           ACCOUNT NO.   202

| DATE | ITEM | POST. REF. | DEBIT | CREDIT | BALANCE | |
|---|---|---|---|---|---|---|
| | | | | | DEBIT | CREDIT |
| | | | | | | |
| | | | | | | |
| | | | | | | |
| | | | | | | |
| | | | | | | |
| | | | | | | |
| | | | | | | |
| | | | | | | |
| | | | | | | |
| | | | | | | |
| | | | | | | |
| | | | | | | |

**Problem 11-11A (Continued)**

ACCOUNT  Purchases                                    ACCOUNT NO.  501

| DATE | ITEM | POST. REF. | DEBIT | CREDIT | BALANCE DEBIT | CREDIT |
|------|------|------------|-------|--------|---------------|--------|
|      |      |            |       |        |               |        |
|      |      |            |       |        |               |        |
|      |      |            |       |        |               |        |
|      |      |            |       |        |               |        |
|      |      |            |       |        |               |        |
|      |      |            |       |        |               |        |
|      |      |            |       |        |               |        |
|      |      |            |       |        |               |        |

ACCOUNT  Purchases Returns and Allowances              ACCOUNT NO.  501.1

| DATE | ITEM | POST. REF. | DEBIT | CREDIT | BALANCE DEBIT | CREDIT |
|------|------|------------|-------|--------|---------------|--------|
|      |      |            |       |        |               |        |
|      |      |            |       |        |               |        |
|      |      |            |       |        |               |        |

ACCOUNT  Purchases Discounts                           ACCOUNT NO.  501.2

| DATE | ITEM | POST. REF. | DEBIT | CREDIT | BALANCE DEBIT | CREDIT |
|------|------|------------|-------|--------|---------------|--------|
|      |      |            |       |        |               |        |
|      |      |            |       |        |               |        |
|      |      |            |       |        |               |        |
|      |      |            |       |        |               |        |

ACCOUNT  Rent Expense                                  ACCOUNT NO.  521

| DATE | ITEM | POST. REF. | DEBIT | CREDIT | BALANCE DEBIT | CREDIT |
|------|------|------------|-------|--------|---------------|--------|
|      |      |            |       |        |               |        |
|      |      |            |       |        |               |        |
|      |      |            |       |        |               |        |

## Problem 11-11A (Concluded)

**ACCOUNTS PAYABLE LEDGER**

**NAME**

**ADDRESS**

| DATE | ITEM | POST. REF. | DEBIT | CREDIT | BALANCE |
|---|---|---|---|---|---|
|  |  |  |  |  |  |
|  |  |  |  |  |  |
|  |  |  |  |  |  |
|  |  |  |  |  |  |

**NAME**

**ADDRESS**

| DATE | ITEM | POST. REF. | DEBIT | CREDIT | BALANCE |
|---|---|---|---|---|---|
|  |  |  |  |  |  |
|  |  |  |  |  |  |
|  |  |  |  |  |  |
|  |  |  |  |  |  |

**NAME**

**ADDRESS**

| DATE | ITEM | POST. REF. | DEBIT | CREDIT | BALANCE |
|---|---|---|---|---|---|
|  |  |  |  |  |  |
|  |  |  |  |  |  |
|  |  |  |  |  |  |
|  |  |  |  |  |  |

**NAME**

**ADDRESS**

| DATE | ITEM | POST. REF. | DEBIT | CREDIT | BALANCE |
|---|---|---|---|---|---|
|  |  |  |  |  |  |
|  |  |  |  |  |  |
|  |  |  |  |  |  |
|  |  |  |  |  |  |

**Problem 11-12A**

## Exercise 11-1B

1. _____
2. _____
3. _____
4. _____

## Exercise 11-2B

**1.**

_____
_____
_____
_____

**2.**

_____
_____
_____
_____

**3.**

### GENERAL JOURNAL                    PAGE

| | DATE | | DESCRIPTION | POST. REF. | DEBIT | CREDIT | |
|---|---|---|---|---|---|---|---|
| 1 | | | | | | | 1 |
| 2 | | | | | | | 2 |
| 3 | | | | | | | 3 |
| 4 | | | | | | | 4 |
| 5 | | | | | | | 5 |
| 6 | | | | | | | 6 |
| 7 | | | | | | | 7 |
| 8 | | | | | | | 8 |
| 9 | | | | | | | 9 |
| 10 | | | | | | | 10 |
| 11 | | | | | | | 11 |
| 12 | | | | | | | 12 |
| 13 | | | | | | | 13 |
| 15 | | | | | | | 15 |

**Exercise 11-6B**

## GENERAL JOURNAL

PAGE  3

| | DATE | DESCRIPTION | POST. REF. | DEBIT | CREDIT | |
|---|---|---|---|---|---|---|
| 1 | | | | | | 1 |
| 2 | | | | | | 2 |
| 3 | | | | | | 3 |
| 4 | | | | | | 4 |
| 5 | | | | | | 5 |
| 6 | | | | | | 6 |
| 7 | | | | | | 7 |
| 8 | | | | | | 8 |
| 9 | | | | | | 9 |
| 10 | | | | | | 10 |
| 11 | | | | | | 11 |
| 12 | | | | | | 12 |

## GENERAL LEDGER

ACCOUNT   Accounts Payable                                    ACCOUNT NO.   202

| DATE | ITEM | POST. REF. | DEBIT | CREDIT | BALANCE DEBIT | BALANCE CREDIT |
|---|---|---|---|---|---|---|
| 20-- Mar. 1 | Balance | ✓ | | | | 8 3 5 0 00 |
| | | | | | | |
| | | | | | | |
| | | | | | | |

ACCOUNT   Purchases Returns and Allowances                   ACCOUNT NO.   501.1

| DATE | ITEM | POST. REF. | DEBIT | CREDIT | BALANCE DEBIT | BALANCE CREDIT |
|---|---|---|---|---|---|---|
| | | | | | | |
| | | | | | | |
| | | | | | | |
| | | | | | | |

## Exercise 11-6B (Concluded)

### ACCOUNTS PAYABLE LEDGER

**NAME** A & D Arms

**ADDRESS**

| DATE | | ITEM | POST. REF. | DEBIT | CREDIT | BALANCE |
|---|---|---|---|---|---|---|
| 20--<br>Mar. | 1 | Balance | ✓ | | | 2 3 0 0 00 |
| | | | | | | |
| | | | | | | |
| | | | | | | |

**NAME** Mighty Mansion

**ADDRESS**

| DATE | | ITEM | POST. REF. | DEBIT | CREDIT | BALANCE |
|---|---|---|---|---|---|---|
| 20--<br>Mar. | 1 | Balance | ✓ | | | 1 4 5 0 00 |
| | | | | | | |
| | | | | | | |
| | | | | | | |

**NAME** Tower Industries

**ADDRESS**

| DATE | | ITEM | POST. REF. | DEBIT | CREDIT | BALANCE |
|---|---|---|---|---|---|---|
| 20--<br>Mar. | 1 | Balance | ✓ | | | 4 6 0 0 00 |
| | | | | | | |
| | | | | | | |
| | | | | | | |

**Exercise 11-7B**

## GENERAL JOURNAL

| | DATE | | DESCRIPTION | POST. REF. | DEBIT | CREDIT | |
|---|---|---|---|---|---|---|---|
| 1 | | | | | | | 1 |
| 2 | | | | | | | 2 |
| 3 | | | | | | | 3 |
| 4 | | | | | | | 4 |
| 5 | | | | | | | 5 |
| 6 | | | | | | | 6 |
| 7 | | | | | | | 7 |
| 8 | | | | | | | 8 |
| 9 | | | | | | | 9 |
| 10 | | | | | | | 10 |
| 11 | | | | | | | 11 |
| 12 | | | | | | | 12 |
| 13 | | | | | | | 13 |
| 14 | | | | | | | 14 |
| 15 | | | | | | | 15 |
| 16 | | | | | | | 16 |
| 17 | | | | | | | 17 |
| 18 | | | | | | | 18 |
| 19 | | | | | | | 19 |
| 20 | | | | | | | 20 |
| 21 | | | | | | | 21 |

**Exercise 11-8B**

**Problem 11-9B**

1.

## GENERAL JOURNAL

| | DATE | | DESCRIPTION | POST. REF. | DEBIT | CREDIT | |
|---|---|---|---|---|---|---|---|
| 1 | | | | | | | 1 |
| 2 | | | | | | | 2 |
| 3 | | | | | | | 3 |
| 4 | | | | | | | 4 |
| 5 | | | | | | | 5 |
| 6 | | | | | | | 6 |
| 7 | | | | | | | 7 |
| 8 | | | | | | | 8 |
| 9 | | | | | | | 9 |
| 10 | | | | | | | 10 |
| 11 | | | | | | | 11 |
| 12 | | | | | | | 12 |
| 13 | | | | | | | 13 |
| 14 | | | | | | | 14 |
| 15 | | | | | | | 15 |
| 16 | | | | | | | 16 |
| 17 | | | | | | | 17 |
| 18 | | | | | | | 18 |
| 19 | | | | | | | 19 |
| 20 | | | | | | | 20 |
| 21 | | | | | | | 21 |
| 22 | | | | | | | 22 |
| 23 | | | | | | | 23 |
| 24 | | | | | | | 24 |
| 25 | | | | | | | 25 |
| 26 | | | | | | | 26 |
| 27 | | | | | | | 27 |
| 28 | | | | | | | 28 |
| 29 | | | | | | | 29 |
| 30 | | | | | | | 30 |
| 31 | | | | | | | 31 |
| 32 | | | | | | | 32 |
| 33 | | | | | | | 33 |
| 34 | | | | | | | 34 |

**Problem 11-9B (Continued)**

**2.**

## GENERAL LEDGER

ACCOUNT    Accounts Payable                                    ACCOUNT NO.  202

| DATE | | ITEM | POST. REF. | DEBIT | CREDIT | BALANCE | |
|------|--|------|-----------|-------|--------|---------|--|
| | | | | | | DEBIT | CREDIT |
| | | | | | | | |
| | | | | | | | |
| | | | | | | | |
| | | | | | | | |
| | | | | | | | |
| | | | | | | | |
| | | | | | | | |

ACCOUNT    Purchases                                          ACCOUNT NO.  501

| DATE | | ITEM | POST. REF. | DEBIT | CREDIT | BALANCE | |
|------|--|------|-----------|-------|--------|---------|--|
| | | | | | | DEBIT | CREDIT |
| | | | | | | | |
| | | | | | | | |
| | | | | | | | |
| | | | | | | | |
| | | | | | | | |
| | | | | | | | |
| | | | | | | | |

## ACCOUNTS PAYABLE LEDGER

**NAME** _____

**ADDRESS** _____

| DATE | | ITEM | POST. REF. | DEBIT | CREDIT | BALANCE |
|------|--|------|-----------|-------|--------|---------|
| | | | | | | |
| | | | | | | |
| | | | | | | |
| | | | | | | |

## Problem 11-9B (Concluded)

**NAME**

**ADDRESS**

| DATE | | ITEM | POST. REF. | DEBIT | CREDIT | BALANCE |
|---|---|---|---|---|---|---|
| | | | | | | |
| | | | | | | |
| | | | | | | |
| | | | | | | |

**NAME**

**ADDRESS**

| DATE | | ITEM | POST. REF. | DEBIT | CREDIT | BALANCE |
|---|---|---|---|---|---|---|
| | | | | | | |
| | | | | | | |
| | | | | | | |
| | | | | | | |

**NAME**

**ADDRESS**

| DATE | | ITEM | POST. REF. | DEBIT | CREDIT | BALANCE |
|---|---|---|---|---|---|---|
| | | | | | | |
| | | | | | | |
| | | | | | | |
| | | | | | | |

**NAME**

**ADDRESS**

| DATE | | ITEM | POST. REF. | DEBIT | CREDIT | BALANCE |
|---|---|---|---|---|---|---|
| | | | | | | |
| | | | | | | |
| | | | | | | |
| | | | | | | |

**Problem 11-10B**

**1.**

## GENERAL JOURNAL

| | DATE | | DESCRIPTION | POST. REF. | DEBIT | CREDIT | |
|---|---|---|---|---|---|---|---|
| 1 | | | | | | | 1 |
| 2 | | | | | | | 2 |
| 3 | | | | | | | 3 |
| 4 | | | | | | | 4 |
| 5 | | | | | | | 5 |
| 6 | | | | | | | 6 |
| 7 | | | | | | | 7 |
| 8 | | | | | | | 8 |
| 9 | | | | | | | 9 |
| 10 | | | | | | | 10 |
| 11 | | | | | | | 11 |
| 12 | | | | | | | 12 |
| 13 | | | | | | | 13 |
| 14 | | | | | | | 14 |
| 15 | | | | | | | 15 |
| 16 | | | | | | | 16 |
| 17 | | | | | | | 17 |
| 18 | | | | | | | 18 |
| 19 | | | | | | | 19 |
| 20 | | | | | | | 20 |
| 21 | | | | | | | 21 |
| 22 | | | | | | | 22 |
| 23 | | | | | | | 23 |
| 24 | | | | | | | 24 |
| 25 | | | | | | | 25 |
| 26 | | | | | | | 26 |
| 27 | | | | | | | 27 |
| 28 | | | | | | | 28 |
| 29 | | | | | | | 29 |
| 30 | | | | | | | 30 |
| 31 | | | | | | | 31 |
| 32 | | | | | | | 32 |
| 33 | | | | | | | 33 |
| 34 | | | | | | | 34 |

## Problem 11-10B (Continued)

### GENERAL JOURNAL

PAGE 10

| | DATE | DESCRIPTION | POST. REF. | DEBIT | CREDIT | |
|---|---|---|---|---|---|---|
| 1 | | | | | | 1 |
| 2 | | | | | | 2 |
| 3 | | | | | | 3 |
| 4 | | | | | | 4 |
| 5 | | | | | | 5 |

2.

### GENERAL LEDGER

ACCOUNT  Cash  ACCOUNT NO.  101

| DATE | | ITEM | POST. REF. | DEBIT | CREDIT | BALANCE DEBIT | BALANCE CREDIT |
|---|---|---|---|---|---|---|---|
| 20-- May | 1 | Balance | ✓ | | | 40 0 0 0 00 | |
| | | | | | | | |
| | | | | | | | |
| | | | | | | | |
| | | | | | | | |
| | | | | | | | |
| | | | | | | | |
| | | | | | | | |
| | | | | | | | |
| | | | | | | | |
| | | | | | | | |

ACCOUNT  Accounts Payable  ACCOUNT NO.  202

| DATE | | ITEM | POST. REF. | DEBIT | CREDIT | BALANCE DEBIT | BALANCE CREDIT |
|---|---|---|---|---|---|---|---|
| 20-- May | 1 | Balance | ✓ | | | | 20 0 0 0 00 |
| | | | | | | | |
| | | | | | | | |
| | | | | | | | |
| | | | | | | | |

**Problem 11-10B (Continued)**

ACCOUNT  Purchases                                          ACCOUNT NO.  501

| DATE | ITEM | POST. REF. | DEBIT | CREDIT | BALANCE DEBIT | BALANCE CREDIT |
|------|------|------------|-------|--------|---------------|----------------|
|      |      |            |       |        |               |                |
|      |      |            |       |        |               |                |
|      |      |            |       |        |               |                |
|      |      |            |       |        |               |                |

ACCOUNT  Purchases Discounts                                ACCOUNT NO.  501.2

| DATE | ITEM | POST. REF. | DEBIT | CREDIT | BALANCE DEBIT | BALANCE CREDIT |
|------|------|------------|-------|--------|---------------|----------------|
|      |      |            |       |        |               |                |
|      |      |            |       |        |               |                |
|      |      |            |       |        |               |                |
|      |      |            |       |        |               |                |

ACCOUNT  Freight-In                                         ACCOUNT NO.  502

| DATE | ITEM | POST. REF. | DEBIT | CREDIT | BALANCE DEBIT | BALANCE CREDIT |
|------|------|------------|-------|--------|---------------|----------------|
|      |      |            |       |        |               |                |
|      |      |            |       |        |               |                |
|      |      |            |       |        |               |                |
|      |      |            |       |        |               |                |

ACCOUNT  Rent Expense                                       ACCOUNT NO.  521

| DATE | ITEM | POST. REF. | DEBIT | CREDIT | BALANCE DEBIT | BALANCE CREDIT |
|------|------|------------|-------|--------|---------------|----------------|
|      |      |            |       |        |               |                |
|      |      |            |       |        |               |                |
|      |      |            |       |        |               |                |
|      |      |            |       |        |               |                |

ACCOUNT  Utilities Expense                                  ACCOUNT NO.  533

| DATE | ITEM | POST. REF. | DEBIT | CREDIT | BALANCE DEBIT | BALANCE CREDIT |
|------|------|------------|-------|--------|---------------|----------------|
|      |      |            |       |        |               |                |
|      |      |            |       |        |               |                |
|      |      |            |       |        |               |                |
|      |      |            |       |        |               |                |

## Problem 11-10B (Concluded)

### ACCOUNTS PAYABLE LEDGER

**NAME** Cortez Distributors

**ADDRESS**

| DATE | | ITEM | POST. REF. | DEBIT | CREDIT | BALANCE |
|---|---|---|---|---|---|---|
| 20--<br>May | 1 | Balance | ✓ | | | 4 2 0 0 00 |
| | | | | | | |
| | | | | | | |

**NAME** Indra & Velga

**ADDRESS**

| DATE | | ITEM | POST. REF. | DEBIT | CREDIT | BALANCE |
|---|---|---|---|---|---|---|
| 20--<br>May | 1 | Balance | ✓ | | | 6 8 0 0 00 |
| | | | | | | |
| | | | | | | |
| | | | | | | |

**NAME** Toy Corner

**ADDRESS**

| DATE | | ITEM | POST. REF. | DEBIT | CREDIT | BALANCE |
|---|---|---|---|---|---|---|
| 20--<br>May | 1 | Balance | ✓ | | | 4 6 0 0 00 |
| | | | | | | |
| | | | | | | |

**NAME** Troutman Outlet

**ADDRESS**

| DATE | | ITEM | POST. REF. | DEBIT | CREDIT | BALANCE |
|---|---|---|---|---|---|---|
| 20--<br>May | 1 | Balance | ✓ | | | 4 4 0 0 00 |
| | | | | | | |
| | | | | | | |

**Exercise 11Apx-1A**

1.

**GENERAL JOURNAL**    PAGE _____

| | DATE | DESCRIPTION | POST. REF. | DEBIT | CREDIT | |
|---|---|---|---|---|---|---|
| 1 | | | | | | 1 |
| 2 | | | | | | 2 |
| 3 | | | | | | 3 |
| 4 | | | | | | 4 |
| 5 | | | | | | 5 |
| 6 | | | | | | 6 |
| 7 | | | | | | 7 |
| 8 | | | | | | 8 |
| 9 | | | | | | 9 |
| 10 | | | | | | 10 |
| 11 | | | | | | 11 |
| 12 | | | | | | 12 |
| 13 | | | | | | 13 |
| 14 | | | | | | 14 |
| 15 | | | | | | 15 |
| 16 | | | | | | 16 |

2.

| | | | | | | |
|---|---|---|---|---|---|---|
| 1 | | | | | | 1 |
| 2 | | | | | | 2 |
| 3 | | | | | | 3 |
| 4 | | | | | | 4 |
| 5 | | | | | | 5 |
| 6 | | | | | | 6 |
| 7 | | | | | | 7 |
| 8 | | | | | | 8 |
| 9 | | | | | | 9 |
| 10 | | | | | | 10 |
| 11 | | | | | | 11 |
| 12 | | | | | | 12 |
| 13 | | | | | | 13 |
| 14 | | | | | | 14 |
| 15 | | | | | | 15 |
| 16 | | | | | | 16 |

## Exercise 11Apx-1B

**1.**

### GENERAL JOURNAL

PAGE

| | DATE | | DESCRIPTION | POST. REF. | DEBIT | CREDIT | |
|---|---|---|---|---|---|---|---|
| 1 | | | | | | | 1 |
| 2 | | | | | | | 2 |
| 3 | | | | | | | 3 |
| 4 | | | | | | | 4 |
| 5 | | | | | | | 5 |
| 6 | | | | | | | 6 |
| 7 | | | | | | | 7 |
| 8 | | | | | | | 8 |
| 9 | | | | | | | 9 |
| 10 | | | | | | | 10 |
| 11 | | | | | | | 11 |
| 12 | | | | | | | 12 |
| 13 | | | | | | | 13 |
| 14 | | | | | | | 14 |
| 15 | | | | | | | 15 |
| 16 | | | | | | | 16 |

**2.**

| | | | | | | | |
|---|---|---|---|---|---|---|---|
| 1 | | | | | | | 1 |
| 2 | | | | | | | 2 |
| 3 | | | | | | | 3 |
| 4 | | | | | | | 4 |
| 5 | | | | | | | 5 |
| 6 | | | | | | | 6 |
| 7 | | | | | | | 7 |
| 8 | | | | | | | 8 |
| 9 | | | | | | | 9 |
| 10 | | | | | | | 10 |
| 11 | | | | | | | 11 |
| 12 | | | | | | | 12 |
| 13 | | | | | | | 13 |
| 14 | | | | | | | 14 |
| 15 | | | | | | | 15 |
| 16 | | | | | | | 16 |

## Exercise 12-1A

**Journal**

a.   Sold merchandise on account.                                          _____

b.   Purchased delivery truck on account for use in the business.          _____

c.   Received payment from customer on account.                            _____

d.   Purchased merchandise on account.                                     _____

e.   Issued check in payment of electric bill.                             _____

f.   Recorded depreciation on factory building.                            _____

## Exercise 12-2A

**SALES JOURNAL**                                                          PAGE

| DATE | SALE NO. | TO WHOM SOLD | POST. REF. | ACCOUNTS RECEIVABLE DEBIT | SALES CREDIT | SALES TAX PAYABLE CREDIT |
|------|----------|--------------|------------|---------------------------|--------------|--------------------------|
|      |          |              |            |                           |              |                          |
|      |          |              |            |                           |              |                          |
|      |          |              |            |                           |              |                          |
|      |          |              |            |                           |              |                          |
|      |          |              |            |                           |              |                          |
|      |          |              |            |                           |              |                          |
|      |          |              |            |                           |              |                          |

## Exercise 12-3A

**CASH RECEIPTS JOURNAL**                                                  PAGE

| DATE | ACCOUNT CREDITED | POST. REF. | GENERAL CREDIT | ACCOUNTS RECEIVABLE CREDIT | SALES CREDIT | SALES TAX PAYABLE CREDIT | CASH DEBIT | |
|------|------------------|------------|----------------|----------------------------|--------------|--------------------------|------------|---|
| 1 |  |  |  |  |  |  |  | 1 |
| 2 |  |  |  |  |  |  |  | 2 |
| 3 |  |  |  |  |  |  |  | 3 |
| 4 |  |  |  |  |  |  |  | 4 |
| 5 |  |  |  |  |  |  |  | 5 |
| 6 |  |  |  |  |  |  |  | 6 |
| 7 |  |  |  |  |  |  |  | 7 |
| 8 |  |  |  |  |  |  |  | 8 |
| 9 |  |  |  |  |  |  |  | 9 |
| 10 |  |  |  |  |  |  |  | 10 |
| 11 |  |  |  |  |  |  |  | 11 |

## Exercise 12-4A

### PURCHASES JOURNAL                                        PAGE

| | DATE | INVOICE NO. | FROM WHOM PURCHASED | POST. REF. | PURCHASES DEBIT ACCTS. PAY. CREDIT | |
|---|---|---|---|---|---|---|
| 1 | | | | | | 1 |
| 2 | | | | | | 2 |
| 3 | | | | | | 3 |
| 4 | | | | | | 4 |
| 5 | | | | | | 5 |
| 6 | | | | | | 6 |
| 7 | | | | | | 7 |
| 8 | | | | | | 8 |
| 9 | | | | | | 9 |
| 10 | | | | | | 10 |
| 11 | | | | | | 11 |

## Exercise 12-5A

### CASH PAYMENTS JOURNAL                                        PAGE

| | DATE | CK. NO. | ACCOUNT DEBITED | POST. REF. | GENERAL DEBIT | ACCOUNTS PAYABLE DEBIT | PURCHASES DEBIT | PURCHASES DISCOUNTS CREDIT | CASH CREDIT | |
|---|---|---|---|---|---|---|---|---|---|---|
| 1 | | | | | | | | | | 1 |
| 2 | | | | | | | | | | 2 |
| 3 | | | | | | | | | | 3 |
| 4 | | | | | | | | | | 4 |
| 5 | | | | | | | | | | 5 |
| 6 | | | | | | | | | | 6 |
| 7 | | | | | | | | | | 7 |
| 8 | | | | | | | | | | 8 |
| 9 | | | | | | | | | | 9 |
| 10 | | | | | | | | | | 10 |
| 11 | | | | | | | | | | 11 |
| 12 | | | | | | | | | | 12 |
| 13 | | | | | | | | | | 13 |

**Problem 12-6A**

**1.**

SALES JOURNAL

PAGE  8

| DATE | SALE NO. | TO WHOM SOLD | POST. REF. | ACCOUNTS RECEIVABLE DEBIT | SALES CREDIT | SALES TAX PAYABLE CREDIT |
|---|---|---|---|---|---|---|
|  |  |  |  |  |  |  |
|  |  |  |  |  |  |  |
|  |  |  |  |  |  |  |
|  |  |  |  |  |  |  |
|  |  |  |  |  |  |  |
|  |  |  |  |  |  |  |
|  |  |  |  |  |  |  |
|  |  |  |  |  |  |  |
|  |  |  |  |  |  |  |
|  |  |  |  |  |  |  |

**2.**

GENERAL LEDGER

ACCOUNT   Accounts Receivable                                      ACCOUNT NO.   122

| DATE | ITEM | POST. REF. | DEBIT | CREDIT | BALANCE DEBIT | BALANCE CREDIT |
|---|---|---|---|---|---|---|
|  |  |  |  |  |  |  |
|  |  |  |  |  |  |  |
|  |  |  |  |  |  |  |

ACCOUNT   Sales Tax Payable                                        ACCOUNT NO.   231

| DATE | ITEM | POST. REF. | DEBIT | CREDIT | BALANCE DEBIT | BALANCE CREDIT |
|---|---|---|---|---|---|---|
|  |  |  |  |  |  |  |
|  |  |  |  |  |  |  |
|  |  |  |  |  |  |  |

## Problem 12-6A (Concluded)

ACCOUNT  Sales                                                    ACCOUNT NO.  401

| DATE | ITEM | POST. REF. | DEBIT | CREDIT | BALANCE | |
|---|---|---|---|---|---|---|
| | | | | | DEBIT | CREDIT |
| | | | | | | |
| | | | | | | |
| | | | | | | |
| | | | | | | |

### ACCOUNTS RECEIVABLE LEDGER

**NAME**  Hassad Co.

**ADDRESS**  1225 W. Temperance Street, Ellettsville, IN 47429-9976

| DATE | ITEM | POST. REF. | DEBIT | CREDIT | BALANCE |
|---|---|---|---|---|---|
| | | | | | |
| | | | | | |
| | | | | | |

**NAME**  Helsinki, Inc.

**ADDRESS**  125 Fishers Dr., Noblesville, IN 47870-8867

| DATE | ITEM | POST. REF. | DEBIT | CREDIT | BALANCE |
|---|---|---|---|---|---|
| | | | | | |
| | | | | | |
| | | | | | |
| | | | | | |

**NAME**  Jung Manufacturing Co.

**ADDRESS**  8825 Old State Road, Bloomington, IN 47401-8823

| DATE | ITEM | POST. REF. | DEBIT | CREDIT | BALANCE |
|---|---|---|---|---|---|
| | | | | | |
| | | | | | |
| | | | | | |
| | | | | | |

**NAME**  Ardis Myler

**ADDRESS**  2100 Greer Lane, Bedford, IN 47421-8876

| DATE | ITEM | POST. REF. | DEBIT | CREDIT | BALANCE |
|---|---|---|---|---|---|
| | | | | | |
| | | | | | |
| | | | | | |
| | | | | | |

**Problem 12-7A**

**1.**

## GENERAL JOURNAL

| | DATE | | DESCRIPTION | POST. REF. | DEBIT | CREDIT | |
|---|---|---|---|---|---|---|---|
| 1 | | | | | | | 1 |
| 2 | | | | | | | 2 |
| 3 | | | | | | | 3 |
| 4 | | | | | | | 4 |
| 5 | | | | | | | 5 |
| 6 | | | | | | | 6 |
| 7 | | | | | | | 7 |
| 8 | | | | | | | 8 |
| 9 | | | | | | | 9 |
| 10 | | | | | | | 10 |
| 11 | | | | | | | 11 |
| 12 | | | | | | | 12 |
| 13 | | | | | | | 13 |
| 14 | | | | | | | 14 |
| 15 | | | | | | | 15 |
| 16 | | | | | | | 16 |
| 17 | | | | | | | 17 |
| 18 | | | | | | | 18 |
| 19 | | | | | | | 19 |
| 20 | | | | | | | 20 |
| 21 | | | | | | | 21 |
| 22 | | | | | | | 22 |
| 23 | | | | | | | 23 |
| 24 | | | | | | | 24 |
| 25 | | | | | | | 25 |
| 26 | | | | | | | 26 |
| 27 | | | | | | | 27 |
| 28 | | | | | | | 28 |
| 29 | | | | | | | 29 |
| 30 | | | | | | | 30 |
| 31 | | | | | | | 31 |
| 32 | | | | | | | 32 |
| 33 | | | | | | | 33 |
| 34 | | | | | | | 34 |

## Problem 12-7A (Continued)

### CASH RECEIPTS JOURNAL

| | DATE | | ACCOUNT CREDITED | POST. REF. | GENERAL CREDIT | ACCOUNTS RECEIVABLE CREDIT |
|---|---|---|---|---|---|---|
| 1 | | | | | | |
| 2 | | | | | | |
| 3 | | | | | | |
| 4 | | | | | | |
| 5 | | | | | | |
| 6 | | | | | | |
| 7 | | | | | | |
| 8 | | | | | | |
| 9 | | | | | | |
| 10 | | | | | | |
| 11 | | | | | | |
| 12 | | | | | | |
| 13 | | | | | | |
| 14 | | | | | | |
| 15 | | | | | | |
| 16 | | | | | | |
| 17 | | | | | | |
| 18 | | | | | | |
| 19 | | | | | | |
| 20 | | | | | | |
| 21 | | | | | | |
| 22 | | | | | | |
| 23 | | | | | | |
| 24 | | | | | | |
| 25 | | | | | | |
| 26 | | | | | | |
| 27 | | | | | | |
| 28 | | | | | | |

**Problem 12-7A (Continued)**

PAGE  10

| SALES CREDIT | | | SALES TAX PAYABLE CREDIT | | | BANK CREDIT CARD EXPENSE DEBIT | | | CASH DEBIT | | | |
|---|---|---|---|---|---|---|---|---|---|---|---|---|
| | | | | | | | | | | | | 1 |
| | | | | | | | | | | | | 2 |
| | | | | | | | | | | | | 3 |
| | | | | | | | | | | | | 4 |
| | | | | | | | | | | | | 5 |
| | | | | | | | | | | | | 6 |
| | | | | | | | | | | | | 7 |
| | | | | | | | | | | | | 8 |
| | | | | | | | | | | | | 9 |
| | | | | | | | | | | | | 10 |
| | | | | | | | | | | | | 11 |
| | | | | | | | | | | | | 12 |
| | | | | | | | | | | | | 13 |
| | | | | | | | | | | | | 14 |
| | | | | | | | | | | | | 15 |
| | | | | | | | | | | | | 16 |
| | | | | | | | | | | | | 17 |
| | | | | | | | | | | | | 18 |
| | | | | | | | | | | | | 19 |
| | | | | | | | | | | | | 20 |
| | | | | | | | | | | | | 21 |
| | | | | | | | | | | | | 22 |
| | | | | | | | | | | | | 23 |
| | | | | | | | | | | | | 24 |
| | | | | | | | | | | | | 25 |
| | | | | | | | | | | | | 26 |
| | | | | | | | | | | | | 27 |
| | | | | | | | | | | | | 28 |

## Problem 12-7A (Continued)

2.

### GENERAL LEDGER

ACCOUNT  Cash                                                 ACCOUNT NO.  101

| DATE | | ITEM | POST. REF. | DEBIT | CREDIT | BALANCE | |
|---|---|---|---|---|---|---|---|
| | | | | | | DEBIT | CREDIT |
| 20--<br>Dec. | 1 | Balance | ✓ | | | 9 8 6 2 00 | |
| | | | | | | | |
| | | | | | | | |
| | | | | | | | |
| | | | | | | | |

ACCOUNT  Accounts Receivable                                  ACCOUNT NO.  122

| DATE | | ITEM | POST. REF. | DEBIT | CREDIT | BALANCE | |
|---|---|---|---|---|---|---|---|
| | | | | | | DEBIT | CREDIT |
| 20--<br>Dec. | 1 | Balance | ✓ | | | 9 3 5 2 00 | |
| | | | | | | | |
| | | | | | | | |
| | | | | | | | |
| | | | | | | | |

ACCOUNT  Sales Tax Payable                                    ACCOUNT NO.  231

| DATE | | ITEM | POST. REF. | DEBIT | CREDIT | BALANCE | |
|---|---|---|---|---|---|---|---|
| | | | | | | DEBIT | CREDIT |
| | | | | | | | |
| | | | | | | | |
| | | | | | | | |
| | | | | | | | |

ACCOUNT  Sales                                                ACCOUNT NO.  401

| DATE | | ITEM | POST. REF. | DEBIT | CREDIT | BALANCE | |
|---|---|---|---|---|---|---|---|
| | | | | | | DEBIT | CREDIT |
| | | | | | | | |
| | | | | | | | |
| | | | | | | | |

**Problem 12-7A (Continued)**

ACCOUNT Sales Returns and Allowances     ACCOUNT NO. 401.1

| DATE | ITEM | POST. REF. | DEBIT | CREDIT | BALANCE DEBIT | BALANCE CREDIT |
|---|---|---|---|---|---|---|
| | | | | | | |
| | | | | | | |
| | | | | | | |
| | | | | | | |

ACCOUNT Bank Credit Card Expense     ACCOUNT NO. 513

| DATE | ITEM | POST. REF. | DEBIT | CREDIT | BALANCE DEBIT | BALANCE CREDIT |
|---|---|---|---|---|---|---|
| | | | | | | |
| | | | | | | |
| | | | | | | |
| | | | | | | |

## ACCOUNTS RECEIVABLE LEDGER

**NAME** Michael Anderson

**ADDRESS** 233 West 11th Avenue, Detroit, MI 59500-1154

| DATE | ITEM | POST. REF. | DEBIT | CREDIT | BALANCE |
|---|---|---|---|---|---|
| 20-- Dec. 1 | Balance | ✓ | | | 2 4 8 0 00 |
| | | | | | |
| | | | | | |
| | | | | | |

**NAME** Ansel Manufacturing

**ADDRESS** 284 West 88 Street, Detroit, MI 59522-1168

| DATE | ITEM | POST. REF. | DEBIT | CREDIT | BALANCE |
|---|---|---|---|---|---|
| 20-- Dec. 1 | Balance | ✓ | | | 9 8 2 00 |
| | | | | | |
| | | | | | |
| | | | | | |

## Problem 12-7A (Concluded)

**NAME**  J. Gorbea

**ADDRESS**  P.O. Box 864, Detroit, MI 59552-0864

| DATE | | ITEM | POST. REF. | DEBIT | CREDIT | BALANCE |
|---|---|---|---|---|---|---|
| 20-- Dec. | 1 | Balance | ✓ | | | 8 8 0 00 |
| | | | | | | |
| | | | | | | |
| | | | | | | |
| | | | | | | |

**NAME**  Rachel Carson

**ADDRESS**  11312 Fourteenth Avenue South, Detroit, MI 59221-1142

| DATE | | ITEM | POST. REF. | DEBIT | CREDIT | BALANCE |
|---|---|---|---|---|---|---|
| 20-- Dec. | 1 | Balance | ✓ | | | 3 2 0 0 00 |
| | | | | | | |
| | | | | | | |
| | | | | | | |
| | | | | | | |

**NAME**  Tom Wilson

**ADDRESS**  100 NW Seward St., Detroit, MI 59210-1337

| DATE | | ITEM | POST. REF. | DEBIT | CREDIT | BALANCE |
|---|---|---|---|---|---|---|
| 20-- Dec. | 1 | Balance | ✓ | | | 1 8 1 0 00 |
| | | | | | | |
| | | | | | | |
| | | | | | | |
| | | | | | | |

**Problem 12-8A**

1.

**SALES JOURNAL**

PAGE 6

| DATE | SALE NO. | TO WHOM SOLD | POST. REF. | ACCOUNTS RECEIVABLE DEBIT | SALES CREDIT | SALES TAX PAYABLE CREDIT |
|---|---|---|---|---|---|---|
| | | | | | | |
| | | | | | | |
| | | | | | | |
| | | | | | | |
| | | | | | | |
| | | | | | | |
| | | | | | | |
| | | | | | | |

**CASH RECEIPTS JOURNAL**

PAGE 9

| | DATE | ACCOUNT CREDITED | POST. REF. | GENERAL CREDIT | ACCOUNTS RECEIVABLE CREDIT | SALES CREDIT | SALES TAX PAYABLE CREDIT | CASH DEBIT | |
|---|---|---|---|---|---|---|---|---|---|
| 1 | | | | | | | | | 1 |
| 2 | | | | | | | | | 2 |
| 3 | | | | | | | | | 3 |
| 4 | | | | | | | | | 4 |
| 5 | | | | | | | | | 5 |
| 6 | | | | | | | | | 6 |
| 7 | | | | | | | | | 7 |
| 8 | | | | | | | | | 8 |
| 9 | | | | | | | | | 9 |

## Problem 12-8A (Continued)

**GENERAL JOURNAL**                                                           PAGE 5

| | DATE | | DESCRIPTION | POST. REF. | DEBIT | CREDIT | |
|---|---|---|---|---|---|---|---|
| 1 | | | | | | | 1 |
| 2 | | | | | | | 2 |
| 3 | | | | | | | 3 |
| 4 | | | | | | | 4 |
| 5 | | | | | | | 5 |
| 6 | | | | | | | 6 |
| 7 | | | | | | | 7 |
| 8 | | | | | | | 8 |
| 9 | | | | | | | 9 |
| 10 | | | | | | | 10 |
| 11 | | | | | | | 11 |
| 12 | | | | | | | 12 |
| 13 | | | | | | | 13 |
| 14 | | | | | | | 14 |

**2.**

**GENERAL LEDGER**

ACCOUNT  Cash                                              ACCOUNT NO.  101

| DATE | | ITEM | POST. REF. | DEBIT | CREDIT | BALANCE DEBIT | BALANCE CREDIT |
|---|---|---|---|---|---|---|---|
| 20-- Mar. | 1 | Balance | ✓ | | | 9 7 4 1 00 | |
| | | | | | | | |
| | | | | | | | |

ACCOUNT  Accounts Receivable                               ACCOUNT NO.  122

| DATE | | ITEM | POST. REF. | DEBIT | CREDIT | BALANCE DEBIT | BALANCE CREDIT |
|---|---|---|---|---|---|---|---|
| 20-- Mar. | 1 | Balance | ✓ | | | 1 0 5 8 25 | |
| | | | | | | | |
| | | | | | | | |
| | | | | | | | |

## Problem 12-8A (Continued)

ACCOUNT   Sales Tax Payable                                   ACCOUNT NO.   231

| DATE | | ITEM | POST. REF. | DEBIT | CREDIT | BALANCE | |
|---|---|---|---|---|---|---|---|
| | | | | | | DEBIT | CREDIT |
| | | | | | | | |
| | | | | | | | |
| | | | | | | | |
| | | | | | | | |
| | | | | | | | |
| | | | | | | | |
| | | | | | | | |
| | | | | | | | |
| | | | | | | | |

ACCOUNT   Sales                                               ACCOUNT NO.   401

| DATE | | ITEM | POST. REF. | DEBIT | CREDIT | BALANCE | |
|---|---|---|---|---|---|---|---|
| | | | | | | DEBIT | CREDIT |
| | | | | | | | |
| | | | | | | | |
| | | | | | | | |
| | | | | | | | |
| | | | | | | | |
| | | | | | | | |
| | | | | | | | |
| | | | | | | | |

ACCOUNT   Sales Returns and Allowances                        ACCOUNT NO.   401.1

| DATE | | ITEM | POST. REF. | DEBIT | CREDIT | BALANCE | |
|---|---|---|---|---|---|---|---|
| | | | | | | DEBIT | CREDIT |
| | | | | | | | |
| | | | | | | | |
| | | | | | | | |
| | | | | | | | |
| | | | | | | | |
| | | | | | | | |
| | | | | | | | |

**Problem 12-8A (Concluded)**

## ACCOUNTS RECEIVABLE LEDGER

**NAME**  Able & Co.

**ADDRESS**  1424 Jackson Creek Road, Nashville, IN 47448-2245

| DATE | | ITEM | POST. REF. | DEBIT | CREDIT | BALANCE |
|---|---|---|---|---|---|---|
| | | | | | | |
| | | | | | | |
| | | | | | | |
| | | | | | | |
| | | | | | | |

**NAME**  Blevins Bakery

**ADDRESS**  6422 E. Bender Road, Bloomington, IN 47401-7756

| DATE | | ITEM | POST. REF. | DEBIT | CREDIT | BALANCE |
|---|---|---|---|---|---|---|
| | | | | | | |
| | | | | | | |
| | | | | | | |
| | | | | | | |
| | | | | | | |

**NAME**  R. J. Kalas, Inc.

**ADDRESS**  3315 Longview Avenue, Bloomington, IN 47401-7223

| DATE | | ITEM | POST. REF. | DEBIT | CREDIT | BALANCE |
|---|---|---|---|---|---|---|
| | | | | | | |
| | | | | | | |
| | | | | | | |
| | | | | | | |
| | | | | | | |

**NAME**  Thompson Group

**ADDRESS**  2300 E. National Road, Cumberland, IN 46229-4824

| DATE | | ITEM | POST. REF. | DEBIT | CREDIT | BALANCE |
|---|---|---|---|---|---|---|
| 20--<br>Mar. | 1 | Balance | ✓ | | | 1 0 5 8 25 |
| | | | | | | |
| | | | | | | |
| | | | | | | |

**Problem 12-9A**

**1.**

**PURCHASES JOURNAL**          PAGE 7

| | DATE | INVOICE NO. | FROM WHOM PURCHASED | POST. REF. | PURCHASES DEBIT ACCTS. PAY. CREDIT | |
|---|---|---|---|---|---|---|
| 1 | | | | | | 1 |
| 2 | | | | | | 2 |
| 3 | | | | | | 3 |
| 4 | | | | | | 4 |
| 5 | | | | | | 5 |
| 6 | | | | | | 6 |
| 7 | | | | | | 7 |
| 8 | | | | | | 8 |
| 9 | | | | | | 9 |
| 10 | | | | | | 10 |
| 11 | | | | | | 11 |
| 12 | | | | | | 12 |
| 13 | | | | | | 13 |
| 14 | | | | | | 14 |

**2.**

**GENERAL LEDGER**

ACCOUNT   Accounts Payable                                ACCOUNT NO.   202

| | | | | | BALANCE | |
|---|---|---|---|---|---|---|
| DATE | ITEM | POST. REF. | DEBIT | CREDIT | DEBIT | CREDIT |
| | | | | | | |
| | | | | | | |
| | | | | | | |
| | | | | | | |

ACCOUNT   Purchases                                       ACCOUNT NO.   501

| | | | | | BALANCE | |
|---|---|---|---|---|---|---|
| DATE | ITEM | POST. REF. | DEBIT | CREDIT | DEBIT | CREDIT |
| | | | | | | |
| | | | | | | |
| | | | | | | |
| | | | | | | |

## Problem 12-9A (Concluded)

### ACCOUNTS PAYABLE LEDGER

**NAME**

**ADDRESS**

| DATE | ITEM | POST. REF. | DEBIT | CREDIT | BALANCE |
|------|------|------------|-------|--------|---------|
|      |      |            |       |        |         |
|      |      |            |       |        |         |

**NAME**

**ADDRESS**

| DATE | ITEM | POST. REF. | DEBIT | CREDIT | BALANCE |
|------|------|------------|-------|--------|---------|
|      |      |            |       |        |         |
|      |      |            |       |        |         |

**NAME**

**ADDRESS**

| DATE | ITEM | POST. REF. | DEBIT | CREDIT | BALANCE |
|------|------|------------|-------|--------|---------|
|      |      |            |       |        |         |
|      |      |            |       |        |         |
|      |      |            |       |        |         |

**NAME**

**ADDRESS**

| DATE | ITEM | POST. REF. | DEBIT | CREDIT | BALANCE |
|------|------|------------|-------|--------|---------|
|      |      |            |       |        |         |
|      |      |            |       |        |         |
|      |      |            |       |        |         |

**NAME**

**ADDRESS**

| DATE | ITEM | POST. REF. | DEBIT | CREDIT | BALANCE |
|------|------|------------|-------|--------|---------|
|      |      |            |       |        |         |
|      |      |            |       |        |         |
|      |      |            |       |        |         |

**Problem 12-10A**

**1.**

## GENERAL LEDGER

ACCOUNT   Accounts Payable                                              ACCOUNT NO.   202

| DATE | ITEM | POST. REF. | DEBIT | CREDIT | BALANCE | |
|------|------|-----------|-------|--------|---------|---|
| | | | | | DEBIT | CREDIT |
| | | | | | | |
| | | | | | | |
| | | | | | | |
| | | | | | | |

ACCOUNT   Purchases                                                     ACCOUNT NO.   501

| DATE | ITEM | POST. REF. | DEBIT | CREDIT | BALANCE | |
|------|------|-----------|-------|--------|---------|---|
| | | | | | DEBIT | CREDIT |
| | | | | | | |
| | | | | | | |
| | | | | | | |
| | | | | | | |

**2.**

## ACCOUNTS PAYABLE LEDGER

**NAME**

**ADDRESS**

| DATE | ITEM | POST. REF. | DEBIT | CREDIT | BALANCE |
|------|------|-----------|-------|--------|---------|
| | | | | | |
| | | | | | |
| | | | | | |
| | | | | | |

**NAME**

**ADDRESS**

| DATE | ITEM | POST. REF. | DEBIT | CREDIT | BALANCE |
|------|------|-----------|-------|--------|---------|
| | | | | | |
| | | | | | |
| | | | | | |
| | | | | | |

## Problem 12-10A (Concluded)

**NAME**

**ADDRESS**

| DATE | | ITEM | POST. REF. | DEBIT | CREDIT | BALANCE |
|---|---|---|---|---|---|---|
| | | | | | | |
| | | | | | | |
| | | | | | | |
| | | | | | | |
| | | | | | | |

**NAME**

**ADDRESS**

| DATE | | ITEM | POST. REF. | DEBIT | CREDIT | BALANCE |
|---|---|---|---|---|---|---|
| | | | | | | |
| | | | | | | |
| | | | | | | |
| | | | | | | |
| | | | | | | |

**NAME**

**ADDRESS**

| DATE | | ITEM | POST. REF. | DEBIT | CREDIT | BALANCE |
|---|---|---|---|---|---|---|
| | | | | | | |
| | | | | | | |
| | | | | | | |
| | | | | | | |

**Problem 12-11A**

**1.**

| | | CASH PAYMENTS JOURNAL | | | | | | | PAGE 6 | |
|---|---|---|---|---|---|---|---|---|---|---|

| | DATE | CK. NO. | ACCOUNT DEBITED | POST. REF. | GENERAL DEBIT | ACCOUNTS PAYABLE DEBIT | PURCHASES DEBIT | PURCHASES DISCOUNTS CREDIT | CASH CREDIT | |
|---|---|---|---|---|---|---|---|---|---|---|
| 1 | | | | | | | | | | 1 |
| 2 | | | | | | | | | | 2 |
| 3 | | | | | | | | | | 3 |
| 4 | | | | | | | | | | 4 |
| 5 | | | | | | | | | | 5 |
| 6 | | | | | | | | | | 6 |
| 7 | | | | | | | | | | 7 |
| 8 | | | | | | | | | | 8 |
| 9 | | | | | | | | | | 9 |
| 10 | | | | | | | | | | 10 |
| 11 | | | | | | | | | | 11 |
| 12 | | | | | | | | | | 12 |

**2.**

## GENERAL LEDGER

ACCOUNT  Cash                                    ACCOUNT NO.  101

| DATE | ITEM | POST. REF. | DEBIT | CREDIT | BALANCE DEBIT | BALANCE CREDIT |
|---|---|---|---|---|---|---|
| 20-- May 1 | Balance | ✓ | | | 40 0 0 0 00 | |
| | | | | | | |
| | | | | | | |

ACCOUNT  Accounts Payable                        ACCOUNT NO.  202

| DATE | ITEM | POST. REF. | DEBIT | CREDIT | BALANCE DEBIT | BALANCE CREDIT |
|---|---|---|---|---|---|---|
| 20-- May 1 | Balance | ✓ | | | | 20 0 0 0 00 |
| | | | | | | |
| | | | | | | |

## Problem 12-11A (Continued)

ACCOUNT   Purchases                                    ACCOUNT NO.   501

| DATE | ITEM | POST. REF. | DEBIT | CREDIT | BALANCE | |
|------|------|------------|-------|--------|---------|---|
| | | | | | DEBIT | CREDIT |
| | | | | | | |
| | | | | | | |
| | | | | | | |
| | | | | | | |

ACCOUNT   Purchases Discounts                          ACCOUNT NO.   501.2

| DATE | ITEM | POST. REF. | DEBIT | CREDIT | BALANCE | |
|------|------|------------|-------|--------|---------|---|
| | | | | | DEBIT | CREDIT |
| | | | | | | |
| | | | | | | |
| | | | | | | |
| | | | | | | |

ACCOUNT   Freight-In                                   ACCOUNT NO.   502

| DATE | ITEM | POST. REF. | DEBIT | CREDIT | BALANCE | |
|------|------|------------|-------|--------|---------|---|
| | | | | | DEBIT | CREDIT |
| | | | | | | |
| | | | | | | |
| | | | | | | |

ACCOUNT   Rent Expense                                 ACCOUNT NO.   521

| DATE | ITEM | POST. REF. | DEBIT | CREDIT | BALANCE | |
|------|------|------------|-------|--------|---------|---|
| | | | | | DEBIT | CREDIT |
| | | | | | | |
| | | | | | | |
| | | | | | | |

ACCOUNT   Utilities Expense                            ACCOUNT NO.   533

| DATE | ITEM | POST. REF. | DEBIT | CREDIT | BALANCE | |
|------|------|------------|-------|--------|---------|---|
| | | | | | DEBIT | CREDIT |
| | | | | | | |
| | | | | | | |
| | | | | | | |

**Problem 12-11A (Concluded)**

## ACCOUNTS PAYABLE LEDGER

**NAME** Fantastic Toys

**ADDRESS**

| DATE | | ITEM | POST. REF. | DEBIT | CREDIT | BALANCE |
|---|---|---|---|---|---|---|
| 20--<br>May | 1 | Balance | ✓ | | | 5 2 0 0 00 |
| | | | | | | |
| | | | | | | |

**NAME** Goya Outlet

**ADDRESS**

| DATE | | ITEM | POST. REF. | DEBIT | CREDIT | BALANCE |
|---|---|---|---|---|---|---|
| 20--<br>May | 1 | Balance | ✓ | | | 3 8 0 0 00 |
| | | | | | | |
| | | | | | | |

**NAME** Mueller's Distributors

**ADDRESS**

| DATE | | ITEM | POST. REF. | DEBIT | CREDIT | BALANCE |
|---|---|---|---|---|---|---|
| 20--<br>May | 1 | Balance | ✓ | | | 3 6 0 0 00 |
| | | | | | | |
| | | | | | | |

**NAME** Van Kooning

**ADDRESS**

| DATE | | ITEM | POST. REF. | DEBIT | CREDIT | BALANCE |
|---|---|---|---|---|---|---|
| 20--<br>May | 1 | Balance | ✓ | | | 7 4 0 0 00 |
| | | | | | | |
| | | | | | | |

**Problem 12-12A**

**1.**                                          **PURCHASES JOURNAL**                                     PAGE  7

| | DATE | INVOICE NO. | FROM WHOM PURCHASED | POST. REF. | PURCHASES DEBIT ACCTS. PAY. CREDIT | |
|---|---|---|---|---|---|---|
| 1 | | | | | | 1 |
| 2 | | | | | | 2 |
| 3 | | | | | | 3 |
| 4 | | | | | | 4 |
| 5 | | | | | | 5 |
| 6 | | | | | | 6 |
| 7 | | | | | | 7 |
| 8 | | | | | | 8 |
| 9 | | | | | | 9 |
| 10 | | | | | | 10 |

**CASH PAYMENTS JOURNAL**                                     PAGE  9

| | DATE | CK. NO. | ACCOUNT DEBITED | POST. REF. | GENERAL DEBIT | ACCOUNTS PAYABLE DEBIT | PURCHASES DEBIT | PURCHASES DISCOUNTS CREDIT | CASH CREDIT | |
|---|---|---|---|---|---|---|---|---|---|---|
| 1 | | | | | | | | | | 1 |
| 2 | | | | | | | | | | 2 |
| 3 | | | | | | | | | | 3 |
| 4 | | | | | | | | | | 4 |
| 5 | | | | | | | | | | 5 |
| 6 | | | | | | | | | | 6 |
| 7 | | | | | | | | | | 7 |
| 8 | | | | | | | | | | 8 |
| 9 | | | | | | | | | | 9 |
| 10 | | | | | | | | | | 10 |
| 11 | | | | | | | | | | 11 |
| 12 | | | | | | | | | | 12 |

**Problem 12-12A (Continued)**

## GENERAL JOURNAL

PAGE  3

| | DATE | DESCRIPTION | POST. REF. | DEBIT | CREDIT | |
|---|---|---|---|---|---|---|
| 1 | | | | | | 1 |
| 2 | | | | | | 2 |
| 3 | | | | | | 3 |
| 4 | | | | | | 4 |
| 5 | | | | | | 5 |
| 6 | | | | | | 6 |
| 7 | | | | | | 7 |
| 8 | | | | | | 8 |
| 9 | | | | | | 9 |
| 10 | | | | | | 10 |

**2.**

## GENERAL LEDGER

ACCOUNT   Cash                                                    ACCOUNT NO.   101

| DATE | ITEM | POST. REF. | DEBIT | CREDIT | BALANCE DEBIT | BALANCE CREDIT |
|---|---|---|---|---|---|---|
| 20-- July 1 | Balance | ✓ | | | 20 0 0 0 00 | |
| | | | | | | |
| | | | | | | |
| | | | | | | |
| | | | | | | |
| | | | | | | |

ACCOUNT   Accounts Payable                                        ACCOUNT NO.   202

| DATE | ITEM | POST. REF. | DEBIT | CREDIT | BALANCE DEBIT | BALANCE CREDIT |
|---|---|---|---|---|---|---|
| | | | | | | |
| | | | | | | |
| | | | | | | |
| | | | | | | |
| | | | | | | |
| | | | | | | |

## Problem 12-12A (Continued)

ACCOUNT   F. Flint, Drawing                                                                          ACCOUNT NO.   312

| DATE | ITEM | POST. REF. | DEBIT | CREDIT | BALANCE | |
|------|------|-----------|-------|--------|---------|--------|
| | | | | | DEBIT | CREDIT |
| | | | | | | |
| | | | | | | |
| | | | | | | |
| | | | | | | |
| | | | | | | |

ACCOUNT   Purchases                                                                          ACCOUNT NO.   501

| DATE | ITEM | POST. REF. | DEBIT | CREDIT | BALANCE | |
|------|------|-----------|-------|--------|---------|--------|
| | | | | | DEBIT | CREDIT |
| | | | | | | |
| | | | | | | |
| | | | | | | |
| | | | | | | |
| | | | | | | |

ACCOUNT   Purchases Returns and Allowances                                         ACCOUNT NO.   501.1

| DATE | ITEM | POST. REF. | DEBIT | CREDIT | BALANCE | |
|------|------|-----------|-------|--------|---------|--------|
| | | | | | DEBIT | CREDIT |
| | | | | | | |
| | | | | | | |
| | | | | | | |
| | | | | | | |
| | | | | | | |

ACCOUNT   Purchases Discounts                                                           ACCOUNT NO.   501.2

| DATE | ITEM | POST. REF. | DEBIT | CREDIT | BALANCE | |
|------|------|-----------|-------|--------|---------|--------|
| | | | | | DEBIT | CREDIT |
| | | | | | | |
| | | | | | | |
| | | | | | | |
| | | | | | | |

ACCOUNT   Rent Expense                                                                    ACCOUNT NO.   521

| DATE | ITEM | POST. REF. | DEBIT | CREDIT | BALANCE | |
|------|------|-----------|-------|--------|---------|--------|
| | | | | | DEBIT | CREDIT |
| | | | | | | |
| | | | | | | |
| | | | | | | |
| | | | | | | |

**Problem 12-12A (Concluded)**

## ACCOUNTS PAYABLE LEDGER

**NAME** _____

**ADDRESS** _____

| DATE | ITEM | POST. REF. | DEBIT | CREDIT | BALANCE |
|------|------|-----------|-------|--------|---------|
|      |      |           |       |        |         |
|      |      |           |       |        |         |
|      |      |           |       |        |         |
|      |      |           |       |        |         |

**NAME** _____

**ADDRESS** _____

| DATE | ITEM | POST. REF. | DEBIT | CREDIT | BALANCE |
|------|------|-----------|-------|--------|---------|
|      |      |           |       |        |         |
|      |      |           |       |        |         |
|      |      |           |       |        |         |
|      |      |           |       |        |         |

**NAME** _____

**ADDRESS** _____

| DATE | ITEM | POST. REF. | DEBIT | CREDIT | BALANCE |
|------|------|-----------|-------|--------|---------|
|      |      |           |       |        |         |
|      |      |           |       |        |         |
|      |      |           |       |        |         |
|      |      |           |       |        |         |

**NAME** _____

**ADDRESS** _____

| DATE | ITEM | POST. REF. | DEBIT | CREDIT | BALANCE |
|------|------|-----------|-------|--------|---------|
|      |      |           |       |        |         |
|      |      |           |       |        |         |
|      |      |           |       |        |         |
|      |      |           |       |        |         |

### Exercise 12-1B

**Journal**

a.  Issued credit memo to customer for merchandise returned.  _____

b.  Sold merchandise for cash.  _____

c.  Purchased merchandise on account.  _____

d.  Issued checks to employees in payment of wages.  _____

e.  Purchased factory supplies on account.  _____

f.  Sold merchandise on account.  _____

### Exercise 12-2B

**SALES JOURNAL**  PAGE

| DATE | SALE NO. | TO WHOM SOLD | POST. REF. | ACCOUNTS RECEIVABLE DEBIT | SALES CREDIT | SALES TAX PAYABLE CREDIT |
|------|----------|--------------|------------|---------------------------|--------------|--------------------------|
|      |          |              |            |                           |              |                          |
|      |          |              |            |                           |              |                          |
|      |          |              |            |                           |              |                          |
|      |          |              |            |                           |              |                          |
|      |          |              |            |                           |              |                          |
|      |          |              |            |                           |              |                          |
|      |          |              |            |                           |              |                          |
|      |          |              |            |                           |              |                          |

### Exercise 12-3B

**CASH RECEIPTS JOURNAL**  PAGE

| | DATE | ACCOUNT CREDITED | POST. REF. | GENERAL CREDIT | ACCOUNTS RECEIVABLE CREDIT | SALES CREDIT | SALES TAX PAYABLE CREDIT | CASH DEBIT | |
|---|------|------------------|------------|----------------|----------------------------|--------------|--------------------------|------------|---|
| 1 |  |  |  |  |  |  |  |  | 1 |
| 2 |  |  |  |  |  |  |  |  | 2 |
| 3 |  |  |  |  |  |  |  |  | 3 |
| 4 |  |  |  |  |  |  |  |  | 4 |
| 5 |  |  |  |  |  |  |  |  | 5 |
| 6 |  |  |  |  |  |  |  |  | 6 |
| 7 |  |  |  |  |  |  |  |  | 7 |
| 8 |  |  |  |  |  |  |  |  | 8 |
| 9 |  |  |  |  |  |  |  |  | 9 |
| 10 |  |  |  |  |  |  |  |  | 10 |
| 11 |  |  |  |  |  |  |  |  | 11 |

**Exercise 12-4B**

## PURCHASES JOURNAL

PAGE _____

| | DATE | INVOICE NO. | FROM WHOM PURCHASED | POST. REF. | PURCHASES DEBIT ACCTS. PAY. CREDIT | |
|---|---|---|---|---|---|---|
| 1 | | | | | | 1 |
| 2 | | | | | | 2 |
| 3 | | | | | | 3 |
| 4 | | | | | | 4 |
| 5 | | | | | | 5 |
| 6 | | | | | | 6 |
| 7 | | | | | | 7 |
| 8 | | | | | | 8 |
| 9 | | | | | | 9 |
| 10 | | | | | | 10 |
| 11 | | | | | | 11 |

**Exercise 12-5B**

## CASH PAYMENTS JOURNAL

PAGE _____

| | DATE | CK. NO. | ACCOUNT DEBITED | POST. REF. | GENERAL DEBIT | ACCOUNTS PAYABLE DEBIT | PURCHASES DEBIT | PURCHASES DISCOUNTS CREDIT | CASH CREDIT | |
|---|---|---|---|---|---|---|---|---|---|---|
| 1 | | | | | | | | | | 1 |
| 2 | | | | | | | | | | 2 |
| 3 | | | | | | | | | | 3 |
| 4 | | | | | | | | | | 4 |
| 5 | | | | | | | | | | 5 |
| 6 | | | | | | | | | | 6 |
| 7 | | | | | | | | | | 7 |
| 8 | | | | | | | | | | 8 |
| 9 | | | | | | | | | | 9 |
| 10 | | | | | | | | | | 10 |
| 11 | | | | | | | | | | 11 |
| 12 | | | | | | | | | | 12 |
| 13 | | | | | | | | | | 13 |

## Problem 12-6B

**1.**

**SALES JOURNAL**  PAGE 8

| DATE | SALE NO. | TO WHOM SOLD | POST. REF. | ACCOUNTS RECEIVABLE DEBIT | SALES CREDIT | SALES TAX PAYABLE CREDIT |
|------|----------|--------------|-----------|---------------------------|--------------|--------------------------|
| | | | | | | |
| | | | | | | |
| | | | | | | |
| | | | | | | |
| | | | | | | |
| | | | | | | |
| | | | | | | |
| | | | | | | |
| | | | | | | |

**2.**

## GENERAL LEDGER

ACCOUNT  Accounts Receivable  ACCOUNT NO. 122

| DATE | ITEM | POST. REF. | DEBIT | CREDIT | BALANCE DEBIT | CREDIT |
|------|------|-----------|-------|--------|---------------|--------|
| | | | | | | |
| | | | | | | |
| | | | | | | |

ACCOUNT  Sales Tax Payable  ACCOUNT NO. 231

| DATE | ITEM | POST. REF. | DEBIT | CREDIT | BALANCE DEBIT | CREDIT |
|------|------|-----------|-------|--------|---------------|--------|
| | | | | | | |
| | | | | | | |
| | | | | | | |

## Problem 12-6B (Concluded)

ACCOUNT   Sales                                                                    ACCOUNT NO.   401

| DATE | ITEM | POST. REF. | DEBIT | CREDIT | BALANCE DEBIT | BALANCE CREDIT |
|------|------|-----------|-------|--------|-------|--------|
|      |      |           |       |        |       |        |
|      |      |           |       |        |       |        |
|      |      |           |       |        |       |        |

### ACCOUNTS RECEIVABLE LEDGER

**NAME**  Dvorak Manufacturing Co.

**ADDRESS**  2105 Williams Drive, Muncie, IN 47304-2437

| DATE | ITEM | POST. REF. | DEBIT | CREDIT | BALANCE |
|------|------|-----------|-------|--------|---------|
|      |      |           |       |        |         |
|      |      |           |       |        |         |
|      |      |           |       |        |         |

**NAME**  Saga, Inc.

**ADDRESS**  1453 Parnell Avenue, Indianapolis, IN 46201-6870

| DATE | ITEM | POST. REF. | DEBIT | CREDIT | BALANCE |
|------|------|-----------|-------|--------|---------|
|      |      |           |       |        |         |
|      |      |           |       |        |         |
|      |      |           |       |        |         |

**NAME**  Vinnie Ward

**ADDRESS**  308 So. Muirhead Drive, Okemos, MI 48864-5356

| DATE | ITEM | POST. REF. | DEBIT | CREDIT | BALANCE |
|------|------|-----------|-------|--------|---------|
|      |      |           |       |        |         |
|      |      |           |       |        |         |
|      |      |           |       |        |         |

**NAME**  Zapata Co.

**ADDRESS**  789 N. Stafford Dr., Bloomington, IN 47401-6201

| DATE | ITEM | POST. REF. | DEBIT | CREDIT | BALANCE |
|------|------|-----------|-------|--------|---------|
|      |      |           |       |        |         |
|      |      |           |       |        |         |

**Problem 12-7B**

1.

## CASH RECEIPTS JOURNAL

| | DATE | | ACCOUNT CREDITED | POST. REF. | GENERAL CREDIT | | ACCOUNTS RECEIVABLE CREDIT | |
|---|---|---|---|---|---|---|---|---|
| 1 | | | | | | | | |
| 2 | | | | | | | | |
| 3 | | | | | | | | |
| 4 | | | | | | | | |
| 5 | | | | | | | | |
| 6 | | | | | | | | |
| 7 | | | | | | | | |
| 8 | | | | | | | | |
| 9 | | | | | | | | |
| 10 | | | | | | | | |
| 11 | | | | | | | | |
| 12 | | | | | | | | |
| 13 | | | | | | | | |
| 14 | | | | | | | | |
| 15 | | | | | | | | |
| 16 | | | | | | | | |
| 17 | | | | | | | | |
| 18 | | | | | | | | |
| 19 | | | | | | | | |
| 20 | | | | | | | | |
| 21 | | | | | | | | |
| 22 | | | | | | | | |
| 23 | | | | | | | | |
| 24 | | | | | | | | |
| 25 | | | | | | | | |
| 26 | | | | | | | | |
| 27 | | | | | | | | |
| 28 | | | | | | | | |

## Problem 12-7B (Continued)

PAGE  10

| SALES CREDIT | | | | SALES TAX PAYABLE CREDIT | | | | BANK CREDIT CARD EXPENSE DEBIT | | | | CASH DEBIT | | | | |
|---|---|---|---|---|---|---|---|---|---|---|---|---|---|---|---|---|
| | | | | | | | | | | | | | | | | 1 |
| | | | | | | | | | | | | | | | | 2 |
| | | | | | | | | | | | | | | | | 3 |
| | | | | | | | | | | | | | | | | 4 |
| | | | | | | | | | | | | | | | | 5 |
| | | | | | | | | | | | | | | | | 6 |
| | | | | | | | | | | | | | | | | 7 |
| | | | | | | | | | | | | | | | | 8 |
| | | | | | | | | | | | | | | | | 9 |
| | | | | | | | | | | | | | | | | 10 |
| | | | | | | | | | | | | | | | | 11 |
| | | | | | | | | | | | | | | | | 12 |
| | | | | | | | | | | | | | | | | 13 |
| | | | | | | | | | | | | | | | | 14 |
| | | | | | | | | | | | | | | | | 15 |
| | | | | | | | | | | | | | | | | 16 |
| | | | | | | | | | | | | | | | | 17 |
| | | | | | | | | | | | | | | | | 18 |
| | | | | | | | | | | | | | | | | 19 |
| | | | | | | | | | | | | | | | | 20 |
| | | | | | | | | | | | | | | | | 21 |
| | | | | | | | | | | | | | | | | 22 |
| | | | | | | | | | | | | | | | | 23 |
| | | | | | | | | | | | | | | | | 24 |
| | | | | | | | | | | | | | | | | 25 |
| | | | | | | | | | | | | | | | | 26 |
| | | | | | | | | | | | | | | | | 27 |
| | | | | | | | | | | | | | | | | 28 |

## Problem 12-7B (Continued)

### GENERAL JOURNAL

| | DATE | DESCRIPTION | POST. REF. | DEBIT | CREDIT | |
|---|---|---|---|---|---|---|
| 1 | | | | | | 1 |
| 2 | | | | | | 2 |
| 3 | | | | | | 3 |
| 4 | | | | | | 4 |
| 5 | | | | | | 5 |
| 6 | | | | | | 6 |
| 7 | | | | | | 7 |
| 8 | | | | | | 8 |
| 9 | | | | | | 9 |
| 10 | | | | | | 10 |
| 11 | | | | | | 11 |
| 12 | | | | | | 12 |
| 13 | | | | | | 13 |
| 14 | | | | | | 14 |
| 15 | | | | | | 15 |
| 16 | | | | | | 16 |
| 17 | | | | | | 17 |
| 18 | | | | | | 18 |
| 19 | | | | | | 19 |
| 20 | | | | | | 20 |
| 21 | | | | | | 21 |
| 22 | | | | | | 22 |
| 23 | | | | | | 23 |
| 24 | | | | | | 24 |
| 25 | | | | | | 25 |
| 26 | | | | | | 26 |
| 27 | | | | | | 27 |
| 28 | | | | | | 28 |
| 29 | | | | | | 29 |
| 30 | | | | | | 30 |
| 31 | | | | | | 31 |
| 32 | | | | | | 32 |
| 33 | | | | | | 33 |
| 34 | | | | | | 34 |

Name _____

**Problem 12-7B (Continued)**

2.

## GENERAL LEDGER

ACCOUNT  Cash                                        ACCOUNT NO.  101

| DATE | | ITEM | POST. REF. | DEBIT | CREDIT | BALANCE DEBIT | BALANCE CREDIT |
|---|---|---|---|---|---|---|---|
| 20-- Jan. | 1 | Balance | ✓ | | | 2 8 9 0 75 | |
| | | | | | | | |
| | | | | | | | |
| | | | | | | | |

ACCOUNT  Accounts Receivable                          ACCOUNT NO.  122

| DATE | | ITEM | POST. REF. | DEBIT | CREDIT | BALANCE DEBIT | BALANCE CREDIT |
|---|---|---|---|---|---|---|---|
| 20-- Jan. | 1 | Balance | ✓ | | | 6 3 0 0 00 | |
| | | | | | | | |
| | | | | | | | |

ACCOUNT  Sales Tax Payable                            ACCOUNT NO.  231

| DATE | ITEM | POST. REF. | DEBIT | CREDIT | BALANCE DEBIT | BALANCE CREDIT |
|---|---|---|---|---|---|---|

ACCOUNT  Sales                                        ACCOUNT NO.  401

| DATE | ITEM | POST. REF. | DEBIT | CREDIT | BALANCE DEBIT | BALANCE CREDIT |
|---|---|---|---|---|---|---|

## Problem 12-7B (Continued)

ACCOUNT  Sales Returns and Allowances          ACCOUNT NO.  401.1

| DATE | ITEM | POST. REF. | DEBIT | CREDIT | BALANCE DEBIT | BALANCE CREDIT |
|---|---|---|---|---|---|---|
| | | | | | | |
| | | | | | | |
| | | | | | | |

ACCOUNT  Bank Credit Card Expense          ACCOUNT NO.  513

| DATE | ITEM | POST. REF. | DEBIT | CREDIT | BALANCE DEBIT | BALANCE CREDIT |
|---|---|---|---|---|---|---|
| | | | | | | |
| | | | | | | |
| | | | | | | |
| | | | | | | |

### ACCOUNTS RECEIVABLE LEDGER

**NAME** Ray Boyd

**ADDRESS** 229 SE 65th Avenue, Portland, OR 97215-1451

| DATE | ITEM | POST. REF. | DEBIT | CREDIT | BALANCE |
|---|---|---|---|---|---|
| 20-- Jan. 1 | Balance | ✓ | | | 1 4 0 0 00 |
| | | | | | |
| | | | | | |
| | | | | | |
| | | | | | |

**NAME** Dazai Manufacturing

**ADDRESS** 447 6th Avenue, Flagstaff, AZ 86004-6842

| DATE | ITEM | POST. REF. | DEBIT | CREDIT | BALANCE |
|---|---|---|---|---|---|
| 20-- Jan. 1 | Balance | ✓ | | | 3 1 8 00 |
| | | | | | |
| | | | | | |
| | | | | | |
| | | | | | |

**Problem 12-7B (Concluded)**

**NAME** Clint Hassell

**ADDRESS** 1462 N. Steves Blvd., Los Cruces, NM 88012-7791

| DATE | | ITEM | POST. REF. | DEBIT | CREDIT | BALANCE |
|---|---|---|---|---|---|---|
| 20-- Jan. | 1 | Balance | ✓ | | | 8 1 5 00 |
| | | | | | | |
| | | | | | | |
| | | | | | | |
| | | | | | | |

**NAME** Jan Sowada

**ADDRESS** 5997 Blackgold Lane, Grapevine, TX 76051-2366

| DATE | | ITEM | POST. REF. | DEBIT | CREDIT | BALANCE |
|---|---|---|---|---|---|---|
| 20-- Jan. | 1 | Balance | ✓ | | | 1 4 8 1 00 |
| | | | | | | |
| | | | | | | |
| | | | | | | |
| | | | | | | |

**NAME** Robert Zehnle

**ADDRESS** 6881 Seneca Drive, San Diego, CA 92127-8671

| DATE | | ITEM | POST. REF. | DEBIT | CREDIT | BALANCE |
|---|---|---|---|---|---|---|
| 20-- Jan. | 1 | Balance | ✓ | | | 2 2 8 6 00 |
| | | | | | | |
| | | | | | | |
| | | | | | | |

## Problem 12-8B

**1.**

### SALES JOURNAL

| DATE | SALE NO. | TO WHOM SOLD | POST. REF. | ACCOUNTS RECEIVABLE DEBIT | SALES CREDIT | SALES TAX PAYABLE CREDIT |
|------|----------|--------------|------------|---------------------------|--------------|--------------------------|
|  |  |  |  |  |  |  |
|  |  |  |  |  |  |  |
|  |  |  |  |  |  |  |
|  |  |  |  |  |  |  |
|  |  |  |  |  |  |  |
|  |  |  |  |  |  |  |
|  |  |  |  |  |  |  |
|  |  |  |  |  |  |  |

### CASH RECEIPTS JOURNAL

| | DATE | ACCOUNT CREDITED | POST. REF. | GENERAL CREDIT | ACCOUNTS RECEIVABLE CREDIT | SALES CREDIT | SALES TAX PAYABLE CREDIT | CASH DEBIT | |
|---|------|------------------|------------|----------------|----------------------------|--------------|--------------------------|------------|---|
| 1 |  |  |  |  |  |  |  |  | 1 |
| 2 |  |  |  |  |  |  |  |  | 2 |
| 3 |  |  |  |  |  |  |  |  | 3 |
| 4 |  |  |  |  |  |  |  |  | 4 |
| 5 |  |  |  |  |  |  |  |  | 5 |
| 6 |  |  |  |  |  |  |  |  | 6 |
| 7 |  |  |  |  |  |  |  |  | 7 |
| 8 |  |  |  |  |  |  |  |  | 8 |
| 9 |  |  |  |  |  |  |  |  | 9 |

**Problem 12-8B (Continued)**

## GENERAL JOURNAL

PAGE 5

| | DATE | DESCRIPTION | POST. REF. | DEBIT | CREDIT | |
|---|---|---|---|---|---|---|
| 1 | | | | | | 1 |
| 2 | | | | | | 2 |
| 3 | | | | | | 3 |
| 4 | | | | | | 4 |
| 5 | | | | | | 5 |
| 6 | | | | | | 6 |
| 7 | | | | | | 7 |
| 8 | | | | | | 8 |
| 9 | | | | | | 9 |
| 10 | | | | | | 10 |
| 11 | | | | | | 11 |
| 12 | | | | | | 12 |
| 13 | | | | | | 13 |
| 14 | | | | | | 14 |

**2.**

## GENERAL LEDGER

ACCOUNT  Cash    ACCOUNT NO.  101

| DATE | ITEM | POST. REF. | DEBIT | CREDIT | BALANCE DEBIT | BALANCE CREDIT |
|---|---|---|---|---|---|---|
| 20-- Apr. 1 | Balance | ✓ | | | 2 8 6 4 54 | |

ACCOUNT  Accounts Receivable    ACCOUNT NO.  122

| DATE | ITEM | POST. REF. | DEBIT | CREDIT | BALANCE DEBIT | BALANCE CREDIT |
|---|---|---|---|---|---|---|
| 20-- Apr. 1 | Balance | ✓ | | | 2 7 2 6 25 | |

## Problem 12-8B (Continued)

ACCOUNT   Sales Tax Payable                                          ACCOUNT NO.   231

| DATE | ITEM | POST. REF. | DEBIT | CREDIT | BALANCE DEBIT | BALANCE CREDIT |
|------|------|------------|-------|--------|-------|--------|
|  |  |  |  |  |  |  |
|  |  |  |  |  |  |  |
|  |  |  |  |  |  |  |
|  |  |  |  |  |  |  |
|  |  |  |  |  |  |  |
|  |  |  |  |  |  |  |
|  |  |  |  |  |  |  |
|  |  |  |  |  |  |  |

ACCOUNT   Sales                                                     ACCOUNT NO.   401

| DATE | ITEM | POST. REF. | DEBIT | CREDIT | BALANCE DEBIT | BALANCE CREDIT |
|------|------|------------|-------|--------|-------|--------|
|  |  |  |  |  |  |  |
|  |  |  |  |  |  |  |
|  |  |  |  |  |  |  |
|  |  |  |  |  |  |  |
|  |  |  |  |  |  |  |
|  |  |  |  |  |  |  |
|  |  |  |  |  |  |  |

ACCOUNT   Sales Returns and Allowances                              ACCOUNT NO.   401.1

| DATE | ITEM | POST. REF. | DEBIT | CREDIT | BALANCE DEBIT | BALANCE CREDIT |
|------|------|------------|-------|--------|-------|--------|
|  |  |  |  |  |  |  |
|  |  |  |  |  |  |  |
|  |  |  |  |  |  |  |
|  |  |  |  |  |  |  |
|  |  |  |  |  |  |  |
|  |  |  |  |  |  |  |

## Problem 12-8B (Concluded)

### ACCOUNTS RECEIVABLE LEDGER

**NAME** O. L. Meyers

**ADDRESS** 119 Hartford Turnpike, Vernon, CT 06066-0113

| DATE | | ITEM | POST. REF. | DEBIT | CREDIT | BALANCE |
|---|---|---|---|---|---|---|
| 20--<br>Apr. | 1 | Balance | ✓ | | | 2 1 8 6 00 |
| | | | | | | |
| | | | | | | |
| | | | | | | |
| | | | | | | |

**NAME** Kelsay Munkres

**ADDRESS** 233 Cambridge Dr., Branford, CT 06405-9276

| DATE | | ITEM | POST. REF. | DEBIT | CREDIT | BALANCE |
|---|---|---|---|---|---|---|
| 20--<br>Apr. | 1 | Balance | ✓ | | | 4 8 2 00 |
| | | | | | | |
| | | | | | | |
| | | | | | | |
| | | | | | | |

**NAME** Andrew Plaa

**ADDRESS** 51 Bissell Ave., Old Saybrook, CT 06475-0212

| DATE | | ITEM | POST. REF. | DEBIT | CREDIT | BALANCE |
|---|---|---|---|---|---|---|
| | | | | | | |
| | | | | | | |
| | | | | | | |
| | | | | | | |
| | | | | | | |

**NAME** Melissa Richfield

**ADDRESS** 1107 Silver Lane, East Hartford, CT 06108-1907

| DATE | | ITEM | POST. REF. | DEBIT | CREDIT | BALANCE |
|---|---|---|---|---|---|---|
| 20--<br>Apr. | 1 | Balance | ✓ | | | 5 8 25 |
| | | | | | | |
| | | | | | | |
| | | | | | | |

## Problem 12-9B

**1.**

**PURCHASES JOURNAL**                                   PAGE  7

| | DATE | INVOICE NO. | FROM WHOM PURCHASED | POST. REF. | PURCHASES DEBIT ACCTS. PAY. CREDIT | |
|---|---|---|---|---|---|---|
| 1 | | | | | | 1 |
| 2 | | | | | | 2 |
| 3 | | | | | | 3 |
| 4 | | | | | | 4 |
| 5 | | | | | | 5 |
| 6 | | | | | | 6 |
| 7 | | | | | | 7 |
| 8 | | | | | | 8 |
| 9 | | | | | | 9 |
| 10 | | | | | | 10 |
| 11 | | | | | | 11 |
| 12 | | | | | | 12 |
| 13 | | | | | | 13 |
| 14 | | | | | | 14 |

**2.**

### GENERAL LEDGER

ACCOUNT  Accounts Payable                      ACCOUNT NO.  202

| DATE | ITEM | POST. REF. | DEBIT | CREDIT | BALANCE DEBIT | BALANCE CREDIT |
|---|---|---|---|---|---|---|
| | | | | | | |
| | | | | | | |
| | | | | | | |
| | | | | | | |

ACCOUNT  Purchases                             ACCOUNT NO.  501

| DATE | ITEM | POST. REF. | DEBIT | CREDIT | BALANCE DEBIT | BALANCE CREDIT |
|---|---|---|---|---|---|---|
| | | | | | | |
| | | | | | | |
| | | | | | | |
| | | | | | | |

**Problem 12-9B (Concluded)**

## ACCOUNTS PAYABLE LEDGER

**NAME**

**ADDRESS**

| DATE | ITEM | POST. REF. | DEBIT | CREDIT | BALANCE |
|------|------|------------|-------|--------|---------|
| | | | | | |
| | | | | | |
| | | | | | |

**NAME**

**ADDRESS**

| DATE | ITEM | POST. REF. | DEBIT | CREDIT | BALANCE |
|------|------|------------|-------|--------|---------|
| | | | | | |
| | | | | | |
| | | | | | |

**NAME**

**ADDRESS**

| DATE | ITEM | POST. REF. | DEBIT | CREDIT | BALANCE |
|------|------|------------|-------|--------|---------|
| | | | | | |
| | | | | | |
| | | | | | |

**NAME**

**ADDRESS**

| DATE | ITEM | POST. REF. | DEBIT | CREDIT | BALANCE |
|------|------|------------|-------|--------|---------|
| | | | | | |
| | | | | | |
| | | | | | |

**NAME**

**ADDRESS**

| DATE | ITEM | POST. REF. | DEBIT | CREDIT | BALANCE |
|------|------|------------|-------|--------|---------|
| | | | | | |
| | | | | | |
| | | | | | |

## Problem 12-10B

**1.**

## GENERAL LEDGER

ACCOUNT   Accounts Payable                                          ACCOUNT NO.   202

| DATE | ITEM | POST. REF. | DEBIT | CREDIT | BALANCE | |
|------|------|-----------|-------|--------|---------|---|
| | | | | | DEBIT | CREDIT |
| | | | | | | |
| | | | | | | |
| | | | | | | |
| | | | | | | |

ACCOUNT   Purchases                                                 ACCOUNT NO.   501

| DATE | ITEM | POST. REF. | DEBIT | CREDIT | BALANCE | |
|------|------|-----------|-------|--------|---------|---|
| | | | | | DEBIT | CREDIT |
| | | | | | | |
| | | | | | | |
| | | | | | | |
| | | | | | | |

**2.**

## ACCOUNTS PAYABLE LEDGER

**NAME**

**ADDRESS**

| DATE | ITEM | POST. REF. | DEBIT | CREDIT | BALANCE |
|------|------|-----------|-------|--------|---------|
| | | | | | |
| | | | | | |
| | | | | | |
| | | | | | |

**NAME**

**ADDRESS**

| DATE | ITEM | POST. REF. | DEBIT | CREDIT | BALANCE |
|------|------|-----------|-------|--------|---------|
| | | | | | |
| | | | | | |
| | | | | | |
| | | | | | |

**Problem 12-10B (Concluded)**

**NAME** _____

**ADDRESS** _____

| DATE | | ITEM | POST. REF. | DEBIT | CREDIT | BALANCE |
|---|---|---|---|---|---|---|
| | | | | | | |
| | | | | | | |
| | | | | | | |
| | | | | | | |
| | | | | | | |

**NAME** _____

**ADDRESS** _____

| DATE | | ITEM | POST. REF. | DEBIT | CREDIT | BALANCE |
|---|---|---|---|---|---|---|
| | | | | | | |
| | | | | | | |
| | | | | | | |
| | | | | | | |
| | | | | | | |

**NAME** _____

**ADDRESS** _____

| DATE | | ITEM | POST. REF. | DEBIT | CREDIT | BALANCE |
|---|---|---|---|---|---|---|
| | | | | | | |
| | | | | | | |
| | | | | | | |
| | | | | | | |

## Problem 12-11B

**1.**

**CASH PAYMENTS JOURNAL**                                                    PAGE 6

| | DATE | CK. NO. | ACCOUNT DEBITED | POST. REF. | GENERAL DEBIT | ACCOUNTS PAYABLE DEBIT | PURCHASES DEBIT | PURCHASES DISCOUNTS CREDIT | CASH CREDIT | |
|---|---|---|---|---|---|---|---|---|---|---|
| 1 | | | | | | | | | | 1 |
| 2 | | | | | | | | | | 2 |
| 3 | | | | | | | | | | 3 |
| 4 | | | | | | | | | | 4 |
| 5 | | | | | | | | | | 5 |
| 6 | | | | | | | | | | 6 |
| 7 | | | | | | | | | | 7 |
| 8 | | | | | | | | | | 8 |
| 9 | | | | | | | | | | 9 |
| 10 | | | | | | | | | | 10 |
| 11 | | | | | | | | | | 11 |
| 12 | | | | | | | | | | 12 |

**2.**

## GENERAL LEDGER

ACCOUNT  Cash                                                      ACCOUNT NO. 101

| DATE | | ITEM | POST. REF. | DEBIT | CREDIT | BALANCE DEBIT | BALANCE CREDIT |
|---|---|---|---|---|---|---|---|
| 20-- May | 1 | Balance | ✓ | | | 40 0 0 0 00 | |
| | | | | | | | |
| | | | | | | | |

ACCOUNT  Accounts Payable                                          ACCOUNT NO. 202

| DATE | | ITEM | POST. REF. | DEBIT | CREDIT | BALANCE DEBIT | BALANCE CREDIT |
|---|---|---|---|---|---|---|---|
| 20-- May | 1 | Balance | ✓ | | | | 20 0 0 0 00 |
| | | | | | | | |
| | | | | | | | |

**Problem 12-11B (Continued)**

ACCOUNT    Purchases                                                            ACCOUNT NO.    501

| DATE | ITEM | POST. REF. | DEBIT | CREDIT | BALANCE | |
|------|------|-----------|-------|--------|---------|--|
| | | | | | DEBIT | CREDIT |
| | | | | | | |
| | | | | | | |
| | | | | | | |
| | | | | | | |

ACCOUNT    Purchases Discounts                                                  ACCOUNT NO.    501.2

| DATE | ITEM | POST. REF. | DEBIT | CREDIT | BALANCE | |
|------|------|-----------|-------|--------|---------|--|
| | | | | | DEBIT | CREDIT |
| | | | | | | |
| | | | | | | |
| | | | | | | |
| | | | | | | |

ACCOUNT    Freight-In                                                           ACCOUNT NO.    502

| DATE | ITEM | POST. REF. | DEBIT | CREDIT | BALANCE | |
|------|------|-----------|-------|--------|---------|--|
| | | | | | DEBIT | CREDIT |
| | | | | | | |
| | | | | | | |
| | | | | | | |

ACCOUNT    Rent Expense                                                         ACCOUNT NO.    521

| DATE | ITEM | POST. REF. | DEBIT | CREDIT | BALANCE | |
|------|------|-----------|-------|--------|---------|--|
| | | | | | DEBIT | CREDIT |
| | | | | | | |
| | | | | | | |
| | | | | | | |

ACCOUNT    Utilities Expense                                                    ACCOUNT NO.    533

| DATE | ITEM | POST. REF. | DEBIT | CREDIT | BALANCE | |
|------|------|-----------|-------|--------|---------|--|
| | | | | | DEBIT | CREDIT |
| | | | | | | |
| | | | | | | |
| | | | | | | |

## Problem 12-11B (Concluded)

### ACCOUNTS PAYABLE LEDGER

**NAME**  Cortez Distributors

**ADDRESS**

| DATE | | ITEM | POST. REF. | DEBIT | CREDIT | BALANCE |
|---|---|---|---|---|---|---|
| 20--<br>May | 1 | Balance | ✓ | | | 4 2 0 0 00 |
| | | | | | | |
| | | | | | | |
| | | | | | | |

**NAME**  Indra & Velga

**ADDRESS**

| DATE | | ITEM | POST. REF. | DEBIT | CREDIT | BALANCE |
|---|---|---|---|---|---|---|
| 20--<br>May | 1 | Balance | ✓ | | | 6 8 0 0 00 |
| | | | | | | |
| | | | | | | |
| | | | | | | |

**NAME**  Toy Corner

**ADDRESS**

| DATE | | ITEM | POST. REF. | DEBIT | CREDIT | BALANCE |
|---|---|---|---|---|---|---|
| 20--<br>May | 1 | Balance | ✓ | | | 4 6 0 0 00 |
| | | | | | | |
| | | | | | | |
| | | | | | | |

**NAME**  Troutman Outlet

**ADDRESS**

| DATE | | ITEM | POST. REF. | DEBIT | CREDIT | BALANCE |
|---|---|---|---|---|---|---|
| 20--<br>May | 1 | Balance | ✓ | | | 4 4 0 0 00 |
| | | | | | | |
| | | | | | | |
| | | | | | | |

**Problem 12-12B**

**1.**

## PURCHASES JOURNAL

| | DATE | INVOICE NO. | FROM WHOM PURCHASED | POST. REF. | PURCHASES DEBIT ACCTS. PAY. CREDIT | |
|---|---|---|---|---|---|---|
| 1 | | | | | | 1 |
| 2 | | | | | | 2 |
| 3 | | | | | | 3 |
| 4 | | | | | | 4 |
| 5 | | | | | | 5 |
| 6 | | | | | | 6 |
| 7 | | | | | | 7 |
| 8 | | | | | | 8 |
| 9 | | | | | | 9 |
| 10 | | | | | | 10 |

## CASH PAYMENTS JOURNAL

| | DATE | CK. NO. | ACCOUNT DEBITED | POST. REF. | GENERAL DEBIT | ACCOUNTS PAYABLE DEBIT | PURCHASES DEBIT | PURCHASES DISCOUNTS CREDIT | CASH CREDIT | |
|---|---|---|---|---|---|---|---|---|---|---|
| 1 | | | | | | | | | | 1 |
| 2 | | | | | | | | | | 2 |
| 3 | | | | | | | | | | 3 |
| 4 | | | | | | | | | | 4 |
| 5 | | | | | | | | | | 5 |
| 6 | | | | | | | | | | 6 |
| 7 | | | | | | | | | | 7 |
| 8 | | | | | | | | | | 8 |
| 9 | | | | | | | | | | 9 |
| 10 | | | | | | | | | | 10 |
| 11 | | | | | | | | | | 11 |
| 12 | | | | | | | | | | 12 |

## Problem 12-12B (Continued)

**GENERAL JOURNAL**                                    PAGE  3

| | DATE | DESCRIPTION | POST. REF. | DEBIT | CREDIT | |
|---|---|---|---|---|---|---|
| 1 | | | | | | 1 |
| 2 | | | | | | 2 |
| 3 | | | | | | 3 |
| 4 | | | | | | 4 |
| 5 | | | | | | 5 |
| 6 | | | | | | 6 |
| 7 | | | | | | 7 |
| 8 | | | | | | 8 |
| 9 | | | | | | 9 |
| 10 | | | | | | 10 |

**2.**

### GENERAL LEDGER

ACCOUNT  Cash                              ACCOUNT NO.  101

| DATE | ITEM | POST. REF. | DEBIT | CREDIT | BALANCE DEBIT | BALANCE CREDIT |
|---|---|---|---|---|---|---|
| 20--<br>July 1 | Balance | ✓ | | | 20 0 0 0 00 | |
| | | | | | | |
| | | | | | | |
| | | | | | | |
| | | | | | | |

ACCOUNT  Accounts Payable                  ACCOUNT NO.  202

| DATE | ITEM | POST. REF. | DEBIT | CREDIT | BALANCE DEBIT | BALANCE CREDIT |
|---|---|---|---|---|---|---|
| | | | | | | |
| | | | | | | |
| | | | | | | |
| | | | | | | |
| | | | | | | |
| | | | | | | |

## Problem 12-12B (Continued)

ACCOUNT  D. Mueller, Drawing                                                      ACCOUNT NO.  312

| DATE | ITEM | POST. REF. | DEBIT | CREDIT | BALANCE DEBIT | BALANCE CREDIT |
|------|------|------------|-------|--------|---------------|----------------|
|      |      |            |       |        |               |                |
|      |      |            |       |        |               |                |
|      |      |            |       |        |               |                |
|      |      |            |       |        |               |                |

ACCOUNT  Purchases                                                                ACCOUNT NO.  501

| DATE | ITEM | POST. REF. | DEBIT | CREDIT | BALANCE DEBIT | BALANCE CREDIT |
|------|------|------------|-------|--------|---------------|----------------|
|      |      |            |       |        |               |                |
|      |      |            |       |        |               |                |
|      |      |            |       |        |               |                |
|      |      |            |       |        |               |                |
|      |      |            |       |        |               |                |

ACCOUNT  Purchases Returns and Allowances                                         ACCOUNT NO.  501.1

| DATE | ITEM | POST. REF. | DEBIT | CREDIT | BALANCE DEBIT | BALANCE CREDIT |
|------|------|------------|-------|--------|---------------|----------------|
|      |      |            |       |        |               |                |
|      |      |            |       |        |               |                |
|      |      |            |       |        |               |                |
|      |      |            |       |        |               |                |

ACCOUNT  Purchases Discounts                                                      ACCOUNT NO.  501.2

| DATE | ITEM | POST. REF. | DEBIT | CREDIT | BALANCE DEBIT | BALANCE CREDIT |
|------|------|------------|-------|--------|---------------|----------------|
|      |      |            |       |        |               |                |
|      |      |            |       |        |               |                |
|      |      |            |       |        |               |                |

ACCOUNT  Rent Expense                                                             ACCOUNT NO.  521

| DATE | ITEM | POST. REF. | DEBIT | CREDIT | BALANCE DEBIT | BALANCE CREDIT |
|------|------|------------|-------|--------|---------------|----------------|
|      |      |            |       |        |               |                |
|      |      |            |       |        |               |                |
|      |      |            |       |        |               |                |

## Problem 12-12B (Concluded)

### ACCOUNTS PAYABLE LEDGER

**NAME**

**ADDRESS**

| DATE | | ITEM | POST. REF. | DEBIT | CREDIT | BALANCE |
|------|--|------|-----------|-------|--------|---------|
| | | | | | | |
| | | | | | | |
| | | | | | | |
| | | | | | | |

**NAME**

**ADDRESS**

| DATE | | ITEM | POST. REF. | DEBIT | CREDIT | BALANCE |
|------|--|------|-----------|-------|--------|---------|
| | | | | | | |
| | | | | | | |
| | | | | | | |
| | | | | | | |

**NAME**

**ADDRESS**

| DATE | | ITEM | POST. REF. | DEBIT | CREDIT | BALANCE |
|------|--|------|-----------|-------|--------|---------|
| | | | | | | |
| | | | | | | |
| | | | | | | |
| | | | | | | |

**NAME**

**ADDRESS**

| DATE | | ITEM | POST. REF. | DEBIT | CREDIT | BALANCE |
|------|--|------|-----------|-------|--------|---------|
| | | | | | | |
| | | | | | | |
| | | | | | | |
| | | | | | | |

**Mastery Problem**

1.

## SALES JOURNAL

| | DATE | SALE NO. | TO WHOM SOLD | POST. REF. | ACCOUNTS RECEIVABLE DEBIT | SALES CREDIT | SALES TAX PAYABLE CREDIT | |
|---|---|---|---|---|---|---|---|---|
| 1 | | | | | | | | 1 |
| 2 | | | | | | | | 2 |
| 3 | | | | | | | | 3 |
| 4 | | | | | | | | 4 |
| 5 | | | | | | | | 5 |
| 6 | | | | | | | | 6 |
| 7 | | | | | | | | 7 |
| 8 | | | | | | | | 8 |

## CASH RECEIPTS JOURNAL

| | DATE | ACCOUNT CREDITED | POST. REF. | GENERAL CREDIT | ACCOUNTS RECEIVABLE CREDIT | SALES CREDIT | SALES TAX PAYABLE CREDIT | CASH DEBIT | |
|---|---|---|---|---|---|---|---|---|---|
| 1 | | | | | | | | | 1 |
| 2 | | | | | | | | | 2 |
| 3 | | | | | | | | | 3 |
| 4 | | | | | | | | | 4 |
| 5 | | | | | | | | | 5 |
| 6 | | | | | | | | | 6 |
| 7 | | | | | | | | | 7 |
| 8 | | | | | | | | | 8 |
| 9 | | | | | | | | | 9 |
| 10 | | | | | | | | | 10 |
| 11 | | | | | | | | | 11 |
| 12 | | | | | | | | | 12 |
| 13 | | | | | | | | | 13 |

## Mastery Problem (Continued)

**PURCHASES JOURNAL**

| | DATE | INVOICE NO. | FROM WHOM PURCHASED | POST. REF. | PURCHASES DEBIT ACCTS. PAY. CREDIT | |
|---|---|---|---|---|---|---|
| 1 | | | | | | 1 |
| 2 | | | | | | 2 |
| 3 | | | | | | 3 |
| 4 | | | | | | 4 |
| 5 | | | | | | 5 |
| 6 | | | | | | 6 |
| 7 | | | | | | 7 |
| 8 | | | | | | 8 |
| 9 | | | | | | 9 |
| 10 | | | | | | 10 |
| 11 | | | | | | 11 |

**CASH PAYMENTS JOURNAL**

| | DATE | CK. NO. | ACCOUNT DEBITED | POST. REF. | GENERAL DEBIT | ACCOUNTS PAYABLE DEBIT | PURCHASES DEBIT | PURCHASES DISCOUNTS CREDIT | CASH CREDIT | |
|---|---|---|---|---|---|---|---|---|---|---|
| 1 | | | | | | | | | | 1 |
| 2 | | | | | | | | | | 2 |
| 3 | | | | | | | | | | 3 |
| 4 | | | | | | | | | | 4 |
| 5 | | | | | | | | | | 5 |
| 6 | | | | | | | | | | 6 |
| 7 | | | | | | | | | | 7 |
| 8 | | | | | | | | | | 8 |
| 9 | | | | | | | | | | 9 |
| 10 | | | | | | | | | | 10 |
| 11 | | | | | | | | | | 11 |
| 12 | | | | | | | | | | 12 |
| 13 | | | | | | | | | | 13 |

**Mastery Problem (Continued)**

## GENERAL JOURNAL

| | DATE | DESCRIPTION | POST. REF. | DEBIT | CREDIT | |
|---|------|-------------|-----------|-------|--------|---|
| 1 | | | | | | 1 |
| 2 | | | | | | 2 |
| 3 | | | | | | 3 |
| 4 | | | | | | 4 |
| 5 | | | | | | 5 |
| 6 | | | | | | 6 |
| 7 | | | | | | 7 |
| 8 | | | | | | 8 |
| 9 | | | | | | 9 |
| 10 | | | | | | 10 |
| 11 | | | | | | 11 |
| 12 | | | | | | 12 |

**2.**

## GENERAL LEDGER

ACCOUNT  Cash                                    ACCOUNT NO.  101

| DATE | | ITEM | POST. REF. | DEBIT | CREDIT | BALANCE DEBIT | BALANCE CREDIT |
|------|---|------|-----------|-------|--------|---------------|----------------|
| 20-- Oct. | 1 | Balance | ✓ | | | 18 2 2 5 00 | |
| | | | | | | | |
| | | | | | | | |
| | | | | | | | |
| | | | | | | | |

ACCOUNT  Accounts Receivable                     ACCOUNT NO.  122

| DATE | | ITEM | POST. REF. | DEBIT | CREDIT | BALANCE DEBIT | BALANCE CREDIT |
|------|---|------|-----------|-------|--------|---------------|----------------|
| 20-- Oct. | 1 | Balance | ✓ | | | 9 6 1 9 00 | |
| | | | | | | | |
| | | | | | | | |
| | | | | | | | |
| | | | | | | | |

## Mastery Problem (Continued)

ACCOUNT  Accounts Payable                                          ACCOUNT NO.  202

| DATE | ITEM | POST. REF. | DEBIT | CREDIT | BALANCE DEBIT | BALANCE CREDIT |
|------|------|-----------|-------|--------|-------|--------|
| 20-- Oct. 1 | Balance | ✓ | | | | 5 1 2 0 00 |
| | | | | | | |
| | | | | | | |
| | | | | | | |
| | | | | | | |

ACCOUNT  Sales Tax Payable                                         ACCOUNT NO.  231

| DATE | ITEM | POST. REF. | DEBIT | CREDIT | BALANCE DEBIT | BALANCE CREDIT |
|------|------|-----------|-------|--------|-------|--------|
| | | | | | | |
| | | | | | | |
| | | | | | | |
| | | | | | | |
| | | | | | | |
| | | | | | | |

ACCOUNT  Sales                                                     ACCOUNT NO.  401

| DATE | ITEM | POST. REF. | DEBIT | CREDIT | BALANCE DEBIT | BALANCE CREDIT |
|------|------|-----------|-------|--------|-------|--------|
| | | | | | | |
| | | | | | | |
| | | | | | | |
| | | | | | | |

ACCOUNT  Sales Returns and Allowances                             ACCOUNT NO.  401.1

| DATE | ITEM | POST. REF. | DEBIT | CREDIT | BALANCE DEBIT | BALANCE CREDIT |
|------|------|-----------|-------|--------|-------|--------|
| | | | | | | |
| | | | | | | |
| | | | | | | |
| | | | | | | |

**Mastery Problem (Continued)**

ACCOUNT   Purchases                                                                 ACCOUNT NO.   501

| DATE | ITEM | POST. REF. | DEBIT | CREDIT | BALANCE DEBIT | BALANCE CREDIT |
|---|---|---|---|---|---|---|
| | | | | | | |
| | | | | | | |
| | | | | | | |
| | | | | | | |

ACCOUNT   Purchases Returns and Allowances                                          ACCOUNT NO.   501.1

| DATE | ITEM | POST. REF. | DEBIT | CREDIT | BALANCE DEBIT | BALANCE CREDIT |
|---|---|---|---|---|---|---|
| | | | | | | |
| | | | | | | |
| | | | | | | |
| | | | | | | |

ACCOUNT   Purchases Discounts                                                       ACCOUNT NO.   501.2

| DATE | ITEM | POST. REF. | DEBIT | CREDIT | BALANCE DEBIT | BALANCE CREDIT |
|---|---|---|---|---|---|---|
| | | | | | | |
| | | | | | | |
| | | | | | | |
| | | | | | | |

ACCOUNT   Wages Expense                                                             ACCOUNT NO.   511

| DATE | ITEM | POST. REF. | DEBIT | CREDIT | BALANCE DEBIT | BALANCE CREDIT |
|---|---|---|---|---|---|---|
| | | | | | | |
| | | | | | | |
| | | | | | | |

ACCOUNT   Telephone Expense                                                         ACCOUNT NO.   525

| DATE | ITEM | POST. REF. | DEBIT | CREDIT | BALANCE DEBIT | BALANCE CREDIT |
|---|---|---|---|---|---|---|
| | | | | | | |
| | | | | | | |
| | | | | | | |

**Mastery Problem (Continued)**

## ACCOUNTS RECEIVABLE LEDGER

**NAME** David's Decorating

**ADDRESS** 12 Jude Lane, Hartford, CT 06117

| DATE | | ITEM | POST. REF. | DEBIT | CREDIT | BALANCE |
|---|---|---|---|---|---|---|
| 20-- Oct. | 1 | Balance | ✓ | | | 3 3 4 0 00 |
| | | | | | | |
| | | | | | | |

**NAME** Meg Johnson

**ADDRESS** 700 Hobbes Dr., Avon, CT 06108

| DATE | | ITEM | POST. REF. | DEBIT | CREDIT | BALANCE |
|---|---|---|---|---|---|---|
| 20-- Oct. | 1 | Balance | ✓ | | | 4 0 0 0 00 |
| | | | | | | |
| | | | | | | |
| | | | | | | |

**NAME** Elizabeth Shoemaker

**ADDRESS** 52 Juniper Road, Hartford, CT 06118

| DATE | | ITEM | POST. REF. | DEBIT | CREDIT | BALANCE |
|---|---|---|---|---|---|---|
| 20-- Oct. | 1 | Balance | ✓ | | | 2 7 9 00 |
| | | | | | | |
| | | | | | | |
| | | | | | | |

**NAME** Leigh Summers

**ADDRESS** 5200 Hamilton Ave., Hartford, CT 06111

| DATE | | ITEM | POST. REF. | DEBIT | CREDIT | BALANCE |
|---|---|---|---|---|---|---|
| 20-- Oct. | 1 | Balance | ✓ | | | 2 0 0 0 00 |
| | | | | | | |
| | | | | | | |
| | | | | | | |

**Mastery Problem (Concluded)**

### ACCOUNTS PAYABLE LEDGER

**NAME** Flower Wholesalers

**ADDRESS** 43 Lucky Lane, Bristol, CT 06007

| DATE | | ITEM | POST. REF. | DEBIT | CREDIT | BALANCE |
|---|---|---|---|---|---|---|
| 20--<br>Oct. | 1 | Balance | ✓ | | | 1 5 0 0 00 |
| | | | | | | |
| | | | | | | |
| | | | | | | |

**NAME** Jill Hand

**ADDRESS** 1009 Drake Rd., Farmington, CT 06082

| DATE | | ITEM | POST. REF. | DEBIT | CREDIT | BALANCE |
|---|---|---|---|---|---|---|
| 20--<br>Oct. | 1 | Balance | ✓ | | | 5 0 0 00 |
| | | | | | | |
| | | | | | | |
| | | | | | | |

**NAME** Seidl Enterprises

**ADDRESS** 888 Anders Street, Newington, CT 06789

| DATE | | ITEM | POST. REF. | DEBIT | CREDIT | BALANCE |
|---|---|---|---|---|---|---|
| | | | | | | |
| | | | | | | |
| | | | | | | |
| | | | | | | |

**NAME** Vases Etc.

**ADDRESS** 34 Harry Ave., East Hartford, CT 05234

| DATE | | ITEM | POST. REF. | DEBIT | CREDIT | BALANCE |
|---|---|---|---|---|---|---|
| 20--<br>Oct. | 1 | Balance | ✓ | | | 3 1 2 0 00 |
| | | | | | | |
| | | | | | | |
| | | | | | | |

**Challenge Problem**

**1.**

## GENERAL JOURNAL

PAGE

| | DATE | DESCRIPTION | POST. REF. | DEBIT | CREDIT | |
|---|---|---|---|---|---|---|
| 1 | | | | | | 1 |
| 2 | | | | | | 2 |
| 3 | | | | | | 3 |
| 4 | | | | | | 4 |
| 5 | | | | | | 5 |
| 6 | | | | | | 6 |
| 7 | | | | | | 7 |
| 8 | | | | | | 8 |
| 9 | | | | | | 9 |
| 10 | | | | | | 10 |
| 11 | | | | | | 11 |
| 12 | | | | | | 12 |
| 13 | | | | | | 13 |
| 14 | | | | | | 14 |
| 15 | | | | | | 15 |
| 16 | | | | | | 16 |
| 17 | | | | | | 17 |
| 18 | | | | | | 18 |
| 19 | | | | | | 19 |
| 20 | | | | | | 20 |
| 21 | | | | | | 21 |
| 22 | | | | | | 22 |
| 23 | | | | | | 23 |
| 24 | | | | | | 24 |
| 25 | | | | | | 25 |
| 26 | | | | | | 26 |
| 27 | | | | | | 27 |
| 28 | | | | | | 28 |
| 29 | | | | | | 29 |
| 30 | | | | | | 30 |
| 31 | | | | | | 31 |
| 32 | | | | | | 32 |
| 33 | | | | | | 33 |
| 34 | | | | | | 34 |

## Challenge Problem (Continued)

### GENERAL JOURNAL

PAGE

| | DATE | | DESCRIPTION | POST. REF. | DEBIT | CREDIT | |
|---|---|---|---|---|---|---|---|
| 1 | | | | | | | 1 |
| 2 | | | | | | | 2 |
| 3 | | | | | | | 3 |
| 4 | | | | | | | 4 |
| 5 | | | | | | | 5 |
| 6 | | | | | | | 6 |
| 7 | | | | | | | 7 |
| 8 | | | | | | | 8 |
| 9 | | | | | | | 9 |
| 10 | | | | | | | 10 |
| 11 | | | | | | | 11 |
| 12 | | | | | | | 12 |
| 13 | | | | | | | 13 |
| 14 | | | | | | | 14 |
| 15 | | | | | | | 15 |
| 16 | | | | | | | 16 |
| 17 | | | | | | | 17 |
| 18 | | | | | | | 18 |
| 19 | | | | | | | 19 |
| 20 | | | | | | | 20 |
| 21 | | | | | | | 21 |
| 22 | | | | | | | 22 |
| 23 | | | | | | | 23 |
| 24 | | | | | | | 24 |
| 25 | | | | | | | 25 |
| 26 | | | | | | | 26 |
| 27 | | | | | | | 27 |
| 28 | | | | | | | 28 |
| 29 | | | | | | | 29 |
| 30 | | | | | | | 30 |
| 31 | | | | | | | 31 |
| 32 | | | | | | | 32 |
| 33 | | | | | | | 33 |
| 34 | | | | | | | 34 |

**Challenge Problem (Continued)**

## GENERAL JOURNAL

PAGE

| | DATE | DESCRIPTION | POST. REF. | DEBIT | CREDIT | |
|---|---|---|---|---|---|---|
| 1 | | | | | | 1 |
| 2 | | | | | | 2 |
| 3 | | | | | | 3 |
| 4 | | | | | | 4 |
| 5 | | | | | | 5 |
| 6 | | | | | | 6 |
| 7 | | | | | | 7 |
| 8 | | | | | | 8 |
| 9 | | | | | | 9 |
| 10 | | | | | | 10 |
| 11 | | | | | | 11 |
| 12 | | | | | | 12 |
| 13 | | | | | | 13 |
| 14 | | | | | | 14 |
| 15 | | | | | | 15 |
| 16 | | | | | | 16 |
| 17 | | | | | | 17 |
| 18 | | | | | | 18 |
| 19 | | | | | | 19 |
| 20 | | | | | | 20 |
| 21 | | | | | | 21 |
| 22 | | | | | | 22 |
| 23 | | | | | | 23 |
| 24 | | | | | | 24 |
| 25 | | | | | | 25 |
| 26 | | | | | | 26 |
| 27 | | | | | | 27 |
| 28 | | | | | | 28 |
| 29 | | | | | | 29 |
| 30 | | | | | | 30 |
| 31 | | | | | | 31 |
| 32 | | | | | | 32 |
| 33 | | | | | | 33 |
| 34 | | | | | | 34 |

**Challenge Problem (Concluded)**
**2.**

**SALES JOURNAL**                                    PAGE ____

| | | | | | | |
|---|---|---|---|---|---|---|
| | | | | | | |

**CASH RECEIPTS JOURNAL**                           PAGE ____

| | | | | | | | |
|---|---|---|---|---|---|---|---|
| | | | | | | | |

**PURCHASES JOURNAL**                               PAGE ____

| | | | | | | |
|---|---|---|---|---|---|---|
| | | | | | | |

**CASH PAYMENTS JOURNAL**                           PAGE ____

| | | | | | | | |
|---|---|---|---|---|---|---|---|
| | | | | | | | |

## Exercise 13-1A

|  | Year 1 | Year 2 |
|---|---|---|
| Ending merchandise inventory . . . . . . . . . . . . | | |
| Beginning merchandise inventory . . . . . . . . . | | |
| Cost of goods sold . . . . . . . . . . . . . . . . . . . . | | |
| Gross profit . . . . . . . . . . . . . . . . . . . . . . . . | | |
| Net income . . . . . . . . . . . . . . . . . . . . . . . . . | | |
| Ending owner's capital . . . . . . . . . . . . . . . . | | |

## Exercise 13-2A

### GENERAL JOURNAL

PAGE

| | DATE | DESCRIPTION | POST. REF. | DEBIT | CREDIT | |
|---|---|---|---|---|---|---|
| 1 | | | | | | 1 |
| 2 | | | | | | 2 |
| 3 | | | | | | 3 |
| 4 | | | | | | 4 |
| 5 | | | | | | 5 |
| 6 | | | | | | 6 |
| 7 | | | | | | 7 |
| 8 | | | | | | 8 |
| 9 | | | | | | 9 |
| 10 | | | | | | 10 |
| 11 | | | | | | 11 |
| 12 | | | | | | 12 |
| 13 | | | | | | 13 |
| 14 | | | | | | 14 |
| 15 | | | | | | 15 |
| 16 | | | | | | 16 |
| 17 | | | | | | 17 |
| 18 | | | | | | 18 |
| 19 | | | | | | 19 |
| 20 | | | | | | 20 |
| 21 | | | | | | 21 |
| 22 | | | | | | 22 |
| 23 | | | | | | 23 |

## Exercise 13-3A

| | | | GENERAL JOURNAL | | | PAGE | | |
|---|---|---|---|---|---|---|---|---|
| | DATE | | DESCRIPTION | POST. REF. | DEBIT | CREDIT | | |
| 1 | | | | | | | | 1 |
| 2 | | | | | | | | 2 |
| 3 | | | | | | | | 3 |
| 4 | | | | | | | | 4 |
| 5 | | | | | | | | 5 |
| 6 | | | | | | | | 6 |
| 7 | | | | | | | | 7 |
| 8 | | | | | | | | 8 |
| 9 | | | | | | | | 9 |
| 10 | | | | | | | | 10 |
| 11 | | | | | | | | 11 |
| 12 | | | | | | | | 12 |
| 13 | | | | | | | | 13 |
| 14 | | | | | | | | 14 |
| 15 | | | | | | | | 15 |
| 16 | | | | | | | | 16 |
| 17 | | | | | | | | 17 |
| 18 | | | | | | | | 18 |
| 19 | | | | | | | | 19 |
| 20 | | | | | | | | 20 |
| 21 | | | | | | | | 21 |
| 22 | | | | | | | | 22 |
| 23 | | | | | | | | 23 |

## Exercise 13-4A

**Exercise 13-5A**

## Problem 13-6A

### 1. FIFO Inventory Method

| Date 20-1/ 20-2 | | Cost of Goods Sold | | | Cost of Ending Inventory | | |
|---|---|---|---|---|---|---|---|
| | | Units | Unit Price | Total | Units | Unit Price | Total |
| | | | | | | | |
| | | | | | | | |
| | | | | | | | |
| | | | | | | | |
| | | | | | | | |
| | | | | | | | |
| | | | | | | | |
| | | | | | | | |
| | | | | | | | |
| | | | | | | | |

### 2. LIFO Inventory Method

| Date 20-1/ 20-2 | | Cost of Goods Sold | | | Cost of Ending Inventory | | |
|---|---|---|---|---|---|---|---|
| | | Units | Unit Price | Total | Units | Unit Price | Total |
| | | | | | | | |
| | | | | | | | |
| | | | | | | | |
| | | | | | | | |
| | | | | | | | |
| | | | | | | | |
| | | | | | | | |
| | | | | | | | |
| | | | | | | | |
| | | | | | | | |

**Problem 13-6A (Concluded)**

3. _____

_____

_____

_____

_____

_____

_____

_____

_____

_____

_____

_____

_____

_____

_____

_____

_____

**4. Specific Identification Method**

| Date 20-1/ 20-2 | | Cost of Goods Sold | | | Cost of Ending Inventory | | |
|---|---|---|---|---|---|---|---|
| | | Units | Unit Price | Total | Units | Unit Price | Total |
| | | | | | | | |
| | | | | | | | |
| | | | | | | | |
| | | | | | | | |
| | | | | | | | |
| | | | | | | | |
| | | | | | | | |
| | | | | | | | |
| | | | | | | | |

## Problem 13-7A

1.

### a. FIFO Inventory Method

| Date | | Cost of Goods Sold | | | Cost of Ending Inventory | | |
|---|---|---|---|---|---|---|---|
| 20-- | | Units | Unit Price | Total | Units | Unit Price | Total |
| | | | | | | | |
| | | | | | | | |
| | | | | | | | |
| | | | | | | | |
| | | | | | | | |
| | | | | | | | |
| | | | | | | | |
| | | | | | | | |
| | | | | | | | |
| | | | | | | | |

### b. LIFO Inventory Method

| Date | | Cost of Goods Sold | | | Cost of Ending Inventory | | |
|---|---|---|---|---|---|---|---|
| 20-- | | Units | Unit Price | Total | Units | Unit Price | Total |
| | | | | | | | |
| | | | | | | | |
| | | | | | | | |
| | | | | | | | |
| | | | | | | | |
| | | | | | | | |
| | | | | | | | |
| | | | | | | | |
| | | | | | | | |
| | | | | | | | |

**Problem 13-7A (Concluded)**

**c.** _____

_____

_____

_____

_____

**2.** _____

**a.** _____

_____

_____

_____

_____

**b.** _____

_____

_____

_____

_____

_____

_____

**Problem 13-8A**

_____

_____

_____

_____

_____

_____

_____

_____

_____

_____

_____

## Problem 13-9A

**1. and 2.**

|  | Cost | Retail |
|---|---|---|
|  |  |  |
|  |  |  |
|  |  |  |
|  |  |  |
|  |  |  |
|  |  |  |
|  |  |  |
|  |  |  |
|  |  |  |
|  |  |  |
|  |  |  |
|  |  |  |
|  |  |  |
|  |  |  |
|  |  |  |
|  |  |  |
|  |  |  |
|  |  |  |
|  |  |  |
|  |  |  |

## Exercise 13-1B

|  | Year 1 | Year 2 |
|---|---|---|
| Ending merchandise inventory . . . . . . . . . . . |  |  |
| Beginning merchandise inventory . . . . . . . . . |  |  |
| Cost of goods sold  . . . . . . . . . . . . . . . . . . |  |  |
| Gross profit . . . . . . . . . . . . . . . . . . . . . . . . |  |  |
| Net income . . . . . . . . . . . . . . . . . . . . . . . . |  |  |
| Ending owner's capital . . . . . . . . . . . . . . . . |  |  |

**Exercise 13-2B**

## GENERAL JOURNAL

PAGE _____

| | DATE | DESCRIPTION | POST. REF. | DEBIT | CREDIT | |
|---|---|---|---|---|---|---|
| 1 | | | | | | 1 |
| 2 | | | | | | 2 |
| 3 | | | | | | 3 |
| 4 | | | | | | 4 |
| 5 | | | | | | 5 |
| 6 | | | | | | 6 |
| 7 | | | | | | 7 |
| 8 | | | | | | 8 |
| 9 | | | | | | 9 |
| 10 | | | | | | 10 |
| 11 | | | | | | 11 |
| 12 | | | | | | 12 |
| 13 | | | | | | 13 |
| 14 | | | | | | 14 |
| 15 | | | | | | 15 |
| 16 | | | | | | 16 |
| 17 | | | | | | 17 |
| 18 | | | | | | 18 |
| 19 | | | | | | 19 |
| 20 | | | | | | 20 |
| 21 | | | | | | 21 |
| 22 | | | | | | 22 |
| 23 | | | | | | 23 |
| 24 | | | | | | 24 |
| 25 | | | | | | 25 |
| 26 | | | | | | 26 |
| 27 | | | | | | 27 |
| 28 | | | | | | 28 |
| 29 | | | | | | 29 |
| 30 | | | | | | 30 |
| 31 | | | | | | 31 |
| 32 | | | | | | 32 |
| 33 | | | | | | 33 |
| 34 | | | | | | 34 |
| 35 | | | | | | 35 |

## Exercise 13-3B

| | DATE | | DESCRIPTION | POST. REF. | DEBIT | CREDIT | |
|---|---|---|---|---|---|---|---|
| 1 | | | | | | | 1 |
| 2 | | | | | | | 2 |
| 3 | | | | | | | 3 |
| 4 | | | | | | | 4 |
| 5 | | | | | | | 5 |
| 6 | | | | | | | 6 |
| 7 | | | | | | | 7 |
| 8 | | | | | | | 8 |
| 9 | | | | | | | 9 |
| 10 | | | | | | | 10 |
| 11 | | | | | | | 11 |
| 12 | | | | | | | 12 |
| 13 | | | | | | | 13 |
| 14 | | | | | | | 14 |
| 15 | | | | | | | 15 |
| 16 | | | | | | | 16 |
| 17 | | | | | | | 17 |
| 18 | | | | | | | 18 |
| 19 | | | | | | | 19 |
| 20 | | | | | | | 20 |
| 21 | | | | | | | 21 |
| 22 | | | | | | | 22 |
| 23 | | | | | | | 23 |

**GENERAL JOURNAL** PAGE

## Exercise 13-4B

**Exercise 13-5B**

## Problem 13-6B

### 1. FIFO Inventory Method

| Date 20-1/ 20-2 | | Cost of Goods Sold | | | Cost of Ending Inventory | | |
| --- | --- | --- | --- | --- | --- | --- | --- |
| | | Units | Unit Price | Total | Units | Unit Price | Total |
| | | | | | | | |
| | | | | | | | |
| | | | | | | | |
| | | | | | | | |
| | | | | | | | |
| | | | | | | | |
| | | | | | | | |
| | | | | | | | |
| | | | | | | | |
| | | | | | | | |

### 2. LIFO Inventory Method

| Date 20-1/ 20-2 | | Cost of Goods Sold | | | Cost of Ending Inventory | | |
| --- | --- | --- | --- | --- | --- | --- | --- |
| | | Units | Unit Price | Total | Units | Unit Price | Total |
| | | | | | | | |
| | | | | | | | |
| | | | | | | | |
| | | | | | | | |
| | | | | | | | |
| | | | | | | | |
| | | | | | | | |
| | | | | | | | |
| | | | | | | | |
| | | | | | | | |

**Problem 13-6B (Concluded)**

3. _____

_____

_____

_____

_____

_____

_____

_____

_____

_____

_____

_____

_____

_____

_____

_____

_____

_____

_____

**4. Specific Identification Method**

| Date 20-1/ 20-2 | | Cost of Goods Sold | | | Cost of Ending Inventory | | |
|---|---|---|---|---|---|---|---|
| | | Units | Unit Price | Total | Units | Unit Price | Total |
| | | | | | | | |
| | | | | | | | |
| | | | | | | | |
| | | | | | | | |
| | | | | | | | |
| | | | | | | | |
| | | | | | | | |
| | | | | | | | |
| | | | | | | | |
| | | | | | | | |

## Problem 13-7B

1.

### a. FIFO Inventory Method

| Date | | Cost of Goods Sold | | | Cost of Ending Inventory | | |
|---|---|---|---|---|---|---|---|
| | | Units | Unit Price | Total | Units | Unit Price | Total |
| 20-- | | | | | | | |
| | | | | | | | |
| | | | | | | | |
| | | | | | | | |
| | | | | | | | |
| | | | | | | | |
| | | | | | | | |
| | | | | | | | |
| | | | | | | | |
| | | | | | | | |

### b. LIFO Inventory Method

| Date | | Cost of Goods Sold | | | Cost of Ending Inventory | | |
|---|---|---|---|---|---|---|---|
| | | Units | Unit Price | Total | Units | Unit Price | Total |
| 20-- | | | | | | | |
| | | | | | | | |
| | | | | | | | |
| | | | | | | | |
| | | | | | | | |
| | | | | | | | |
| | | | | | | | |
| | | | | | | | |
| | | | | | | | |
| | | | | | | | |

**Problem 13-7B (Concluded)**

**c.** _____

_____

_____

_____

**2.** _____

**a.** _____

_____

_____

_____

**b.** _____

_____

_____

_____

_____

**Problem 13-8B**

_____

_____

_____

_____

_____

_____

_____

_____

_____

_____

_____

_____

## Problem 13-9B

**1. and 2.**

|  | Cost | Retail |
|---|---|---|

## Mastery Problem

**1.**

### a. FIFO Inventory Method

| Date 20-2 | | Cost of Goods Sold | | | Cost of Ending Inventory | | |
|---|---|---|---|---|---|---|---|
| | | Units | Unit Price | Total | Units | Unit Price | Total |
| | | | | | | | |
| | | | | | | | |
| | | | | | | | |
| | | | | | | | |
| | | | | | | | |
| | | | | | | | |
| | | | | | | | |
| | | | | | | | |
| | | | | | | | |
| | | | | | | | |

### b. LIFO Inventory Method

| Date 20-2 | | Cost of Goods Sold | | | Cost of Ending Inventory | | |
|---|---|---|---|---|---|---|---|
| | | Units | Unit Price | Total | Units | Unit Price | Total |
| | | | | | | | |
| | | | | | | | |
| | | | | | | | |
| | | | | | | | |
| | | | | | | | |
| | | | | | | | |
| | | | | | | | |
| | | | | | | | |
| | | | | | | | |
| | | | | | | | |

**Mastery Problem (Concluded)**

c.

2.

a.

b.

3.

## Challenge Problem

| 20-1 | FIFO Units | Cost/Unit | Cost | LIFO Units | Cost/Unit | Cost |
|---|---|---|---|---|---|---|
| | | | | | | |
| | | | | | | |
| | | | | | | |
| | | | | | | |
| | | | | | | |
| | | | | | | |
| | | | | | | |

| Details of Cost of Goods Sold 20-1 | FIFO Units | Cost/Unit | Cost | LIFO Units | Cost/Unit | Cost |
|---|---|---|---|---|---|---|
| | | | | | | |
| | | | | | | |
| | | | | | | |
| | | | | | | |

## Challenge Problem (Concluded)

| 20-2 | FIFO Units | FIFO Cost/Unit | FIFO Cost | LIFO Units | LIFO Cost/Unit | LIFO Cost |
|------|------------|----------------|-----------|------------|----------------|-----------|
|      |            |                |           |            |                |           |
|      |            |                |           |            |                |           |
|      |            |                |           |            |                |           |
|      |            |                |           |            |                |           |
|      |            |                |           |            |                |           |
|      |            |                |           |            |                |           |
|      |            |                |           |            |                |           |
|      |            |                |           |            |                |           |

| Details of Cost of Goods Sold 20-2 | FIFO Units | FIFO Cost/Unit | FIFO Cost | LIFO Units | LIFO Cost/Unit | LIFO Cost |
|------------------------------------|------------|----------------|-----------|------------|----------------|-----------|
|      |            |                |           |            |                |           |
|      |            |                |           |            |                |           |
|      |            |                |           |            |                |           |
|      |            |                |           |            |                |           |
|      |            |                |           |            |                |           |
|      |            |                |           |            |                |           |

## APPENDIX: PERPETUAL INVENTORY METHOD:
## LIFO AND MOVING-AVERAGE METHODS

## Exercise 13Apx-1A

### 1. Perpetual LIFO

| Date | Purchases Units | Cost/ Unit | Total | Cost of Goods Sold Units | Cost/ Unit | CGS | Cum. CGS | Inventory on Hand Layer | Units | Cost/ Unit | Layer Cost | Total |
|------|------|------|------|------|------|------|------|------|------|------|------|------|
|  |  |  |  |  |  |  |  |  |  |  |  |  |
|  |  |  |  |  |  |  |  |  |  |  |  |  |
|  |  |  |  |  |  |  |  |  |  |  |  |  |
|  |  |  |  |  |  |  |  |  |  |  |  |  |
|  |  |  |  |  |  |  |  |  |  |  |  |  |
|  |  |  |  |  |  |  |  |  |  |  |  |  |
|  |  |  |  |  |  |  |  |  |  |  |  |  |
|  |  |  |  |  |  |  |  |  |  |  |  |  |
|  |  |  |  |  |  |  |  |  |  |  |  |  |
|  |  |  |  |  |  |  |  |  |  |  |  |  |
|  |  |  |  |  |  |  |  |  |  |  |  |  |
|  |  |  |  |  |  |  |  |  |  |  |  |  |

### 2. Perpetual Moving-Average

| Date | Purchases Units | Cost/ Unit | Total | Cost of Goods Sold Units | Cost/ Unit | CGS | Cum. CGS | Inventory on Hand and Average Cost per Unit Cost of Purchase or (Sale) | Cost of Inventory on Hand | Units on Hand | Average Cost/ Unit |
|------|------|------|------|------|------|------|------|------|------|------|------|
|  |  |  |  |  |  |  |  |  |  |  |  |
|  |  |  |  |  |  |  |  |  |  |  |  |
|  |  |  |  |  |  |  |  |  |  |  |  |
|  |  |  |  |  |  |  |  |  |  |  |  |
|  |  |  |  |  |  |  |  |  |  |  |  |

## Problem 13Apx-2A

### 1. Perpetual LIFO

| Date | Purchases | | | Cost of Goods Sold | | | | Inventory on Hand | | | | |
|------|-------|---------------|-------|-------|---------------|-----|-------------|-------|-------|---------------|---------------|-------|
| | Units | Cost/<br>Unit | Total | Units | Cost/<br>Unit | CGS | Cum.<br>CGS | Layer | Units | Cost/<br>Unit | Layer<br>Cost | Total |
| | | | | | | | | | | | | |
| | | | | | | | | | | | | |
| | | | | | | | | | | | | |
| | | | | | | | | | | | | |
| | | | | | | | | | | | | |
| | | | | | | | | | | | | |
| | | | | | | | | | | | | |
| | | | | | | | | | | | | |
| | | | | | | | | | | | | |
| | | | | | | | | | | | | |
| | | | | | | | | | | | | |
| | | | | | | | | | | | | |
| | | | | | | | | | | | | |
| | | | | | | | | | | | | |
| | | | | | | | | | | | | |
| | | | | | | | | | | | | |
| | | | | | | | | | | | | |
| | | | | | | | | | | | | |
| | | | | | | | | | | | | |
| | | | | | | | | | | | | |
| | | | | | | | | | | | | |
| | | | | | | | | | | | | |
| | | | | | | | | | | | | |
| | | | | | | | | | | | | |
| | | | | | | | | | | | | |
| | | | | | | | | | | | | |
| | | | | | | | | | | | | |
| | | | | | | | | | | | | |

**Problem 13Apx-2A (Concluded)**

**2. Perpetual Moving-Average**

| Date | Purchases | | | Cost of Goods Sold | | | | Inventory on Hand and Average Cost per Unit | | | |
|---|---|---|---|---|---|---|---|---|---|---|---|
| | Units | Cost/ Unit | Total | Units | Cost/ Unit | CGS | Cum. CGS | Cost of Purchase or (Sale) | Cost of Inventory on Hand | Units on Hand | Average Cost/ Unit |
| | | | | | | | | | | | |
| | | | | | | | | | | | |
| | | | | | | | | | | | |
| | | | | | | | | | | | |
| | | | | | | | | | | | |
| | | | | | | | | | | | |
| | | | | | | | | | | | |
| | | | | | | | | | | | |
| | | | | | | | | | | | |
| | | | | | | | | | | | |
| | | | | | | | | | | | |
| | | | | | | | | | | | |
| | | | | | | | | | | | |

## Exercise 13Apx-1B

### 1. Perpetual LIFO

| | Purchases | | | Cost of Goods Sold | | | | Inventory on Hand | | | | |
|---|---|---|---|---|---|---|---|---|---|---|---|---|
| Date | Units | Cost/ Unit | Total | Units | Cost/ Unit | CGS | Cum. CGS | Layer | Units | Cost/ Unit | Layer Cost | Total |
| | | | | | | | | | | | | |
| | | | | | | | | | | | | |
| | | | | | | | | | | | | |
| | | | | | | | | | | | | |
| | | | | | | | | | | | | |
| | | | | | | | | | | | | |
| | | | | | | | | | | | | |
| | | | | | | | | | | | | |
| | | | | | | | | | | | | |
| | | | | | | | | | | | | |
| | | | | | | | | | | | | |
| | | | | | | | | | | | | |

### 2. Perpetual Moving-Average

| | Purchases | | | Cost of Goods Sold | | | | Inventory on Hand and Average Cost per Unit | | | |
|---|---|---|---|---|---|---|---|---|---|---|---|
| Date | Units | Cost/ Unit | Total | Units | Cost/ Unit | CGS | Cum. CGS | Cost of Purchase or (Sale) | Cost of Inventory on Hand | Units on Hand | Average Cost/ Unit |
| | | | | | | | | | | | |
| | | | | | | | | | | | | |
| | | | | | | | | | | | | |
| | | | | | | | | | | | | |
| | | | | | | | | | | | | |

## Problem 13Apx-2B

### 1. Perpetual LIFO

| Date | Purchases | | | Cost of Goods Sold | | | | Inventory on Hand | | | | |
|---|---|---|---|---|---|---|---|---|---|---|---|---|
| | Units | Cost/ Unit | Total | Units | Cost/ Unit | CGS | Cum. CGS | Layer | Units | Cost/ Unit | Layer Cost | Total |
| | | | | | | | | | | | | |
| | | | | | | | | | | | | |
| | | | | | | | | | | | | |
| | | | | | | | | | | | | |
| | | | | | | | | | | | | |
| | | | | | | | | | | | | |
| | | | | | | | | | | | | |
| | | | | | | | | | | | | |
| | | | | | | | | | | | | |
| | | | | | | | | | | | | |
| | | | | | | | | | | | | |
| | | | | | | | | | | | | |
| | | | | | | | | | | | | |
| | | | | | | | | | | | | |
| | | | | | | | | | | | | |
| | | | | | | | | | | | | |
| | | | | | | | | | | | | |
| | | | | | | | | | | | | |
| | | | | | | | | | | | | |
| | | | | | | | | | | | | |
| | | | | | | | | | | | | |
| | | | | | | | | | | | | |
| | | | | | | | | | | | | |
| | | | | | | | | | | | | |

## Problem 13Apx-2B (Concluded)

### 2. Perpetual Moving-Average

| Date | Purchases | | | Cost of Goods Sold | | | | Inventory on Hand and Average Cost per Unit | | | |
|---|---|---|---|---|---|---|---|---|---|---|---|
| | Units | Cost/ Unit | Total | Units | Cost/ Unit | CGS | Cum. CGS | Cost of Purchase or (Sale) | Cost of Inventory on Hand | Units on Hand | Average Cost/ Unit |
| | | | | | | | | | | | |
| | | | | | | | | | | | |
| | | | | | | | | | | | |
| | | | | | | | | | | | |
| | | | | | | | | | | | |
| | | | | | | | | | | | |
| | | | | | | | | | | | |
| | | | | | | | | | | | |
| | | | | | | | | | | | |
| | | | | | | | | | | | |

© 2011 Cengage Learning. All Rights Reserved. May not be scanned, copied or duplicated, or posted to a publicly accessible website, in whole or in part.

**Exercise 14-1A**

| Merchandise Inventory | Income Summary |
|---|---|
| | |

**Exercise 14-2A**

| | | | | | |
|---|---|---|---|---|---|
| | | | | | |

**Exercise 14-3A**

| Cash | Unearned Ticket Revenue |
|---|---|
| | |

| Ticket Revenue |
|---|
| |

**Exercise 14-4A**

1., 2., and 3.

Kevin's

Work

For Year Ended

| | ACCOUNT TITLE | TRIAL BALANCE | | | | | | | | | | ADJUSTMENTS | | | | | | | | |
|---|---|---|---|---|---|---|---|---|---|---|---|---|---|---|---|---|---|---|---|---|
| | | DEBIT | | | | | CREDIT | | | | | DEBIT | | | | CREDIT | | | | |
| 1 | Merchandise Inventory | 40 | 0 | 0 | 0 | 00 | | | | | | | | | | | | | | |
| 12 | Income Summary | | | | | | | | | | | | | | | | | | | |
| 13 | Purchases | 90 | 0 | 0 | 0 | 00 | | | | | | | | | | | | | | |
| 14 | Purchases Returns and Allow. | | | | | | 2 | 0 | 0 | 0 | 00 | | | | | | | | | |
| 15 | Purchases Discounts | | | | | | 3 | 0 | 0 | 0 | 00 | | | | | | | | | |
| 16 | Freight-In | | 5 | 0 | 0 | 00 | | | | | | | | | | | | | | |
| 17 | | | | | | | | | | | | | | | | | | | | |
| 18 | | | | | | | | | | | | | | | | | | | | |

**Exercise 14-4A (Concluded)**

Gift Shop

Sheet (Partial)

December 31, 20--

| | ADJUSTED TRIAL BALANCE | | INCOME STATEMENT | | BALANCE SHEET | | |
|---|---|---|---|---|---|---|---|
| | DEBIT | CREDIT | DEBIT | CREDIT | DEBIT | CREDIT | |
| | | | | | | | 1 |
| | | | | | | | 12 |
| | | | | | | | 13 |
| | | | | | | | 14 |
| | | | | | | | 15 |
| | | | | | | | 16 |
| | | | | | | | 17 |
| | | | | | | | 18 |

**4.**

## Exercise 14-5A

## Exercise 14-6A

### GENERAL JOURNAL

PAGE

| | DATE | DESCRIPTION | POST. REF. | DEBIT | CREDIT | |
|---|---|---|---|---|---|---|
| 1 | | | | | | 1 |
| 2 | | | | | | 2 |
| 3 | | | | | | 3 |
| 4 | | | | | | 4 |
| 5 | | | | | | 5 |
| 6 | | | | | | 6 |
| 7 | | | | | | 7 |
| 8 | | | | | | 8 |
| 9 | | | | | | 9 |
| 10 | | | | | | 10 |
| 11 | | | | | | 11 |
| 12 | | | | | | 12 |
| 13 | | | | | | 13 |
| 14 | | | | | | 14 |
| 15 | | | | | | 15 |
| 16 | | | | | | 16 |
| 17 | | | | | | 17 |
| 18 | | | | | | 18 |
| 19 | | | | | | 19 |
| 20 | | | | | | 20 |
| 21 | | | | | | 21 |
| 22 | | | | | | 22 |
| 23 | | | | | | 23 |
| 24 | | | | | | 24 |
| 25 | | | | | | 25 |
| 26 | | | | | | 26 |
| 27 | | | | | | 27 |

## Exercise 14-7A

**GENERAL JOURNAL**                    PAGE

| | DATE | DESCRIPTION | POST. REF. | DEBIT | CREDIT | |
|---|---|---|---|---|---|---|
| 1 | | | | | | 1 |
| 2 | | | | | | 2 |
| 3 | | | | | | 3 |
| 4 | | | | | | 4 |
| 5 | | | | | | 5 |
| 6 | | | | | | 6 |
| 7 | | | | | | 7 |
| 8 | | | | | | 8 |
| 9 | | | | | | 9 |
| 10 | | | | | | 10 |
| 11 | | | | | | 11 |
| 12 | | | | | | 12 |
| 13 | | | | | | 13 |
| 14 | | | | | | 14 |
| 15 | | | | | | 15 |
| 16 | | | | | | 16 |
| 17 | | | | | | 17 |
| 18 | | | | | | 18 |
| 19 | | | | | | 19 |

## Exercise 14-8A

**GENERAL JOURNAL**                    PAGE

| | DATE | DESCRIPTION | POST. REF. | DEBIT | CREDIT | |
|---|---|---|---|---|---|---|
| 1 | | | | | | 1 |
| 2 | | | | | | 2 |
| 3 | | | | | | 3 |
| 4 | | | | | | 4 |
| 5 | | | | | | 5 |
| 6 | | | | | | 6 |
| 7 | | | | | | 7 |
| 8 | | | | | | 8 |
| 9 | | | | | | 9 |
| 10 | | | | | | 10 |
| 11 | | | | | | 11 |

## Problem 14-9A

### 1. and 2.

Seaside Kite

Work

For Year Ended

| | ACCOUNT TITLE | TRIAL BALANCE | | ADJUSTMENTS | |
|---|---|---|---|---|---|
| | | DEBIT | CREDIT | DEBIT | CREDIT |
| 1 | Cash | 20 0 0 0 00 | | | |
| 2 | Accounts Receivable | 14 0 0 0 00 | | | |
| 3 | Merchandise Inventory | 25 0 0 0 00 | | | |
| 4 | Supplies | 8 0 0 0 00 | | | |
| 5 | Prepaid Insurance | 5 4 0 0 00 | | | |
| 6 | Land | 30 0 0 0 00 | | | |
| 7 | Building | 50 0 0 0 00 | | | |
| 8 | Accumulated Depr.—Building | | 20 0 0 0 00 | | |
| 9 | Store Equipment | 35 0 0 0 00 | | | |
| 10 | Accumulated Depr.—Store Equip. | | 14 0 0 0 00 | | |
| 11 | Accounts Payable | | 9 6 0 0 00 | | |
| 12 | Wages Payable | | | | |
| 13 | Sales Tax Payable | | 5 9 0 0 00 | | |
| 14 | Unearned Rent Revenue | | 8 9 0 0 00 | | |
| 15 | Mortgage Payable | | 45 0 0 0 00 | | |
| 16 | J. Kennington, Capital | | 65 4 1 0 00 | | |
| 17 | J. Kennington, Drawing | 26 0 0 0 00 | | | |
| 18 | Income Summary | | | | |
| 19 | Sales | | 118 0 0 0 00 | | |
| 20 | Sales Returns and Allowances | 1 7 0 0 00 | | | |
| 21 | Rent Revenue | | | | |
| 22 | Purchases | 27 0 0 0 00 | | | |
| 23 | Purchases Returns and Allow. | | 1 4 0 0 00 | | |
| 24 | Purchases Discounts | | 1 8 0 0 00 | | |
| 25 | Freight-In | 2 1 0 0 00 | | | |
| 26 | Wages Expense | 32 0 0 0 00 | | | |
| 27 | Advertising Expense | 3 6 0 0 00 | | | |
| 28 | Supplies Expense | | | | |
| 29 | Telephone Expense | 1 3 5 0 00 | | | |
| 30 | Utilities Expense | 8 0 0 0 00 | | | |
| 31 | Insurance Expense | | | | |
| 32 | Depreciation Expense—Building | | | | |
| 33 | Depreciation Exp.—Store Equip. | | | | |
| 34 | Miscellaneous Expense | 8 6 0 00 | | | |
| 35 | | 290 0 1 0 00 | 290 0 1 0 00 | | |
| 36 | | | | | |
| 37 | | | | | |
| 38 | | | | | |

## Problem 14-9A (Continued)

Shop _____

Sheet _____

December 31, 20-- _____

| ADJUSTED TRIAL BALANCE | | INCOME STATEMENT | | BALANCE SHEET | | |
|---|---|---|---|---|---|---|
| DEBIT | CREDIT | DEBIT | CREDIT | DEBIT | CREDIT | |
| | | | | | | 1 |
| | | | | | | 2 |
| | | | | | | 3 |
| | | | | | | 4 |
| | | | | | | 5 |
| | | | | | | 6 |
| | | | | | | 7 |
| | | | | | | 8 |
| | | | | | | 9 |
| | | | | | | 10 |
| | | | | | | 11 |
| | | | | | | 12 |
| | | | | | | 13 |
| | | | | | | 14 |
| | | | | | | 15 |
| | | | | | | 16 |
| | | | | | | 17 |
| | | | | | | 18 |
| | | | | | | 19 |
| | | | | | | 20 |
| | | | | | | 21 |
| | | | | | | 22 |
| | | | | | | 23 |
| | | | | | | 24 |
| | | | | | | 25 |
| | | | | | | 26 |
| | | | | | | 27 |
| | | | | | | 28 |
| | | | | | | 29 |
| | | | | | | 30 |
| | | | | | | 31 |
| | | | | | | 32 |
| | | | | | | 33 |
| | | | | | | 34 |
| | | | | | | 35 |
| | | | | | | 36 |
| | | | | | | 37 |
| | | | | | | 38 |

## Problem 14-9A (Concluded)

**3.**

**GENERAL JOURNAL**                                            PAGE

| | DATE | | DESCRIPTION | POST. REF. | DEBIT | CREDIT | |
|---|---|---|---|---|---|---|---|
| 1 | | | | | | | 1 |
| 2 | | | | | | | 2 |
| 3 | | | | | | | 3 |
| 4 | | | | | | | 4 |
| 5 | | | | | | | 5 |
| 6 | | | | | | | 6 |
| 7 | | | | | | | 7 |
| 8 | | | | | | | 8 |
| 9 | | | | | | | 9 |
| 10 | | | | | | | 10 |
| 11 | | | | | | | 11 |
| 12 | | | | | | | 12 |
| 13 | | | | | | | 13 |
| 14 | | | | | | | 14 |
| 15 | | | | | | | 15 |
| 16 | | | | | | | 16 |
| 17 | | | | | | | 17 |
| 18 | | | | | | | 18 |
| 19 | | | | | | | 19 |
| 20 | | | | | | | 20 |
| 21 | | | | | | | 21 |
| 22 | | | | | | | 22 |
| 23 | | | | | | | 23 |
| 24 | | | | | | | 24 |
| 25 | | | | | | | 25 |
| 26 | | | | | | | 26 |
| 27 | | | | | | | 27 |
| 28 | | | | | | | 28 |
| 29 | | | | | | | 29 |
| 30 | | | | | | | 30 |
| 31 | | | | | | | 31 |
| 32 | | | | | | | 32 |
| 33 | | | | | | | 33 |
| 34 | | | | | | | 34 |

**Problem 14-10A**

1. and 2. (See pages 518 and 519.)

3.

### GENERAL JOURNAL

PAGE _____

| | DATE | | DESCRIPTION | POST. REF. | DEBIT | CREDIT | |
|---|---|---|---|---|---|---|---|
| 1 | | | | | | | 1 |
| 2 | | | | | | | 2 |
| 3 | | | | | | | 3 |
| 4 | | | | | | | 4 |
| 5 | | | | | | | 5 |
| 6 | | | | | | | 6 |
| 7 | | | | | | | 7 |
| 8 | | | | | | | 8 |
| 9 | | | | | | | 9 |
| 10 | | | | | | | 10 |
| 11 | | | | | | | 11 |
| 12 | | | | | | | 12 |
| 13 | | | | | | | 13 |
| 14 | | | | | | | 14 |
| 15 | | | | | | | 15 |
| 16 | | | | | | | 16 |
| 17 | | | | | | | 17 |
| 18 | | | | | | | 18 |
| 19 | | | | | | | 19 |
| 20 | | | | | | | 20 |
| 21 | | | | | | | 21 |
| 22 | | | | | | | 22 |
| 23 | | | | | | | 23 |
| 24 | | | | | | | 24 |
| 25 | | | | | | | 25 |
| 26 | | | | | | | 26 |
| 27 | | | | | | | 27 |
| 28 | | | | | | | 28 |
| 29 | | | | | | | 29 |
| 30 | | | | | | | 30 |
| 31 | | | | | | | 31 |
| 32 | | | | | | | 32 |
| 33 | | | | | | | 33 |
| 34 | | | | | | | 34 |

## Problem 14-10A (Continued)
### 1. and 2.

Cascade Bicycle

Work

For Year Ended

| | ACCOUNT TITLE | TRIAL BALANCE | | ADJUSTMENTS | |
|---|---|---|---|---|---|
| | | DEBIT | CREDIT | DEBIT | CREDIT |
| 1 | Cash | 23 0 0 0 00 | | | |
| 2 | Accounts Receivable | 15 0 0 0 00 | | | |
| 3 | Merchandise Inventory | 31 0 0 0 00 | | | |
| 4 | Supplies | 7 2 0 0 00 | | | |
| 5 | Prepaid Insurance | 4 6 0 0 00 | | | |
| 6 | Land | 28 0 0 0 00 | | | |
| 7 | Building | 53 0 0 0 00 | | | |
| 8 | Accumulated Depr.—Building | | 17 0 0 0 00 | | |
| 9 | Store Equipment | 27 0 0 0 00 | | | |
| 10 | Accumulated Depr.—Store Equip. | | 9 0 0 0 00 | | |
| 11 | Accounts Payable | | 3 8 0 0 00 | | |
| 12 | Wages Payable | | | | |
| 13 | Sales Tax Payable | | 3 0 5 0 00 | | |
| 14 | Unearned Storage Revenue | | 5 6 0 0 00 | | |
| 15 | Mortgage Payable | | 42 0 0 0 00 | | |
| 16 | D. Lamond, Capital | | 165 7 6 0 00 | | |
| 17 | D. Lamond, Drawing | 33 0 0 0 00 | | | |
| 18 | Income Summary | | | | |
| 19 | Sales | | 51 0 0 0 00 | | |
| 20 | Sales Returns and Allowances | 2 4 0 0 00 | | | |
| 21 | Storage Revenue | | | | |
| 22 | Purchases | 21 0 0 0 00 | | | |
| 23 | Purchases Returns and Allow. | | 1 3 0 0 00 | | |
| 24 | Purchases Discounts | | 1 9 0 0 00 | | |
| 25 | Freight-In | 1 8 0 0 00 | | | |
| 26 | Wages Expense | 35 0 0 0 00 | | | |
| 27 | Advertising Expense | 5 7 0 0 00 | | | |
| 28 | Supplies Expense | | | | |
| 29 | Telephone Expense | 2 2 0 0 00 | | | |
| 30 | Utilities Expense | 9 6 0 0 00 | | | |
| 31 | Insurance Expense | | | | |
| 32 | Depreciation Expense—Building | | | | |
| 33 | Depreciation Exp.—Store Equip. | | | | |
| 34 | Miscellaneous Expense | 9 1 0 00 | | | |
| 35 | | 300 4 1 0 00 | 300 4 1 0 00 | | |
| 36 | | | | | |
| 37 | | | | | |
| 38 | | | | | |

## Problem 14-10A (Concluded)

Shop _____

Sheet _____

December 31, 20-- _____

| ADJUSTED TRIAL BALANCE | | INCOME STATEMENT | | BALANCE SHEET | | |
|---|---|---|---|---|---|---|
| DEBIT | CREDIT | DEBIT | CREDIT | DEBIT | CREDIT | |
| | | | | | | 1 |
| | | | | | | 2 |
| | | | | | | 3 |
| | | | | | | 4 |
| | | | | | | 5 |
| | | | | | | 6 |
| | | | | | | 7 |
| | | | | | | 8 |
| | | | | | | 9 |
| | | | | | | 10 |
| | | | | | | 11 |
| | | | | | | 12 |
| | | | | | | 13 |
| | | | | | | 14 |
| | | | | | | 15 |
| | | | | | | 16 |
| | | | | | | 17 |
| | | | | | | 18 |
| | | | | | | 19 |
| | | | | | | 20 |
| | | | | | | 21 |
| | | | | | | 22 |
| | | | | | | 23 |
| | | | | | | 24 |
| | | | | | | 25 |
| | | | | | | 26 |
| | | | | | | 27 |
| | | | | | | 28 |
| | | | | | | 29 |
| | | | | | | 30 |
| | | | | | | 31 |
| | | | | | | 32 |
| | | | | | | 33 |
| | | | | | | 34 |
| | | | | | | 35 |
| | | | | | | 36 |
| | | | | | | 37 |
| | | | | | | 38 |

## Problem 14-11A

1.

Stark Street Computers

Work Sheet (Partial)

For Year Ended December 31, 20--

| | ACCOUNT TITLE | TRIAL BALANCE DEBIT | TRIAL BALANCE CREDIT | ADJUSTMENTS DEBIT | ADJUSTMENTS CREDIT | ADJUSTED TRIAL BALANCE DEBIT | ADJUSTED TRIAL BALANCE CREDIT | |
|---|---|---|---|---|---|---|---|---|
| 1 | Cash | 18 0 0 0 00 | | | | 18 0 0 0 00 | | 1 |
| 2 | Accounts Receivable | 11 0 0 0 00 | | | | 11 0 0 0 00 | | 2 |
| 3 | Merchandise Inventory | 25 0 0 0 00 | | | | 35 0 0 0 00 | | 3 |
| 4 | Supplies | 8 0 0 0 00 | | | | 2 8 2 0 00 | | 4 |
| 5 | Prepaid Insurance | 5 4 0 0 00 | | | | 1 2 2 5 00 | | 5 |
| 6 | Land | 27 0 0 0 00 | | | | 27 0 0 0 00 | | 6 |
| 7 | Building | 48 0 0 0 00 | | | | 48 0 0 0 00 | | 7 |
| 8 | Accum. Depr.—Building | | 20 0 0 0 00 | | | | 27 0 0 0 00 | 8 |
| 9 | Store Equipment | 33 0 0 0 00 | | | | 33 0 0 0 00 | | 9 |
| 10 | Accum. Depr.—Store Equip. | | 8 7 0 0 00 | | | | 12 8 0 0 00 | 10 |
| 11 | Accounts Payable | | 6 4 0 0 00 | | | | 6 4 0 0 00 | 11 |
| 12 | Wages Payable | | | | | | 1 3 0 0 00 | 12 |
| 13 | Sales Tax Payable | | 5 7 0 0 00 | | | | 5 7 0 0 00 | 13 |
| 14 | Unearned Repair Rev. | | 8 2 0 0 00 | | | | 1 8 0 0 00 | 14 |
| 15 | Mortgage Payable | | 44 0 0 0 00 | | | | 44 0 0 0 00 | 15 |
| 16 | L. Cowart, Capital | | 80 0 2 5 00 | | | | 80 0 2 5 00 | 16 |
| 17 | L. Cowart, Drawing | 35 0 0 0 00 | | | | 35 0 0 0 00 | | 17 |
| 18 | Income Summary | | | | | 25 0 0 0 00 | 35 0 0 0 00 | 18 |
| 19 | Sales | | 122 0 0 0 00 | | | | 122 0 0 0 00 | 19 |
| 20 | Sales Returns and Allow. | 2 2 5 0 00 | | | | 2 2 5 0 00 | | 20 |
| 21 | Repair Revenue | | | | | | 6 4 0 0 00 | 21 |
| 22 | Purchases | 29 7 5 0 00 | | | | 29 7 5 0 00 | | 22 |
| 23 | Purchases Ret. and Allow. | | 1 8 5 0 00 | | | | 1 8 5 0 00 | 23 |
| 24 | Purchases Discounts | | 1 4 2 5 00 | | | | 1 4 2 5 00 | 24 |
| 25 | Freight-In | 3 2 0 0 00 | | | | 3 2 0 0 00 | | 25 |
| 26 | Wages Expense | 37 0 0 0 00 | | | | 38 3 0 0 00 | | 26 |
| 27 | Advertising Expense | 4 1 2 5 00 | | | | 4 1 2 5 00 | | 27 |
| 28 | Supplies Expense | | | | | 5 1 8 0 00 | | 28 |
| 29 | Telephone Expense | 1 6 5 0 00 | | | | 1 6 5 0 00 | | 29 |
| 30 | Utilities Expense | 9 1 5 0 00 | | | | 9 1 5 0 00 | | 30 |
| 31 | Insurance Expense | | | | | 4 1 7 5 00 | | 31 |
| 32 | Depr. Exp.—Building | | | | | 7 0 0 0 00 | | 32 |
| 33 | Depr. Exp.—Store Equip. | | | | | 4 1 0 0 00 | | 33 |
| 34 | Miscellaneous Expense | 7 7 5 00 | | | | 7 7 5 00 | | 34 |
| 35 | | 298 3 0 0 00 | 298 3 0 0 00 | | | 345 7 0 0 00 | 345 7 0 0 00 | 35 |
| 36 | | | | | | | | 36 |
| 37 | | | | | | | | 37 |
| 38 | | | | | | | | 38 |

**Problem 14-11A (Concluded)**

**2.**

## GENERAL JOURNAL

| | DATE | | DESCRIPTION | POST. REF. | DEBIT | CREDIT | |
|---|---|---|---|---|---|---|---|
| 1 | | | | | | | 1 |
| 2 | | | | | | | 2 |
| 3 | | | | | | | 3 |
| 4 | | | | | | | 4 |
| 5 | | | | | | | 5 |
| 6 | | | | | | | 6 |
| 7 | | | | | | | 7 |
| 8 | | | | | | | 8 |
| 9 | | | | | | | 9 |
| 10 | | | | | | | 10 |
| 11 | | | | | | | 11 |
| 12 | | | | | | | 12 |
| 13 | | | | | | | 13 |
| 14 | | | | | | | 14 |
| 15 | | | | | | | 15 |
| 16 | | | | | | | 16 |
| 17 | | | | | | | 17 |
| 18 | | | | | | | 18 |
| 19 | | | | | | | 19 |
| 20 | | | | | | | 20 |
| 21 | | | | | | | 21 |
| 22 | | | | | | | 22 |
| 23 | | | | | | | 23 |
| 24 | | | | | | | 24 |
| 25 | | | | | | | 25 |
| 26 | | | | | | | 26 |
| 27 | | | | | | | 27 |
| 28 | | | | | | | 28 |
| 29 | | | | | | | 29 |
| 30 | | | | | | | 30 |
| 31 | | | | | | | 31 |
| 32 | | | | | | | 32 |
| 33 | | | | | | | 33 |
| 34 | | | | | | | 34 |
| 35 | | | | | | | 35 |

## Problem 14-12A

1.

Lewis Music

Work

For Year Ended

| | ACCOUNT TITLE | TRIAL BALANCE | | | | | | | | | | ADJUSTMENTS | | | | | | | |
|---|---|---|---|---|---|---|---|---|---|---|---|---|---|---|---|---|---|---|---|
| | | DEBIT | | | | | CREDIT | | | | | DEBIT | | | | | CREDIT | | |
| 1 | Cash | 27 | 0 | 0 | 0 | 00 | | | | | | | | | | | | | |
| 2 | Accounts Receivable | 13 | 3 | 0 | 0 | 00 | | | | | | | | | | | | | |
| 3 | Merchandise Inventory | 34 | 0 | 0 | 0 | 00 | | | | | | | | | | | | | |
| 4 | Supplies | 5 | 3 | 0 | 0 | 00 | | | | | | | | | | | | | |
| 5 | Prepaid Insurance | 6 | 1 | 0 | 0 | 00 | | | | | | | | | | | | | |
| 6 | Land | 31 | 0 | 0 | 0 | 00 | | | | | | | | | | | | | |
| 7 | Building | 52 | 0 | 0 | 0 | 00 | | | | | | | | | | | | | |
| 8 | Accumulated Depr.—Building | | | | | | 17 | 0 | 0 | 0 | 00 | | | | | | | | |
| 9 | Store Equipment | 39 | 0 | 0 | 0 | 00 | | | | | | | | | | | | | |
| 10 | Accumulated Depr.—Store Equip. | | | | | | 11 | 9 | 0 | 0 | 00 | | | | | | | | |
| 11 | Accounts Payable | | | | | | 6 | 2 | 5 | 0 | 00 | | | | | | | | |
| 12 | Wages Payable | | | | | | | | | | | | | | | | | | |
| 13 | Sales Tax Payable | | | | | | 6 | 2 | 0 | 0 | 00 | | | | | | | | |
| 14 | Unearned Rent Revenue | | | | | | 7 | 4 | 0 | 0 | 00 | | | | | | | | |
| 15 | Mortgage Payable | | | | | | 46 | 0 | 0 | 0 | 00 | | | | | | | | |
| 16 | H. Lewis, Capital | | | | | | 111 | 6 | 2 | 0 | 00 | | | | | | | | |
| 17 | H. Lewis, Drawing | 37 | 0 | 0 | 0 | 00 | | | | | | | | | | | | | |
| 18 | Income Summary | | | | | | | | | | | | | | | | | | |
| 19 | Sales | | | | | | 136 | 0 | 0 | 0 | 00 | | | | | | | | |
| 20 | Sales Returns and Allowances | 3 | 5 | 0 | 0 | 00 | | | | | | | | | | | | | |
| 21 | Rent Revenue | | | | | | | | | | | | | | | | | | |
| 22 | Purchases | 39 | 0 | 0 | 0 | 00 | | | | | | | | | | | | | |
| 23 | Purchases Returns and Allow. | | | | | | 2 | 5 | 3 | 0 | 00 | | | | | | | | |
| 24 | Purchases Discounts | | | | | | 1 | 9 | 7 | 5 | 00 | | | | | | | | |
| 25 | Freight-In | 2 | 6 | 5 | 0 | 00 | | | | | | | | | | | | | |
| 26 | Wages Expense | 42 | 0 | 0 | 0 | 00 | | | | | | | | | | | | | |
| 27 | Advertising Expense | 4 | 1 | 7 | 5 | 00 | | | | | | | | | | | | | |
| 28 | Supplies Expense | | | | | | | | | | | | | | | | | | |
| 29 | Telephone Expense | 1 | 9 | 8 | 0 | 00 | | | | | | | | | | | | | |
| 30 | Utilities Expense | 7 | 9 | 4 | 5 | 00 | | | | | | | | | | | | | |
| 31 | Insurance Expense | | | | | | | | | | | | | | | | | | |
| 32 | Depreciation Expense—Building | | | | | | | | | | | | | | | | | | |
| 33 | Depreciation Exp.—Store Equip. | | | | | | | | | | | | | | | | | | |
| 34 | Miscellaneous Expense | | 9 | 2 | 5 | 00 | | | | | | | | | | | | | |
| 35 | | 346 | 8 | 7 | 5 | 00 | 346 | 8 | 7 | 5 | 00 | | | | | | | | |
| 36 | Net Income | | | | | | | | | | | | | | | | | | |
| 37 | | | | | | | | | | | | | | | | | | | |
| 38 | | | | | | | | | | | | | | | | | | | |

**Problem 14-12A (Continued)**

Store _____

Sheet _____

December 31, 20--

| ADJUSTED TRIAL BALANCE DEBIT | ADJUSTED TRIAL BALANCE CREDIT | INCOME STATEMENT DEBIT | INCOME STATEMENT CREDIT | BALANCE SHEET DEBIT | BALANCE SHEET CREDIT | |
|---|---|---|---|---|---|---|
| | | | | 27 0 0 0 00 | | 1 |
| | | | | 13 3 0 0 00 | | 2 |
| | | | | 38 0 0 0 00 | | 3 |
| | | | | 1 5 0 0 00 | | 4 |
| | | | | 1 7 8 5 00 | | 5 |
| | | | | 31 0 0 0 00 | | 6 |
| | | | | 52 0 0 0 00 | | 7 |
| | | | | | 21 1 4 5 00 | 8 |
| | | | | 39 0 0 0 00 | | 9 |
| | | | | | 14 8 7 5 00 | 10 |
| | | | | | 6 2 5 0 00 | 11 |
| | | | | | 8 7 5 00 | 12 |
| | | | | | 6 2 0 0 00 | 13 |
| | | | | | 3 1 7 5 00 | 14 |
| | | | | | 46 0 0 0 00 | 15 |
| | | | | | 111 6 2 0 00 | 16 |
| | | | | 37 0 0 0 00 | | 17 |
| | | 34 0 0 0 00 | 38 0 0 0 00 | | | 18 |
| | | | 136 0 0 0 00 | | | 19 |
| | | 3 5 0 0 00 | | | | 20 |
| | | | 4 2 2 5 00 | | | 21 |
| | | 39 0 0 0 00 | | | | 22 |
| | | | 2 5 3 0 00 | | | 23 |
| | | | 1 9 7 5 00 | | | 24 |
| | | 2 6 5 0 00 | | | | 25 |
| | | 42 8 7 5 00 | | | | 26 |
| | | 4 1 7 5 00 | | | | 27 |
| | | 3 8 0 0 00 | | | | 28 |
| | | 1 9 8 0 00 | | | | 29 |
| | | 7 9 4 5 00 | | | | 30 |
| | | 4 3 1 5 00 | | | | 31 |
| | | 4 1 4 5 00 | | | | 32 |
| | | 2 9 7 5 00 | | | | 33 |
| | | 9 2 5 00 | | | | 34 |
| | | 152 2 8 5 00 | 182 7 3 0 00 | 240 5 8 5 00 | 210 1 4 0 00 | 35 |
| | | 30 4 4 5 00 | | | 30 4 4 5 00 | 36 |
| | | 182 7 3 0 00 | 182 7 3 0 00 | 240 5 8 5 00 | 240 5 8 5 00 | 37 |
| | | | | | | 38 |

**Problem 14-12A (Continued)**

2.

## GENERAL JOURNAL

PAGE

| | DATE | | DESCRIPTION | POST. REF. | DEBIT | CREDIT | |
|---|---|---|---|---|---|---|---|
| 1 | | | | | | | 1 |
| 2 | | | | | | | 2 |
| 3 | | | | | | | 3 |
| 4 | | | | | | | 4 |
| 5 | | | | | | | 5 |
| 6 | | | | | | | 6 |
| 7 | | | | | | | 7 |
| 8 | | | | | | | 8 |
| 9 | | | | | | | 9 |
| 10 | | | | | | | 10 |
| 11 | | | | | | | 11 |
| 12 | | | | | | | 12 |
| 13 | | | | | | | 13 |
| 14 | | | | | | | 14 |
| 15 | | | | | | | 15 |
| 16 | | | | | | | 16 |
| 17 | | | | | | | 17 |
| 18 | | | | | | | 18 |
| 19 | | | | | | | 19 |
| 20 | | | | | | | 20 |
| 21 | | | | | | | 21 |
| 22 | | | | | | | 22 |
| 23 | | | | | | | 23 |
| 24 | | | | | | | 24 |
| 25 | | | | | | | 25 |
| 26 | | | | | | | 26 |
| 27 | | | | | | | 27 |
| 28 | | | | | | | 28 |
| 29 | | | | | | | 29 |
| 30 | | | | | | | 30 |
| 31 | | | | | | | 31 |
| 32 | | | | | | | 32 |
| 33 | | | | | | | 33 |
| 34 | | | | | | | 34 |

**Problem 14-12A (Concluded)**

3.

|  |  |  |  |  |  |
|---|---|---|---|---|---|
|  |  |  |  |  |  |
|  |  |  |  |  |  |
|  |  |  |  |  |  |
|  |  |  |  |  |  |
|  |  |  |  |  |  |
|  |  |  |  |  |  |
|  |  |  |  |  |  |
|  |  |  |  |  |  |
|  |  |  |  |  |  |
|  |  |  |  |  |  |
|  |  |  |  |  |  |
|  |  |  |  |  |  |
|  |  |  |  |  |  |
|  |  |  |  |  |  |
|  |  |  |  |  |  |
|  |  |  |  |  |  |
|  |  |  |  |  |  |
|  |  |  |  |  |  |
|  |  |  |  |  |  |
|  |  |  |  |  |  |
|  |  |  |  |  |  |
|  |  |  |  |  |  |
|  |  |  |  |  |  |
|  |  |  |  |  |  |
|  |  |  |  |  |  |
|  |  |  |  |  |  |
|  |  |  |  |  |  |
|  |  |  |  |  |  |

**Exercise 14-1B**

| Merchandise Inventory | Income Summary |
|---|---|

**Exercise 14-2B**

| | | | | | |
|---|---|---|---|---|---|
| | | | | | |

**Exercise 14-3B**

| Cash | Unearned Ticket Revenue |
|---|---|

| Ticket Revenue |
|---|

**Exercise 14-4B**

**1., 2., 3., and 4.  (See pages 528 and 529.)**

**Exercise 14-5B**

_____

_____

_____

_____

**Exercise 14-6B**

**GENERAL JOURNAL**                                          PAGE _____

| | DATE | DESCRIPTION | POST. REF. | DEBIT | CREDIT | |
|---|---|---|---|---|---|---|
| 1 | | | | | | 1 |
| 2 | | | | | | 2 |
| 3 | | | | | | 3 |
| 4 | | | | | | 4 |
| 5 | | | | | | 5 |
| 6 | | | | | | 6 |
| 7 | | | | | | 7 |
| 8 | | | | | | 8 |
| 9 | | | | | | 9 |
| 10 | | | | | | 10 |
| 11 | | | | | | 11 |
| 12 | | | | | | 12 |
| 13 | | | | | | 13 |
| 14 | | | | | | 14 |
| 15 | | | | | | 15 |
| 16 | | | | | | 16 |
| 17 | | | | | | 17 |
| 18 | | | | | | 18 |
| 19 | | | | | | 19 |
| 20 | | | | | | 20 |
| 21 | | | | | | 21 |
| 22 | | | | | | 22 |
| 23 | | | | | | 23 |
| 24 | | | | | | 24 |
| 25 | | | | | | 25 |
| 26 | | | | | | 26 |
| 27 | | | | | | 27 |

## Exercise 14-4B

### 1., 2., and 3.

Nicole's

Work

For Year Ended

| | ACCOUNT TITLE | TRIAL BALANCE | | ADJUSTMENTS | | |
|---|---|---|---|---|---|---|
| | | DEBIT | CREDIT | DEBIT | CREDIT | |
| 1 | Merchandise Inventory | 30 0 0 0 00 | | | | |
| 12 | Income Summary | | | | | |
| 13 | Purchases | 85 0 0 0 00 | | | | |
| 14 | Purchases Returns and Allow. | | 2 2 0 0 00 | | | |
| 15 | Purchases Discounts | | 2 5 0 0 00 | | | |
| 16 | Freight-In | 1 0 0 00 | | | | |
| 17 | | | | | | |
| 18 | | | | | | |

## Exercise 14-4B  (Concluded)

Gift Shop

Sheet (Partial)

December 31, 20--

| ADJUSTED TRIAL BALANCE | | INCOME STATEMENT | | BALANCE SHEET | | |
|---|---|---|---|---|---|---|
| DEBIT | CREDIT | DEBIT | CREDIT | DEBIT | CREDIT | |
| | | | | | | 1 |
| | | | | | | 12 |
| | | | | | | 13 |
| | | | | | | 14 |
| | | | | | | 15 |
| | | | | | | 16 |
| | | | | | | 17 |
| | | | | | | 18 |

**4.**

## Exercise 14-7B

**GENERAL JOURNAL**                                   PAGE

| | DATE | | DESCRIPTION | POST. REF. | DEBIT | CREDIT | |
|---|---|---|---|---|---|---|---|
| 1 | | | | | | | 1 |
| 2 | | | | | | | 2 |
| 3 | | | | | | | 3 |
| 4 | | | | | | | 4 |
| 5 | | | | | | | 5 |
| 6 | | | | | | | 6 |
| 7 | | | | | | | 7 |
| 8 | | | | | | | 8 |
| 9 | | | | | | | 9 |
| 10 | | | | | | | 10 |
| 11 | | | | | | | 11 |
| 12 | | | | | | | 12 |
| 13 | | | | | | | 13 |
| 14 | | | | | | | 14 |
| 15 | | | | | | | 15 |
| 16 | | | | | | | 16 |
| 17 | | | | | | | 17 |
| 18 | | | | | | | 18 |
| 19 | | | | | | | 19 |
| 20 | | | | | | | 20 |
| 21 | | | | | | | 21 |

## Exercise 14-8B

**GENERAL JOURNAL**                                   PAGE

| | DATE | | DESCRIPTION | POST. REF. | DEBIT | CREDIT | |
|---|---|---|---|---|---|---|---|
| 1 | | | | | | | 1 |
| 2 | | | | | | | 2 |
| 3 | | | | | | | 3 |
| 4 | | | | | | | 4 |
| 5 | | | | | | | 5 |
| 6 | | | | | | | 6 |
| 7 | | | | | | | 7 |
| 8 | | | | | | | 8 |
| 9 | | | | | | | 9 |
| 10 | | | | | | | 10 |

**Problem 14-9B**

**1. and 2.  (See pages 532 and 533.)**

**3.**

## GENERAL JOURNAL

PAGE

| | DATE | | DESCRIPTION | POST. REF. | DEBIT | CREDIT | |
|---|---|---|---|---|---|---|---|
| 1 | | | | | | | 1 |
| 2 | | | | | | | 2 |
| 3 | | | | | | | 3 |
| 4 | | | | | | | 4 |
| 5 | | | | | | | 5 |
| 6 | | | | | | | 6 |
| 7 | | | | | | | 7 |
| 8 | | | | | | | 8 |
| 9 | | | | | | | 9 |
| 10 | | | | | | | 10 |
| 11 | | | | | | | 11 |
| 12 | | | | | | | 12 |
| 13 | | | | | | | 13 |
| 14 | | | | | | | 14 |
| 15 | | | | | | | 15 |
| 16 | | | | | | | 16 |
| 17 | | | | | | | 17 |
| 18 | | | | | | | 18 |
| 19 | | | | | | | 19 |
| 20 | | | | | | | 20 |
| 21 | | | | | | | 21 |
| 22 | | | | | | | 22 |
| 23 | | | | | | | 23 |
| 24 | | | | | | | 24 |
| 25 | | | | | | | 25 |
| 26 | | | | | | | 26 |
| 27 | | | | | | | 27 |
| 28 | | | | | | | 28 |
| 29 | | | | | | | 29 |
| 30 | | | | | | | 30 |
| 31 | | | | | | | 31 |
| 32 | | | | | | | 32 |
| 33 | | | | | | | 33 |
| 34 | | | | | | | 34 |

## Problem 14-9B (Continued)
**1. and 2.**

Basket

Work

For Year Ended

| | ACCOUNT TITLE | TRIAL BALANCE | | ADJUSTMENTS | |
|---|---|---|---|---|---|
| | | DEBIT | CREDIT | DEBIT | CREDIT |
| 1 | Cash | 25 0 0 0 00 | | | |
| 2 | Accounts Receivable | 8 1 0 0 00 | | | |
| 3 | Merchandise Inventory | 32 0 0 0 00 | | | |
| 4 | Supplies | 7 1 0 0 00 | | | |
| 5 | Prepaid Insurance | 3 6 0 0 00 | | | |
| 6 | Land | 40 0 0 0 00 | | | |
| 7 | Building | 45 0 0 0 00 | | | |
| 8 | Accumulated Depr.—Building | | 16 0 0 0 00 | | |
| 9 | Store Equipment | 27 0 0 0 00 | | | |
| 10 | Accumulated Depr.—Store Equip. | | 5 5 0 0 00 | | |
| 11 | Accounts Payable | | 3 6 0 0 00 | | |
| 12 | Wages Payable | | | | |
| 13 | Sales Tax Payable | | 6 2 0 0 00 | | |
| 14 | Unearned Decorating Revenue | | 6 3 0 0 00 | | |
| 15 | Mortgage Payable | | 36 0 0 0 00 | | |
| 16 | L. Palermo, Capital | | 112 0 5 0 00 | | |
| 17 | L. Palermo, Drawing | 31 0 0 0 00 | | | |
| 18 | Income Summary | | | | |
| 19 | Sales | | 125 0 0 0 00 | | |
| 20 | Sales Returns and Allowances | 2 6 0 0 00 | | | |
| 21 | Decorating Revenue | | | | |
| 22 | Purchases | 38 0 0 0 00 | | | |
| 23 | Purchases Returns and Allow. | | 2 2 0 0 00 | | |
| 24 | Purchases Discounts | | 1 7 0 0 00 | | |
| 25 | Freight-In | 1 9 0 0 00 | | | |
| 26 | Wages Expense | 38 0 0 0 00 | | | |
| 27 | Advertising Expense | 4 2 0 0 00 | | | |
| 28 | Supplies Expense | | | | |
| 29 | Telephone Expense | 1 8 7 0 00 | | | |
| 30 | Utilities Expense | 8 4 0 0 00 | | | |
| 31 | Insurance Expense | | | | |
| 32 | Depreciation Expense—Building | | | | |
| 33 | Depreciation Exp.—Store Equip. | | | | |
| 34 | Miscellaneous Expense | 7 8 0 00 | | | |
| 35 | | 314 5 5 0 00 | 314 5 5 0 00 | | |
| 36 | | | | | |
| 37 | | | | | |
| 38 | | | | | |

**Problem 14-9B (Concluded)**

Corner
_____

Sheet
_____

December 31, 20--
_____

| | ADJUSTED TRIAL BALANCE | | INCOME STATEMENT | | BALANCE SHEET | | |
| --- | --- | --- | --- | --- | --- | --- | --- |
| | DEBIT | CREDIT | DEBIT | CREDIT | DEBIT | CREDIT | |
| | | | | | | | 1 |
| | | | | | | | 2 |
| | | | | | | | 3 |
| | | | | | | | 4 |
| | | | | | | | 5 |
| | | | | | | | 6 |
| | | | | | | | 7 |
| | | | | | | | 8 |
| | | | | | | | 9 |
| | | | | | | | 10 |
| | | | | | | | 11 |
| | | | | | | | 12 |
| | | | | | | | 13 |
| | | | | | | | 14 |
| | | | | | | | 15 |
| | | | | | | | 16 |
| | | | | | | | 17 |
| | | | | | | | 18 |
| | | | | | | | 19 |
| | | | | | | | 20 |
| | | | | | | | 21 |
| | | | | | | | 22 |
| | | | | | | | 23 |
| | | | | | | | 24 |
| | | | | | | | 25 |
| | | | | | | | 26 |
| | | | | | | | 27 |
| | | | | | | | 28 |
| | | | | | | | 29 |
| | | | | | | | 30 |
| | | | | | | | 31 |
| | | | | | | | 32 |
| | | | | | | | 33 |
| | | | | | | | 34 |
| | | | | | | | 35 |
| | | | | | | | 36 |
| | | | | | | | 37 |
| | | | | | | | 38 |

## Problem 14-10B

### 1. and 2.

Oregon Bike

Work

For Year Ended

| | ACCOUNT TITLE | TRIAL BALANCE DEBIT | | | | | TRIAL BALANCE CREDIT | | | | | ADJUSTMENTS DEBIT | | | ADJUSTMENTS CREDIT | | |
|---|---|---|---|---|---|---|---|---|---|---|---|---|---|---|---|---|---|
| 1 | Cash | 27 | 0 | 0 | 0 | 00 | | | | | | | | | | | |
| 2 | Accounts Receivable | 12 | 0 | 0 | 0 | 00 | | | | | | | | | | | |
| 3 | Merchandise Inventory | 39 | 0 | 0 | 0 | 00 | | | | | | | | | | | |
| 4 | Supplies | 6 | 2 | 0 | 0 | 00 | | | | | | | | | | | |
| 5 | Prepaid Insurance | 5 | 8 | 0 | 0 | 00 | | | | | | | | | | | |
| 6 | Land | 32 | 0 | 0 | 0 | 00 | | | | | | | | | | | |
| 7 | Building | 58 | 0 | 0 | 0 | 00 | | | | | | | | | | | |
| 8 | Accumulated Depr.—Building | | | | | | 27 | 0 | 0 | 0 | 00 | | | | | | |
| 9 | Store Equipment | 31 | 0 | 0 | 0 | 00 | | | | | | | | | | | |
| 10 | Accumulated Depr.—Store Equip. | | | | | | 14 | 0 | 0 | 0 | 00 | | | | | | |
| 11 | Accounts Payable | | | | | | 4 | 9 | 0 | 0 | 00 | | | | | | |
| 12 | Wages Payable | | | | | | | | | | | | | | | | |
| 13 | Sales Tax Payable | | | | | | 2 | 9 | 0 | 0 | 00 | | | | | | |
| 14 | Unearned Rent Revenue | | | | | | 6 | 1 | 0 | 0 | 00 | | | | | | |
| 15 | Mortgage Payable | | | | | | 49 | 0 | 0 | 0 | 00 | | | | | | |
| 16 | C. Moody, Capital | | | | | | 169 | 5 | 0 | 0 | 00 | | | | | | |
| 17 | C. Moody, Drawing | 36 | 0 | 0 | 0 | 00 | | | | | | | | | | | |
| 18 | Income Summary | | | | | | | | | | | | | | | | |
| 19 | Sales | | | | | | 58 | 0 | 0 | 0 | 00 | | | | | | |
| 20 | Sales Returns and Allowances | 3 | 3 | 0 | 0 | 00 | | | | | | | | | | | |
| 21 | Rent Revenue | | | | | | | | | | | | | | | | |
| 22 | Purchases | 19 | 0 | 0 | 0 | 00 | | | | | | | | | | | |
| 23 | Purchases Returns and Allow. | | | | | | | 9 | 0 | 0 | 00 | | | | | | |
| 24 | Purchases Discounts | | | | | | 1 | 4 | 5 | 0 | 00 | | | | | | |
| 25 | Freight-In | | 8 | 0 | 0 | 00 | | | | | | | | | | | |
| 26 | Wages Expense | 47 | 0 | 0 | 0 | 00 | | | | | | | | | | | |
| 27 | Advertising Expense | 6 | 2 | 0 | 0 | 00 | | | | | | | | | | | |
| 28 | Supplies Expense | | | | | | | | | | | | | | | | |
| 29 | Telephone Expense | 1 | 8 | 6 | 0 | 00 | | | | | | | | | | | |
| 30 | Utilities Expense | 8 | 1 | 0 | 0 | 00 | | | | | | | | | | | |
| 31 | Insurance Expense | | | | | | | | | | | | | | | | |
| 32 | Depreciation Expense—Building | | | | | | | | | | | | | | | | |
| 33 | Depreciation Exp.—Store Equip. | | | | | | | | | | | | | | | | |
| 34 | Miscellaneous Expense | | 4 | 9 | 0 | 00 | | | | | | | | | | | |
| 35 | | 333 | 7 | 5 | 0 | 00 | 333 | 7 | 5 | 0 | 00 | | | | | | |
| 36 | | | | | | | | | | | | | | | | | |
| 37 | | | | | | | | | | | | | | | | | |
| 38 | | | | | | | | | | | | | | | | | |

**Problem 14-10B (Continued)**

Company _____

Sheet _____

December 31, 20--

| ADJUSTED TRIAL BALANCE | | INCOME STATEMENT | | BALANCE SHEET | | |
|---|---|---|---|---|---|---|
| DEBIT | CREDIT | DEBIT | CREDIT | DEBIT | CREDIT | |
| | | | | | | 1 |
| | | | | | | 2 |
| | | | | | | 3 |
| | | | | | | 4 |
| | | | | | | 5 |
| | | | | | | 6 |
| | | | | | | 7 |
| | | | | | | 8 |
| | | | | | | 9 |
| | | | | | | 10 |
| | | | | | | 11 |
| | | | | | | 12 |
| | | | | | | 13 |
| | | | | | | 14 |
| | | | | | | 15 |
| | | | | | | 16 |
| | | | | | | 17 |
| | | | | | | 18 |
| | | | | | | 19 |
| | | | | | | 20 |
| | | | | | | 21 |
| | | | | | | 22 |
| | | | | | | 23 |
| | | | | | | 24 |
| | | | | | | 25 |
| | | | | | | 26 |
| | | | | | | 27 |
| | | | | | | 28 |
| | | | | | | 29 |
| | | | | | | 30 |
| | | | | | | 31 |
| | | | | | | 32 |
| | | | | | | 33 |
| | | | | | | 34 |
| | | | | | | 35 |
| | | | | | | 36 |
| | | | | | | 37 |
| | | | | | | 38 |

## Problem 14-10B (Concluded)

**3.**

**GENERAL JOURNAL** PAGE

| | DATE | DESCRIPTION | POST. REF. | DEBIT | CREDIT | |
|---|---|---|---|---|---|---|
| 1 | | | | | | 1 |
| 2 | | | | | | 2 |
| 3 | | | | | | 3 |
| 4 | | | | | | 4 |
| 5 | | | | | | 5 |
| 6 | | | | | | 6 |
| 7 | | | | | | 7 |
| 8 | | | | | | 8 |
| 9 | | | | | | 9 |
| 10 | | | | | | 10 |
| 11 | | | | | | 11 |
| 12 | | | | | | 12 |
| 13 | | | | | | 13 |
| 14 | | | | | | 14 |
| 15 | | | | | | 15 |
| 16 | | | | | | 16 |
| 17 | | | | | | 17 |
| 18 | | | | | | 18 |
| 19 | | | | | | 19 |
| 20 | | | | | | 20 |
| 21 | | | | | | 21 |
| 22 | | | | | | 22 |
| 23 | | | | | | 23 |
| 24 | | | | | | 24 |
| 25 | | | | | | 25 |
| 26 | | | | | | 26 |
| 27 | | | | | | 27 |
| 28 | | | | | | 28 |
| 29 | | | | | | 29 |
| 30 | | | | | | 30 |
| 31 | | | | | | 31 |
| 32 | | | | | | 32 |
| 33 | | | | | | 33 |
| 34 | | | | | | 34 |

## Problem 14-11B

1.

Burnside Auto Parts

Work Sheet (Partial)

For Year Ended December 31, 20--

| # | ACCOUNT TITLE | TRIAL BALANCE DEBIT | TRIAL BALANCE CREDIT | ADJUSTMENTS DEBIT | ADJUSTMENTS CREDIT | ADJUSTED TRIAL BALANCE DEBIT | ADJUSTED TRIAL BALANCE CREDIT | # |
|---|---|---|---|---|---|---|---|---|
| 1 | Cash | 21 0 0 0 00 | | | | 21 0 0 0 00 | | 1 |
| 2 | Accounts Receivable | 8 3 0 0 00 | | | | 8 3 0 0 00 | | 2 |
| 3 | Merchandise Inventory | 32 0 0 0 00 | | | | 36 0 0 0 00 | | 3 |
| 4 | Supplies | 6 1 5 0 00 | | | | 1 8 6 5 00 | | 4 |
| 5 | Prepaid Insurance | 5 9 2 5 00 | | | | 1 8 3 5 00 | | 5 |
| 6 | Land | 41 7 5 0 00 | | | | 41 7 5 0 00 | | 6 |
| 7 | Building | 43 0 0 0 00 | | | | 43 0 0 0 00 | | 7 |
| 8 | Accum. Depr.—Building | | 24 0 0 0 00 | | | | 27 5 0 0 00 | 8 |
| 9 | Store Equipment | 25 4 0 0 00 | | | | 25 4 0 0 00 | | 9 |
| 10 | Accum. Depr.—Store Equip. | | 12 4 0 0 00 | | | | 14 7 5 0 00 | 10 |
| 11 | Accounts Payable | | 8 1 0 0 00 | | | | 8 1 0 0 00 | 11 |
| 12 | Wages Payable | | | | | | 9 8 0 00 | 12 |
| 13 | Sales Tax Payable | | 5 2 0 0 00 | | | | 5 2 0 0 00 | 13 |
| 14 | Unearn. Rent-A-Junk Rev. | | 7 9 5 0 00 | | | | 2 3 5 0 00 | 14 |
| 15 | Mortgage Payable | | 26 0 0 0 00 | | | | 26 0 0 0 00 | 15 |
| 16 | B. Davis, Capital | | 109 1 3 0 00 | | | | 109 1 3 0 00 | 16 |
| 17 | B. Davis, Drawing | 40 0 0 0 00 | | | | 40 0 0 0 00 | | 17 |
| 18 | Income Summary | | | | | 32 0 0 0 00 | 36 0 0 0 00 | 18 |
| 19 | Sales | | 123 5 0 0 00 | | | | 123 5 0 0 00 | 19 |
| 20 | Sales Returns and Allow. | 2 8 6 0 00 | | | | 2 8 6 0 00 | | 20 |
| 21 | Rent-A-Junk Revenue | | | | | | 5 6 0 0 00 | 21 |
| 22 | Purchases | 32 5 2 5 00 | | | | 32 5 2 5 00 | | 22 |
| 23 | Purchases Ret. and Allow. | | 2 1 5 0 00 | | | | 2 1 5 0 00 | 23 |
| 24 | Purchases Discounts | | 2 4 0 0 00 | | | | 2 4 0 0 00 | 24 |
| 25 | Freight-In | 3 1 7 5 00 | | | | 3 1 7 5 00 | | 25 |
| 26 | Wages Expense | 44 1 7 5 00 | | | | 45 1 5 5 00 | | 26 |
| 27 | Advertising Expense | 3 2 7 5 00 | | | | 3 2 7 5 00 | | 27 |
| 28 | Supplies Expense | | | | | 4 2 8 5 00 | | 28 |
| 29 | Telephone Expense | 2 2 0 0 00 | | | | 2 2 0 0 00 | | 29 |
| 30 | Utilities Expense | 8 2 5 0 00 | | | | 8 2 5 0 00 | | 30 |
| 31 | Insurance Expense | | | | | 4 0 9 0 00 | | 31 |
| 32 | Depr. Exp.—Building | | | | | 3 5 0 0 00 | | 32 |
| 33 | Depr. Exp.—Store Equip. | | | | | 2 3 5 0 00 | | 33 |
| 34 | Miscellaneous Expense | 8 4 5 00 | | | | 8 4 5 00 | | 34 |
| 35 | | 320 8 3 0 00 | 320 8 3 0 00 | | | 363 6 6 0 00 | 363 6 6 0 00 | 35 |
| 36 | | | | | | | | 36 |
| 37 | | | | | | | | 37 |
| 38 | | | | | | | | 38 |

## Problem 14-11B (Concluded)

**2.**

### GENERAL JOURNAL

| | DATE | | DESCRIPTION | POST. REF. | DEBIT | CREDIT | |
|---|---|---|---|---|---|---|---|
| 1 | | | | | | | 1 |
| 2 | | | | | | | 2 |
| 3 | | | | | | | 3 |
| 4 | | | | | | | 4 |
| 5 | | | | | | | 5 |
| 6 | | | | | | | 6 |
| 7 | | | | | | | 7 |
| 8 | | | | | | | 8 |
| 9 | | | | | | | 9 |
| 10 | | | | | | | 10 |
| 11 | | | | | | | 11 |
| 12 | | | | | | | 12 |
| 13 | | | | | | | 13 |
| 14 | | | | | | | 14 |
| 15 | | | | | | | 15 |
| 16 | | | | | | | 16 |
| 17 | | | | | | | 17 |
| 18 | | | | | | | 18 |
| 19 | | | | | | | 19 |
| 20 | | | | | | | 20 |
| 21 | | | | | | | 21 |
| 22 | | | | | | | 22 |
| 23 | | | | | | | 23 |
| 24 | | | | | | | 24 |
| 25 | | | | | | | 25 |
| 26 | | | | | | | 26 |
| 27 | | | | | | | 27 |
| 28 | | | | | | | 28 |
| 29 | | | | | | | 29 |
| 30 | | | | | | | 30 |
| 31 | | | | | | | 31 |
| 32 | | | | | | | 32 |
| 33 | | | | | | | 33 |
| 34 | | | | | | | 34 |

**Problem 14-12B**

1. (See pages 540 and 541.)
2.

### GENERAL JOURNAL

PAGE _____

| | DATE | | DESCRIPTION | POST. REF. | DEBIT | CREDIT | |
|---|---|---|---|---|---|---|---|
| 1 | | | | | | | 1 |
| 2 | | | | | | | 2 |
| 3 | | | | | | | 3 |
| 4 | | | | | | | 4 |
| 5 | | | | | | | 5 |
| 6 | | | | | | | 6 |
| 7 | | | | | | | 7 |
| 8 | | | | | | | 8 |
| 9 | | | | | | | 9 |
| 10 | | | | | | | 10 |
| 11 | | | | | | | 11 |
| 12 | | | | | | | 12 |
| 13 | | | | | | | 13 |
| 14 | | | | | | | 14 |
| 15 | | | | | | | 15 |
| 16 | | | | | | | 16 |
| 17 | | | | | | | 17 |
| 18 | | | | | | | 18 |
| 19 | | | | | | | 19 |
| 20 | | | | | | | 20 |
| 21 | | | | | | | 21 |
| 22 | | | | | | | 22 |
| 23 | | | | | | | 23 |
| 24 | | | | | | | 24 |
| 25 | | | | | | | 25 |
| 26 | | | | | | | 26 |
| 27 | | | | | | | 27 |
| 28 | | | | | | | 28 |
| 29 | | | | | | | 29 |
| 30 | | | | | | | 30 |
| 31 | | | | | | | 31 |
| 32 | | | | | | | 32 |
| 33 | | | | | | | 33 |
| 34 | | | | | | | 34 |

## Problem 14-12B  (Continued)

1.

Diamond Music

Work

For Year Ended

| | ACCOUNT TITLE | TRIAL BALANCE | | ADJUSTMENTS | |
|---|---|---|---|---|---|
| | | DEBIT | CREDIT | DEBIT | CREDIT |
| 1 | Cash | 31 0 0 0 00 | | | |
| 2 | Accounts Receivable | 11 9 8 0 00 | | | |
| 3 | Merchandise Inventory | 33 6 0 0 00 | | | |
| 4 | Supplies | 7 1 4 0 00 | | | |
| 5 | Prepaid Insurance | 5 9 8 5 00 | | | |
| 6 | Land | 36 2 0 0 00 | | | |
| 7 | Building | 51 8 5 0 00 | | | |
| 8 | Accumulated Depr.—Building | | 13 5 9 0 00 | | |
| 9 | Store Equipment | 32 6 7 5 00 | | | |
| 10 | Accumulated Depr.—Store Equip. | | 10 2 9 0 00 | | |
| 11 | Accounts Payable | | 5 8 9 5 00 | | |
| 12 | Wages Payable | | | | |
| 13 | Sales Tax Payable | | 6 3 7 5 00 | | |
| 14 | Unearned Rent Revenue | | 8 8 5 0 00 | | |
| 15 | Mortgage Payable | | 42 4 0 0 00 | | |
| 16 | N. Diamond, Capital | | 116 3 5 0 00 | | |
| 17 | N. Diamond, Drawing | 39 5 0 0 00 | | | |
| 18 | Income Summary | | | | |
| 19 | Sales | | 148 0 0 0 00 | | |
| 20 | Sales Returns and Allowances | 2 8 0 0 00 | | | |
| 21 | Rent Revenue | | | | |
| 22 | Purchases | 40 7 0 0 00 | | | |
| 23 | Purchases Returns and Allow. | | 2 7 7 5 00 | | |
| 24 | Purchases Discounts | | 2 3 2 5 00 | | |
| 25 | Freight-In | 1 8 7 5 00 | | | |
| 26 | Wages Expense | 47 0 0 0 00 | | | |
| 27 | Advertising Expense | 4 6 9 5 00 | | | |
| 28 | Supplies Expense | | | | |
| 29 | Telephone Expense | 2 2 5 0 00 | | | |
| 30 | Utilities Expense | 6 8 2 5 00 | | | |
| 31 | Insurance Expense | | | | |
| 32 | Depreciation Expense—Building | | | | |
| 33 | Depreciation Exp.—Store Equip. | | | | |
| 34 | Miscellaneous Expense | 7 7 5 00 | | | |
| 35 | | 356 8 5 0 00 | 356 8 5 0 00 | | |
| 36 | Net Income | | | | |
| 37 | | | | | |
| 38 | | | | | |

## Problem 14-12B (Continued)

Store _____

Sheet _____

December 31, 20--

| | ADJUSTED TRIAL BALANCE DEBIT | ADJUSTED TRIAL BALANCE CREDIT | INCOME STATEMENT DEBIT | INCOME STATEMENT CREDIT | BALANCE SHEET DEBIT | BALANCE SHEET CREDIT | |
|---|---|---|---|---|---|---|---|
| | | | | | 31 0 0 0 00 | | 1 |
| | | | | | 11 9 8 0 00 | | 2 |
| | | | | | 39 1 0 0 00 | | 3 |
| | | | | | 1 9 6 5 00 | | 4 |
| | | | | | 1 2 3 5 00 | | 5 |
| | | | | | 36 2 0 0 00 | | 6 |
| | | | | | 51 8 5 0 00 | | 7 |
| | | | | | | 18 8 7 5 00 | 8 |
| | | | | | 32 6 7 5 00 | | 9 |
| | | | | | | 14 7 5 5 00 | 10 |
| | | | | | | 5 8 9 5 00 | 11 |
| | | | | | | 1 2 5 0 00 | 12 |
| | | | | | | 6 3 7 5 00 | 13 |
| | | | | | | 2 9 3 0 00 | 14 |
| | | | | | | 42 4 0 0 00 | 15 |
| | | | | | | 116 3 5 0 00 | 16 |
| | | | | | 39 5 0 0 00 | | 17 |
| | | | 33 6 0 0 00 | 39 1 0 0 00 | | | 18 |
| | | | | 148 0 0 0 00 | | | 19 |
| | | | 2 8 0 0 00 | | | | 20 |
| | | | | 5 9 2 0 00 | | | 21 |
| | | | 40 7 0 0 00 | | | | 22 |
| | | | | 2 7 7 5 00 | | | 23 |
| | | | | 2 3 2 5 00 | | | 24 |
| | | | 1 8 7 5 00 | | | | 25 |
| | | | 48 2 5 0 00 | | | | 26 |
| | | | 4 6 9 5 00 | | | | 27 |
| | | | 5 1 7 5 00 | | | | 28 |
| | | | 2 2 5 0 00 | | | | 29 |
| | | | 6 8 2 5 00 | | | | 30 |
| | | | 4 7 5 0 00 | | | | 31 |
| | | | 5 2 8 5 00 | | | | 32 |
| | | | 4 4 6 5 00 | | | | 33 |
| | | | 7 7 5 00 | | | | 34 |
| | | | 161 4 4 5 00 | 198 1 2 0 00 | 245 5 0 5 00 | 208 8 3 0 00 | 35 |
| | | | 36 6 7 5 00 | | | 36 6 7 5 00 | 36 |
| | | | 198 1 2 0 00 | 198 1 2 0 00 | 245 5 0 5 00 | 245 5 0 5 00 | 37 |
| | | | | | | | 38 |

## Problem 14-12B (Concluded)

3.

**Mastery Problem**

1. (See pages 544 and 545 for work sheet.)
2.

## GENERAL JOURNAL

PAGE

| | DATE | | DESCRIPTION | POST. REF. | DEBIT | CREDIT | |
|---|---|---|---|---|---|---|---|
| 1 | | | | | | | 1 |
| 2 | | | | | | | 2 |
| 3 | | | | | | | 3 |
| 4 | | | | | | | 4 |
| 5 | | | | | | | 5 |
| 6 | | | | | | | 6 |
| 7 | | | | | | | 7 |
| 8 | | | | | | | 8 |
| 9 | | | | | | | 9 |
| 10 | | | | | | | 10 |
| 11 | | | | | | | 11 |
| 12 | | | | | | | 12 |
| 13 | | | | | | | 13 |
| 14 | | | | | | | 14 |
| 15 | | | | | | | 15 |
| 16 | | | | | | | 16 |
| 17 | | | | | | | 17 |
| 18 | | | | | | | 18 |
| 19 | | | | | | | 19 |
| 20 | | | | | | | 20 |
| 21 | | | | | | | 21 |
| 22 | | | | | | | 22 |
| 23 | | | | | | | 23 |
| 24 | | | | | | | 24 |
| 25 | | | | | | | 25 |
| 26 | | | | | | | 26 |
| 27 | | | | | | | 27 |
| 28 | | | | | | | 28 |
| 29 | | | | | | | 29 |
| 30 | | | | | | | 30 |
| 31 | | | | | | | 31 |
| 32 | | | | | | | 32 |
| 33 | | | | | | | 33 |
| 34 | | | | | | | 34 |

## Mastery Problem  (Continued)
1.

Waikiki Surf

Work

For Year Ended

| | ACCOUNT TITLE | TRIAL BALANCE | | ADJUSTMENTS | |
|---|---|---|---|---|---|
| | | DEBIT | CREDIT | DEBIT | CREDIT |
| 1 | Cash | 30 0 0 0 00 | | | |
| 2 | Accounts Receivable | 22 5 0 0 00 | | | |
| 3 | Merchandise Inventory | 57 0 0 0 00 | | | |
| 4 | Supplies | 2 7 0 0 00 | | | |
| 5 | Prepaid Insurance | 3 6 0 0 00 | | | |
| 6 | Land | 15 0 0 0 00 | | | |
| 7 | Building | 135 0 0 0 00 | | | |
| 8 | Accumulated Depr.—Building | | 24 0 0 0 00 | | |
| 9 | Store Equipment | 75 0 0 0 00 | | | |
| 10 | Accumulated Depr.—Store Equip. | | 22 5 0 0 00 | | |
| 11 | Notes Payable | | 7 5 0 0 00 | | |
| 12 | Accounts Payable | | 15 0 0 0 00 | | |
| 13 | Wages Payable | | | | |
| 14 | Unearned Boat Rental Revenue | | 33 0 0 0 00 | | |
| 15 | J. Neff, Capital | | 233 7 0 0 00 | | |
| 16 | J. Neff, Drawing | 30 0 0 0 00 | | | |
| 17 | Income Summary | | | | |
| 18 | Sales | | 300 7 5 0 00 | | |
| 19 | Sales Returns and Allowances | 1 8 0 0 00 | | | |
| 20 | Boat Rental Revenue | | | | |
| 21 | Purchases | 157 5 0 0 00 | | | |
| 22 | Purchases Returns and Allow. | | 1 2 0 0 00 | | |
| 23 | Purchases Discounts | | 1 5 0 0 00 | | |
| 24 | Freight-In | 4 5 0 00 | | | |
| 25 | Wages Expense | 63 0 0 0 00 | | | |
| 26 | Advertising Expense | 11 2 5 0 00 | | | |
| 27 | Supplies Expense | | | | |
| 28 | Telephone Expense | 5 2 5 0 00 | | | |
| 29 | Utilities Expense | 18 0 0 0 00 | | | |
| 30 | Insurance Expense | | | | |
| 31 | Depreciation Expense—Building | | | | |
| 32 | Depreciation Exp.—Store Equip. | | | | |
| 33 | Miscellaneous Expense | 10 8 7 5 00 | | | |
| 34 | Interest Expense | 2 2 5 00 | | | |
| 35 | | 639 1 5 0 00 | 639 1 5 0 00 | | |
| 36 | | | | | |
| 37 | | | | | |
| 38 | | | | | |

**Mastery Problem (Concluded)**

Shop _____

Sheet _____

December 31, 20-- _____

| ADJUSTED TRIAL BALANCE | | INCOME STATEMENT | | BALANCE SHEET | | |
|---|---|---|---|---|---|---|
| DEBIT | CREDIT | DEBIT | CREDIT | DEBIT | CREDIT | |
| | | | | | | 1 |
| | | | | | | 2 |
| | | | | | | 3 |
| | | | | | | 4 |
| | | | | | | 5 |
| | | | | | | 6 |
| | | | | | | 7 |
| | | | | | | 8 |
| | | | | | | 9 |
| | | | | | | 10 |
| | | | | | | 11 |
| | | | | | | 12 |
| | | | | | | 13 |
| | | | | | | 14 |
| | | | | | | 15 |
| | | | | | | 16 |
| | | | | | | 17 |
| | | | | | | 18 |
| | | | | | | 19 |
| | | | | | | 20 |
| | | | | | | 21 |
| | | | | | | 22 |
| | | | | | | 23 |
| | | | | | | 24 |
| | | | | | | 25 |
| | | | | | | 26 |
| | | | | | | 27 |
| | | | | | | 28 |
| | | | | | | 29 |
| | | | | | | 30 |
| | | | | | | 31 |
| | | | | | | 32 |
| | | | | | | 33 |
| | | | | | | 34 |
| | | | | | | 35 |
| | | | | | | 36 |
| | | | | | | 37 |
| | | | | | | 38 |

**Challenge Problem**

# APPENDIX: EXPENSE METHOD OF ACCOUNTING FOR PREPAID EXPENSES

## Exercise 14Apx-1A

### GENERAL JOURNAL                    PAGE _____

| | DATE | DESCRIPTION | POST. REF. | DEBIT | CREDIT | |
|---|---|---|---|---|---|---|
| 1 | | | | | | 1 |
| 2 | | | | | | 2 |
| 3 | | | | | | 3 |
| 4 | | | | | | 4 |
| 5 | | | | | | 5 |
| 6 | | | | | | 6 |
| 7 | | | | | | 7 |
| 8 | | | | | | 8 |
| 9 | | | | | | 9 |
| 10 | | | | | | 10 |
| 11 | | | | | | 11 |
| 12 | | | | | | 12 |

## Exercise 14Apx-1B

### GENERAL JOURNAL                    PAGE _____

| | DATE | DESCRIPTION | POST. REF. | DEBIT | CREDIT | |
|---|---|---|---|---|---|---|
| 1 | | | | | | 1 |
| 2 | | | | | | 2 |
| 3 | | | | | | 3 |
| 4 | | | | | | 4 |
| 5 | | | | | | 5 |
| 6 | | | | | | 6 |
| 7 | | | | | | 7 |
| 8 | | | | | | 8 |
| 9 | | | | | | 9 |
| 10 | | | | | | 10 |
| 11 | | | | | | 11 |
| 12 | | | | | | 12 |

## Exercise 15-1A

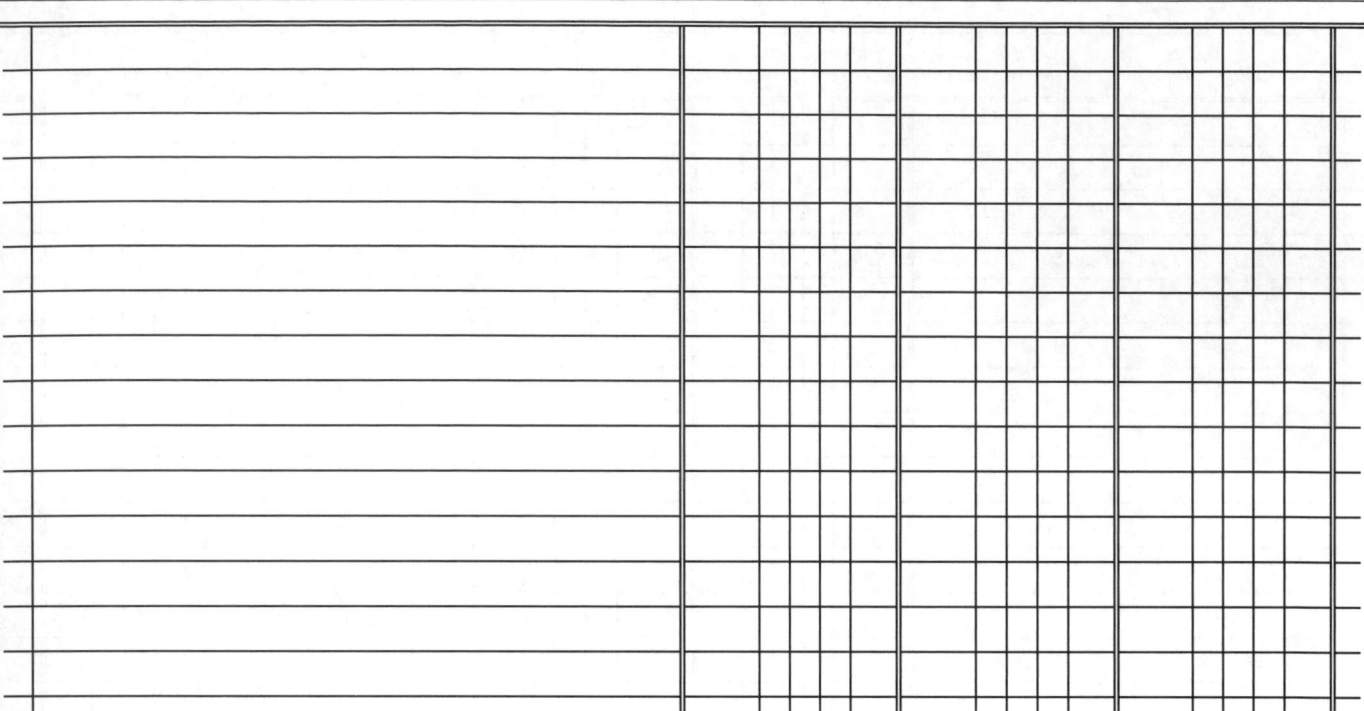

## Exercise 15-2A

**Exercise 15-3A**

**Exercise 15-4A**

**Exercise 15-5A**

**1.**

## GENERAL JOURNAL

| | DATE | | DESCRIPTION | POST. REF. | DEBIT | CREDIT | |
|---|---|---|---|---|---|---|---|
| 1 | | | | | | | 1 |
| 2 | | | | | | | 2 |
| 3 | | | | | | | 3 |
| 4 | | | | | | | 4 |
| 5 | | | | | | | 5 |
| 6 | | | | | | | 6 |
| 7 | | | | | | | 7 |
| 8 | | | | | | | 8 |
| 9 | | | | | | | 9 |
| 10 | | | | | | | 10 |
| 11 | | | | | | | 11 |
| 12 | | | | | | | 12 |
| 13 | | | | | | | 13 |
| 14 | | | | | | | 14 |
| 15 | | | | | | | 15 |
| 16 | | | | | | | 16 |
| 17 | | | | | | | 17 |
| 18 | | | | | | | 18 |
| 19 | | | | | | | 19 |
| 20 | | | | | | | 20 |
| 21 | | | | | | | 21 |
| 22 | | | | | | | 22 |
| 23 | | | | | | | 23 |
| 24 | | | | | | | 24 |
| 25 | | | | | | | 25 |
| 26 | | | | | | | 26 |
| 27 | | | | | | | 27 |
| 28 | | | | | | | 28 |
| 29 | | | | | | | 29 |
| 30 | | | | | | | 30 |
| 31 | | | | | | | 31 |
| 32 | | | | | | | 32 |
| 33 | | | | | | | 33 |
| 34 | | | | | | | 34 |

**Exercise 15-5A (Concluded)**

**2.**

| | | | | |
|---|---|---|---|---|
| | | | | |
| | | | | |
| | | | | |
| | | | | |
| | | | | |
| | | | | |
| | | | | |
| | | | | |
| | | | | |
| | | | | |
| | | | | |
| | | | | |
| | | | | |
| | | | | |
| | | | | |

J. M. Gimbel, Capital

## Exercise 15-6A

**GENERAL JOURNAL**                                                          PAGE

| | DATE | DESCRIPTION | POST. REF. | DEBIT | CREDIT | |
|---|---|---|---|---|---|---|
| 1 | | | | | | 1 |
| 2 | | | | | | 2 |
| 3 | | | | | | 3 |
| 4 | | | | | | 4 |
| 5 | | | | | | 5 |

## Exercise 15-7A

| DATE | WITHOUT REVERSING ENTRY | WITH REVERSING ENTRY |
|---|---|---|
| Adjusting Entry: | | |
| Closing Entry: | | |
| Reversing Entry: | | |
| Payment of Payroll: | | |

Wages Expense                                    Wages Expense

Wages Payable                                    Wages Payable

**Problem 15-8A**

1.

**Problem 15-8A (Continued)**

2.

**Problem 15-8A (Concluded)**

3.

## Problem 15-9A

**Problem 15-10A**

**1. (See pages 562 and 563)**

**2., 3., and 5.**

**GENERAL JOURNAL** PAGE _____

| | DATE | | DESCRIPTION | POST. REF. | DEBIT | CREDIT | |
|---|---|---|---|---|---|---|---|
| 1 | | | | | | | 1 |
| 2 | | | | | | | 2 |
| 3 | | | | | | | 3 |
| 4 | | | | | | | 4 |
| 5 | | | | | | | 5 |
| 6 | | | | | | | 6 |
| 7 | | | | | | | 7 |
| 8 | | | | | | | 8 |
| 9 | | | | | | | 9 |
| 10 | | | | | | | 10 |
| 11 | | | | | | | 11 |
| 12 | | | | | | | 12 |
| 13 | | | | | | | 13 |
| 14 | | | | | | | 14 |
| 15 | | | | | | | 15 |
| 16 | | | | | | | 16 |
| 17 | | | | | | | 17 |
| 18 | | | | | | | 18 |
| 19 | | | | | | | 19 |
| 20 | | | | | | | 20 |
| 21 | | | | | | | 21 |
| 22 | | | | | | | 22 |
| 23 | | | | | | | 23 |
| 24 | | | | | | | 24 |
| 25 | | | | | | | 25 |
| 26 | | | | | | | 26 |
| 27 | | | | | | | 27 |
| 28 | | | | | | | 28 |
| 29 | | | | | | | 29 |
| 30 | | | | | | | 30 |
| 31 | | | | | | | 31 |
| 32 | | | | | | | 32 |
| 33 | | | | | | | 33 |
| 34 | | | | | | | 34 |

**Problem 15-10A (Continued)**

**GENERAL JOURNAL**                                    PAGE

| | DATE | DESCRIPTION | POST. REF. | DEBIT | CREDIT | |
|---|---|---|---|---|---|---|
| 1 | | | | | | 1 |
| 2 | | | | | | 2 |
| 3 | | | | | | 3 |
| 4 | | | | | | 4 |
| 5 | | | | | | 5 |
| 6 | | | | | | 6 |
| 7 | | | | | | 7 |
| 8 | | | | | | 8 |
| 9 | | | | | | 9 |
| 10 | | | | | | 10 |
| 11 | | | | | | 11 |
| 12 | | | | | | 12 |
| 13 | | | | | | 13 |
| 14 | | | | | | 14 |
| 15 | | | | | | 15 |
| 16 | | | | | | 16 |
| 17 | | | | | | 17 |
| 18 | | | | | | 18 |
| 19 | | | | | | 19 |
| 20 | | | | | | 20 |
| 21 | | | | | | 21 |
| 22 | | | | | | 22 |
| 23 | | | | | | 23 |
| 24 | | | | | | 24 |
| 25 | | | | | | 25 |
| 26 | | | | | | 26 |
| 27 | | | | | | 27 |
| 28 | | | | | | 28 |
| 29 | | | | | | 29 |
| 30 | | | | | | 30 |
| 31 | | | | | | 31 |
| 32 | | | | | | 32 |
| 33 | | | | | | 33 |
| 34 | | | | | | 34 |

**Problem 15-10A (Concluded)**

**4.**

| ACCOUNT | DEBIT BALANCE | CREDIT BALANCE |
|---------|---------------|----------------|
|  |  |  |
|  |  |  |
|  |  |  |
|  |  |  |
|  |  |  |
|  |  |  |
|  |  |  |
|  |  |  |
|  |  |  |
|  |  |  |
|  |  |  |
|  |  |  |
|  |  |  |
|  |  |  |
|  |  |  |
|  |  |  |
|  |  |  |
|  |  |  |
|  |  |  |
|  |  |  |
|  |  |  |
|  |  |  |
|  |  |  |
|  |  |  |
|  |  |  |
|  |  |  |
|  |  |  |
|  |  |  |
|  |  |  |
|  |  |  |

## Problem 15-10A (Continued)
1.

Ellis Fabric

Work

For Year Ended

| | | TRIAL BALANCE | | | | | | | | | ADJUSTMENTS | | | | | | | | |
|---|---|---|---|---|---|---|---|---|---|---|---|---|---|---|---|---|---|---|---|
| | | DEBIT | | | | | CREDIT | | | | | DEBIT | | | | | CREDIT | | | |
| 1 | Cash | 28 | 0 | 0 | 0 | 00 | | | | | | | | | | | | | | |
| 2 | Accounts Receivable | 14 | 2 | 0 | 0 | 00 | | | | | | | | | | | | | | |
| 3 | Merchandise Inventory | 33 | 0 | 0 | 0 | 00 | | | | | | | | | | | | | | |
| 4 | Supplies | 1 | 6 | 0 | 0 | 00 | | | | | | | | | | | | | | |
| 5 | Prepaid Insurance | | 9 | 0 | 0 | 00 | | | | | | | | | | | | | | |
| 6 | Equipment | 6 | 6 | 0 | 0 | 00 | | | | | | | | | | | | | | |
| 7 | Accumulated Depr.—Equipment | | | | | | 1 | 0 | 0 | 0 | 00 | | | | | | | | | |
| 8 | Accounts Payable | | | | | | 15 | 6 | 2 | 0 | 00 | | | | | | | | | |
| 9 | Wages Payable | | | | | | | | | | | | | | | | | | | |
| 10 | Sales Tax Payable | | | | | | | 8 | 5 | 0 | 00 | | | | | | | | | |
| 11 | Unearned Revenue | | | | | | | 5 | 0 | 0 | 00 | | | | | | | | | |
| 12 | W. P. Ellis, Capital | | | | | | 71 | 2 | 0 | 0 | 00 | | | | | | | | | |
| 13 | W. P. Ellis, Drawing | 21 | 6 | 1 | 0 | 00 | | | | | | | | | | | | | | |
| 14 | Income Summary | | | | | | | | | | | | | | | | | | | |
| 15 | Sales | | | | | | 74 | 5 | 0 | 0 | 00 | | | | | | | | | |
| 16 | Sales Returns and Allowances | 1 | 8 | 5 | 0 | 00 | | | | | | | | | | | | | | |
| 17 | Interest Revenue | | | | | | 1 | 2 | 0 | 0 | 00 | | | | | | | | | |
| 18 | Purchases | 41 | 5 | 0 | 0 | 00 | | | | | | | | | | | | | | |
| 19 | Purchases Returns and Allow. | | | | | | 1 | 8 | 0 | 0 | 00 | | | | | | | | | |
| 20 | Purchases Discounts | | | | | | | 8 | 3 | 0 | 00 | | | | | | | | | |
| 21 | Freight-In | | 6 | 6 | 0 | 00 | | | | | | | | | | | | | | |
| 22 | Wages Expense | 14 | 8 | 8 | 0 | 00 | | | | | | | | | | | | | | |
| 23 | Advertising Expense | | 8 | 1 | 0 | 00 | | | | | | | | | | | | | | |
| 24 | Supplies Expense | | | | | | | | | | | | | | | | | | | |
| 25 | Telephone Expense | 1 | 2 | 1 | 0 | 00 | | | | | | | | | | | | | | |
| 26 | Utilities Expense | 3 | 2 | 4 | 0 | 00 | | | | | | | | | | | | | | |
| 27 | Insurance Expense | | | | | | | | | | | | | | | | | | | |
| 28 | Depreciation Expense—Equip. | | | | | | | | | | | | | | | | | | | |
| 29 | Miscellaneous Expense | | 9 | 2 | 0 | 00 | | | | | | | | | | | | | | |
| 30 | Interest Expense | 1 | 0 | 2 | 0 | 00 | | | | | | | | | | | | | | |
| 31 | | 172 | 0 | 0 | 0 | 00 | 172 | 0 | 0 | 0 | 00 | | | | | | | | | |
| 32 | | | | | | | | | | | | | | | | | | | | |
| 33 | | | | | | | | | | | | | | | | | | | | |

**Problem 15-10A (Concluded)**

Store _____

Sheet _____

December 31, 20-1 _____

| | ADJUSTED TRIAL BALANCE | | INCOME STATEMENT | | BALANCE SHEET | | |
|---|---|---|---|---|---|---|---|
| | DEBIT | CREDIT | DEBIT | CREDIT | DEBIT | CREDIT | |
| | | | | | | | 1 |
| | | | | | | | 2 |
| | | | | | | | 3 |
| | | | | | | | 4 |
| | | | | | | | 5 |
| | | | | | | | 6 |
| | | | | | | | 7 |
| | | | | | | | 8 |
| | | | | | | | 9 |
| | | | | | | | 10 |
| | | | | | | | 11 |
| | | | | | | | 12 |
| | | | | | | | 13 |
| | | | | | | | 14 |
| | | | | | | | 15 |
| | | | | | | | 16 |
| | | | | | | | 17 |
| | | | | | | | 18 |
| | | | | | | | 19 |
| | | | | | | | 20 |
| | | | | | | | 21 |
| | | | | | | | 22 |
| | | | | | | | 23 |
| | | | | | | | 24 |
| | | | | | | | 25 |
| | | | | | | | 26 |
| | | | | | | | 27 |
| | | | | | | | 28 |
| | | | | | | | 29 |
| | | | | | | | 30 |
| | | | | | | | 31 |
| | | | | | | | 32 |
| | | | | | | | 33 |

**Exercise 15-1B**

**Exercise 15-2B**

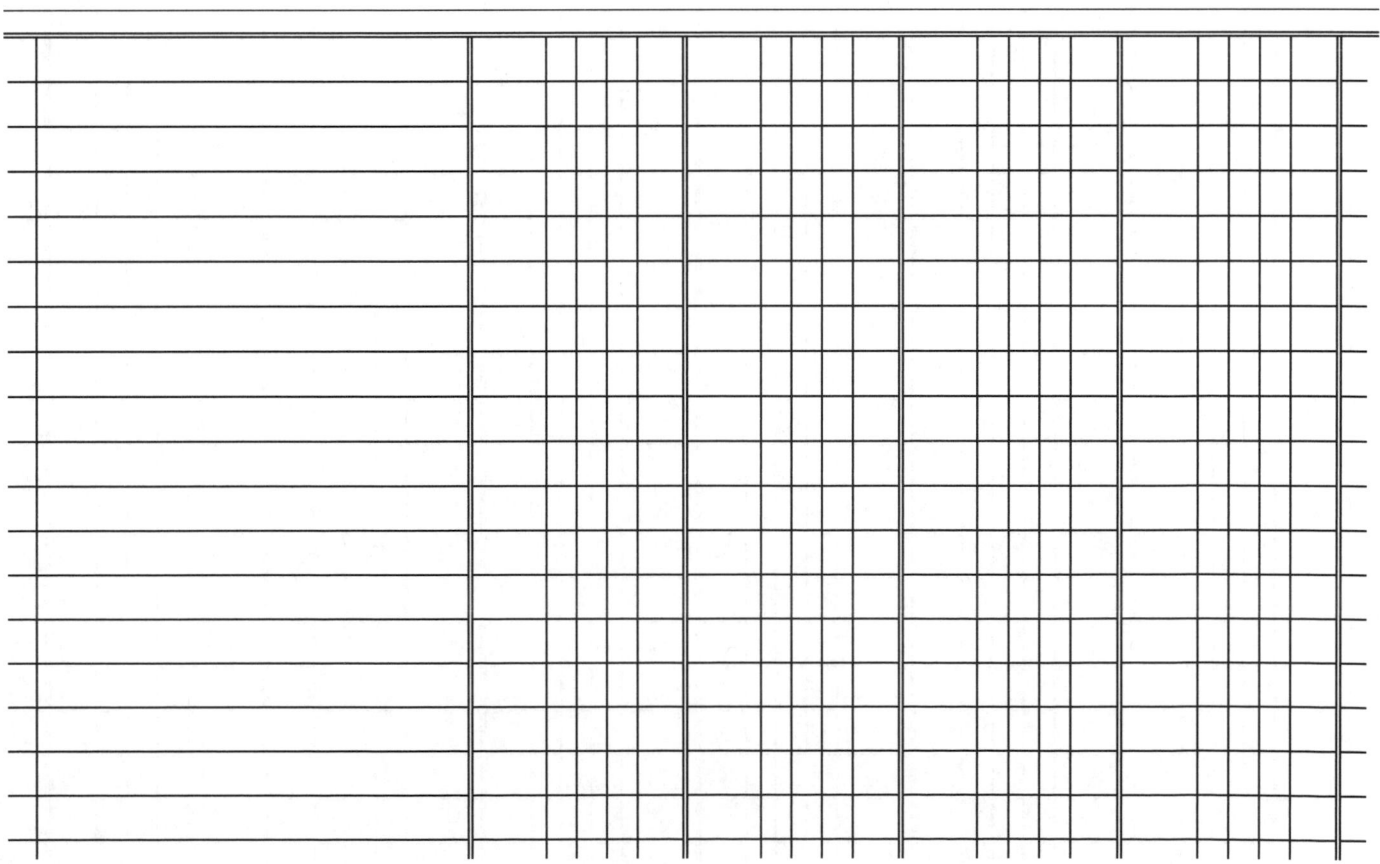

**Exercise 15-3B**

| | | | | | | | | | | | | | | |
|---|---|---|---|---|---|---|---|---|---|---|---|---|---|---|
| | | | | | | | | | | | | | | |
| | | | | | | | | | | | | | | |
| | | | | | | | | | | | | | | |
| | | | | | | | | | | | | | | |
| | | | | | | | | | | | | | | |
| | | | | | | | | | | | | | | |
| | | | | | | | | | | | | | | |
| | | | | | | | | | | | | | | |
| | | | | | | | | | | | | | | |
| | | | | | | | | | | | | | | |
| | | | | | | | | | | | | | | |
| | | | | | | | | | | | | | | |
| | | | | | | | | | | | | | | |
| | | | | | | | | | | | | | | |
| | | | | | | | | | | | | | | |
| | | | | | | | | | | | | | | |
| | | | | | | | | | | | | | | |
| | | | | | | | | | | | | | | |
| | | | | | | | | | | | | | | |
| | | | | | | | | | | | | | | |
| | | | | | | | | | | | | | | |
| | | | | | | | | | | | | | | |
| | | | | | | | | | | | | | | |
| | | | | | | | | | | | | | | |
| | | | | | | | | | | | | | | |
| | | | | | | | | | | | | | | |
| | | | | | | | | | | | | | | |

## Exercise 15-4B

**Exercise 15-5B**

## GENERAL JOURNAL

PAGE _____

| | DATE | | DESCRIPTION | POST. REF. | DEBIT | CREDIT | |
|---|---|---|---|---|---|---|---|
| 1 | | | | | | | 1 |
| 2 | | | | | | | 2 |
| 3 | | | | | | | 3 |
| 4 | | | | | | | 4 |
| 5 | | | | | | | 5 |
| 6 | | | | | | | 6 |
| 7 | | | | | | | 7 |
| 8 | | | | | | | 8 |
| 9 | | | | | | | 9 |
| 10 | | | | | | | 10 |
| 11 | | | | | | | 11 |
| 12 | | | | | | | 12 |
| 13 | | | | | | | 13 |
| 14 | | | | | | | 14 |
| 15 | | | | | | | 15 |
| 16 | | | | | | | 16 |
| 17 | | | | | | | 17 |
| 18 | | | | | | | 18 |
| 19 | | | | | | | 19 |
| 20 | | | | | | | 20 |
| 21 | | | | | | | 21 |
| 22 | | | | | | | 22 |
| 23 | | | | | | | 23 |
| 24 | | | | | | | 24 |
| 25 | | | | | | | 25 |
| 26 | | | | | | | 26 |
| 27 | | | | | | | 27 |
| 28 | | | | | | | 28 |
| 29 | | | | | | | 29 |
| 30 | | | | | | | 30 |
| 31 | | | | | | | 31 |
| 32 | | | | | | | 32 |
| 33 | | | | | | | 33 |
| 34 | | | | | | | 34 |

**Exercise 15-5B (Concluded)**

**2.**

| | | | |
|---|---|---|---|
| | | | |
| | | | |
| | | | |
| | | | |
| | | | |
| | | | |
| | | | |
| | | | |
| | | | |
| | | | |
| | | | |
| | | | |
| | | | |
| | | | |
| | | | |
| | | | |
| | | | |
| | | | |

L. Marlow, Capital

**Exercise 15-6B**

### GENERAL JOURNAL

PAGE ___

| | DATE | DESCRIPTION | POST. REF. | DEBIT | CREDIT | |
|---|---|---|---|---|---|---|
| 1 | | | | | | 1 |
| 2 | | | | | | 2 |
| 3 | | | | | | 3 |
| 4 | | | | | | 4 |
| 5 | | | | | | 5 |

**Exercise 15-7B**

| DATE | WITHOUT REVERSING ENTRY | WITH REVERSING ENTRY |
|---|---|---|
| Adjusting Entry: | | |
| Closing Entry: | | |
| Reversing Entry: | | |
| Payment of Payroll: | | |

Wages Expense

Wages Expense

Wages Payable

Wages Payable

## Problem 15-8B

1.

**Problem 15-8B (Continued)**

2.

**Problem 15-8B (Concluded)**

3.

**Problem 15-9B**

## Problem 15-10B
1.

Darby Kite

Work

For Year Ended

| | | TRIAL BALANCE | | | | | | | | | ADJUSTMENTS | | | | | | | | |
|---|---|---|---|---|---|---|---|---|---|---|---|---|---|---|---|---|---|---|---|
| | | DEBIT | | | | | CREDIT | | | | | DEBIT | | | | CREDIT | | | |
| 1 | Cash | 11 | 7 | 0 | 0 | 00 | | | | | | | | | | | | | |
| 2 | Accounts Receivable | 11 | 2 | 0 | 0 | 00 | | | | | | | | | | | | | |
| 3 | Merchandise Inventory | 25 | 0 | 0 | 0 | 00 | | | | | | | | | | | | | |
| 4 | Supplies | 1 | 2 | 0 | 0 | 00 | | | | | | | | | | | | | |
| 5 | Prepaid Insurance | | 8 | 0 | 0 | 00 | | | | | | | | | | | | | |
| 6 | Equipment | 5 | 4 | 0 | 0 | 00 | | | | | | | | | | | | | |
| 7 | Accumulated Depr.—Equipment | | | | | | | 8 | 0 | 0 | 00 | | | | | | | | |
| 8 | Accounts Payable | | | | | | | 7 | 1 | 0 | 0 | 00 | | | | | | | |
| 9 | Wages Payable | | | | | | | | | | | | | | | | | | |
| 10 | Sales Tax Payable | | | | | | | 2 | 5 | 0 | 00 | | | | | | | | |
| 11 | Unearned Revenue | | | | | | | 3 | 0 | 0 | 0 | 00 | | | | | | | |
| 12 | M. D. Akins, Capital | | | | | | 50 | 0 | 0 | 0 | 00 | | | | | | | | |
| 13 | M. D. Akins, Drawing | 10 | 5 | 0 | 0 | 00 | | | | | | | | | | | | | |
| 14 | Income Summary | | | | | | | | | | | | | | | | | | |
| 15 | Sales | | | | | | 55 | 4 | 9 | 0 | 00 | | | | | | | | |
| 16 | Sales Returns and Allowances | 1 | 4 | 5 | 0 | 00 | | | | | | | | | | | | | |
| 17 | Purchases | 34 | 5 | 0 | 0 | 00 | | | | | | | | | | | | | |
| 18 | Purchases Returns and Allow. | | | | | | 1 | 1 | 0 | 0 | 00 | | | | | | | | |
| 19 | Purchases Discounts | | | | | | | 6 | 3 | 0 | 00 | | | | | | | | |
| 20 | Freight-In | | 3 | 6 | 0 | 00 | | | | | | | | | | | | | |
| 21 | Wages Expense | 10 | 8 | 8 | 0 | 00 | | | | | | | | | | | | | |
| 22 | Advertising Expense | | 7 | 4 | 0 | 00 | | | | | | | | | | | | | |
| 23 | Supplies Expense | | | | | | | | | | | | | | | | | | |
| 24 | Telephone Expense | 1 | 1 | 0 | 0 | 00 | | | | | | | | | | | | | |
| 25 | Utilities Expense | 2 | 3 | 0 | 0 | 00 | | | | | | | | | | | | | |
| 26 | Insurance Expense | | | | | | | | | | | | | | | | | | |
| 27 | Depreciation Expense—Equip. | | | | | | | | | | | | | | | | | | |
| 28 | Miscellaneous Expense | | 3 | 2 | 0 | 00 | | | | | | | | | | | | | |
| 29 | Interest Expense | | 9 | 2 | 0 | 00 | | | | | | | | | | | | | |
| 30 | | 118 | 3 | 7 | 0 | 00 | 118 | 3 | 7 | 0 | 00 | | | | | | | | |
| 31 | | | | | | | | | | | | | | | | | | | |
| 33 | | | | | | | | | | | | | | | | | | | |

## Problem 15-10B  (Continued)

Store _____

Sheet _____

December 31, 20-1

| ADJUSTED TRIAL BALANCE | | INCOME STATEMENT | | BALANCE SHEET | | |
|---|---|---|---|---|---|---|
| DEBIT | CREDIT | DEBIT | CREDIT | DEBIT | CREDIT | |
| | | | | | | 1 |
| | | | | | | 2 |
| | | | | | | 3 |
| | | | | | | 4 |
| | | | | | | 5 |
| | | | | | | 6 |
| | | | | | | 7 |
| | | | | | | 8 |
| | | | | | | 9 |
| | | | | | | 10 |
| | | | | | | 11 |
| | | | | | | 12 |
| | | | | | | 13 |
| | | | | | | 14 |
| | | | | | | 15 |
| | | | | | | 16 |
| | | | | | | 17 |
| | | | | | | 18 |
| | | | | | | 19 |
| | | | | | | 20 |
| | | | | | | 21 |
| | | | | | | 22 |
| | | | | | | 23 |
| | | | | | | 24 |
| | | | | | | 25 |
| | | | | | | 26 |
| | | | | | | 27 |
| | | | | | | 28 |
| | | | | | | 29 |
| | | | | | | 30 |
| | | | | | | 31 |
| | | | | | | 32 |

## Problem 15-10B (Continued)
2., 3., and 5.

### GENERAL JOURNAL

PAGE

| | DATE | DESCRIPTION | POST. REF. | DEBIT | CREDIT | |
|---|---|---|---|---|---|---|
| 1 | | | | | | 1 |
| 2 | | | | | | 2 |
| 3 | | | | | | 3 |
| 4 | | | | | | 4 |
| 5 | | | | | | 5 |
| 6 | | | | | | 6 |
| 7 | | | | | | 7 |
| 8 | | | | | | 8 |
| 9 | | | | | | 9 |
| 10 | | | | | | 10 |
| 11 | | | | | | 11 |
| 12 | | | | | | 12 |
| 13 | | | | | | 13 |
| 14 | | | | | | 14 |
| 15 | | | | | | 15 |
| 16 | | | | | | 16 |
| 17 | | | | | | 17 |
| 18 | | | | | | 18 |
| 19 | | | | | | 19 |
| 20 | | | | | | 20 |
| 21 | | | | | | 21 |
| 22 | | | | | | 22 |
| 23 | | | | | | 23 |
| 24 | | | | | | 24 |
| 25 | | | | | | 25 |
| 26 | | | | | | 26 |
| 27 | | | | | | 27 |
| 28 | | | | | | 28 |
| 29 | | | | | | 29 |
| 30 | | | | | | 30 |
| 31 | | | | | | 31 |
| 32 | | | | | | 32 |
| 33 | | | | | | 33 |
| 34 | | | | | | 34 |

**Problem 15-10B (Continued)**

## GENERAL JOURNAL

PAGE

| | DATE | | DESCRIPTION | POST. REF. | DEBIT | CREDIT | |
|---|---|---|---|---|---|---|---|
| 1 | | | | | | | 1 |
| 2 | | | | | | | 2 |
| 3 | | | | | | | 3 |
| 4 | | | | | | | 4 |
| 5 | | | | | | | 5 |
| 6 | | | | | | | 6 |
| 7 | | | | | | | 7 |
| 8 | | | | | | | 8 |
| 9 | | | | | | | 9 |
| 10 | | | | | | | 10 |
| 11 | | | | | | | 11 |
| 12 | | | | | | | 12 |
| 13 | | | | | | | 13 |
| 14 | | | | | | | 14 |
| 15 | | | | | | | 15 |
| 16 | | | | | | | 16 |
| 17 | | | | | | | 17 |
| 18 | | | | | | | 18 |
| 19 | | | | | | | 19 |
| 20 | | | | | | | 20 |
| 21 | | | | | | | 21 |
| 22 | | | | | | | 22 |
| 23 | | | | | | | 23 |
| 24 | | | | | | | 24 |
| 25 | | | | | | | 25 |
| 26 | | | | | | | 26 |
| 27 | | | | | | | 27 |
| 28 | | | | | | | 28 |
| 29 | | | | | | | 29 |
| 30 | | | | | | | 30 |
| 31 | | | | | | | 31 |
| 32 | | | | | | | 32 |
| 33 | | | | | | | 33 |
| 34 | | | | | | | 34 |

## Problem 15-10B (Concluded)

**4.**

| ACCOUNT | DEBIT BALANCE | CREDIT BALANCE |
|---|---|---|
| | | |
| | | |
| | | |
| | | |
| | | |
| | | |
| | | |
| | | |
| | | |
| | | |
| | | |
| | | |
| | | |
| | | |
| | | |
| | | |
| | | |
| | | |
| | | |
| | | |
| | | |
| | | |
| | | |
| | | |
| | | |
| | | |
| | | |
| | | |
| | | |

**Mastery Problem**

**1.**

**Mastery Problem (Continued)**

2.

**Mastery Problem (Continued)**

**3.**

**Mastery Problem (Continued)**

**4.**

**Mastery Problem (Continued)**

**5.**

## GENERAL JOURNAL

| | DATE | | DESCRIPTION | POST. REF. | DEBIT | CREDIT | |
|---|---|---|---|---|---|---|---|
| 1 | | | | | | | 1 |
| 2 | | | | | | | 2 |
| 3 | | | | | | | 3 |
| 4 | | | | | | | 4 |
| 5 | | | | | | | 5 |
| 6 | | | | | | | 6 |
| 7 | | | | | | | 7 |
| 8 | | | | | | | 8 |
| 9 | | | | | | | 9 |
| 10 | | | | | | | 10 |
| 11 | | | | | | | 11 |
| 12 | | | | | | | 12 |
| 13 | | | | | | | 13 |
| 14 | | | | | | | 14 |
| 15 | | | | | | | 15 |
| 16 | | | | | | | 16 |
| 17 | | | | | | | 17 |
| 18 | | | | | | | 18 |
| 19 | | | | | | | 19 |
| 20 | | | | | | | 20 |
| 21 | | | | | | | 21 |
| 22 | | | | | | | 22 |

Should the adjustment be reversed? _____

_____

_____

_____

_____

_____

_____

_____

## Mastery Problem (Concluded)
### 6. and 7.

**GENERAL JOURNAL**  PAGE 4

| | DATE | DESCRIPTION | POST. REF. | DEBIT | CREDIT | |
|---|---|---|---|---|---|---|
| 1 | | | | | | 1 |
| 2 | | | | | | 2 |
| 3 | | | | | | 3 |
| 4 | | | | | | 4 |
| 5 | | | | | | 5 |
| 6 | | | | | | 6 |
| 7 | | | | | | 7 |
| 8 | | | | | | 8 |
| 9 | | | | | | 9 |
| 10 | | | | | | 10 |
| 11 | | | | | | 11 |
| 12 | | | | | | 12 |
| 13 | | | | | | 13 |
| 14 | | | | | | 14 |
| 15 | | | | | | 15 |
| 16 | | | | | | 16 |
| 17 | | | | | | 17 |
| 18 | | | | | | 18 |
| 19 | | | | | | 19 |
| 20 | | | | | | 20 |
| 21 | | | | | | 21 |
| 22 | | | | | | 22 |
| 23 | | | | | | 23 |
| 24 | | | | | | 24 |
| 25 | | | | | | 25 |
| 26 | | | | | | 26 |
| 27 | | | | | | 27 |
| 28 | | | | | | 28 |
| 29 | | | | | | 29 |
| 30 | | | | | | 30 |
| 31 | | | | | | 31 |
| 32 | | | | | | 32 |
| 33 | | | | | | 33 |
| 34 | | | | | | 34 |
| 35 | | | | | | 35 |

**Challenge Problem**

**Comprehensive Problem 2—General Journal Based, Part 1**

| Requirements 2. and 3. | **GENERAL JOURNAL** | PAGE 3 |

| | DATE | DESCRIPTION | POST. REF. | DEBIT | CREDIT | |
|---|---|---|---|---|---|---|
| 1 | | | | | | 1 |
| 2 | | | | | | 2 |
| 3 | | | | | | 3 |
| 4 | | | | | | 4 |
| 5 | | | | | | 5 |
| 6 | | | | | | 6 |
| 7 | | | | | | 7 |
| 8 | | | | | | 8 |
| 9 | | | | | | 9 |
| 10 | | | | | | 10 |
| 11 | | | | | | 11 |
| 12 | | | | | | 12 |
| 13 | | | | | | 13 |
| 14 | | | | | | 14 |
| 15 | | | | | | 15 |
| 16 | | | | | | 16 |
| 17 | | | | | | 17 |
| 18 | | | | | | 18 |
| 19 | | | | | | 19 |
| 20 | | | | | | 20 |
| 21 | | | | | | 21 |
| 22 | | | | | | 22 |
| 23 | | | | | | 23 |
| 24 | | | | | | 24 |
| 25 | | | | | | 25 |
| 26 | | | | | | 26 |
| 27 | | | | | | 27 |
| 28 | | | | | | 28 |
| 29 | | | | | | 29 |
| 30 | | | | | | 30 |
| 31 | | | | | | 31 |
| 32 | | | | | | 32 |
| 33 | | | | | | 33 |
| 34 | | | | | | 34 |
| 35 | | | | | | 35 |
| 36 | | | | | | 36 |
| 37 | | | | | | 37 |
| 38 | | | | | | 38 |
| 39 | | | | | | 39 |
| 40 | | | | | | 40 |
| 41 | | | | | | 41 |

## Comprehensive Problem 2—General Journal Based, Part 1
## (Requirements 2. and 3. Concluded)

### GENERAL JOURNAL
PAGE 4

| | DATE | DESCRIPTION | POST. REF. | DEBIT | CREDIT | |
|---|---|---|---|---|---|---|
| 1 | | | | | | 1 |
| 2 | | | | | | 2 |
| 3 | | | | | | 3 |
| 4 | | | | | | 4 |
| 5 | | | | | | 5 |
| 6 | | | | | | 6 |
| 7 | | | | | | 7 |
| 8 | | | | | | 8 |
| 9 | | | | | | 9 |
| 10 | | | | | | 10 |
| 11 | | | | | | 11 |
| 12 | | | | | | 12 |
| 13 | | | | | | 13 |
| 14 | | | | | | 14 |
| 15 | | | | | | 15 |
| 16 | | | | | | 16 |
| 17 | | | | | | 17 |

### Requirements 1., 2., 3., 6., 7., and 9.

### GENERAL LEDGER

ACCOUNT   Cash                          ACCOUNT NO.   101

| DATE | | ITEM | POST. REF. | DEBIT | CREDIT | BALANCE DEBIT | BALANCE CREDIT | |
|---|---|---|---|---|---|---|---|---|
| 20-1 Dec. | 16 | Balance | ✓ | | | 9 7 0 5 00 | | |
| | | | | | | | | |
| | | | | | | | | |
| | | | | | | | | |
| | | | | | | | | |
| | | | | | | | | |
| | | | | | | | | |
| | | | | | | | | |
| | | | | | | | | |

# Comprehensive Problem 2—General Journal Based, Part 1
# (Requirements 1., 2., 3., 6., 7., and 9. Continued)

ACCOUNT  Accounts Receivable                                    ACCOUNT NO.  122

| DATE | | ITEM | POST. REF. | DEBIT | CREDIT | BALANCE DEBIT | BALANCE CREDIT |
|---|---|---|---|---|---|---|---|
| 20-1 Dec. | 16 | Balance | ✓ | | | 10 2 5 6 00 | |
| | | | | | | | |
| | | | | | | | |
| | | | | | | | |
| | | | | | | | |
| | | | | | | | |
| | | | | | | | |
| | | | | | | | |
| | | | | | | | |
| | | | | | | | |
| | | | | | | | |
| | | | | | | | |

ACCOUNT  Merchandise Inventory                                  ACCOUNT NO.  131

| DATE | | ITEM | POST. REF. | DEBIT | CREDIT | BALANCE DEBIT | BALANCE CREDIT |
|---|---|---|---|---|---|---|---|
| 20-1 Dec. | 16 | Balance | ✓ | | | 21 8 0 0 00 | |
| | | | | | | | |
| | | | | | | | |

ACCOUNT  Supplies                                              ACCOUNT NO.  141

| DATE | | ITEM | POST. REF. | DEBIT | CREDIT | BALANCE DEBIT | BALANCE CREDIT |
|---|---|---|---|---|---|---|---|
| 20-1 Dec. | 16 | Balance | ✓ | | | 1 0 3 5 00 | |
| | | | | | | | |
| | | | | | | | |

ACCOUNT  Prepaid Insurance                                     ACCOUNT NO.  145

| DATE | | ITEM | POST. REF. | DEBIT | CREDIT | BALANCE DEBIT | BALANCE CREDIT |
|---|---|---|---|---|---|---|---|
| 20-1 Dec. | 16 | Balance | ✓ | | | 1 3 8 0 00 | |
| | | | | | | | |

## Comprehensive Problem 2—General Journal Based, Part 1
## (Requirements 1., 2., 3., 6., 7., and 9. Continued)

ACCOUNT  Land                                                  ACCOUNT NO.  161

| DATE | | ITEM | POST. REF. | DEBIT | CREDIT | BALANCE DEBIT | BALANCE CREDIT |
|---|---|---|---|---|---|---|---|
| 20-1 Dec. | 16 | Balance | ✓ | | | 8 7 0 0 00 | |

ACCOUNT  Building                                              ACCOUNT NO.  171

| DATE | | ITEM | POST. REF. | DEBIT | CREDIT | BALANCE DEBIT | BALANCE CREDIT |
|---|---|---|---|---|---|---|---|
| 20-1 Dec. | 16 | Balance | ✓ | | | 52 0 0 0 00 | |

ACCOUNT  Accumulated Depreciation—Building                     ACCOUNT NO.  171.1

| DATE | | ITEM | POST. REF. | DEBIT | CREDIT | BALANCE DEBIT | BALANCE CREDIT |
|---|---|---|---|---|---|---|---|
| 20-1 Dec. | 16 | Balance | ✓ | | | | 9 2 0 0 00 |

ACCOUNT  Store Equipment                                       ACCOUNT NO.  181

| DATE | | ITEM | POST. REF. | DEBIT | CREDIT | BALANCE DEBIT | BALANCE CREDIT |
|---|---|---|---|---|---|---|---|
| 20-1 Dec. | 16 | Balance | ✓ | | | 28 7 5 0 00 | |

## Comprehensive Problem 2—General Journal Based, Part 1
## (Requirements 1., 2., 3., 6., 7., and 9. Continued)

ACCOUNT  Accumulated Depreciation—Store Equipment                    ACCOUNT NO.  181.1

| DATE | | ITEM | POST. REF. | DEBIT | CREDIT | BALANCE DEBIT | BALANCE CREDIT |
|---|---|---|---|---|---|---|---|
| 20-1 Dec. | 16 | Balance | ✓ | | | | 9 3 0 0 00 |
| | | | | | | | |
| | | | | | | | |
| | | | | | | | |

ACCOUNT  Accounts Payable                    ACCOUNT NO.  202

| DATE | | ITEM | POST. REF. | DEBIT | CREDIT | BALANCE DEBIT | BALANCE CREDIT |
|---|---|---|---|---|---|---|---|
| 20-1 Dec. | 16 | Balance | ✓ | | | | 3 6 0 0 00 |
| | | | | | | | |
| | | | | | | | |
| | | | | | | | |
| | | | | | | | |
| | | | | | | | |
| | | | | | | | |
| | | | | | | | |
| | | | | | | | |
| | | | | | | | |

ACCOUNT  Wages Payable                    ACCOUNT NO.  219

| DATE | ITEM | POST. REF. | DEBIT | CREDIT | BALANCE DEBIT | BALANCE CREDIT |
|---|---|---|---|---|---|---|
| | | | | | | |
| | | | | | | |
| | | | | | | |
| | | | | | | |

# Comprehensive Problem 2—General Journal Based, Part 1
## (Requirements 1., 2., 3., 6., 7., and 9. Continued)

ACCOUNT   Sales Tax Payable     ACCOUNT NO.   231

| DATE | ITEM | POST. REF. | DEBIT | CREDIT | BALANCE DEBIT | BALANCE CREDIT |
|---|---|---|---|---|---|---|
| 20-1 Dec. 16 | Balance | ✓ | | | | 1 3 7 8 00 |

ACCOUNT   Mortgage Payable     ACCOUNT NO.   251

| DATE | ITEM | POST. REF. | DEBIT | CREDIT | BALANCE DEBIT | BALANCE CREDIT |
|---|---|---|---|---|---|---|
| 20-1 Dec. 16 | Balance | ✓ | | | | 12 5 2 5 00 |

ACCOUNT   Tom Jones, Capital     ACCOUNT NO.   311

| DATE | ITEM | POST. REF. | DEBIT | CREDIT | BALANCE DEBIT | BALANCE CREDIT |
|---|---|---|---|---|---|---|
| 20-1 Dec. 16 | Balance | ✓ | | | | 90 0 0 0 00 |

ACCOUNT   Tom Jones, Drawing     ACCOUNT NO.   312

| DATE | ITEM | POST. REF. | DEBIT | CREDIT | BALANCE DEBIT | BALANCE CREDIT |
|---|---|---|---|---|---|---|
| 20-1 Dec. 16 | Balance | ✓ | | | 8 5 0 0 00 | |

## Comprehensive Problem 2—General Journal Based, Part 1
## (Requirements 1., 2., 3., 6., 7., and 9. Continued)

ACCOUNT  Income Summary                                        ACCOUNT NO.  313

| DATE | ITEM | POST. REF. | DEBIT | CREDIT | BALANCE DEBIT | BALANCE CREDIT |
|------|------|------------|-------|--------|---------------|----------------|
|      |      |            |       |        |               |                |
|      |      |            |       |        |               |                |
|      |      |            |       |        |               |                |
|      |      |            |       |        |               |                |
|      |      |            |       |        |               |                |
|      |      |            |       |        |               |                |

ACCOUNT  Sales                                                 ACCOUNT NO.  401

| DATE | ITEM | POST. REF. | DEBIT | CREDIT | BALANCE DEBIT | BALANCE CREDIT |
|------|------|------------|-------|--------|---------------|----------------|
| 20-1 Dec. 16 | Balance | ✓ |  |  |  | 124 9 0 0 00 |
|      |      |            |       |        |               |                |
|      |      |            |       |        |               |                |
|      |      |            |       |        |               |                |
|      |      |            |       |        |               |                |
|      |      |            |       |        |               |                |
|      |      |            |       |        |               |                |
|      |      |            |       |        |               |                |

ACCOUNT  Sales Returns and Allowances                          ACCOUNT NO.  401.1

| DATE | ITEM | POST. REF. | DEBIT | CREDIT | BALANCE DEBIT | BALANCE CREDIT |
|------|------|------------|-------|--------|---------------|----------------|
| 20-1 Dec. 16 | Balance | ✓ |  |  | 1 4 3 0 00 |  |
|      |      |            |       |        |               |                |
|      |      |            |       |        |               |                |
|      |      |            |       |        |               |                |

## Comprehensive Problem 2—General Journal Based, Part 1
## (Requirements 1., 2., 3., 6., 7., and 9. Continued)

ACCOUNT   Purchases                                        ACCOUNT NO.   501

| DATE | | ITEM | POST. REF. | DEBIT | CREDIT | BALANCE | |
|---|---|---|---|---|---|---|---|
| | | | | | | DEBIT | CREDIT |
| 20-1 Dec. | 16 | Balance | ✓ | | | 64 4 0 0 00 | |
| | | | | | | | |
| | | | | | | | |
| | | | | | | | |
| | | | | | | | |
| | | | | | | | |

ACCOUNT   Purchases Returns and Allowances                 ACCOUNT NO.   501.1

| DATE | | ITEM | POST. REF. | DEBIT | CREDIT | BALANCE | |
|---|---|---|---|---|---|---|---|
| | | | | | | DEBIT | CREDIT |
| 20-1 Dec. | 16 | Balance | ✓ | | | | 4 6 0 00 |
| | | | | | | | |
| | | | | | | | |
| | | | | | | | |
| | | | | | | | |

ACCOUNT   Purchases Discounts                               ACCOUNT NO.   501.2

| DATE | | ITEM | POST. REF. | DEBIT | CREDIT | BALANCE | |
|---|---|---|---|---|---|---|---|
| | | | | | | DEBIT | CREDIT |
| 20-1 Dec. | 16 | Balance | ✓ | | | | 6 9 8 00 |
| | | | | | | | |
| | | | | | | | |
| | | | | | | | |
| | | | | | | | |

ACCOUNT   Freight-In                                        ACCOUNT NO.   502

| DATE | | ITEM | POST. REF. | DEBIT | CREDIT | BALANCE | |
|---|---|---|---|---|---|---|---|
| | | | | | | DEBIT | CREDIT |
| 20-1 Dec. | 16 | Balance | ✓ | | | 1 7 5 00 | |
| | | | | | | | |
| | | | | | | | |
| | | | | | | | |
| | | | | | | | |

# Comprehensive Problem 2—General Journal Based, Part 1
# (Requirements 1., 2., 3., 6., 7., and 9. Continued)

ACCOUNT  Wages Expense                                                                 ACCOUNT NO.  511

| DATE | | ITEM | POST. REF. | DEBIT | CREDIT | BALANCE | |
|---|---|---|---|---|---|---|---|
| | | | | | | DEBIT | CREDIT |
| 20-1 Dec. | 16 | Balance | ✓ | | | 26 1 0 0 00 | |
| | | | | | | | |
| | | | | | | | |
| | | | | | | | |
| | | | | | | | |

ACCOUNT  Advertising Expense                                                           ACCOUNT NO.  512

| DATE | | ITEM | POST. REF. | DEBIT | CREDIT | BALANCE | |
|---|---|---|---|---|---|---|---|
| | | | | | | DEBIT | CREDIT |
| 20-1 Dec. | 16 | Balance | ✓ | | | 4 7 0 0 00 | |
| | | | | | | | |
| | | | | | | | |
| | | | | | | | |
| | | | | | | | |

ACCOUNT  Supplies Expense                                                              ACCOUNT NO.  524

| DATE | | ITEM | POST. REF. | DEBIT | CREDIT | BALANCE | |
|---|---|---|---|---|---|---|---|
| | | | | | | DEBIT | CREDIT |
| | | | | | | | |
| | | | | | | | |
| | | | | | | | |
| | | | | | | | |
| | | | | | | | |

ACCOUNT  Telephone Expense                                                             ACCOUNT NO.  525

| DATE | | ITEM | POST. REF. | DEBIT | CREDIT | BALANCE | |
|---|---|---|---|---|---|---|---|
| | | | | | | DEBIT | CREDIT |
| 20-1 Dec. | 16 | Balance | ✓ | | | 2 1 8 0 00 | |
| | | | | | | | |
| | | | | | | | |

## Comprehensive Problem 2—General Journal Based, Part 1
## (Requirements 1., 2., 3., 6., 7., and 9. Continued)

ACCOUNT  Utilities Expense           ACCOUNT NO.  533

| DATE | | ITEM | POST. REF. | DEBIT | CREDIT | BALANCE DEBIT | BALANCE CREDIT |
|---|---|---|---|---|---|---|---|
| 20-1 Dec. | 16 | Balance | ✓ | | | 6 9 0 0 00 | |
| | | | | | | | |
| | | | | | | | |
| | | | | | | | |

ACCOUNT  Insurance Expense           ACCOUNT NO.  535

| DATE | | ITEM | POST. REF. | DEBIT | CREDIT | BALANCE DEBIT | BALANCE CREDIT |
|---|---|---|---|---|---|---|---|
| | | | | | | | |
| | | | | | | | |
| | | | | | | | |
| | | | | | | | |
| | | | | | | | |

ACCOUNT  Depreciation Expense—Building           ACCOUNT NO.  540

| DATE | | ITEM | POST. REF. | DEBIT | CREDIT | BALANCE DEBIT | BALANCE CREDIT |
|---|---|---|---|---|---|---|---|
| | | | | | | | |
| | | | | | | | |
| | | | | | | | |
| | | | | | | | |
| | | | | | | | |

ACCOUNT  Depreciation Expense—Store Equipment           ACCOUNT NO.  541

| DATE | | ITEM | POST. REF. | DEBIT | CREDIT | BALANCE DEBIT | BALANCE CREDIT |
|---|---|---|---|---|---|---|---|
| | | | | | | | |
| | | | | | | | |
| | | | | | | | |
| | | | | | | | |
| | | | | | | | |

## Comprehensive Problem 2—General Journal Based, Part 1
## (Requirements 1., 2., 3., 6., 7., and 9. Continued)

ACCOUNT **Miscellaneous Expense**                    ACCOUNT NO. **549**

| DATE | | ITEM | POST. REF. | DEBIT | CREDIT | BALANCE DEBIT | BALANCE CREDIT |
|---|---|---|---|---|---|---|---|
| 20-1 Dec. | 16 | Balance | ✓ | | | 2 7 0 0 00 | |
| | | | | | | | |
| | | | | | | | |
| | | | | | | | |
| | | | | | | | |

ACCOUNT **Interest Expense**                    ACCOUNT NO. **551**

| DATE | | ITEM | POST. REF. | DEBIT | CREDIT | BALANCE DEBIT | BALANCE CREDIT |
|---|---|---|---|---|---|---|---|
| 20-1 Dec. | 16 | Balance | ✓ | | | 1 3 5 0 00 | |
| | | | | | | | |
| | | | | | | | |
| | | | | | | | |
| | | | | | | | |

## ACCOUNTS RECEIVABLE LEDGER

**NAME** Martha Boyle

**ADDRESS** 12 Jude Lane, Hartford, CT 06117

| DATE | | ITEM | POST. REF. | DEBIT | CREDIT | BALANCE |
|---|---|---|---|---|---|---|
| 20-1 Dec. | 16 | Balance | ✓ | | | 3 7 9 6 00 |
| | | | | | | |
| | | | | | | |
| | | | | | | |
| | | | | | | |

**NAME** Anne Clark

**ADDRESS** 52 Juniper Road, Hartford, CT 06118

| DATE | | ITEM | POST. REF. | DEBIT | CREDIT | BALANCE |
|---|---|---|---|---|---|---|
| 20-1 Dec. | 16 | Balance | ✓ | | | 2 1 0 0 00 |
| | | | | | | |
| | | | | | | |

## Comprehensive Problem 2—General Journal Based, Part 1
## (Requirements 1., 2., 3., 6., 7., and 9. Continued)

**NAME** John Dempsey

**ADDRESS** 700 Hobbes Dr., Avon, CT  06108

| DATE | | ITEM | POST. REF. | DEBIT | CREDIT | BALANCE |
|---|---|---|---|---|---|---|
| 20-1 Dec. | 16 | Balance | ✓ | | | 1 5 6 0 00 |
| | | | | | | |
| | | | | | | |
| | | | | | | |

**NAME** Kim Fields

**ADDRESS** 5200 Hamilton Ave., Hartford, CT  06117

| DATE | | ITEM | POST. REF. | DEBIT | CREDIT | BALANCE |
|---|---|---|---|---|---|---|
| 20-1 Dec. | 16 | Balance | ✓ | | | — |
| | | | | | | |
| | | | | | | |

**NAME** Lucy Greene

**ADDRESS** 236 Bally Lane, Simsbury, CT  06123

| DATE | | ITEM | POST. REF. | DEBIT | CREDIT | BALANCE |
|---|---|---|---|---|---|---|
| 20-1 Dec. | 16 | Balance | ✓ | | | 2 8 0 0 00 |
| | | | | | | |
| | | | | | | |
| | | | | | | |
| | | | | | | |

# Comprehensive Problem 2—General Journal Based, Part 1
## (Requirements 1., 2., 3., 6., 7., and 9. Concluded)

### ACCOUNTS PAYABLE LEDGER

**NAME** Evans Essentials

**ADDRESS** 34 Harry Ave., East Hartford, CT 05234

| DATE | | ITEM | POST. REF. | DEBIT | CREDIT | BALANCE |
|---|---|---|---|---|---|---|
| 20-1 Dec. | 16 | Balance | ✓ | | | 3 6 0 0 00 |
| | | | | | | |
| | | | | | | |
| | | | | | | |

**NAME** Nathen Co.

**ADDRESS** 1009 Drake Rd., Farmington, CT 06082

| DATE | | ITEM | POST. REF. | DEBIT | CREDIT | BALANCE |
|---|---|---|---|---|---|---|
| 20-1 Dec. | 16 | Balance | ✓ | | | |
| | | | | | | |
| | | | | | | |
| | | | | | | |

**NAME** Owen Enterprises

**ADDRESS** 43 Lucky Lane, Bristol, CT 06007

| DATE | | ITEM | POST. REF. | DEBIT | CREDIT | BALANCE |
|---|---|---|---|---|---|---|
| 20-1 Dec. | 16 | Balance | ✓ | | | |
| | | | | | | |
| | | | | | | |
| | | | | | | |

**NAME** West Wholesalers

**ADDRESS** 888 Anders Street, Newington, CT 06789

| DATE | | ITEM | POST. REF. | DEBIT | CREDIT | BALANCE |
|---|---|---|---|---|---|---|
| 20-1 Dec. | 16 | Balance | ✓ | | | |
| | | | | | | |
| | | | | | | |
| | | | | | | |

## Comprehensive Problem 2—General Journal Based, Part 1

**Requirement 4.**

**This page left intentionally blank.**

## Comprehensive Problem 2—General Journal Based, Part 1
Requirement 5.

| | TRIAL BALANCE | | ADJUSTMENTS | |
|---|---|---|---|---|
| | DEBIT | CREDIT | DEBIT | CREDIT |
| 1 | | | | |
| 2 | | | | |
| 3 | | | | |
| 4 | | | | |
| 5 | | | | |
| 6 | | | | |
| 7 | | | | |
| 8 | | | | |
| 9 | | | | |
| 10 | | | | |
| 11 | | | | |
| 12 | | | | |
| 13 | | | | |
| 14 | | | | |
| 15 | | | | |
| 16 | | | | |
| 17 | | | | |
| 18 | | | | |
| 19 | | | | |
| 20 | | | | |
| 21 | | | | |
| 22 | | | | |
| 23 | | | | |
| 24 | | | | |
| 25 | | | | |
| 26 | | | | |
| 27 | | | | |
| 28 | | | | |
| 29 | | | | |
| 30 | | | | |
| 31 | | | | |
| 32 | | | | |
| 33 | | | | |
| 34 | | | | |
| 35 | | | | |
| 36 | | | | |

**Comprehensive Problem 2—General Journal Based, Part 1
(Requirement 5. Continued)**

| ADJUSTED TRIAL BALANCE | | INCOME STATEMENT | | BALANCE SHEET | | |
|---|---|---|---|---|---|---|
| DEBIT | CREDIT | DEBIT | CREDIT | DEBIT | CREDIT | |
| | | | | | | 1 |
| | | | | | | 2 |
| | | | | | | 3 |
| | | | | | | 4 |
| | | | | | | 5 |
| | | | | | | 6 |
| | | | | | | 7 |
| | | | | | | 8 |
| | | | | | | 9 |
| | | | | | | 10 |
| | | | | | | 11 |
| | | | | | | 12 |
| | | | | | | 13 |
| | | | | | | 14 |
| | | | | | | 15 |
| | | | | | | 16 |
| | | | | | | 17 |
| | | | | | | 18 |
| | | | | | | 19 |
| | | | | | | 20 |
| | | | | | | 21 |
| | | | | | | 22 |
| | | | | | | 23 |
| | | | | | | 24 |
| | | | | | | 25 |
| | | | | | | 26 |
| | | | | | | 27 |
| | | | | | | 28 |
| | | | | | | 29 |
| | | | | | | 30 |
| | | | | | | 31 |
| | | | | | | 32 |
| | | | | | | 33 |
| | | | | | | 34 |
| | | | | | | 35 |
| | | | | | | 36 |

## Comprehensive Problem 2—General Journal Based, Part 1
## (Requirement 5. Continued)

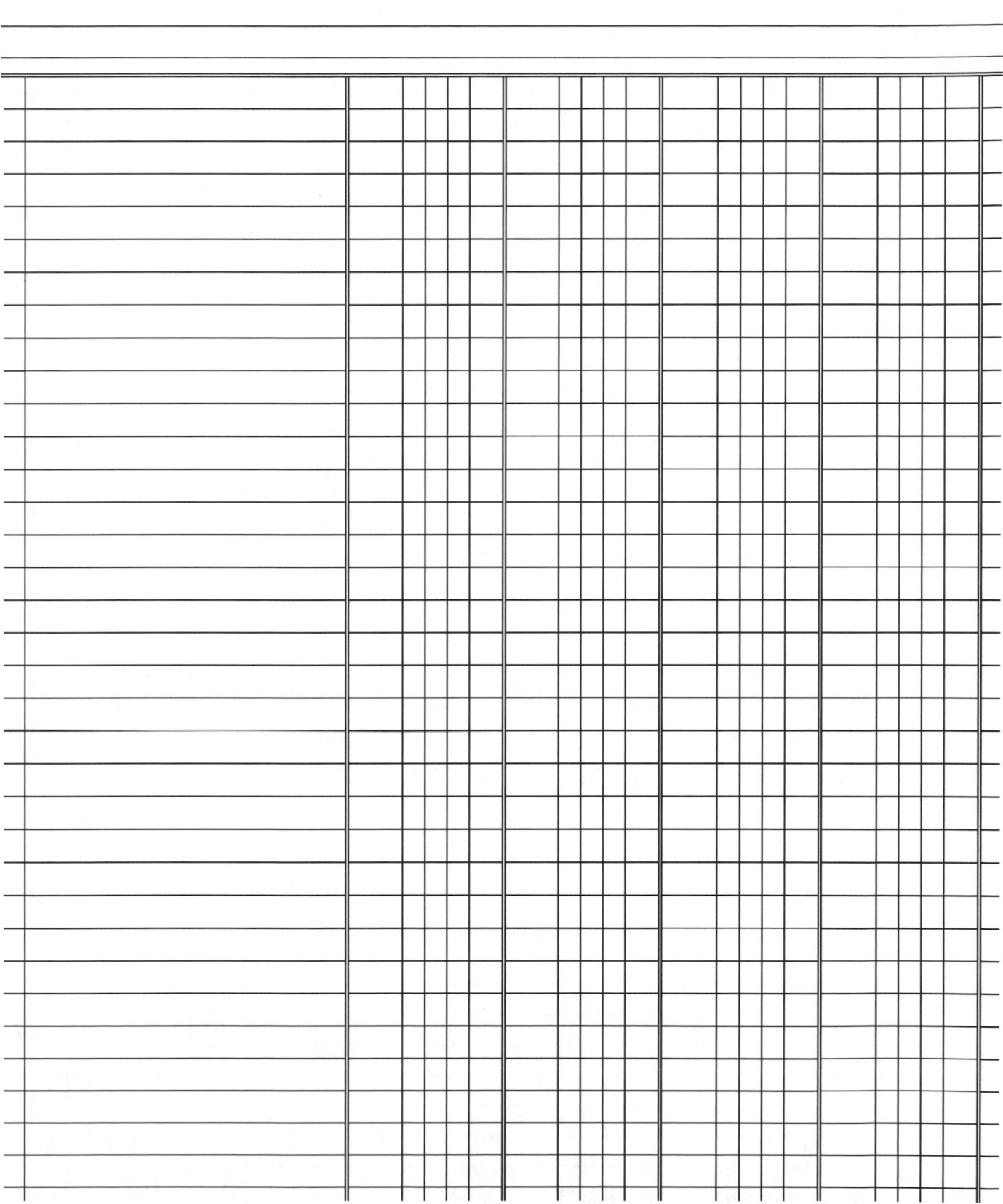

**Comprehensive Problem 2—General Journal Based, Part 1
(Requirement 5. Continued)**

**Comprehensive Problem 2—General Journal Based, Part 1
(Requirement 5. Concluded)**

## Comprehensive Problem 2—General Journal Based, Part 1

Requirement 6.

### GENERAL JOURNAL

PAGE 5

| | DATE | | DESCRIPTION | POST. REF. | DEBIT | CREDIT | |
|---|---|---|---|---|---|---|---|
| 1 | | | | | | | 1 |
| 2 | | | | | | | 2 |
| 3 | | | | | | | 3 |
| 4 | | | | | | | 4 |
| 5 | | | | | | | 5 |
| 6 | | | | | | | 6 |
| 7 | | | | | | | 7 |
| 8 | | | | | | | 8 |
| 9 | | | | | | | 9 |
| 10 | | | | | | | 10 |
| 11 | | | | | | | 11 |
| 12 | | | | | | | 12 |
| 13 | | | | | | | 13 |
| 14 | | | | | | | 14 |
| 15 | | | | | | | 15 |
| 16 | | | | | | | 16 |
| 17 | | | | | | | 17 |
| 18 | | | | | | | 18 |
| 19 | | | | | | | 19 |
| 20 | | | | | | | 20 |
| 21 | | | | | | | 21 |
| 22 | | | | | | | 22 |
| 23 | | | | | | | 23 |
| 24 | | | | | | | 24 |
| 25 | | | | | | | 25 |
| 26 | | | | | | | 26 |
| 27 | | | | | | | 27 |
| 28 | | | | | | | 28 |
| 29 | | | | | | | 29 |
| 30 | | | | | | | 30 |
| 31 | | | | | | | 31 |
| 32 | | | | | | | 32 |
| 33 | | | | | | | 33 |
| 34 | | | | | | | 34 |

## Comprehensive Problem 2—General Journal Based, Part 1

### Requirements 7. and 9.

**GENERAL JOURNAL**                 PAGE 6

| | DATE | DESCRIPTION | POST. REF. | DEBIT | CREDIT | |
|---|---|---|---|---|---|---|
| 1 | | | | | | 1 |
| 2 | | | | | | 2 |
| 3 | | | | | | 3 |
| 4 | | | | | | 4 |
| 5 | | | | | | 5 |
| 6 | | | | | | 6 |
| 7 | | | | | | 7 |
| 8 | | | | | | 8 |
| 9 | | | | | | 9 |
| 10 | | | | | | 10 |
| 11 | | | | | | 11 |
| 12 | | | | | | 12 |
| 13 | | | | | | 13 |
| 14 | | | | | | 14 |
| 15 | | | | | | 15 |
| 16 | | | | | | 16 |
| 17 | | | | | | 17 |
| 18 | | | | | | 18 |
| 19 | | | | | | 19 |
| 20 | | | | | | 20 |
| 21 | | | | | | 21 |
| 22 | | | | | | 22 |
| 23 | | | | | | 23 |
| 24 | | | | | | 24 |
| 25 | | | | | | 25 |
| 26 | | | | | | 26 |
| 27 | | | | | | 27 |
| 28 | | | | | | 28 |
| 29 | | | | | | 29 |
| 30 | | | | | | 30 |
| 31 | | | | | | 31 |
| 32 | | | | | | 32 |
| 33 | | | | | | 33 |
| 34 | | | | | | 34 |

## Comprehensive Problem 2—General Journal Based, Part 1

**Requirement 8.**

| ACCOUNT | DEBIT BALANCE | CREDIT BALANCE |
|---|---|---|
|  |  |  |
|  |  |  |
|  |  |  |
|  |  |  |
|  |  |  |
|  |  |  |
|  |  |  |
|  |  |  |
|  |  |  |
|  |  |  |
|  |  |  |
|  |  |  |
|  |  |  |
|  |  |  |
|  |  |  |
|  |  |  |
|  |  |  |
|  |  |  |
|  |  |  |
|  |  |  |
|  |  |  |
|  |  |  |
|  |  |  |
|  |  |  |
|  |  |  |
|  |  |  |
|  |  |  |
|  |  |  |
|  |  |  |
|  |  |  |
|  |  |  |
|  |  |  |
|  |  |  |

## Comprehensive Problem 2—General Journal Based, Part 2
### Requirements 2. and 3.

**GENERAL JOURNAL**

PAGE  1

| | DATE | | DESCRIPTION | POST. REF. | DEBIT | CREDIT | |
|---|---|---|---|---|---|---|---|
| 1 | | | | | | | 1 |
| 2 | | | | | | | 2 |
| 3 | | | | | | | 3 |
| 4 | | | | | | | 4 |
| 5 | | | | | | | 5 |
| 6 | | | | | | | 6 |
| 7 | | | | | | | 7 |
| 8 | | | | | | | 8 |
| 9 | | | | | | | 9 |
| 10 | | | | | | | 10 |
| 11 | | | | | | | 11 |
| 12 | | | | | | | 12 |
| 13 | | | | | | | 13 |
| 14 | | | | | | | 14 |
| 15 | | | | | | | 15 |
| 16 | | | | | | | 16 |
| 17 | | | | | | | 17 |
| 18 | | | | | | | 18 |
| 19 | | | | | | | 19 |
| 20 | | | | | | | 20 |
| 21 | | | | | | | 21 |
| 22 | | | | | | | 22 |
| 23 | | | | | | | 23 |
| 24 | | | | | | | 24 |
| 25 | | | | | | | 25 |
| 26 | | | | | | | 26 |
| 27 | | | | | | | 27 |
| 28 | | | | | | | 28 |
| 29 | | | | | | | 29 |
| 30 | | | | | | | 30 |
| 31 | | | | | | | 31 |
| 32 | | | | | | | 32 |
| 33 | | | | | | | 33 |
| 34 | | | | | | | 34 |
| 35 | | | | | | | 35 |
| 36 | | | | | | | 36 |
| 37 | | | | | | | 37 |
| 38 | | | | | | | 38 |
| 39 | | | | | | | 39 |

**Comprehensive Problem 2—General Journal Based, Part 2
(Requirements 2. and 3. Concluded)**

### GENERAL JOURNAL

PAGE 2

| | DATE | | DESCRIPTION | POST. REF. | DEBIT | CREDIT | |
|---|---|---|---|---|---|---|---|
| 1 | | | | | | | 1 |
| 2 | | | | | | | 2 |
| 3 | | | | | | | 3 |
| 4 | | | | | | | 4 |
| 5 | | | | | | | 5 |
| 6 | | | | | | | 6 |
| 7 | | | | | | | 7 |
| 8 | | | | | | | 8 |
| 9 | | | | | | | 9 |
| 10 | | | | | | | 10 |
| 11 | | | | | | | 11 |
| 12 | | | | | | | 12 |
| 13 | | | | | | | 13 |
| 14 | | | | | | | 14 |
| 15 | | | | | | | 15 |
| 16 | | | | | | | 16 |
| 17 | | | | | | | 17 |
| 18 | | | | | | | 18 |
| 19 | | | | | | | 19 |
| 20 | | | | | | | 20 |
| 21 | | | | | | | 21 |
| 22 | | | | | | | 22 |
| 23 | | | | | | | 23 |
| 24 | | | | | | | 24 |
| 25 | | | | | | | 25 |
| 26 | | | | | | | 26 |
| 27 | | | | | | | 27 |
| 28 | | | | | | | 28 |
| 29 | | | | | | | 29 |
| 30 | | | | | | | 30 |
| 31 | | | | | | | 31 |
| 32 | | | | | | | 32 |
| 33 | | | | | | | 33 |
| 34 | | | | | | | 34 |
| 35 | | | | | | | 35 |
| 36 | | | | | | | 36 |
| 37 | | | | | | | 37 |
| 38 | | | | | | | 38 |
| 39 | | | | | | | 39 |

## Comprehensive Problem 2—General Journal Based, Part 2
### Requirements 1., 2., 3., 6., and 7.

### GENERAL LEDGER

ACCOUNT  Cash                                          ACCOUNT NO.  101

| DATE | | ITEM | POST. REF. | DEBIT | CREDIT | BALANCE | |
|---|---|---|---|---|---|---|---|
| | | | | | | DEBIT | CREDIT |
| 20-2 Jan. | 1 | Balance | ✓ | | | 12 5 4 8 00 | |
| | | | | | | | |
| | | | | | | | |
| | | | | | | | |
| | | | | | | | |
| | | | | | | | |
| | | | | | | | |
| | | | | | | | |
| | | | | | | | |
| | | | | | | | |
| | | | | | | | |
| | | | | | | | |
| | | | | | | | |
| | | | | | | | |
| | | | | | | | |

ACCOUNT  Accounts Receivable                           ACCOUNT NO.  122

| DATE | | ITEM | POST. REF. | DEBIT | CREDIT | BALANCE | |
|---|---|---|---|---|---|---|---|
| | | | | | | DEBIT | CREDIT |
| 20-2 Jan. | 1 | Balance | ✓ | | | 7 2 0 3 00 | |
| | | | | | | | |
| | | | | | | | |
| | | | | | | | |
| | | | | | | | |
| | | | | | | | |
| | | | | | | | |
| | | | | | | | |
| | | | | | | | |
| | | | | | | | |
| | | | | | | | |
| | | | | | | | |

## Comprehensive Problem 2—General Journal Based, Part 2
## (Requirements 1., 2., 3., 6., and 7. Continued)

ACCOUNT    Merchandise Inventory        ACCOUNT NO.   131

| DATE | | ITEM | POST. REF. | DEBIT | CREDIT | BALANCE DEBIT | BALANCE CREDIT |
|---|---|---|---|---|---|---|---|
| 20-2 Jan. | 1 | Balance | ✓ | | | 19 7 0 0 00 | |
| | | | | | | | |
| | | | | | | | |
| | | | | | | | |
| | | | | | | | |

ACCOUNT    Supplies        ACCOUNT NO.   141

| DATE | | ITEM | POST. REF. | DEBIT | CREDIT | BALANCE DEBIT | BALANCE CREDIT |
|---|---|---|---|---|---|---|---|
| 20-2 Jan. | 1 | Balance | ✓ | | | 5 2 5 00 | |
| | | | | | | | |
| | | | | | | | |
| | | | | | | | |
| | | | | | | | |

ACCOUNT    Prepaid Insurance        ACCOUNT NO.   145

| DATE | | ITEM | POST. REF. | DEBIT | CREDIT | BALANCE DEBIT | BALANCE CREDIT |
|---|---|---|---|---|---|---|---|
| 20-2 Jan. | 1 | Balance | ✓ | | | 1 0 0 0 00 | |
| | | | | | | | |
| | | | | | | | |
| | | | | | | | |
| | | | | | | | |

ACCOUNT    Land        ACCOUNT NO.   161

| DATE | | ITEM | POST. REF. | DEBIT | CREDIT | BALANCE DEBIT | BALANCE CREDIT |
|---|---|---|---|---|---|---|---|
| 20-2 Jan. | 1 | Balance | ✓ | | | 8 7 0 0 00 | |
| | | | | | | | |
| | | | | | | | |
| | | | | | | | |

## Comprehensive Problem 2—General Journal Based, Part 2 (Requirements 1., 2., 3., 6., and 7. Continued)

ACCOUNT  Building                                                                 ACCOUNT NO.  171

| DATE | | ITEM | POST. REF. | DEBIT | CREDIT | BALANCE | |
|---|---|---|---|---|---|---|---|
| | | | | | | DEBIT | CREDIT |
| 20-2 Jan. | 1 | Balance | ✓ | | | 52 0 0 0 00 | |
| | | | | | | | |
| | | | | | | | |
| | | | | | | | |
| | | | | | | | |
| | | | | | | | |

ACCOUNT  Accumulated Depreciation—Building                                        ACCOUNT NO.  171.1

| DATE | | ITEM | POST. REF. | DEBIT | CREDIT | BALANCE | |
|---|---|---|---|---|---|---|---|
| | | | | | | DEBIT | CREDIT |
| 20-2 Jan. | 1 | Balance | ✓ | | | | 10 0 0 0 00 |
| | | | | | | | |
| | | | | | | | |
| | | | | | | | |
| | | | | | | | |
| | | | | | | | |

ACCOUNT  Store Equipment                                                          ACCOUNT NO.  181

| DATE | | ITEM | POST. REF. | DEBIT | CREDIT | BALANCE | |
|---|---|---|---|---|---|---|---|
| | | | | | | DEBIT | CREDIT |
| 20-2 Jan. | 1 | Balance | ✓ | | | 28 7 5 0 00 | |
| | | | | | | | |
| | | | | | | | |
| | | | | | | | |
| | | | | | | | |
| | | | | | | | |

**Comprehensive Problem 2—General Journal Based, Part 2
(Requirements 1., 2., 3., 6., and 7. Continued)**

ACCOUNT  Accumulated Depreciation—Store Equipment          ACCOUNT NO.  181.1

| DATE | | ITEM | POST. REF. | DEBIT | CREDIT | BALANCE | |
|---|---|---|---|---|---|---|---|
| | | | | | | DEBIT | CREDIT |
| 20-2 Jan. | 1 | Balance | ✓ | | | | 9 7 5 0 00 |
| | | | | | | | |
| | | | | | | | |
| | | | | | | | |

ACCOUNT  Accounts Payable          ACCOUNT NO.  202

| DATE | | ITEM | POST. REF. | DEBIT | CREDIT | BALANCE | |
|---|---|---|---|---|---|---|---|
| | | | | | | DEBIT | CREDIT |
| 20-2 Jan. | 1 | Balance | ✓ | | | | 4 3 5 0 00 |
| | | | | | | | |
| | | | | | | | |
| | | | | | | | |
| | | | | | | | |
| | | | | | | | |
| | | | | | | | |
| | | | | | | | |

ACCOUNT  Wages Payable          ACCOUNT NO.  219

| DATE | ITEM | POST. REF. | DEBIT | CREDIT | BALANCE | |
|---|---|---|---|---|---|---|
| | | | | | DEBIT | CREDIT |
| | | | | | | |
| | | | | | | |
| | | | | | | |
| | | | | | | |

# Comprehensive Problem 2—General Journal Based, Part 2
## (Requirements 1., 2., 3., 6., and 7. Continued)

ACCOUNT  Sales Tax Payable                                    ACCOUNT NO.  231

| DATE | | ITEM | POST. REF. | DEBIT | CREDIT | BALANCE DEBIT | BALANCE CREDIT |
|---|---|---|---|---|---|---|---|
| 20-2 Jan. | 1 | Balance | ✓ | | | | 1 5 1 8 00 |
| | | | | | | | |
| | | | | | | | |
| | | | | | | | |
| | | | | | | | |
| | | | | | | | |
| | | | | | | | |

ACCOUNT  Mortgage Payable                                     ACCOUNT NO.  251

| DATE | | ITEM | POST. REF. | DEBIT | CREDIT | BALANCE DEBIT | BALANCE CREDIT |
|---|---|---|---|---|---|---|---|
| 20-2 Jan. | 1 | Balance | ✓ | | | | 12 5 2 5 00 |
| | | | | | | | |
| | | | | | | | |
| | | | | | | | |

ACCOUNT  Tom Jones, Capital                                   ACCOUNT NO.  311

| DATE | | ITEM | POST. REF. | DEBIT | CREDIT | BALANCE DEBIT | BALANCE CREDIT |
|---|---|---|---|---|---|---|---|
| 20-2 Jan. | 1 | Balance | ✓ | | | | 91 9 5 3 00 |
| | | | | | | | |
| | | | | | | | |
| | | | | | | | |
| | | | | | | | |

ACCOUNT  Tom Jones, Drawing                                   ACCOUNT NO.  312

| DATE | | ITEM | POST. REF. | DEBIT | CREDIT | BALANCE DEBIT | BALANCE CREDIT |
|---|---|---|---|---|---|---|---|
| | | | | | | | |
| | | | | | | | |
| | | | | | | | |
| | | | | | | | |
| | | | | | | | |

# Comprehensive Problem 2—General Journal Based, Part 2
## (Requirements 1., 2., 3., 6., and 7. Continued)

ACCOUNT  Income Summary                                              ACCOUNT NO.  313

| DATE | ITEM | POST. REF. | DEBIT | CREDIT | BALANCE DEBIT | BALANCE CREDIT |
|------|------|-----------|-------|--------|-------|--------|
|      |      |           |       |        |       |        |
|      |      |           |       |        |       |        |
|      |      |           |       |        |       |        |
|      |      |           |       |        |       |        |
|      |      |           |       |        |       |        |
|      |      |           |       |        |       |        |

ACCOUNT  Sales                                                        ACCOUNT NO.  401

| DATE | ITEM | POST. REF. | DEBIT | CREDIT | BALANCE DEBIT | BALANCE CREDIT |
|------|------|-----------|-------|--------|-------|--------|
|      |      |           |       |        |       |        |
|      |      |           |       |        |       |        |
|      |      |           |       |        |       |        |
|      |      |           |       |        |       |        |
|      |      |           |       |        |       |        |

ACCOUNT  Sales Returns and Allowances                                ACCOUNT NO.  401.1

| DATE | ITEM | POST. REF. | DEBIT | CREDIT | BALANCE DEBIT | BALANCE CREDIT |
|------|------|-----------|-------|--------|-------|--------|
|      |      |           |       |        |       |        |
|      |      |           |       |        |       |        |
|      |      |           |       |        |       |        |
|      |      |           |       |        |       |        |

ACCOUNT  Purchases                                                   ACCOUNT NO.  501

| DATE | ITEM | POST. REF. | DEBIT | CREDIT | BALANCE DEBIT | BALANCE CREDIT |
|------|------|-----------|-------|--------|-------|--------|
|      |      |           |       |        |       |        |
|      |      |           |       |        |       |        |
|      |      |           |       |        |       |        |
|      |      |           |       |        |       |        |
|      |      |           |       |        |       |        |
|      |      |           |       |        |       |        |

## Comprehensive Problem 2—General Journal Based, Part 2
## (Requirements 1., 2., 3., 6., and 7. Continued)

ACCOUNT  Purchases Returns and Allowances                    ACCOUNT NO.  501.1

| DATE | ITEM | POST. REF. | DEBIT | CREDIT | BALANCE | |
|------|------|------------|-------|--------|---------|---|
| | | | | | DEBIT | CREDIT |
| | | | | | | |
| | | | | | | |
| | | | | | | |
| | | | | | | |
| | | | | | | |
| | | | | | | |

ACCOUNT  Purchases Discounts                                 ACCOUNT NO.  501.2

| DATE | ITEM | POST. REF. | DEBIT | CREDIT | BALANCE | |
|------|------|------------|-------|--------|---------|---|
| | | | | | DEBIT | CREDIT |
| | | | | | | |
| | | | | | | |
| | | | | | | |
| | | | | | | |
| | | | | | | |
| | | | | | | |

ACCOUNT  Freight-In                                          ACCOUNT NO.  502

| DATE | ITEM | POST. REF. | DEBIT | CREDIT | BALANCE | |
|------|------|------------|-------|--------|---------|---|
| | | | | | DEBIT | CREDIT |
| | | | | | | |
| | | | | | | |
| | | | | | | |
| | | | | | | |
| | | | | | | |

**Comprehensive Problem 2—General Journal Based, Part 2**
**(Requirements 1., 2., 3., 6., and 7. Continued)**

ACCOUNT  Wages Expense                                        ACCOUNT NO.  511

| DATE | ITEM | POST. REF. | DEBIT | CREDIT | BALANCE DEBIT | BALANCE CREDIT |
|------|------|-----------|-------|--------|---------------|----------------|
| 20-2 Jan. 1 | Balance | ✓ | | | | 3 3 0 00 |
| | | | | | | |
| | | | | | | |
| | | | | | | |
| | | | | | | |
| | | | | | | |

ACCOUNT  Advertising Expense                                  ACCOUNT NO.  512

| DATE | ITEM | POST. REF. | DEBIT | CREDIT | BALANCE DEBIT | BALANCE CREDIT |
|------|------|-----------|-------|--------|---------------|----------------|
| | | | | | | |
| | | | | | | |
| | | | | | | |
| | | | | | | |
| | | | | | | |

ACCOUNT  Supplies Expense                                     ACCOUNT NO.  524

| DATE | ITEM | POST. REF. | DEBIT | CREDIT | BALANCE DEBIT | BALANCE CREDIT |
|------|------|-----------|-------|--------|---------------|----------------|
| | | | | | | |
| | | | | | | |
| | | | | | | |
| | | | | | | |
| | | | | | | |

ACCOUNT  Telephone Expense                                    ACCOUNT NO.  525

| DATE | ITEM | POST. REF. | DEBIT | CREDIT | BALANCE DEBIT | BALANCE CREDIT |
|------|------|-----------|-------|--------|---------------|----------------|
| | | | | | | |
| | | | | | | |
| | | | | | | |
| | | | | | | |

## Comprehensive Problem 2—General Journal Based, Part 2 (Requirements 1., 2., 3., 6., and 7. Continued)

ACCOUNT   Utilities Expense                                                      ACCOUNT NO.   533

| DATE | ITEM | POST. REF. | DEBIT | CREDIT | BALANCE DEBIT | BALANCE CREDIT |
|------|------|------------|-------|--------|---------------|----------------|
|      |      |            |       |        |               |                |
|      |      |            |       |        |               |                |
|      |      |            |       |        |               |                |
|      |      |            |       |        |               |                |

ACCOUNT   Insurance Expense                                                      ACCOUNT NO.   535

| DATE | ITEM | POST. REF. | DEBIT | CREDIT | BALANCE DEBIT | BALANCE CREDIT |
|------|------|------------|-------|--------|---------------|----------------|
|      |      |            |       |        |               |                |
|      |      |            |       |        |               |                |
|      |      |            |       |        |               |                |
|      |      |            |       |        |               |                |
|      |      |            |       |        |               |                |

ACCOUNT   Depreciation Expense—Building                                          ACCOUNT NO.   540

| DATE | ITEM | POST. REF. | DEBIT | CREDIT | BALANCE DEBIT | BALANCE CREDIT |
|------|------|------------|-------|--------|---------------|----------------|
|      |      |            |       |        |               |                |
|      |      |            |       |        |               |                |
|      |      |            |       |        |               |                |
|      |      |            |       |        |               |                |
|      |      |            |       |        |               |                |

ACCOUNT   Depreciation Expense—Store Equipment                                   ACCOUNT NO.   541

| DATE | ITEM | POST. REF. | DEBIT | CREDIT | BALANCE DEBIT | BALANCE CREDIT |
|------|------|------------|-------|--------|---------------|----------------|
|      |      |            |       |        |               |                |
|      |      |            |       |        |               |                |
|      |      |            |       |        |               |                |
|      |      |            |       |        |               |                |
|      |      |            |       |        |               |                |

## Comprehensive Problem 2—General Journal Based, Part 2
## (Requirements 1., 2., 3., 6., and 7. Continued)

ACCOUNT  Miscellaneous Expense                    ACCOUNT NO.  549

| DATE | ITEM | POST. REF. | DEBIT | CREDIT | BALANCE DEBIT | BALANCE CREDIT |
|------|------|-----------|-------|--------|--------|--------|
|  |  |  |  |  |  |  |
|  |  |  |  |  |  |  |
|  |  |  |  |  |  |  |
|  |  |  |  |  |  |  |
|  |  |  |  |  |  |  |

ACCOUNT  Interest Expense                         ACCOUNT NO.  551

| DATE | ITEM | POST. REF. | DEBIT | CREDIT | BALANCE DEBIT | BALANCE CREDIT |
|------|------|-----------|-------|--------|--------|--------|
|  |  |  |  |  |  |  |
|  |  |  |  |  |  |  |
|  |  |  |  |  |  |  |
|  |  |  |  |  |  |  |
|  |  |  |  |  |  |  |

### ACCOUNTS RECEIVABLE LEDGER

**NAME**  Martha Boyle

**ADDRESS**  12 Jude Lane, Hartford, CT  06117

| DATE | | ITEM | POST. REF. | DEBIT | CREDIT | BALANCE |
|------|---|------|-----------|-------|--------|---------|
| 20-2 Jan. | 1 | Balance | ✓ |  |  | 1 3 2 3 00 |
|  |  |  |  |  |  |  |
|  |  |  |  |  |  |  |
|  |  |  |  |  |  |  |
|  |  |  |  |  |  |  |

**NAME**  Anne Clark

**ADDRESS**  52 Juniper Road, Hartford, CT  06118

| DATE | | ITEM | POST. REF. | DEBIT | CREDIT | BALANCE |
|------|---|------|-----------|-------|--------|---------|
| 20-2 Jan. | 1 | Balance | ✓ |  |  | 2 1 0 0 00 |
|  |  |  |  |  |  |  |
|  |  |  |  |  |  |  |

## Comprehensive Problem 2—General Journal Based, Part 2 (Requirements 1., 2., 3., 6., and 7. Continued)

**NAME** John Dempsey

**ADDRESS** 700 Hobbes Dr., Avon, CT  06108

| DATE | | ITEM | POST. REF. | DEBIT | CREDIT | BALANCE |
|---|---|---|---|---|---|---|
| 20-2 Jan. | 1 | Balance | ✓ | | | 2 1 2 1 00 |
| | | | | | | |
| | | | | | | |
| | | | | | | |

**NAME** Kim Fields

**ADDRESS** 5200 Hamilton Ave., Hartford, CT  06117

| DATE | | ITEM | POST. REF. | DEBIT | CREDIT | BALANCE |
|---|---|---|---|---|---|---|
| 20-2 Jan. | 1 | Balance | ✓ | | | 1 6 8 00 |
| | | | | | | |
| | | | | | | |

**NAME** Lucy Greene

**ADDRESS** 236 Bally Lane, Simsbury, CT  06123

| DATE | | ITEM | POST. REF. | DEBIT | CREDIT | BALANCE |
|---|---|---|---|---|---|---|
| 20-2 Jan. | 1 | Balance | ✓ | | | 1 4 9 1 00 |
| | | | | | | |
| | | | | | | |
| | | | | | | |
| | | | | | | |

**Comprehensive Problem 2—General Journal Based, Part 2**
**(Requirements 1., 2., 3., 6., and 7. Concluded)**

## ACCOUNTS PAYABLE LEDGER

**NAME** Evans Essentials

**ADDRESS** 34 Harry Ave., East Hartford, CT 05234

| DATE | | ITEM | POST. REF. | DEBIT | CREDIT | BALANCE |
|---|---|---|---|---|---|---|
| 20-2 Jan. | 1 | Balance | ✓ | | | 2 3 5 0 00 |
| | | | | | | |
| | | | | | | |

**NAME** Nathen Co.

**ADDRESS** 1009 Drake Rd., Farmington, CT 06082

| DATE | | ITEM | POST. REF. | DEBIT | CREDIT | BALANCE |
|---|---|---|---|---|---|---|
| 20-2 Jan. | 1 | Balance | ✓ | | | 8 0 0 00 |
| | | | | | | |
| | | | | | | |

**NAME** Owen Enterprises

**ADDRESS** 43 Lucky Lane, Bristol, CT 06007

| DATE | | ITEM | POST. REF. | DEBIT | CREDIT | BALANCE |
|---|---|---|---|---|---|---|
| | | | | | | |
| | | | | | | |
| | | | | | | |
| | | | | | | |

**NAME** West Wholesalers

**ADDRESS** 888 Anders Street, Newington, CT 06789

| DATE | | ITEM | POST. REF. | DEBIT | CREDIT | BALANCE |
|---|---|---|---|---|---|---|
| 20-2 Jan. | 1 | Balance | ✓ | | | 1 2 0 0 00 |
| | | | | | | |
| | | | | | | |

**Comprehensive Problem 2—General Journal Based, Part 2**

**Requirement 4.**

**This page left intentionally blank.**

# Comprehensive Problem 2—General Journal Based, Part 2
## Requirement 5.

| | TRIAL BALANCE | | ADJUSTMENTS | |
|---|---|---|---|---|
| | DEBIT | CREDIT | DEBIT | CREDIT |
| 1 | | | | |
| 2 | | | | |
| 3 | | | | |
| 4 | | | | |
| 5 | | | | |
| 6 | | | | |
| 7 | | | | |
| 8 | | | | |
| 9 | | | | |
| 10 | | | | |
| 11 | | | | |
| 12 | | | | |
| 13 | | | | |
| 14 | | | | |
| 15 | | | | |
| 16 | | | | |
| 17 | | | | |
| 18 | | | | |
| 19 | | | | |
| 20 | | | | |
| 21 | | | | |
| 22 | | | | |
| 23 | | | | |
| 24 | | | | |
| 25 | | | | |
| 26 | | | | |
| 27 | | | | |
| 28 | | | | |
| 29 | | | | |
| 30 | | | | |
| 31 | | | | |
| 32 | | | | |
| 33 | | | | |
| 34 | | | | |
| 35 | | | | |
| 36 | | | | |

**Comprehensive Problem 2—General Journal Based, Part 2
(Requirement 5. Continued)**

| ADJUSTED TRIAL BALANCE | | INCOME STATEMENT | | BALANCE SHEET | | |
|---|---|---|---|---|---|---|
| DEBIT | CREDIT | DEBIT | CREDIT | DEBIT | CREDIT | |
| | | | | | | 1 |
| | | | | | | 2 |
| | | | | | | 3 |
| | | | | | | 4 |
| | | | | | | 5 |
| | | | | | | 6 |
| | | | | | | 7 |
| | | | | | | 8 |
| | | | | | | 9 |
| | | | | | | 10 |
| | | | | | | 11 |
| | | | | | | 12 |
| | | | | | | 13 |
| | | | | | | 14 |
| | | | | | | 15 |
| | | | | | | 16 |
| | | | | | | 17 |
| | | | | | | 18 |
| | | | | | | 19 |
| | | | | | | 20 |
| | | | | | | 21 |
| | | | | | | 22 |
| | | | | | | 23 |
| | | | | | | 24 |
| | | | | | | 25 |
| | | | | | | 26 |
| | | | | | | 27 |
| | | | | | | 28 |
| | | | | | | 29 |
| | | | | | | 30 |
| | | | | | | 31 |
| | | | | | | 32 |
| | | | | | | 33 |
| | | | | | | 34 |
| | | | | | | 35 |
| | | | | | | 36 |

# Comprehensive Problem 2—General Journal Based, Part 2
# (Requirement 5. Continued)

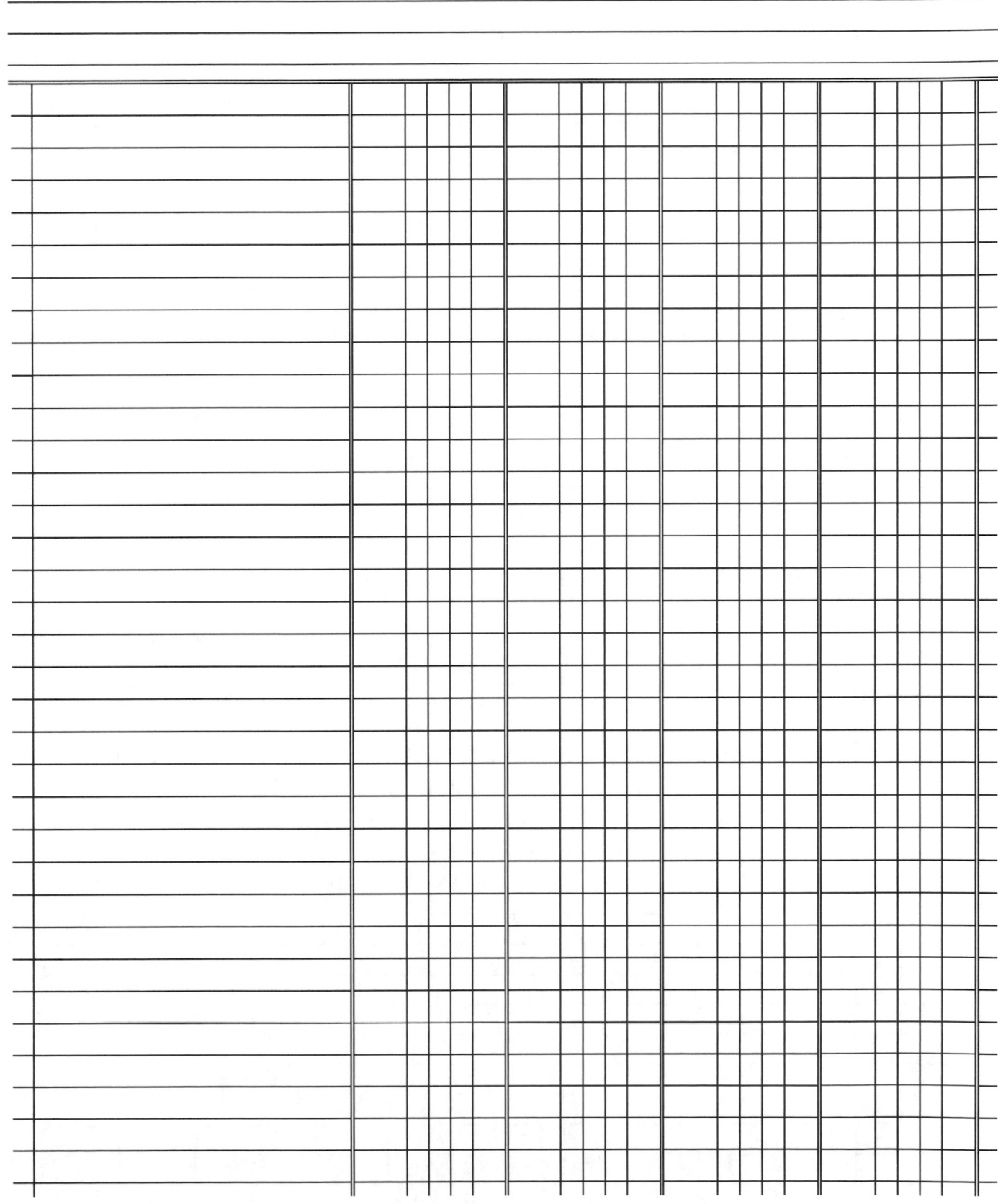

**Comprehensive Problem 2—General Journal Based, Part 2
(Requirement 5. Continued)**

| | | | | |
|---|---|---|---|---|
| | | | | |

## Comprehensive Problem 2—General Journal Based, Part 2
## (Requirement 5. Concluded)

## Comprehensive Problem 2—General Journal Based, Part 2

**Requirement 6.**

### GENERAL JOURNAL

| | DATE | | DESCRIPTION | POST. REF. | DEBIT | CREDIT | |
|---|---|---|---|---|---|---|---|
| 1 | | | | | | | 1 |
| 2 | | | | | | | 2 |
| 3 | | | | | | | 3 |
| 4 | | | | | | | 4 |
| 5 | | | | | | | 5 |
| 6 | | | | | | | 6 |
| 7 | | | | | | | 7 |
| 8 | | | | | | | 8 |
| 9 | | | | | | | 9 |
| 10 | | | | | | | 10 |
| 11 | | | | | | | 11 |
| 12 | | | | | | | 12 |
| 13 | | | | | | | 13 |
| 14 | | | | | | | 14 |
| 15 | | | | | | | 15 |
| 16 | | | | | | | 16 |
| 17 | | | | | | | 17 |
| 18 | | | | | | | 18 |
| 19 | | | | | | | 19 |
| 20 | | | | | | | 20 |
| 21 | | | | | | | 21 |
| 22 | | | | | | | 22 |
| 23 | | | | | | | 23 |
| 24 | | | | | | | 24 |
| 25 | | | | | | | 25 |
| 26 | | | | | | | 26 |
| 27 | | | | | | | 27 |
| 28 | | | | | | | 28 |
| 29 | | | | | | | 29 |
| 30 | | | | | | | 30 |
| 31 | | | | | | | 31 |
| 32 | | | | | | | 32 |
| 33 | | | | | | | 33 |
| 34 | | | | | | | 34 |

## Comprehensive Problem 2—General Journal Based, Part 2

**Requirement 7.**

### GENERAL JOURNAL

| | DATE | | DESCRIPTION | POST. REF. | DEBIT | CREDIT | |
|---|---|---|---|---|---|---|---|
| 1 | | | | | | | 1 |
| 2 | | | | | | | 2 |
| 3 | | | | | | | 3 |
| 4 | | | | | | | 4 |
| 5 | | | | | | | 5 |
| 6 | | | | | | | 6 |
| 7 | | | | | | | 7 |
| 8 | | | | | | | 8 |
| 9 | | | | | | | 9 |
| 10 | | | | | | | 10 |
| 11 | | | | | | | 11 |
| 12 | | | | | | | 12 |
| 13 | | | | | | | 13 |
| 14 | | | | | | | 14 |
| 15 | | | | | | | 15 |
| 16 | | | | | | | 16 |
| 17 | | | | | | | 17 |
| 18 | | | | | | | 18 |
| 19 | | | | | | | 19 |
| 20 | | | | | | | 20 |
| 21 | | | | | | | 21 |
| 22 | | | | | | | 22 |
| 23 | | | | | | | 23 |
| 24 | | | | | | | 24 |
| 25 | | | | | | | 25 |
| 26 | | | | | | | 26 |
| 27 | | | | | | | 27 |
| 28 | | | | | | | 28 |
| 29 | | | | | | | 29 |
| 30 | | | | | | | 30 |
| 31 | | | | | | | 31 |
| 32 | | | | | | | 32 |
| 33 | | | | | | | 33 |
| 34 | | | | | | | 34 |

## Comprehensive Problem 2—General Journal Based, Part 2
**Requirement 8.**

| ACCOUNT | DEBIT BALANCE | CREDIT BALANCE |
|---|---|---|
| | | |
| | | |
| | | |
| | | |
| | | |
| | | |
| | | |
| | | |
| | | |
| | | |
| | | |
| | | |
| | | |
| | | |
| | | |
| | | |
| | | |
| | | |
| | | |
| | | |
| | | |
| | | |
| | | |
| | | |
| | | |
| | | |
| | | |
| | | |
| | | |
| | | |
| | | |
| | | |
| | | |
| | | |
| | | |
| | | |
| | | |
| | | |
| | | |

## Comprehensive Problem 2—Special Journals Based, Part 1
**Requirements 2. and 3.**

### SALES JOURNAL                                                      PAGE  6

| DATE | | SALE NO. | TO WHOM SOLD | POST. REF. | ACCOUNTS RECEIVABLE DEBIT | SALES CREDIT | SALES TAX PAYABLE CREDIT |
|---|---|---|---|---|---|---|---|
| 20-1 Dec. | 1-15 | | Cumulative Amount | ✓ | 4 2 6 3 00 | 4 0 6 0 00 | 2 0 3 00 |
| | | | | | | | |
| | | | | | | | |
| | | | | | | | |
| | | | | | | | |
| | | | | | | | |
| | | | | | | | |
| | | | | | | | |
| | | | | | | | |

### CASH RECEIPTS JOURNAL                                             PAGE  9

| | DATE | | ACCOUNT CREDITED | POST. REF. | GENERAL CREDIT | ACCOUNTS RECEIVABLE CREDIT | SALES CREDIT | SALES TAX PAYABLE CREDIT | CASH DEBIT | |
|---|---|---|---|---|---|---|---|---|---|---|
| 1 | 20-1 Dec. | 1-15 | Cumulative Amt | ✓ | | 1 8 3 0 00 | 4 8 4 0 00 | 2 4 2 00 | 6 9 1 2 00 | 1 |
| 2 | | | | | | | | | | 2 |
| 3 | | | | | | | | | | 3 |
| 4 | | | | | | | | | | 4 |
| 5 | | | | | | | | | | 5 |
| 6 | | | | | | | | | | 6 |
| 7 | | | | | | | | | | 7 |

**Comprehensive Problem 2—Special Journals Based, Part 1
(Requirements 2. and 3. Continued)**

### PURCHASES JOURNAL          PAGE 5

| | DATE | INVOICE NO. | FROM WHOM PURCHASED | POST. REF. | PURCHASES DEBIT ACCTS. PAY. CREDIT | |
|---|---|---|---|---|---|---|
| 1 | 20-1 Dec. 1-15 | | Cumulative Amount | ✓ | 3 9 0 0 00 | 1 |
| 2 | | | | | | 2 |
| 3 | | | | | | 3 |
| 4 | | | | | | 4 |
| 5 | | | | | | 5 |
| 6 | | | | | | 6 |

### CASH PAYMENTS JOURNAL          PAGE 10

| | DATE | CK. NO. | ACCOUNT DEBITED | POST. REF. | GENERAL DEBIT | ACCOUNTS PAYABLE DEBIT | PURCHASES DEBIT | PURCHASES DISCOUNTS CREDIT | CASH CREDIT | |
|---|---|---|---|---|---|---|---|---|---|---|
| 1 | 20-1 Dec. 1-15 | | Cumulative Amount | ✓ | 1 6 8 0 00 | 7 1 5 0 00 | | 1 2 3 00 | 8 7 0 7 00 | 1 |
| 2 | | | | | | | | | | 2 |
| 3 | | | | | | | | | | 3 |
| 4 | | | | | | | | | | 4 |
| 5 | | | | | | | | | | 5 |
| 6 | | | | | | | | | | 6 |
| 7 | | | | | | | | | | 7 |
| 8 | | | | | | | | | | 8 |
| 9 | | | | | | | | | | 9 |
| 10 | | | | | | | | | | 10 |
| 11 | | | | | | | | | | 11 |
| 12 | | | | | | | | | | 12 |
| 13 | | | | | | | | | | 13 |
| 14 | | | | | | | | | | 14 |
| 15 | | | | | | | | | | 15 |

## Comprehensive Problem 2—Special Journals Based, Part 1
## (Requirements 2. and 3. Concluded)

### GENERAL JOURNAL                                             PAGE 3

| | DATE | DESCRIPTION | POST. REF. | DEBIT | CREDIT | |
|---|---|---|---|---|---|---|
| 1 | | | | | | 1 |
| 2 | | | | | | 2 |
| 3 | | | | | | 3 |
| 4 | | | | | | 4 |
| 5 | | | | | | 5 |
| 6 | | | | | | 6 |
| 7 | | | | | | 7 |
| 8 | | | | | | 8 |
| 9 | | | | | | 9 |
| 10 | | | | | | 10 |
| 11 | | | | | | 11 |
| 12 | | | | | | 12 |

## Requirements 1., 2., 3., 6., 7., and 9.
### GENERAL LEDGER

ACCOUNT  Cash                                          ACCOUNT NO.  101

| DATE | | ITEM | POST. REF. | DEBIT | CREDIT | BALANCE DEBIT | BALANCE CREDIT |
|---|---|---|---|---|---|---|---|
| 20-1 Dec. | 16 | Balance | ✓ | | | 11 5 0 0 00 | |
| | | | | | | | |
| | | | | | | | |
| | | | | | | | |
| | | | | | | | |
| | | | | | | | |
| | | | | | | | |

ACCOUNT  Accounts Receivable                            ACCOUNT NO.  122

| DATE | | ITEM | POST. REF. | DEBIT | CREDIT | BALANCE DEBIT | BALANCE CREDIT |
|---|---|---|---|---|---|---|---|
| 20-1 Dec. | 16 | Balance | ✓ | | | 7 8 2 3 00 | |
| | | | | | | | |
| | | | | | | | |
| | | | | | | | |
| | | | | | | | |
| | | | | | | | |

## Comprehensive Problem 2—Special Journals Based, Part 1
## (Requirements 1., 2., 3., 6., 7., and 9. Continued)

ACCOUNT  Merchandise Inventory                                    ACCOUNT NO.  131

| DATE | | ITEM | POST. REF. | DEBIT | CREDIT | BALANCE | |
|---|---|---|---|---|---|---|---|
| | | | | | | DEBIT | CREDIT |
| 20-1 Dec. | 16 | Balance | ✓ | | | 21 8 0 0 00 | |
| | | | | | | | |
| | | | | | | | |
| | | | | | | | |

ACCOUNT  Supplies                                    ACCOUNT NO.  141

| DATE | | ITEM | POST. REF. | DEBIT | CREDIT | BALANCE | |
|---|---|---|---|---|---|---|---|
| | | | | | | DEBIT | CREDIT |
| 20-1 Dec. | 16 | Balance | ✓ | | | 1 0 3 5 00 | |
| | | | | | | | |
| | | | | | | | |
| | | | | | | | |

ACCOUNT  Prepaid Insurance                                    ACCOUNT NO.  145

| DATE | | ITEM | POST. REF. | DEBIT | CREDIT | BALANCE | |
|---|---|---|---|---|---|---|---|
| | | | | | | DEBIT | CREDIT |
| 20-1 Dec. | 16 | Balance | ✓ | | | 1 3 8 0 00 | |
| | | | | | | | |
| | | | | | | | |
| | | | | | | | |

ACCOUNT  Land                                    ACCOUNT NO.  161

| DATE | | ITEM | POST. REF. | DEBIT | CREDIT | BALANCE | |
|---|---|---|---|---|---|---|---|
| | | | | | | DEBIT | CREDIT |
| 20-1 Dec. | 16 | Balance | ✓ | | | 8 7 0 0 00 | |
| | | | | | | | |
| | | | | | | | |
| | | | | | | | |

## Comprehensive Problem 2—Special Journals Based, Part 1 (Requirements 1., 2., 3., 6., 7., and 9. Continued)

ACCOUNT  Building                                         ACCOUNT NO.  171

| DATE | | ITEM | POST. REF. | DEBIT | CREDIT | BALANCE | |
|---|---|---|---|---|---|---|---|
| | | | | | | DEBIT | CREDIT |
| 20-1 Dec. | 16 | Balance | ✓ | | | 52 0 0 0 00 | |
| | | | | | | | |
| | | | | | | | |
| | | | | | | | |

ACCOUNT  Accumulated Depreciation—Building               ACCOUNT NO.  171.1

| DATE | | ITEM | POST. REF. | DEBIT | CREDIT | BALANCE | |
|---|---|---|---|---|---|---|---|
| | | | | | | DEBIT | CREDIT |
| 20-1 Dec. | 16 | Balance | ✓ | | | | 9 2 0 0 00 |
| | | | | | | | |
| | | | | | | | |
| | | | | | | | |

ACCOUNT  Store Equipment                                 ACCOUNT NO.  181

| DATE | | ITEM | POST. REF. | DEBIT | CREDIT | BALANCE | |
|---|---|---|---|---|---|---|---|
| | | | | | | DEBIT | CREDIT |
| 20-1 Dec. | 16 | Balance | ✓ | | | 28 7 5 0 00 | |
| | | | | | | | |
| | | | | | | | |
| | | | | | | | |

ACCOUNT  Accumulated Depreciation—Store Equipment        ACCOUNT NO.  181.1

| DATE | | ITEM | POST. REF. | DEBIT | CREDIT | BALANCE | |
|---|---|---|---|---|---|---|---|
| | | | | | | DEBIT | CREDIT |
| 20-1 Dec. | 16 | Balance | ✓ | | | | 9 3 0 0 00 |
| | | | | | | | |
| | | | | | | | |
| | | | | | | | |

**Comprehensive Problem 2—Special Journals Based, Part 1
(Requirements 1., 2., 3., 6., 7., and 9. Continued)**

ACCOUNT  Accounts Payable                                   ACCOUNT NO.  202

| DATE | | ITEM | POST. REF. | DEBIT | CREDIT | BALANCE DEBIT | BALANCE CREDIT |
|---|---|---|---|---|---|---|---|
| 20-1 Dec. | 16 | Balance | ✓ | | | | 6 8 5 0 00 |
| | | | | | | | |
| | | | | | | | |
| | | | | | | | |

ACCOUNT  Wages Payable                                      ACCOUNT NO.  219

| DATE | ITEM | POST. REF. | DEBIT | CREDIT | BALANCE DEBIT | BALANCE CREDIT |
|---|---|---|---|---|---|---|
| | | | | | | |
| | | | | | | |
| | | | | | | |
| | | | | | | |
| | | | | | | |

ACCOUNT  Sales Tax Payable                                  ACCOUNT NO.  231

| DATE | | ITEM | POST. REF. | DEBIT | CREDIT | BALANCE DEBIT | BALANCE CREDIT |
|---|---|---|---|---|---|---|---|
| 20-1 Dec. | 16 | Balance | ✓ | | | | 9 3 3 00 |
| | | | | | | | |
| | | | | | | | |
| | | | | | | | |
| | | | | | | | |

ACCOUNT  Mortgage Payable                                   ACCOUNT NO.  251

| DATE | | ITEM | POST. REF. | DEBIT | CREDIT | BALANCE DEBIT | BALANCE CREDIT |
|---|---|---|---|---|---|---|---|
| 20-1 Dec. | 16 | Balance | ✓ | | | | 12 5 2 5 00 |
| | | | | | | | |
| | | | | | | | |
| | | | | | | | |

## Comprehensive Problem 2—Special Journals Based, Part 1 (Requirements 1., 2., 3., 6., 7., and 9. Continued)

ACCOUNT   Tom Jones, Capital                                                 ACCOUNT NO.   311

| DATE | | ITEM | POST. REF. | DEBIT | CREDIT | BALANCE DEBIT | BALANCE CREDIT |
|---|---|---|---|---|---|---|---|
| 20-1 Dec. | 16 | Balance | ✓ | | | | 90 0 0 0 00 |
| | | | | | | | |
| | | | | | | | |
| | | | | | | | |

ACCOUNT   Tom Jones, Drawing                                              ACCOUNT NO.   312

| DATE | | ITEM | POST. REF. | DEBIT | CREDIT | BALANCE DEBIT | BALANCE CREDIT |
|---|---|---|---|---|---|---|---|
| 20-1 Dec. | 16 | Balance | ✓ | | | 8 5 0 0 00 | |
| | | | | | | | |
| | | | | | | | |
| | | | | | | | |

ACCOUNT   Income Summary                                                  ACCOUNT NO.   313

| DATE | | ITEM | POST. REF. | DEBIT | CREDIT | BALANCE DEBIT | BALANCE CREDIT |
|---|---|---|---|---|---|---|---|
| | | | | | | | |
| | | | | | | | |
| | | | | | | | |
| | | | | | | | |
| | | | | | | | |
| | | | | | | | |

ACCOUNT   Sales                                                          ACCOUNT NO.   401

| DATE | | ITEM | POST. REF. | DEBIT | CREDIT | BALANCE DEBIT | BALANCE CREDIT |
|---|---|---|---|---|---|---|---|
| 20-1 Dec. | 16 | Balance | ✓ | | | | 116 0 0 0 00 |
| | | | | | | | |
| | | | | | | | |
| | | | | | | | |

**Comprehensive Problem 2—Special Journals Based, Part 1
(Requirements 1., 2., 3., 6., 7., and 9. Continued)**

ACCOUNT    Sales Returns and Allowances                    ACCOUNT NO.    401.1

| DATE | | ITEM | POST. REF. | DEBIT | CREDIT | BALANCE DEBIT | BALANCE CREDIT |
|---|---|---|---|---|---|---|---|
| 20-1 Dec. | 16 | Balance | ✓ | | | 1 4 3 0 00 | |
| | | | | | | | |
| | | | | | | | |
| | | | | | | | |
| | | | | | | | |

ACCOUNT    Purchases                                        ACCOUNT NO.    501

| DATE | | ITEM | POST. REF. | DEBIT | CREDIT | BALANCE DEBIT | BALANCE CREDIT |
|---|---|---|---|---|---|---|---|
| 20-1 Dec. | 16 | Balance | ✓ | | | 60 5 0 0 00 | |
| | | | | | | | |
| | | | | | | | |
| | | | | | | | |
| | | | | | | | |
| | | | | | | | |

ACCOUNT    Purchases Returns and Allowances                ACCOUNT NO.    501.1

| DATE | | ITEM | POST. REF. | DEBIT | CREDIT | BALANCE DEBIT | BALANCE CREDIT |
|---|---|---|---|---|---|---|---|
| 20-1 Dec. | 16 | Balance | ✓ | | | | 4 6 0 00 |
| | | | | | | | |
| | | | | | | | |
| | | | | | | | |
| | | | | | | | |

ACCOUNT    Purchases Discounts                              ACCOUNT NO.    501.2

| DATE | | ITEM | POST. REF. | DEBIT | CREDIT | BALANCE DEBIT | BALANCE CREDIT |
|---|---|---|---|---|---|---|---|
| 20-1 Dec. | 16 | Balance | ✓ | | | | 5 7 5 00 |
| | | | | | | | |
| | | | | | | | |
| | | | | | | | |
| | | | | | | | |

# Comprehensive Problem 2—Special Journals Based, Part 1
## (Requirements 1., 2., 3., 6., 7., and 9. Continued)

ACCOUNT  Freight-In                                                         ACCOUNT NO.  502

| DATE | | ITEM | POST. REF. | DEBIT | CREDIT | BALANCE DEBIT | BALANCE CREDIT |
|---|---|---|---|---|---|---|---|
| 20-1 Dec. | 16 | Balance | ✓ | | | 1 7 5 00 | |
| | | | | | | | |
| | | | | | | | |
| | | | | | | | |

ACCOUNT  Wages Expense                                                      ACCOUNT NO.  511

| DATE | | ITEM | POST. REF. | DEBIT | CREDIT | BALANCE DEBIT | BALANCE CREDIT |
|---|---|---|---|---|---|---|---|
| 20-1 Dec. | 16 | Balance | ✓ | | | 26 1 0 0 00 | |
| | | | | | | | |
| | | | | | | | |
| | | | | | | | |
| | | | | | | | |
| | | | | | | | |

ACCOUNT  Advertising Expense                                               ACCOUNT NO.  512

| DATE | | ITEM | POST. REF. | DEBIT | CREDIT | BALANCE DEBIT | BALANCE CREDIT |
|---|---|---|---|---|---|---|---|
| 20-1 Dec. | 16 | Balance | ✓ | | | 4 7 0 0 00 | |
| | | | | | | | |
| | | | | | | | |
| | | | | | | | |
| | | | | | | | |

ACCOUNT  Supplies Expense                                                  ACCOUNT NO.  524

| DATE | | ITEM | POST. REF. | DEBIT | CREDIT | BALANCE DEBIT | BALANCE CREDIT |
|---|---|---|---|---|---|---|---|
| | | | | | | | |
| | | | | | | | |
| | | | | | | | |
| | | | | | | | |

# Comprehensive Problem 2—Special Journals Based, Part 1
## (Requirements 1., 2., 3., 6., 7., and 9. Continued)

ACCOUNT  Telephone Expense                                    ACCOUNT NO.  525

| DATE | | ITEM | POST. REF. | DEBIT | CREDIT | BALANCE | |
|---|---|---|---|---|---|---|---|
| | | | | | | DEBIT | CREDIT |
| 20-1 Dec. | 16 | Balance | ✓ | | | 2 1 8 0 00 | |
| | | | | | | | |
| | | | | | | | |
| | | | | | | | |
| | | | | | | | |

ACCOUNT  Utilities Expense                                    ACCOUNT NO.  533

| DATE | | ITEM | POST. REF. | DEBIT | CREDIT | BALANCE | |
|---|---|---|---|---|---|---|---|
| | | | | | | DEBIT | CREDIT |
| 20-1 Dec. | 16 | Balance | ✓ | | | 6 9 0 0 00 | |
| | | | | | | | |
| | | | | | | | |
| | | | | | | | |
| | | | | | | | |

ACCOUNT  Insurance Expense                                    ACCOUNT NO.  535

| DATE | ITEM | POST. REF. | DEBIT | CREDIT | BALANCE | |
|---|---|---|---|---|---|---|
| | | | | | DEBIT | CREDIT |
| | | | | | | |
| | | | | | | |
| | | | | | | |
| | | | | | | |

ACCOUNT  Depreciation Expense—Building                        ACCOUNT NO.  540

| DATE | ITEM | POST. REF. | DEBIT | CREDIT | BALANCE | |
|---|---|---|---|---|---|---|
| | | | | | DEBIT | CREDIT |
| | | | | | | |
| | | | | | | |
| | | | | | | |
| | | | | | | |

## Comprehensive Problem 2—Special Journals Based, Part 1
## (Requirements 1., 2., 3., 6., 7., and 9. Continued)

ACCOUNT  Depreciation Expense—Store Equipment         ACCOUNT NO.  541

| DATE | ITEM | POST. REF. | DEBIT | CREDIT | BALANCE DEBIT | BALANCE CREDIT |
|------|------|-----------|-------|--------|-------|--------|
|      |      |           |       |        |       |        |
|      |      |           |       |        |       |        |
|      |      |           |       |        |       |        |
|      |      |           |       |        |       |        |

ACCOUNT  Miscellaneous Expense         ACCOUNT NO.  549

| DATE | ITEM | POST. REF. | DEBIT | CREDIT | BALANCE DEBIT | BALANCE CREDIT |
|------|------|-----------|-------|--------|-------|--------|
| 20-1 Dec. 16 | Balance | ✓ |  |  | 2 7 0 0 00 |  |
|      |      |           |       |        |       |        |
|      |      |           |       |        |       |        |
|      |      |           |       |        |       |        |

ACCOUNT  Interest Expense         ACCOUNT NO.  551

| DATE | ITEM | POST. REF. | DEBIT | CREDIT | BALANCE DEBIT | BALANCE CREDIT |
|------|------|-----------|-------|--------|-------|--------|
| 20-1 Dec. 16 | Balance | ✓ |  |  | 1 3 5 0 00 |  |
|      |      |           |       |        |       |        |
|      |      |           |       |        |       |        |
|      |      |           |       |        |       |        |

## ACCOUNTS RECEIVABLE LEDGER

**NAME**  Martha Boyle

**ADDRESS**  12 Jude Lane, Hartford, CT  06117

| DATE | ITEM | POST. REF. | DEBIT | CREDIT | BALANCE |
|------|------|-----------|-------|--------|---------|
| 20-1 Dec. 16 | Balance | ✓ |  |  | 3 7 9 6 00 |
|      |      |           |       |        |         |
|      |      |           |       |        |         |
|      |      |           |       |        |         |
|      |      |           |       |        |         |

Name _____

**Comprehensive Problem 2—Special Journals Based, Part 1
(Requirements 1., 2., 3., 6., 7., and 9. Continued)**

**NAME** Anne Clark
**ADDRESS** 52 Juniper Road, Hartford, CT 06118

| DATE | | ITEM | POST. REF. | DEBIT | CREDIT | BALANCE |
|---|---|---|---|---|---|---|
| 20-1 Dec. | 16 | Balance | ✓ | | | 2 1 0 0 00 |
| | | | | | | |
| | | | | | | |

**NAME** John Dempsey
**ADDRESS** 700 Hobbes Dr., Avon, CT 06108

| DATE | | ITEM | POST. REF. | DEBIT | CREDIT | BALANCE |
|---|---|---|---|---|---|---|
| 20-1 Dec. | 16 | Balance | ✓ | | | 1 5 6 0 00 |
| | | | | | | |
| | | | | | | |

**NAME** Kim Fields
**ADDRESS** 5200 Hamilton Ave., Hartford, CT 06117

| DATE | | ITEM | POST. REF. | DEBIT | CREDIT | BALANCE |
|---|---|---|---|---|---|---|
| 20-1 Dec. | 16 | Balance | ✓ | | | —|—|—|—|— |
| | | | | | | |
| | | | | | | |

**NAME** Lucy Greene
**ADDRESS** 236 Bally Lane, Simsbury, CT 06123

| DATE | | ITEM | POST. REF. | DEBIT | CREDIT | BALANCE |
|---|---|---|---|---|---|---|
| 20-1 Dec. | 16 | Balance | ✓ | | | 2 8 0 0 00 |
| | | | | | | |
| | | | | | | |
| | | | | | | |
| | | | | | | |

## Comprehensive Problem 2—Special Journals Based, Part 1
## (Requirements 1., 2., 3., 6., 7., and 9. Continued)

### ACCOUNTS PAYABLE LEDGER

**NAME** Evans Essentials

**ADDRESS** 34 Harry Ave., East Hartford, CT 05234

| DATE | | ITEM | POST. REF. | DEBIT | CREDIT | BALANCE |
|------|---|------|------------|-------|--------|---------|
| 20-1 Dec. | 16 | Balance | ✓ | | | 3 6 0 0 00 |
| | | | | | | |
| | | | | | | |
| | | | | | | |
| | | | | | | |
| | | | | | | |

**NAME** Nathen Co.

**ADDRESS** 1009 Drake Rd., Farmington, CT 06082

| DATE | | ITEM | POST. REF. | DEBIT | CREDIT | BALANCE |
|------|---|------|------------|-------|--------|---------|
| 20-1 Dec. | 16 | Balance | ✓ | | | |
| | | | | | | |
| | | | | | | |
| | | | | | | |
| | | | | | | |
| | | | | | | |
| | | | | | | |

**Comprehensive Problem 2—Special Journals Based, Part 1
(Requirements 1., 2., 3., 6., 7., and 9. Concluded)**

**NAME**  Owen Enterprises

**ADDRESS**  43 Lucky Lane, Bristol, CT  06007

| DATE | | ITEM | POST. REF. | DEBIT | CREDIT | BALANCE |
|------|--|------|-----------|-------|--------|---------|
| 20-1 Dec. | 16 | Balance | ✓ | | | |
| | | | | | | |
| | | | | | | |
| | | | | | | |

**NAME**  West Wholesalers

**ADDRESS**  888 Anders Street, Newington, CT  06789

| DATE | | ITEM | POST. REF. | DEBIT | CREDIT | BALANCE |
|------|--|------|-----------|-------|--------|---------|
| 20-1 Dec. | 16 | Balance | ✓ | | | |
| | | | | | | |
| | | | | | | |

**Comprehensive Problem 2—Special Journals Based, Part 1**

Requirement 4.

## Comprehensive Problem 2—Special Journals Based, Part 1
### Requirement 5.

| | TRIAL BALANCE | | ADJUSTMENTS | |
|---|---|---|---|---|
| | DEBIT | CREDIT | DEBIT | CREDIT |
| 1 | | | | |
| 2 | | | | |
| 3 | | | | |
| 4 | | | | |
| 5 | | | | |
| 6 | | | | |
| 7 | | | | |
| 8 | | | | |
| 9 | | | | |
| 10 | | | | |
| 11 | | | | |
| 12 | | | | |
| 13 | | | | |
| 14 | | | | |
| 15 | | | | |
| 16 | | | | |
| 17 | | | | |
| 18 | | | | |
| 19 | | | | |
| 20 | | | | |
| 21 | | | | |
| 22 | | | | |
| 23 | | | | |
| 24 | | | | |
| 25 | | | | |
| 26 | | | | |
| 27 | | | | |
| 28 | | | | |
| 29 | | | | |
| 30 | | | | |
| 31 | | | | |
| 32 | | | | |
| 33 | | | | |
| 34 | | | | |
| 35 | | | | |
| 36 | | | | |

**Comprehensive Problem 2—Special Journals Based, Part 1
(Requirement 5. Continued)**

| ADJUSTED TRIAL BALANCE | | INCOME STATEMENT | | BALANCE SHEET | | |
|---|---|---|---|---|---|---|
| DEBIT | CREDIT | DEBIT | CREDIT | DEBIT | CREDIT | |
| | | | | | | 1 |
| | | | | | | 2 |
| | | | | | | 3 |
| | | | | | | 4 |
| | | | | | | 5 |
| | | | | | | 6 |
| | | | | | | 7 |
| | | | | | | 8 |
| | | | | | | 9 |
| | | | | | | 10 |
| | | | | | | 11 |
| | | | | | | 12 |
| | | | | | | 13 |
| | | | | | | 14 |
| | | | | | | 15 |
| | | | | | | 16 |
| | | | | | | 17 |
| | | | | | | 18 |
| | | | | | | 19 |
| | | | | | | 20 |
| | | | | | | 21 |
| | | | | | | 22 |
| | | | | | | 23 |
| | | | | | | 24 |
| | | | | | | 25 |
| | | | | | | 26 |
| | | | | | | 27 |
| | | | | | | 28 |
| | | | | | | 29 |
| | | | | | | 30 |
| | | | | | | 31 |
| | | | | | | 32 |
| | | | | | | 33 |
| | | | | | | 34 |
| | | | | | | 35 |
| | | | | | | 36 |

**Comprehensive Problem 2—Special Journals Based, Part 1
(Requirement 5. Continued)**

**Comprehensive Problem 2—Special Journals Based, Part 1
(Requirement 5. Continued)**

**Comprehensive Problem 2—Special Journals Based, Part 1**
**(Requirement 5. Concluded)**

## Comprehensive Problem 2—Special Journals Based, Part 1

**Requirement 6.**

### GENERAL JOURNAL

PAGE 5

| | DATE | DESCRIPTION | POST. REF. | DEBIT | CREDIT | |
|---|---|---|---|---|---|---|
| 1 | | | | | | 1 |
| 2 | | | | | | 2 |
| 3 | | | | | | 3 |
| 4 | | | | | | 4 |
| 5 | | | | | | 5 |
| 6 | | | | | | 6 |
| 7 | | | | | | 7 |
| 8 | | | | | | 8 |
| 9 | | | | | | 9 |
| 10 | | | | | | 10 |
| 11 | | | | | | 11 |
| 12 | | | | | | 12 |
| 13 | | | | | | 13 |
| 14 | | | | | | 14 |
| 15 | | | | | | 15 |
| 16 | | | | | | 16 |
| 17 | | | | | | 17 |
| 18 | | | | | | 18 |
| 19 | | | | | | 19 |
| 20 | | | | | | 20 |
| 21 | | | | | | 21 |
| 22 | | | | | | 22 |
| 23 | | | | | | 23 |
| 24 | | | | | | 24 |
| 25 | | | | | | 25 |
| 26 | | | | | | 26 |
| 27 | | | | | | 27 |
| 28 | | | | | | 28 |
| 29 | | | | | | 29 |
| 30 | | | | | | 30 |
| 31 | | | | | | 31 |
| 32 | | | | | | 32 |
| 33 | | | | | | 33 |
| 34 | | | | | | 34 |

**Comprehensive Problem 2—Special Journals Based, Part 1**

**Requirements 7. and 9.**

## GENERAL JOURNAL

PAGE  6

| | DATE | | DESCRIPTION | POST. REF. | DEBIT | CREDIT | |
|---|---|---|---|---|---|---|---|
| 1 | | | | | | | 1 |
| 2 | | | | | | | 2 |
| 3 | | | | | | | 3 |
| 4 | | | | | | | 4 |
| 5 | | | | | | | 5 |
| 6 | | | | | | | 6 |
| 7 | | | | | | | 7 |
| 8 | | | | | | | 8 |
| 9 | | | | | | | 9 |
| 10 | | | | | | | 10 |
| 11 | | | | | | | 11 |
| 12 | | | | | | | 12 |
| 13 | | | | | | | 13 |
| 14 | | | | | | | 14 |
| 15 | | | | | | | 15 |
| 16 | | | | | | | 16 |
| 17 | | | | | | | 17 |
| 18 | | | | | | | 18 |
| 19 | | | | | | | 19 |
| 20 | | | | | | | 20 |
| 21 | | | | | | | 21 |
| 22 | | | | | | | 22 |
| 23 | | | | | | | 23 |
| 24 | | | | | | | 24 |
| 25 | | | | | | | 25 |
| 26 | | | | | | | 26 |
| 27 | | | | | | | 27 |
| 28 | | | | | | | 28 |
| 29 | | | | | | | 29 |
| 30 | | | | | | | 30 |
| 31 | | | | | | | 31 |
| 32 | | | | | | | 32 |
| 33 | | | | | | | 33 |
| 34 | | | | | | | 34 |

## Comprehensive Problem 2—Special Journals Based, Part 1
### Requirement 8.

| ACCOUNT | DEBIT BALANCE | CREDIT BALANCE |
|---|---|---|
| | | |
| | | |
| | | |
| | | |
| | | |
| | | |
| | | |
| | | |
| | | |
| | | |
| | | |
| | | |
| | | |
| | | |
| | | |
| | | |
| | | |
| | | |
| | | |
| | | |
| | | |
| | | |
| | | |
| | | |
| | | |
| | | |
| | | |
| | | |
| | | |

## Comprehensive Problem 2—Special Journals Based, Part 2
Requirements 2. and 3.

### SALES JOURNAL

PAGE 7

| DATE | SALE NO. | TO WHOM SOLD | POST. REF. | ACCOUNTS RECEIVABLE DEBIT | SALES CREDIT | SALES TAX PAYABLE CREDIT |
|------|----------|--------------|-----------|---------------------------|--------------|--------------------------|
|      |          |              |           |                           |              |                          |
|      |          |              |           |                           |              |                          |
|      |          |              |           |                           |              |                          |
|      |          |              |           |                           |              |                          |
|      |          |              |           |                           |              |                          |
|      |          |              |           |                           |              |                          |
|      |          |              |           |                           |              |                          |
|      |          |              |           |                           |              |                          |

### CASH RECEIPTS JOURNAL

PAGE 10

| | DATE | ACCOUNT CREDITED | POST. REF. | GENERAL CREDIT | ACCOUNTS RECEIVABLE CREDIT | SALES CREDIT | SALES TAX PAYABLE CREDIT | CASH DEBIT | |
|---|------|------------------|-----------|----------------|----------------------------|--------------|--------------------------|-----------|---|
| 1 |  |  |  |  |  |  |  |  | 1 |
| 2 |  |  |  |  |  |  |  |  | 2 |
| 3 |  |  |  |  |  |  |  |  | 3 |
| 4 |  |  |  |  |  |  |  |  | 4 |
| 5 |  |  |  |  |  |  |  |  | 5 |
| 6 |  |  |  |  |  |  |  |  | 6 |
| 7 |  |  |  |  |  |  |  |  | 7 |
| 8 |  |  |  |  |  |  |  |  | 8 |
| 9 |  |  |  |  |  |  |  |  | 9 |

## Comprehensive Problem 2—Special Journals Based, Part 2
## (Requirements 2. and 3. Continued)

### PURCHASES JOURNAL

| | DATE | INVOICE NO. | FROM WHOM PURCHASED | POST. REF. | PURCHASES DEBIT ACCTS. PAY. CREDIT | |
|---|---|---|---|---|---|---|
| 1 | | | | | | 1 |
| 2 | | | | | | 2 |
| 3 | | | | | | 3 |
| 4 | | | | | | 4 |
| 5 | | | | | | 5 |
| 6 | | | | | | 6 |
| 7 | | | | | | 7 |
| 8 | | | | | | 8 |
| 9 | | | | | | 9 |

### CASH PAYMENTS JOURNAL

| | DATE | CK. NO. | ACCOUNT DEBITED | POST. REF. | GENERAL DEBIT | ACCOUNTS PAYABLE DEBIT | PURCHASES DEBIT | PURCHASES DISCOUNTS CREDIT | CASH CREDIT | |
|---|---|---|---|---|---|---|---|---|---|---|
| 1 | | | | | | | | | | 1 |
| 2 | | | | | | | | | | 2 |
| 3 | | | | | | | | | | 3 |
| 4 | | | | | | | | | | 4 |
| 5 | | | | | | | | | | 5 |
| 6 | | | | | | | | | | 6 |
| 7 | | | | | | | | | | 7 |
| 8 | | | | | | | | | | 8 |
| 9 | | | | | | | | | | 9 |
| 10 | | | | | | | | | | 10 |
| 11 | | | | | | | | | | 11 |
| 12 | | | | | | | | | | 12 |
| 13 | | | | | | | | | | 13 |

## Comprehensive Problem 2—Special Journals Based, Part 2
### (Requirements 2. and 3. Concluded)

**GENERAL JOURNAL**                                    PAGE 1

| DATE | DESCRIPTION | POST. REF. | DEBIT | CREDIT |
|------|-------------|-----------|-------|--------|
| 1 | | | | |
| 2 | | | | |
| 3 | | | | |
| 4 | | | | |
| 5 | | | | |
| 6 | | | | |
| 7 | | | | |
| 8 | | | | |
| 9 | | | | |
| 10 | | | | |
| 11 | | | | |
| 12 | | | | |

### Requirements 1., 2., 3., 6., and 7.
**GENERAL LEDGER**

ACCOUNT  Cash                                ACCOUNT NO. 101

| DATE | ITEM | POST. REF. | DEBIT | CREDIT | BALANCE DEBIT | BALANCE CREDIT |
|------|------|-----------|-------|--------|--------|--------|
| 20-2 Jan. 1 | Balance | ✓ | | | 12 5 4 8 00 | |

ACCOUNT  Accounts Receivable              ACCOUNT NO. 122

| DATE | ITEM | POST. REF. | DEBIT | CREDIT | BALANCE DEBIT | BALANCE CREDIT |
|------|------|-----------|-------|--------|--------|--------|
| 20-2 Jan. 1 | Balance | ✓ | | | 7 2 0 3 00 | |

## Comprehensive Problem 2—Special Journals Based, Part 2
## (Requirements 1., 2., 3., 6., and 7. Continued)

ACCOUNT   Merchandise Inventory          ACCOUNT NO.   131

| DATE | | ITEM | POST. REF. | DEBIT | CREDIT | BALANCE | |
|---|---|---|---|---|---|---|---|
| | | | | | | DEBIT | CREDIT |
| 20-2 Jan. | 1 | Balance | ✓ | | | 19 7 0 0 00 | |
| | | | | | | | |
| | | | | | | | |
| | | | | | | | |
| | | | | | | | |
| | | | | | | | |

ACCOUNT   Supplies          ACCOUNT NO.   141

| DATE | | ITEM | POST. REF. | DEBIT | CREDIT | BALANCE | |
|---|---|---|---|---|---|---|---|
| | | | | | | DEBIT | CREDIT |
| 20-2 Jan. | 1 | Balance | ✓ | | | 5 2 5 00 | |
| | | | | | | | |
| | | | | | | | |
| | | | | | | | |
| | | | | | | | |

ACCOUNT   Prepaid Insurance          ACCOUNT NO.   145

| DATE | | ITEM | POST. REF. | DEBIT | CREDIT | BALANCE | |
|---|---|---|---|---|---|---|---|
| | | | | | | DEBIT | CREDIT |
| 20-2 Jan. | 1 | Balance | ✓ | | | 1 0 0 0 00 | |
| | | | | | | | |
| | | | | | | | |
| | | | | | | | |
| | | | | | | | |

ACCOUNT   Land          ACCOUNT NO.   161

| DATE | | ITEM | POST. REF. | DEBIT | CREDIT | BALANCE | |
|---|---|---|---|---|---|---|---|
| | | | | | | DEBIT | CREDIT |
| 20-2 Jan. | 1 | Balance | ✓ | | | 8 7 0 0 00 | |
| | | | | | | | |
| | | | | | | | |

**Comprehensive Problem 2—Special Journals Based, Part 2
(Requirements 1., 2., 3., 6., and 7. Continued)**

ACCOUNT  Building                                                          ACCOUNT NO.  171

| DATE | | ITEM | POST. REF. | DEBIT | CREDIT | BALANCE | |
|---|---|---|---|---|---|---|---|
| | | | | | | DEBIT | CREDIT |
| 20-2 Jan. | 1 | Balance | ✓ | | | 52 0 0 0 00 | |
| | | | | | | | |
| | | | | | | | |
| | | | | | | | |

ACCOUNT  Accumulated Depreciation—Building                                 ACCOUNT NO.  171.1

| DATE | | ITEM | POST. REF. | DEBIT | CREDIT | BALANCE | |
|---|---|---|---|---|---|---|---|
| | | | | | | DEBIT | CREDIT |
| 20-2 Jan. | 1 | Balance | ✓ | | | | 10 0 0 0 00 |
| | | | | | | | |
| | | | | | | | |
| | | | | | | | |

ACCOUNT  Store Equipment                                                   ACCOUNT NO.  181

| DATE | | ITEM | POST. REF. | DEBIT | CREDIT | BALANCE | |
|---|---|---|---|---|---|---|---|
| | | | | | | DEBIT | CREDIT |
| 20-2 Jan. | 1 | Balance | ✓ | | | 28 7 5 0 00 | |
| | | | | | | | |
| | | | | | | | |
| | | | | | | | |

ACCOUNT  Accumulated Depreciation—Store Equipment                          ACCOUNT NO.  181.1

| DATE | | ITEM | POST. REF. | DEBIT | CREDIT | BALANCE | |
|---|---|---|---|---|---|---|---|
| | | | | | | DEBIT | CREDIT |
| 20-2 Jan. | 1 | Balance | ✓ | | | | 9 7 5 0 00 |
| | | | | | | | |
| | | | | | | | |
| | | | | | | | |

## Comprehensive Problem 2—Special Journals Based, Part 2
## (Requirements 1., 2., 3., 6., and 7. Continued)

ACCOUNT  Accounts Payable                                    ACCOUNT NO.  202

| DATE | | ITEM | POST. REF. | DEBIT | CREDIT | BALANCE | |
|---|---|---|---|---|---|---|---|
| | | | | | | DEBIT | CREDIT |
| 20-2 Jan. | 1 | Balance | ✓ | | | | 4 3 5 0 00 |
| | | | | | | | |
| | | | | | | | |
| | | | | | | | |
| | | | | | | | |
| | | | | | | | |
| | | | | | | | |

ACCOUNT  Wages Payable                                       ACCOUNT NO.  219

| DATE | ITEM | POST. REF. | DEBIT | CREDIT | BALANCE | |
|---|---|---|---|---|---|---|
| | | | | | DEBIT | CREDIT |
| | | | | | | |
| | | | | | | |
| | | | | | | |

ACCOUNT  Sales Tax Payable                                   ACCOUNT NO.  231

| DATE | | ITEM | POST. REF. | DEBIT | CREDIT | BALANCE | |
|---|---|---|---|---|---|---|---|
| | | | | | | DEBIT | CREDIT |
| 20-2 Jan. | 1 | Balance | ✓ | | | | 1 5 1 8 00 |
| | | | | | | | |
| | | | | | | | |
| | | | | | | | |
| | | | | | | | |
| | | | | | | | |

ACCOUNT  Mortgage Payable                                    ACCOUNT NO.  251

| DATE | | ITEM | POST. REF. | DEBIT | CREDIT | BALANCE | |
|---|---|---|---|---|---|---|---|
| | | | | | | DEBIT | CREDIT |
| 20-2 Jan. | 1 | Balance | ✓ | | | | 12 5 2 5 00 |
| | | | | | | | |
| | | | | | | | |

## Comprehensive Problem 2—Special Journals Based, Part 2
## (Requirements 1., 2., 3., 6., and 7. Continued)

ACCOUNT  Tom Jones, Capital                                  ACCOUNT NO.  311

| DATE | | ITEM | POST. REF. | DEBIT | CREDIT | BALANCE | |
|---|---|---|---|---|---|---|---|
| | | | | | | DEBIT | CREDIT |
| 20-2 Jan. | 1 | Balance | ✓ | | | | 91 9 5 3 00 |
| | | | | | | | |
| | | | | | | | |

ACCOUNT  Tom Jones, Drawing                                  ACCOUNT NO.  312

| DATE | ITEM | POST. REF. | DEBIT | CREDIT | BALANCE | |
|---|---|---|---|---|---|---|
| | | | | | DEBIT | CREDIT |
| | | | | | | |
| | | | | | | |
| | | | | | | |

ACCOUNT  Income Summary                                      ACCOUNT NO.  313

| DATE | ITEM | POST. REF. | DEBIT | CREDIT | BALANCE | |
|---|---|---|---|---|---|---|
| | | | | | DEBIT | CREDIT |
| | | | | | | |
| | | | | | | |
| | | | | | | |
| | | | | | | |
| | | | | | | |
| | | | | | | |

ACCOUNT  Sales                                               ACCOUNT NO.  401

| DATE | ITEM | POST. REF. | DEBIT | CREDIT | BALANCE | |
|---|---|---|---|---|---|---|
| | | | | | DEBIT | CREDIT |
| | | | | | | |
| | | | | | | |
| | | | | | | |
| | | | | | | |

## Comprehensive Problem 2—Special Journals Based, Part 2
## (Requirements 1., 2., 3., 6., and 7. Continued)

ACCOUNT  Sales Returns and Allowances                    ACCOUNT NO.  401.1

| DATE | ITEM | POST. REF. | DEBIT | CREDIT | BALANCE | |
|------|------|------------|-------|--------|---------|---|
| | | | | | DEBIT | CREDIT |
| | | | | | | |
| | | | | | | |
| | | | | | | |
| | | | | | | |
| | | | | | | |

ACCOUNT  Purchases                                       ACCOUNT NO.  501

| DATE | ITEM | POST. REF. | DEBIT | CREDIT | BALANCE | |
|------|------|------------|-------|--------|---------|---|
| | | | | | DEBIT | CREDIT |
| | | | | | | |
| | | | | | | |
| | | | | | | |
| | | | | | | |
| | | | | | | |

ACCOUNT  Purchases Returns and Allowances                ACCOUNT NO.  501.1

| DATE | ITEM | POST. REF. | DEBIT | CREDIT | BALANCE | |
|------|------|------------|-------|--------|---------|---|
| | | | | | DEBIT | CREDIT |
| | | | | | | |
| | | | | | | |
| | | | | | | |
| | | | | | | |
| | | | | | | |

ACCOUNT  Purchases Discounts                             ACCOUNT NO.  501.2

| DATE | ITEM | POST. REF. | DEBIT | CREDIT | BALANCE | |
|------|------|------------|-------|--------|---------|---|
| | | | | | DEBIT | CREDIT |
| | | | | | | |
| | | | | | | |
| | | | | | | |
| | | | | | | |

## Comprehensive Problem 2—Special Journals Based, Part 2
## (Requirements 1., 2., 3., 6., and 7. Continued)

ACCOUNT Freight-In        ACCOUNT NO. 502

| DATE | ITEM | POST. REF. | DEBIT | CREDIT | BALANCE DEBIT | BALANCE CREDIT |
|---|---|---|---|---|---|---|
| | | | | | | |
| | | | | | | |
| | | | | | | |
| | | | | | | |

ACCOUNT Wages Expense        ACCOUNT NO. 511

| DATE | ITEM | POST. REF. | DEBIT | CREDIT | BALANCE DEBIT | BALANCE CREDIT |
|---|---|---|---|---|---|---|
| 20-2 Jan. 1 | Balance | ✓ | | | | 3 3 0 00 |
| | | | | | | |
| | | | | | | |
| | | | | | | |
| | | | | | | |
| | | | | | | |
| | | | | | | |

ACCOUNT Advertising Expense        ACCOUNT NO. 512

| DATE | ITEM | POST. REF. | DEBIT | CREDIT | BALANCE DEBIT | BALANCE CREDIT |
|---|---|---|---|---|---|---|
| | | | | | | |
| | | | | | | |
| | | | | | | |

ACCOUNT Supplies Expense        ACCOUNT NO. 524

| DATE | ITEM | POST. REF. | DEBIT | CREDIT | BALANCE DEBIT | BALANCE CREDIT |
|---|---|---|---|---|---|---|
| | | | | | | |
| | | | | | | |
| | | | | | | |
| | | | | | | |

## Comprehensive Problem 2—Special Journals Based, Part 2
## (Requirements 1., 2., 3., 6., and 7. Continued)

ACCOUNT   Telephone Expense      ACCOUNT NO.   525

| DATE | ITEM | POST. REF. | DEBIT | CREDIT | BALANCE DEBIT | BALANCE CREDIT |
|------|------|-----------|-------|--------|-------|--------|
|      |      |           |       |        |       |        |
|      |      |           |       |        |       |        |
|      |      |           |       |        |       |        |
|      |      |           |       |        |       |        |

ACCOUNT   Utilities Expense      ACCOUNT NO.   533

| DATE | ITEM | POST. REF. | DEBIT | CREDIT | BALANCE DEBIT | BALANCE CREDIT |
|------|------|-----------|-------|--------|-------|--------|
|      |      |           |       |        |       |        |
|      |      |           |       |        |       |        |
|      |      |           |       |        |       |        |
|      |      |           |       |        |       |        |

ACCOUNT   Insurance Expense      ACCOUNT NO.   535

| DATE | ITEM | POST. REF. | DEBIT | CREDIT | BALANCE DEBIT | BALANCE CREDIT |
|------|------|-----------|-------|--------|-------|--------|
|      |      |           |       |        |       |        |
|      |      |           |       |        |       |        |
|      |      |           |       |        |       |        |
|      |      |           |       |        |       |        |

ACCOUNT   Depreciation Expense—Building      ACCOUNT NO.   540

| DATE | ITEM | POST. REF. | DEBIT | CREDIT | BALANCE DEBIT | BALANCE CREDIT |
|------|------|-----------|-------|--------|-------|--------|
|      |      |           |       |        |       |        |
|      |      |           |       |        |       |        |
|      |      |           |       |        |       |        |
|      |      |           |       |        |       |        |

ACCOUNT   Depreciation Expense—Store Equipment      ACCOUNT NO.   541

| DATE | ITEM | POST. REF. | DEBIT | CREDIT | BALANCE DEBIT | BALANCE CREDIT |
|------|------|-----------|-------|--------|-------|--------|
|      |      |           |       |        |       |        |
|      |      |           |       |        |       |        |
|      |      |           |       |        |       |        |
|      |      |           |       |        |       |        |

## Comprehensive Problem 2—Special Journals Based, Part 2
## (Requirements 1., 2., 3., 6., and 7. Continued)

ACCOUNT   Miscellaneous Expense                                          ACCOUNT NO.   549

| DATE | ITEM | POST. REF. | DEBIT | CREDIT | BALANCE DEBIT | BALANCE CREDIT |
|------|------|------------|-------|--------|---------------|----------------|
|      |      |            |       |        |               |                |
|      |      |            |       |        |               |                |
|      |      |            |       |        |               |                |
|      |      |            |       |        |               |                |
|      |      |            |       |        |               |                |
|      |      |            |       |        |               |                |

ACCOUNT   Interest Expense                                               ACCOUNT NO.   551

| DATE | ITEM | POST. REF. | DEBIT | CREDIT | BALANCE DEBIT | BALANCE CREDIT |
|------|------|------------|-------|--------|---------------|----------------|
|      |      |            |       |        |               |                |
|      |      |            |       |        |               |                |
|      |      |            |       |        |               |                |
|      |      |            |       |        |               |                |
|      |      |            |       |        |               |                |

## ACCOUNTS RECEIVABLE LEDGER

**NAME**  Martha Boyle

**ADDRESS**  12 Jude Lane, Hartford, CT  06117

| DATE | ITEM | POST. REF. | DEBIT | CREDIT | BALANCE |
|------|------|------------|-------|--------|---------|
| 20-2 Jan. 1 | Balance | ✓ |  |  | 1 3 2 3 00 |
|      |      |            |       |        |         |
|      |      |            |       |        |         |
|      |      |            |       |        |         |

**NAME**  Anne Clark

**ADDRESS**  52 Juniper Road, Hartford, CT  06118

| DATE | ITEM | POST. REF. | DEBIT | CREDIT | BALANCE |
|------|------|------------|-------|--------|---------|
| 20-2 Jan. 1 | Balance | ✓ |  |  | 2 1 0 0 00 |
|      |      |            |       |        |         |
|      |      |            |       |        |         |
|      |      |            |       |        |         |

**Comprehensive Problem 2—Special Journals Based, Part 2
(Requirements 1., 2., 3., 6., and 7. Continued)**

**NAME** John Dempsey

**ADDRESS** 700 Hobbes Dr., Avon, CT  06108

| DATE | | ITEM | POST. REF. | DEBIT | CREDIT | BALANCE |
|---|---|---|---|---|---|---|
| 20-2 Jan. | 1 | Balance | ✓ | | | 2 1 2 1 00 |
| | | | | | | |
| | | | | | | |
| | | | | | | |

**NAME** Kim Fields

**ADDRESS** 5200 Hamilton Ave., Hartford, CT  06117

| DATE | | ITEM | POST. REF. | DEBIT | CREDIT | BALANCE |
|---|---|---|---|---|---|---|
| 20-2 Jan. | 1 | Balance | ✓ | | | 1 6 8 00 |
| | | | | | | |
| | | | | | | |
| | | | | | | |

**NAME** Lucy Greene

**ADDRESS** 236 Bally Lane, Simsbury, CT  06123

| DATE | | ITEM | POST. REF. | DEBIT | CREDIT | BALANCE |
|---|---|---|---|---|---|---|
| 20-2 Jan. | 1 | Balance | ✓ | | | 1 4 9 1 00 |
| | | | | | | |
| | | | | | | |
| | | | | | | |

**Comprehensive Problem 2—Special Journals Based, Part 2
(Requirements 1., 2., 3., 6., and 7. Concluded)**

## ACCOUNTS PAYABLE LEDGER

**NAME** Evans Essentials

**ADDRESS** 34 Harry Ave., East Hartford, CT 05234

| DATE | | ITEM | POST. REF. | DEBIT | CREDIT | BALANCE |
|---|---|---|---|---|---|---|
| 20-2 Jan. | 1 | Balance | ✓ | | | 2 3 5 0 00 |
| | | | | | | |
| | | | | | | |

**NAME** Nathen Co.

**ADDRESS** 1009 Drake Rd., Farmington, CT 06082

| DATE | | ITEM | POST. REF. | DEBIT | CREDIT | BALANCE |
|---|---|---|---|---|---|---|
| 20-2 Jan. | 1 | Balance | ✓ | | | 8 0 0 00 |
| | | | | | | |
| | | | | | | |

**NAME** Owen Enterprises

**ADDRESS** 43 Lucky Lane, Bristol, CT 06007

| DATE | | ITEM | POST. REF. | DEBIT | CREDIT | BALANCE |
|---|---|---|---|---|---|---|
| | | | | | | |
| | | | | | | |
| | | | | | | |

**NAME** West Wholesalers

**ADDRESS** 888 Anders Street, Newington, CT 06789

| DATE | | ITEM | POST. REF. | DEBIT | CREDIT | BALANCE |
|---|---|---|---|---|---|---|
| 20-2 Jan. | 1 | Balance | ✓ | | | 1 2 0 0 00 |
| | | | | | | |
| | | | | | | |

**Comprehensive Problem 2—Special Journals Based, Part 2**

Requirement 4.

## Comprehensive Problem 2—Special Journals Based, Part 2

**Requirement 5.**

| | TRIAL BALANCE | | ADJUSTMENTS | |
|---|---|---|---|---|
| | DEBIT | CREDIT | DEBIT | CREDIT |
| 1 | | | | |
| 2 | | | | |
| 3 | | | | |
| 4 | | | | |
| 5 | | | | |
| 6 | | | | |
| 7 | | | | |
| 8 | | | | |
| 9 | | | | |
| 10 | | | | |
| 11 | | | | |
| 12 | | | | |
| 13 | | | | |
| 14 | | | | |
| 15 | | | | |
| 16 | | | | |
| 17 | | | | |
| 18 | | | | |
| 19 | | | | |
| 20 | | | | |
| 21 | | | | |
| 22 | | | | |
| 23 | | | | |
| 24 | | | | |
| 25 | | | | |
| 26 | | | | |
| 27 | | | | |
| 28 | | | | |
| 29 | | | | |
| 30 | | | | |
| 31 | | | | |
| 32 | | | | |
| 33 | | | | |
| 34 | | | | |
| 35 | | | | |
| 36 | | | | |

## Comprehensive Problem 2—Special Journals Based, Part 2
## (Requirement 5. Continued)

| ADJUSTED TRIAL BALANCE | | INCOME STATEMENT | | BALANCE SHEET | | |
|---|---|---|---|---|---|---|
| DEBIT | CREDIT | DEBIT | CREDIT | DEBIT | CREDIT | |
| | | | | | | 1 |
| | | | | | | 2 |
| | | | | | | 3 |
| | | | | | | 4 |
| | | | | | | 5 |
| | | | | | | 6 |
| | | | | | | 7 |
| | | | | | | 8 |
| | | | | | | 9 |
| | | | | | | 10 |
| | | | | | | 11 |
| | | | | | | 12 |
| | | | | | | 13 |
| | | | | | | 14 |
| | | | | | | 15 |
| | | | | | | 16 |
| | | | | | | 17 |
| | | | | | | 18 |
| | | | | | | 19 |
| | | | | | | 20 |
| | | | | | | 21 |
| | | | | | | 22 |
| | | | | | | 23 |
| | | | | | | 24 |
| | | | | | | 25 |
| | | | | | | 26 |
| | | | | | | 27 |
| | | | | | | 28 |
| | | | | | | 29 |
| | | | | | | 30 |
| | | | | | | 31 |
| | | | | | | 32 |
| | | | | | | 33 |
| | | | | | | 34 |
| | | | | | | 35 |
| | | | | | | 36 |

**Comprehensive Problem 2—Special Journals Based, Part 2**
**(Requirement 5. Continued)**

**Comprehensive Problem 2—Special Journals Based, Part 2
(Requirement 5. Continued)**

**Comprehensive Problem 2—Special Journals Based, Part 2
(Requirement 5. Concluded)**

## Comprehensive Problem 2—Special Journals Based, Part 2

Requirement 6.

### GENERAL JOURNAL                                             PAGE  2

| | DATE | | DESCRIPTION | POST. REF. | DEBIT | CREDIT | |
|---|---|---|---|---|---|---|---|
| 1 | | | | | | | 1 |
| 2 | | | | | | | 2 |
| 3 | | | | | | | 3 |
| 4 | | | | | | | 4 |
| 5 | | | | | | | 5 |
| 6 | | | | | | | 6 |
| 7 | | | | | | | 7 |
| 8 | | | | | | | 8 |
| 9 | | | | | | | 9 |
| 10 | | | | | | | 10 |
| 11 | | | | | | | 11 |
| 12 | | | | | | | 12 |
| 13 | | | | | | | 13 |
| 14 | | | | | | | 14 |
| 15 | | | | | | | 15 |
| 16 | | | | | | | 16 |
| 17 | | | | | | | 17 |
| 18 | | | | | | | 18 |
| 19 | | | | | | | 19 |
| 20 | | | | | | | 20 |
| 21 | | | | | | | 21 |
| 22 | | | | | | | 22 |
| 23 | | | | | | | 23 |
| 24 | | | | | | | 24 |
| 25 | | | | | | | 25 |
| 26 | | | | | | | 26 |
| 27 | | | | | | | 27 |
| 28 | | | | | | | 28 |
| 29 | | | | | | | 29 |
| 30 | | | | | | | 30 |
| 31 | | | | | | | 31 |
| 32 | | | | | | | 32 |
| 33 | | | | | | | 33 |
| 34 | | | | | | | 34 |

## Comprehensive Problem 2—Special Journals Based, Part 2

**Requirement 7.**

### GENERAL JOURNAL

PAGE 3

| | DATE | | DESCRIPTION | POST. REF. | DEBIT | CREDIT | |
|---|---|---|---|---|---|---|---|
| 1 | | | | | | | 1 |
| 2 | | | | | | | 2 |
| 3 | | | | | | | 3 |
| 4 | | | | | | | 4 |
| 5 | | | | | | | 5 |
| 6 | | | | | | | 6 |
| 7 | | | | | | | 7 |
| 8 | | | | | | | 8 |
| 9 | | | | | | | 9 |
| 10 | | | | | | | 10 |
| 11 | | | | | | | 11 |
| 12 | | | | | | | 12 |
| 13 | | | | | | | 13 |
| 14 | | | | | | | 14 |
| 15 | | | | | | | 15 |
| 16 | | | | | | | 16 |
| 17 | | | | | | | 17 |
| 18 | | | | | | | 18 |
| 19 | | | | | | | 19 |
| 20 | | | | | | | 20 |
| 21 | | | | | | | 21 |
| 22 | | | | | | | 22 |
| 23 | | | | | | | 23 |
| 24 | | | | | | | 24 |
| 25 | | | | | | | 25 |
| 26 | | | | | | | 26 |
| 27 | | | | | | | 27 |
| 28 | | | | | | | 28 |
| 29 | | | | | | | 29 |
| 30 | | | | | | | 30 |
| 31 | | | | | | | 31 |
| 32 | | | | | | | 32 |
| 33 | | | | | | | 33 |
| 34 | | | | | | | 34 |

**Comprehensive Problem 2—Special Journals Based, Part 2**

Requirement 8.

| ACCOUNT | DEBIT BALANCE | CREDIT BALANCE |
|---|---|---|
| | | |
| | | |
| | | |
| | | |
| | | |
| | | |
| | | |
| | | |
| | | |
| | | |
| | | |
| | | |
| | | |
| | | |
| | | |
| | | |
| | | |
| | | |
| | | |
| | | |
| | | |
| | | |
| | | |
| | | |
| | | |
| | | |
| | | |
| | | |
| | | |
| | | |
| | | |
| | | |

# NOTES

END PAGE OF
WORKING PAPERS

# END PAGE OF
# STUDY GUIDE

# NOTES